S0-AEI-972

# *The* DARK GOODBYE

# The Dark Goodbye Vol. 1
## Written by Frank Marraffino
## Illustrated by Drew Rausch

Contributing Editor - Paul Morrissey
Lettering - Lucas Rivera
Cover Design - Christian Lownds

Editor - Bryce P. Coleman
Digital Imaging Manager - Chris Buford
Pre-Production Supervisor - Erika Terriquez
Art Director - Anne Marie Horne
Production Manager - Elisabeth Brizzi
Managing Editor - Vy Nguyen
VP of Production - Ron Klamert
Editor-in-Chief - Rob Tokar
Publisher - Mike Kiley
President and C.O.O. - John Parker
C.E.O. and Chief Creative Officer - Stuart Levy

A  Manga

TOKYOPOP and  are trademarks or registered trademarks of TOKYOPOP Inc.

TOKYOPOP Inc.
5900 Wilshire Blvd. Suite 2000
Los Angeles, CA 90036

E-mail: info@TOKYOPOP.com
Come visit us online at www.TOKYOPOP.com

ISBN: 978-1-59816-972-0

First TOKYOPOP printing: April 2007
10  9  8  7  6  5  4  3  2  1
Printed in the USA

# The DARK GOODBYE

## VOLUME 1

## WRITTEN BY
## FRANK MARRAFFINO

## ILLUSTRATED BY
## DREW RAUSCH

⊙ TOKYOPOP®

HAMBURG // LONDON // LOS ANGELES // TOKYO

# The DARK GOODBYE

## VOLUME ONE
## TABLE OF CONTENTS

# EDITOR'S INTRODUCTION

From an early age, most of us learn to avoid dark alleys. However, there are some of us who tend to seek them out. We need to know what's in there. What's on the other side. And then there are times when those dark, ominous recesses find us.

When I was told about Frank Marraffino's story pitch, I jumped at the chance to edit the book. In fact, I should take this opportunity to apologize to my good friend, and fellow editor, Paul Morrissey. It was Paul who told me about the pitch, and if I recall, I nearly grabbed him by the shirt collar and demanded the project. Paul graciously (maybe too quickly) acquiesced to my plea.

The reason for my nearly pathological reaction was that, years earlier, I, too, had been inspired to try my hand at a similar tale. It had never coalesced into anything more than rambling notes and fevered ideas, but it had remained in the darker corners of my mind, waiting...

And here was Frank's story, better than I could have ever conceived it. A perfect fusion of Chandleresque hard boiled noir and the weird horror of H.P. Lovecraft. Gumshoes and femmes fatale mingling on the same pages as ancient insane deities and things that lurk in the depths. Frank had it down. The language and cadences of the crime pulps intermingled with a terrifying, dark mythology. It was clear that Frank understood the two genres intuitively, but what was impressive was how he tapped into the similar tropes and themes of the two, and melded them so seamlessly.

Now the question was, **"who could possibly draw this madness?"**

Once again, I owe a debt of gratitude to Mr. Morrissey, who'd been (sometimes I think almost too conveniently) hanging on to the portfolio of a certain Drew Rausch for a while.

I can't imagine anyone else drawing the book. Drew's artwork is drenched in shadow. His line work has an unsettling, agitated quality to it, and he frequently frames his panels in an off-kilter manner, much like the German expressionism that informed film noir. It has, and I mean this in the best possible way, a sense of decay about it. It's as if Drew's glimpsed the best possible way, a sense of decay about it. It's as if Drew's glimpsed realms none of us were meant to see, and brought back these nightmarish representations to share with the rest of us.

So here you have it, Dear Reader. The Dark Goodbye.
It's the ink-black alley that found me and beckoned me to enter.
And refuses to let me leave.
And now, here you are. Will you join me?

At this very moment, I can hear Morrissey at his desk behind me... laughing.

Bryce P. Coleman
Los Angeles, CA.
January 2007

# CHAPTER 1:
## THE WAYWARD SISTER

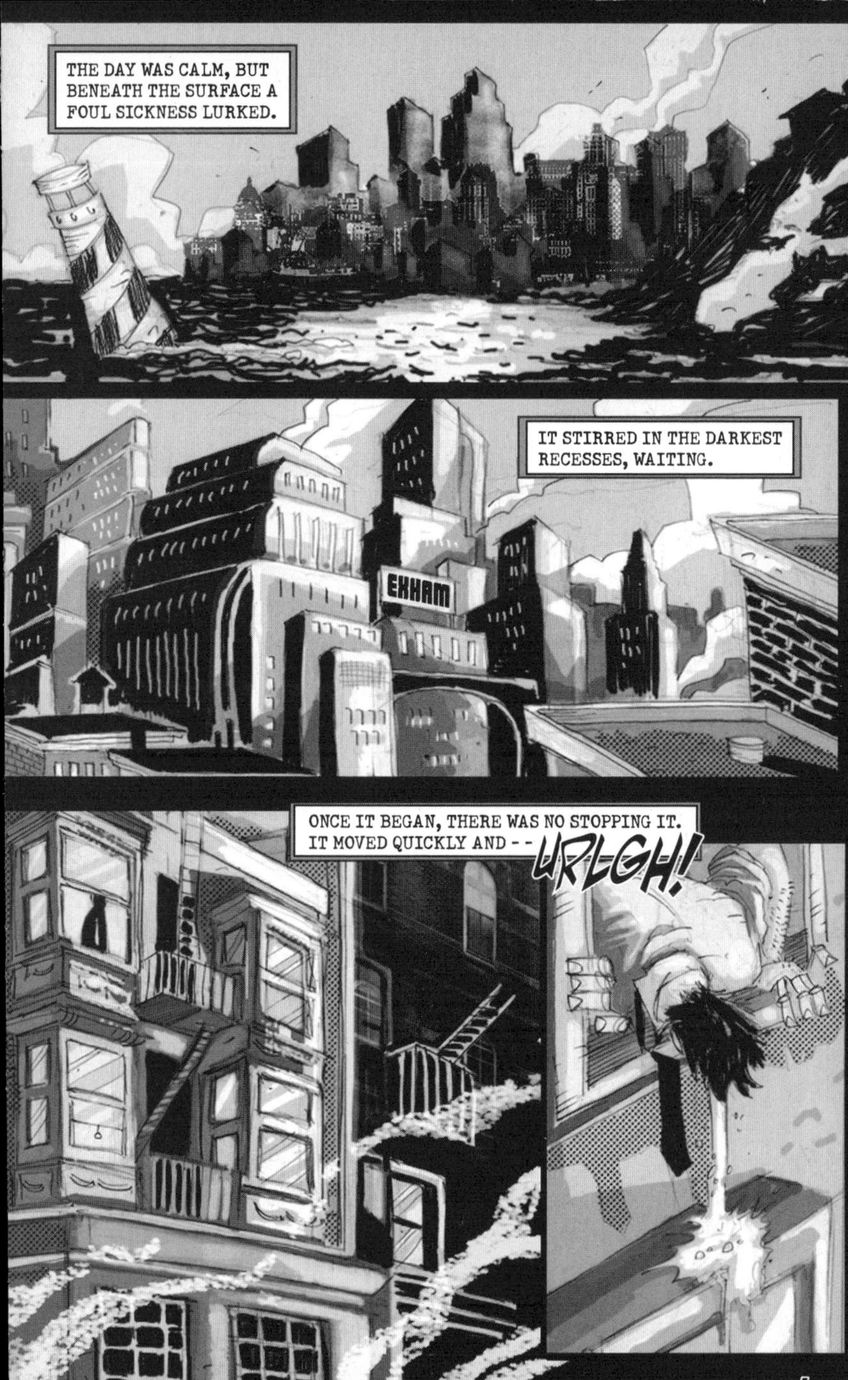
THE DAY WAS CALM, BUT BENEATH THE SURFACE A FOUL SICKNESS LURKED.
IT STIRRED IN THE DARKEST RECESSES, WAITING.
EXHAM
ONCE IT BEGAN, THERE WAS NO STOPPING IT. IT MOVED QUICKLY AND - -
URLGH!

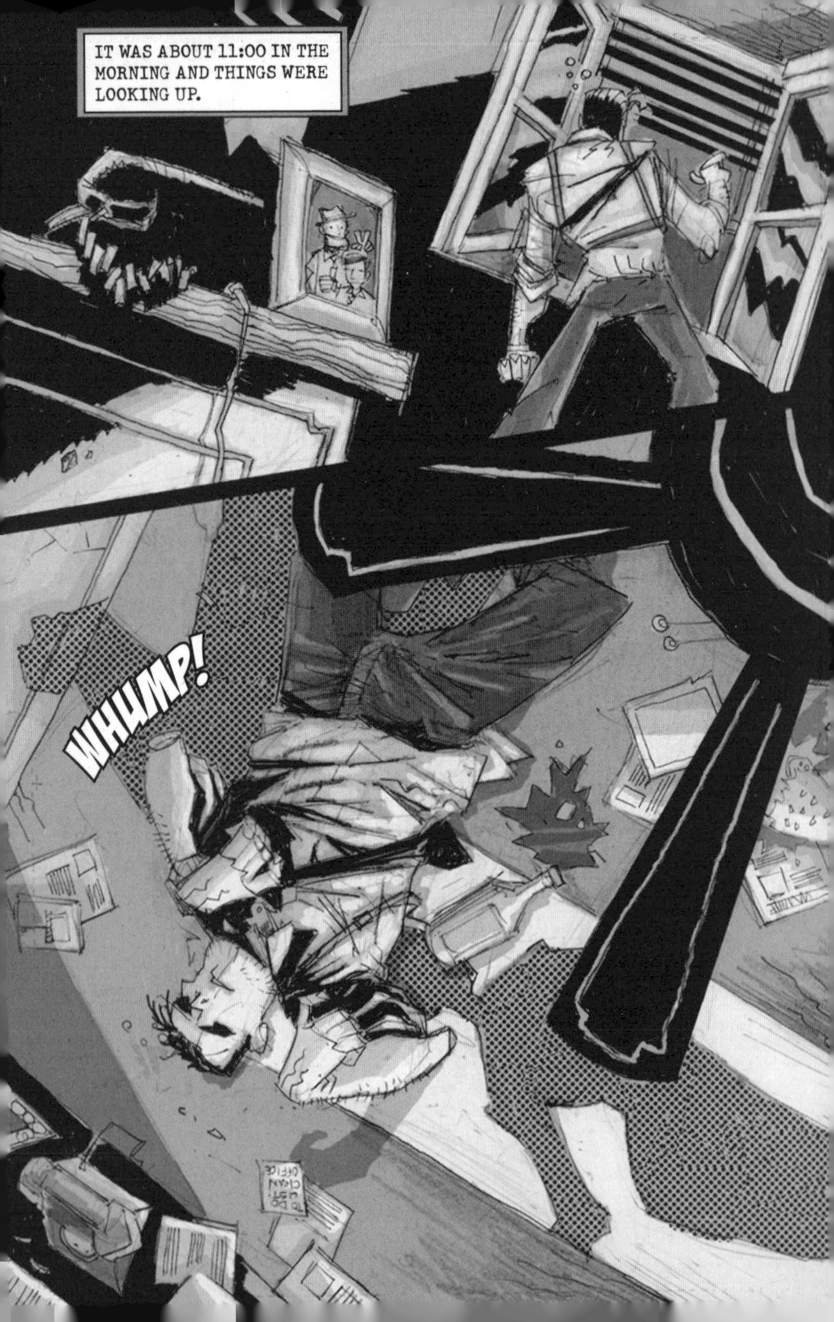
IT WAS ABOUT 11:00 IN THE MORNING AND THINGS WERE LOOKING UP.
WHUMP!
TO DO LIST: CLEAN OFFICE

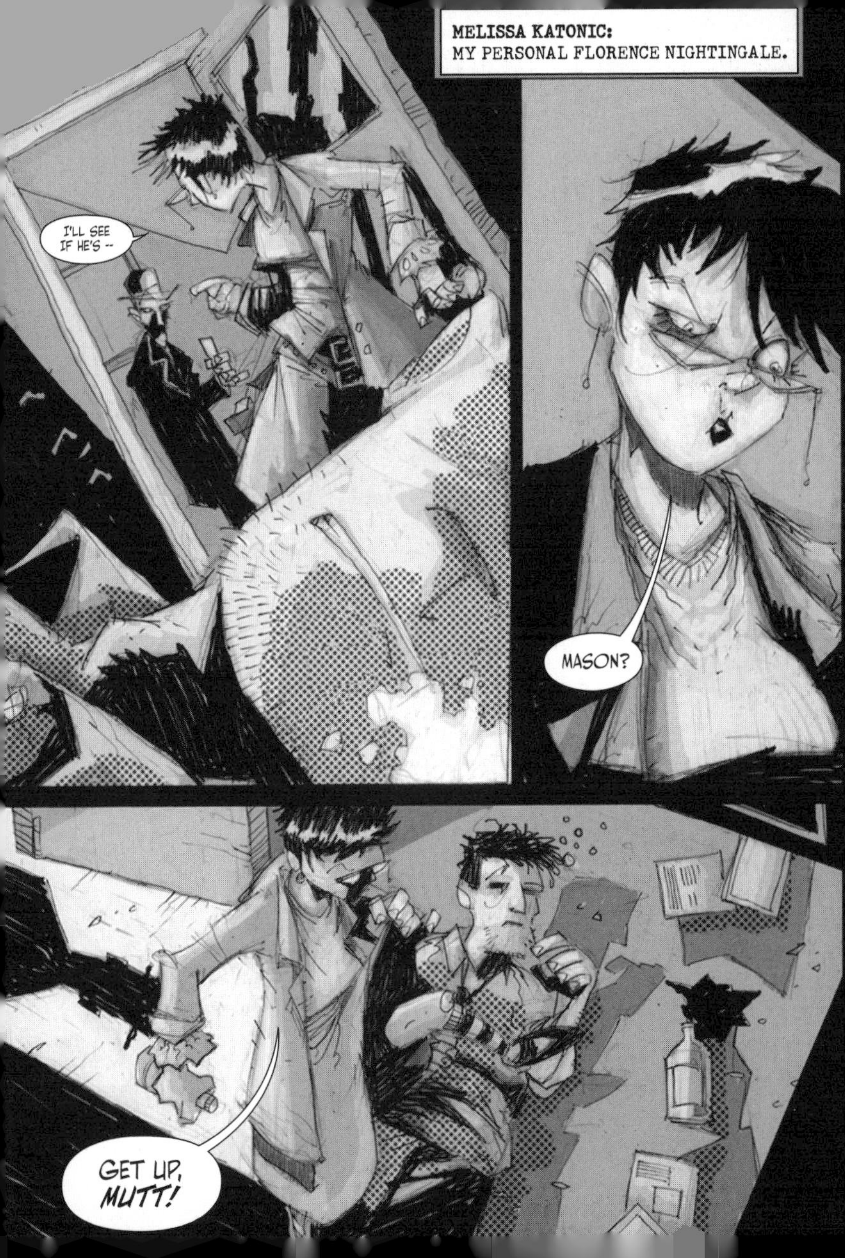
MELISSA KATONIC:
MY PERSONAL FLORENCE NIGHTINGALE.
I'LL SEE IF HE'S --
MASON?
GET UP, MUTT!

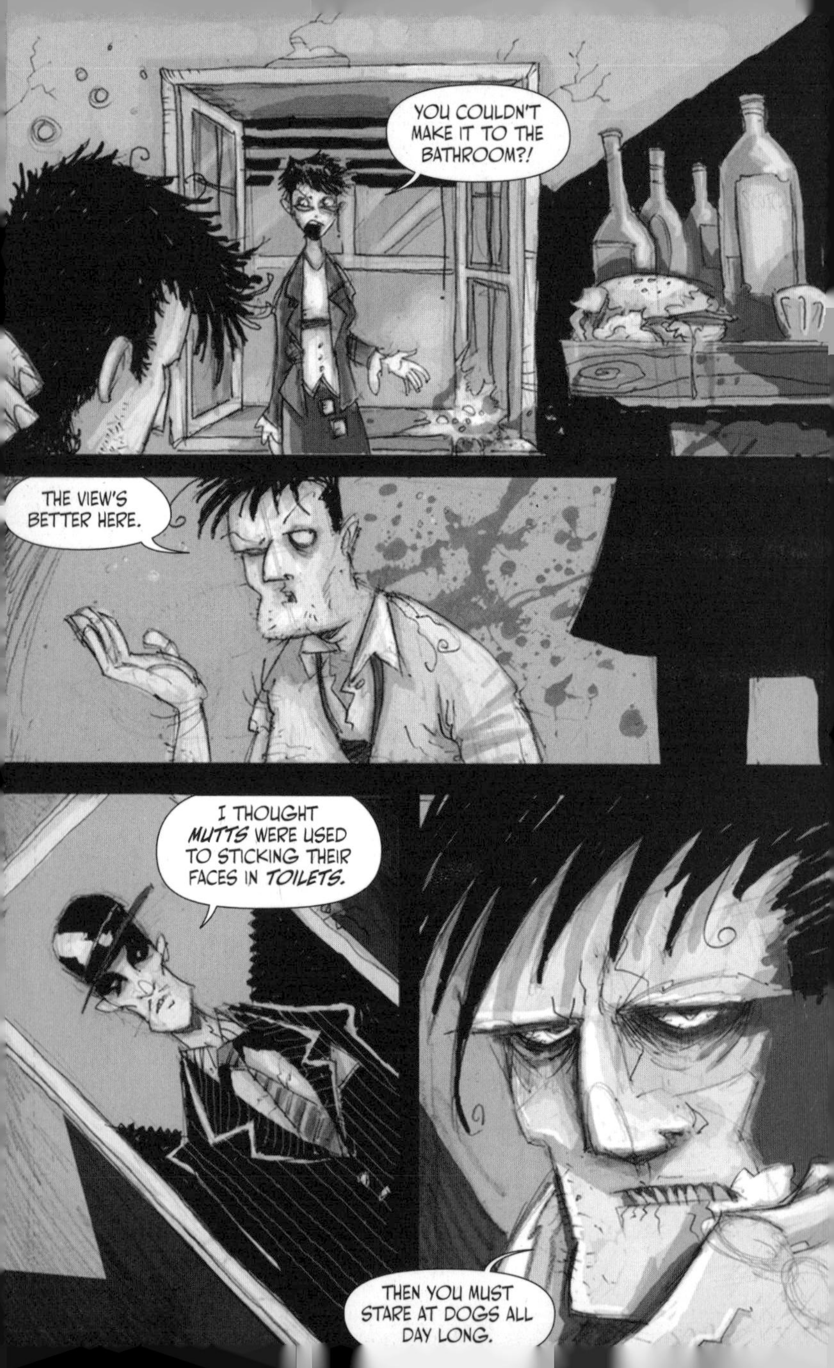
YOU COULDN'T MAKE IT TO THE BATHROOM?!
THE VIEW'S BETTER HERE.
I THOUGHT *MUTTS* WERE USED TO STICKING THEIR FACES IN *TOILETS*.
THEN YOU MUST STARE AT DOGS ALL DAY LONG.

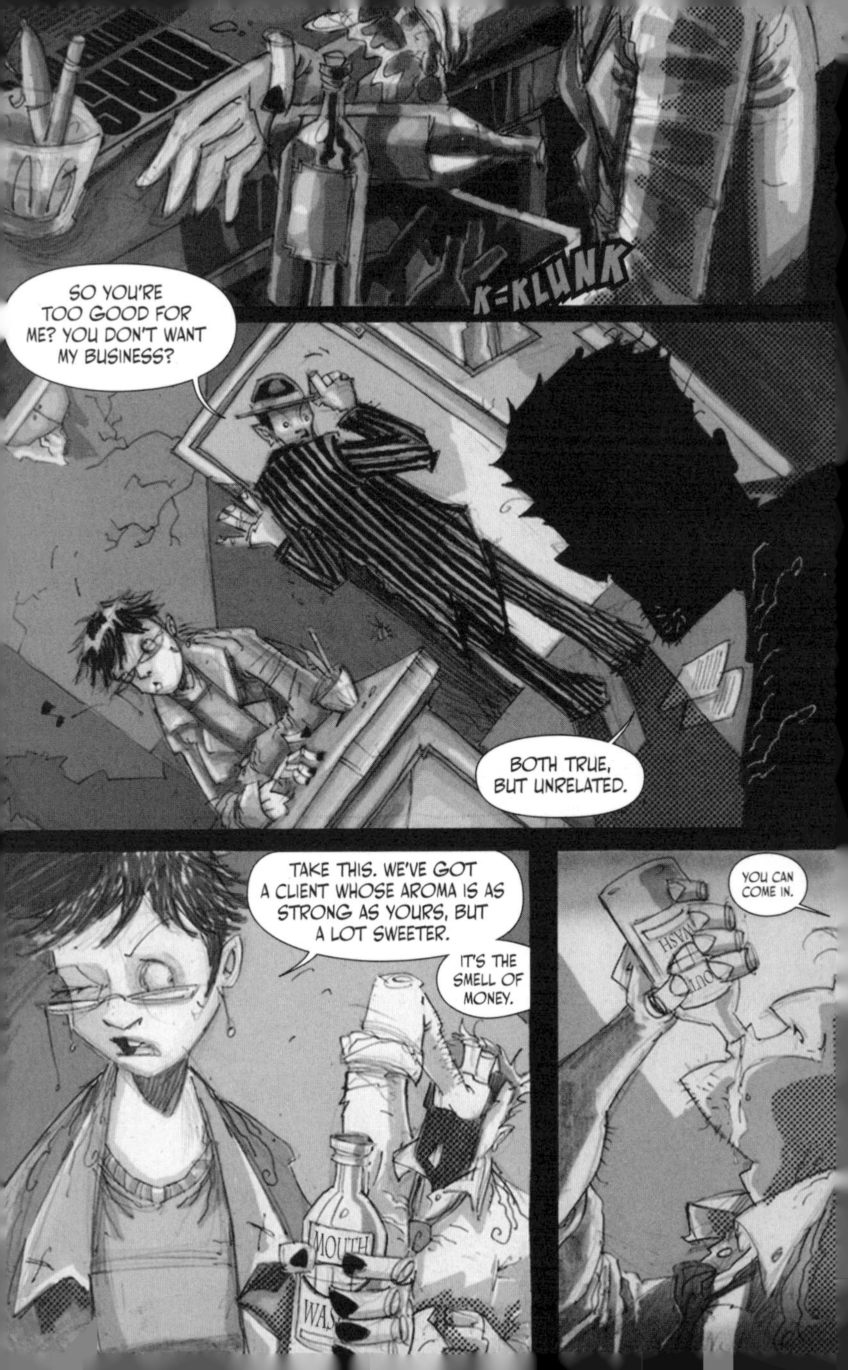
K-KLUNK
SO YOU'RE TOO GOOD FOR ME? YOU DON'T WANT MY BUSINESS?
BOTH TRUE, BUT UNRELATED.
TAKE THIS. WE'VE GOT A CLIENT WHOSE AROMA IS AS STRONG AS YOURS, BUT A LOT SWEETER.
IT'S THE SMELL OF MONEY.
MOUTH WAS
YOU CAN COME IN.

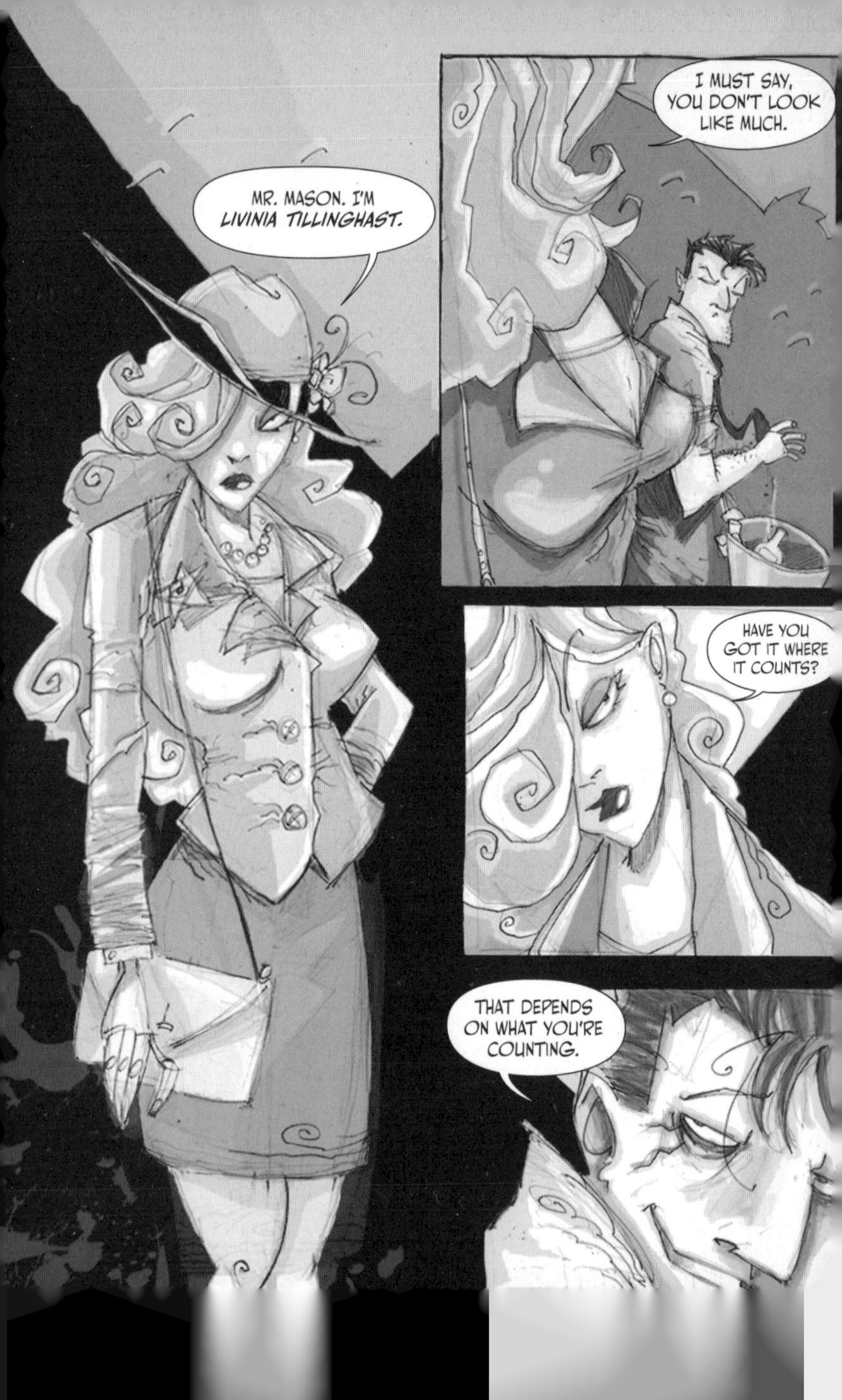

MR. MASON. I'M LIVINIA TILLINGHAST.
I MUST SAY, YOU DON'T LOOK LIKE MUCH.
HAVE YOU GOT IT WHERE IT COUNTS?
THAT DEPENDS ON WHAT YOU'RE COUNTING.

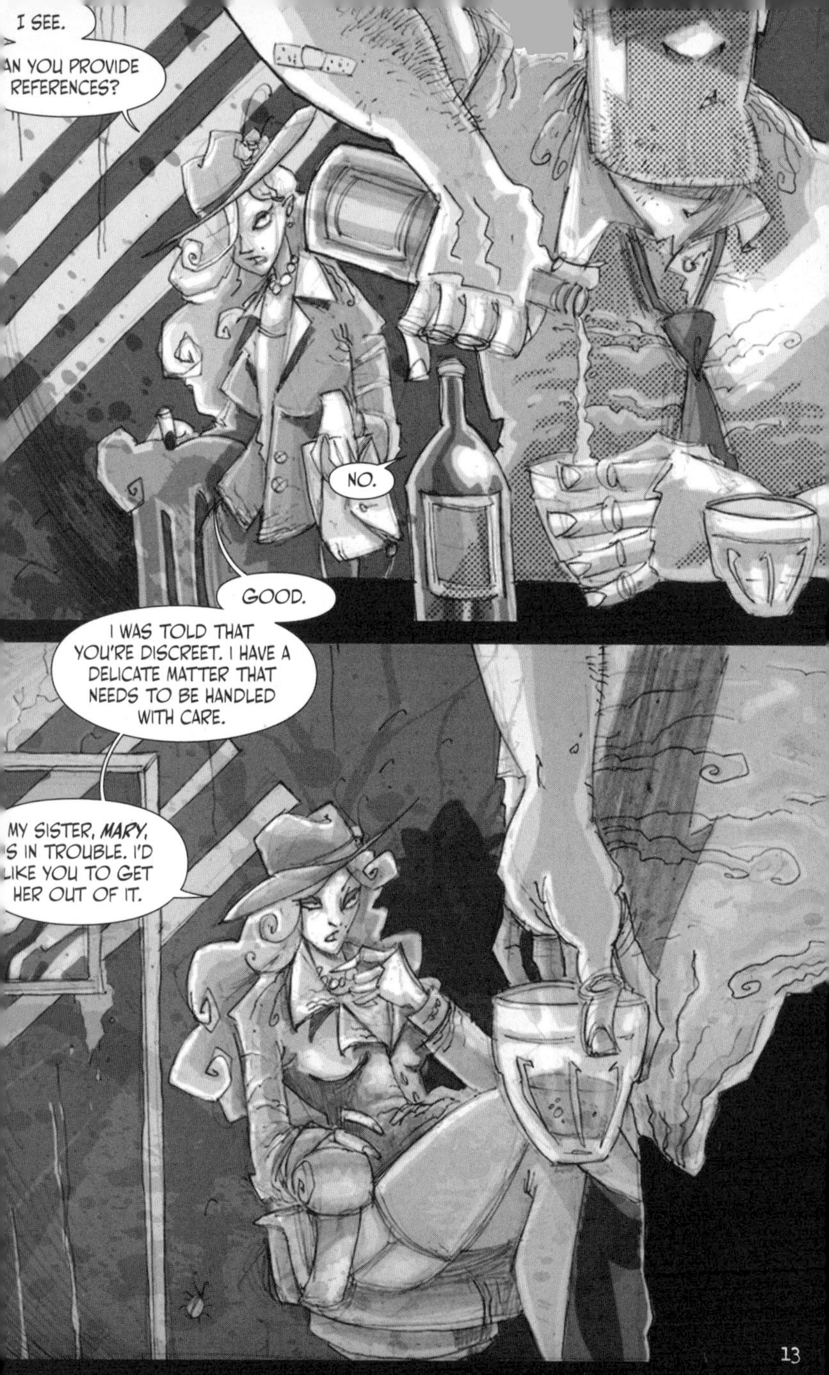
I SEE.
AN YOU PROVIDE REFERENCES?
NO.
GOOD.
I WAS TOLD THAT YOU'RE DISCREET. I HAVE A DELICATE MATTER THAT NEEDS TO BE HANDLED WITH CARE.
MY SISTER, *MARY*, S IN TROUBLE. I'D LIKE YOU TO GET HER OUT OF IT.

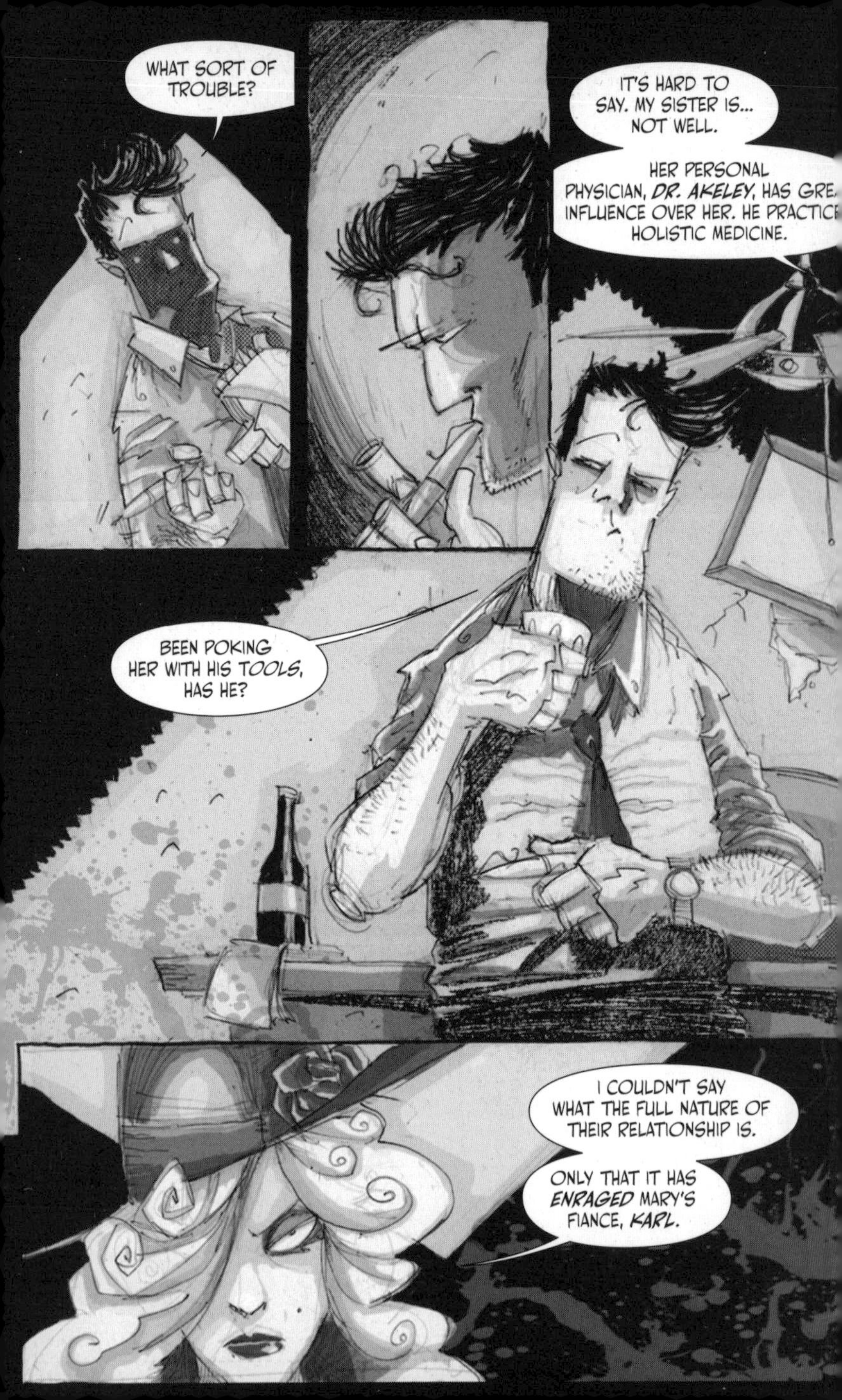
WHAT SORT OF TROUBLE?
IT'S HARD TO SAY. MY SISTER IS... NOT WELL.
HER PERSONAL PHYSICIAN, *DR. AKELEY*, HAS GRE INFLUENCE OVER HER. HE PRACTIC HOLISTIC MEDICINE.
BEEN POKING HER WITH HIS *TOOLS*, HAS HE?
I COULDN'T SAY WHAT THE FULL NATURE OF THEIR RELATIONSHIP IS.
ONLY THAT IT HAS *ENRAGED* MARY'S FIANCE, *KARL*.

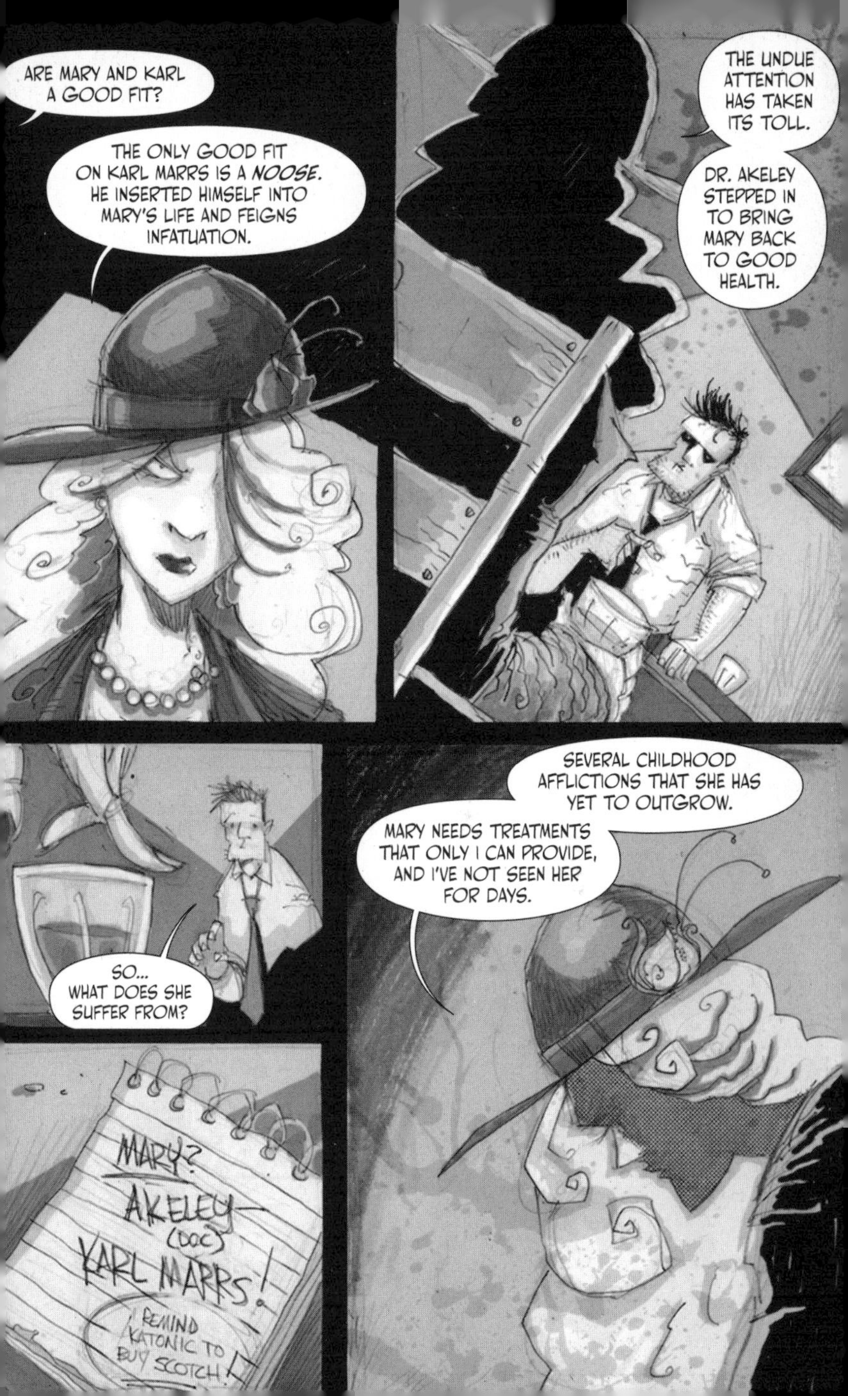
ARE MARY AND KARL A GOOD FIT?
THE ONLY GOOD FIT ON KARL MARRS IS A *NOOSE.* HE INSERTED HIMSELF INTO MARY'S LIFE AND FEIGNS INFATUATION.
THE UNDUE ATTENTION HAS TAKEN ITS TOLL.
DR. AKELEY STEPPED IN TO BRING MARY BACK TO GOOD HEALTH.
SO... WHAT DOES SHE SUFFER FROM?
MARY?
AKELEY (DOC)
KARL MARRS!
REMIND KATONIC TO BUY SCOTCH!
SEVERAL CHILDHOOD AFFLICTIONS THAT SHE HAS YET TO OUTGROW.
MARY NEEDS TREATMENTS THAT ONLY I CAN PROVIDE, AND I'VE NOT SEEN HER FOR DAYS.

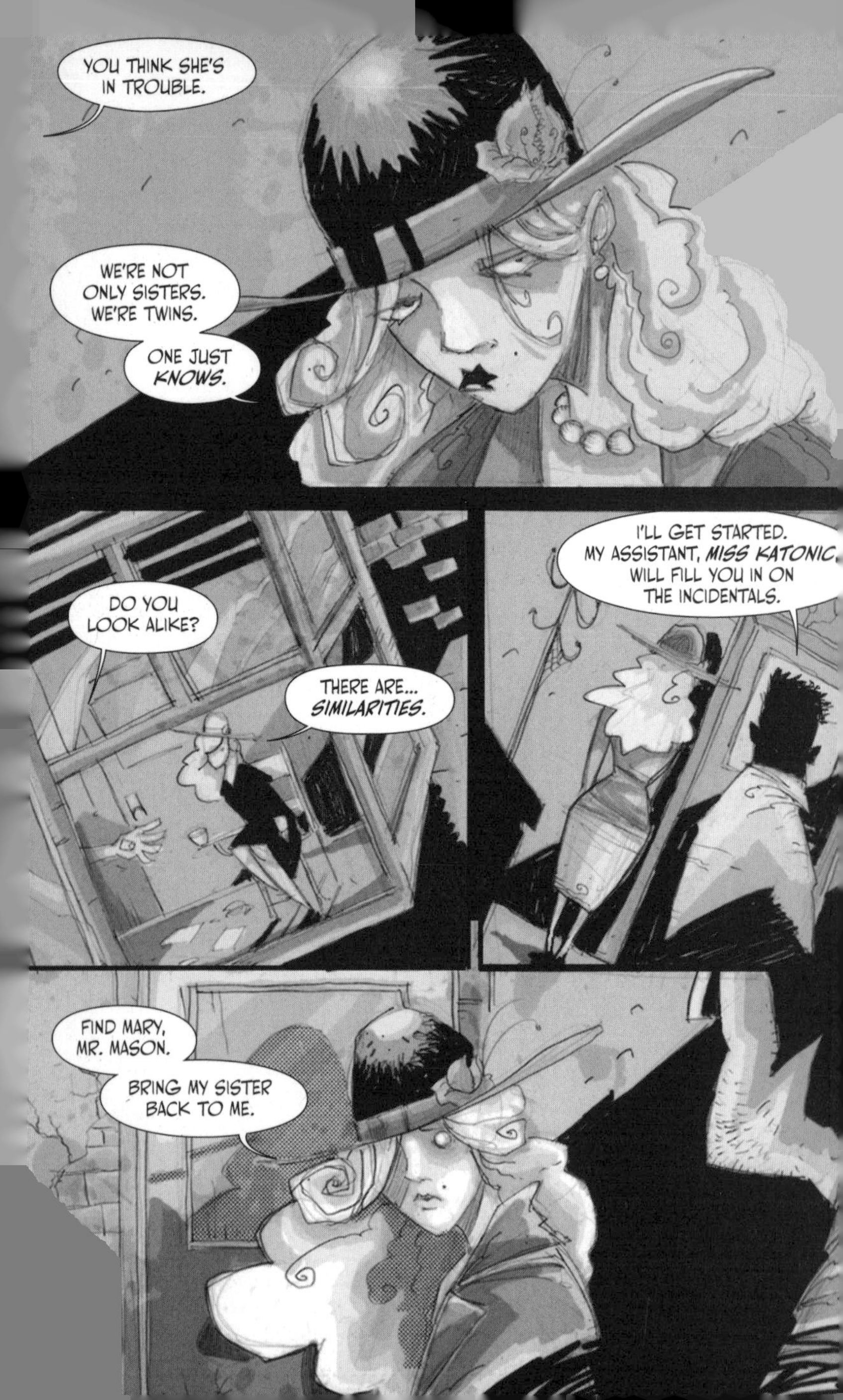
YOU THINK SHE'S IN TROUBLE.
WE'RE NOT ONLY SISTERS. WE'RE TWINS.
ONE JUST *KNOWS.*
DO YOU LOOK ALIKE?
THERE ARE... *SIMILARITIES.*
I'LL GET STARTED. MY ASSISTANT, *MISS KATONIC,* WILL FILL YOU IN ON THE INCIDENTALS.
FIND MARY, MR. MASON.
BRING MY SISTER BACK TO ME.

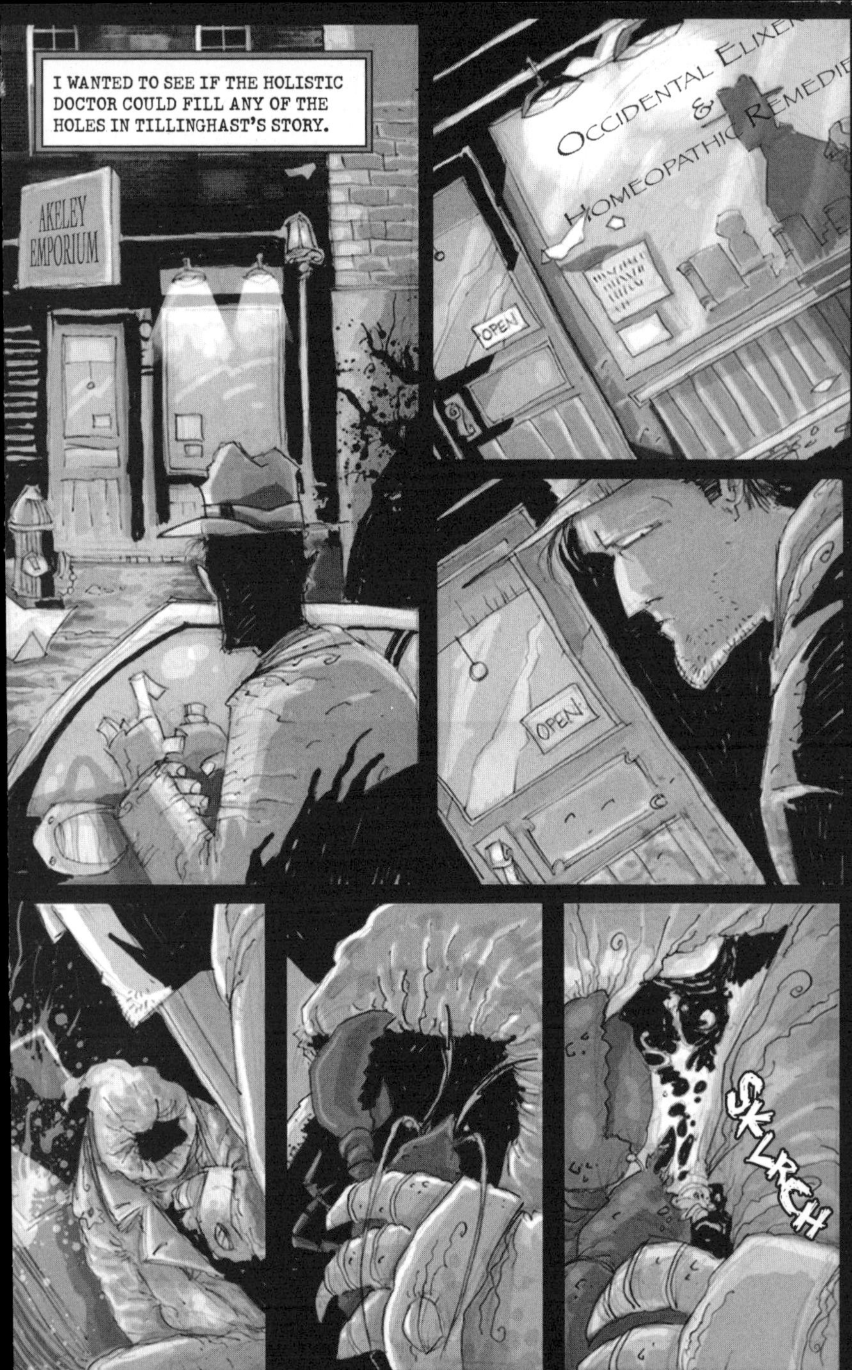
I WANTED TO SEE IF THE HOLISTIC DOCTOR COULD FILL ANY OF THE HOLES IN TILLINGHAST'S STORY.
AKELEY EMPORIUM
OCCIDENTAL ELIXER & HOMEOPATHIC REMEDIE
OPEN
OPEN
SKLRCH

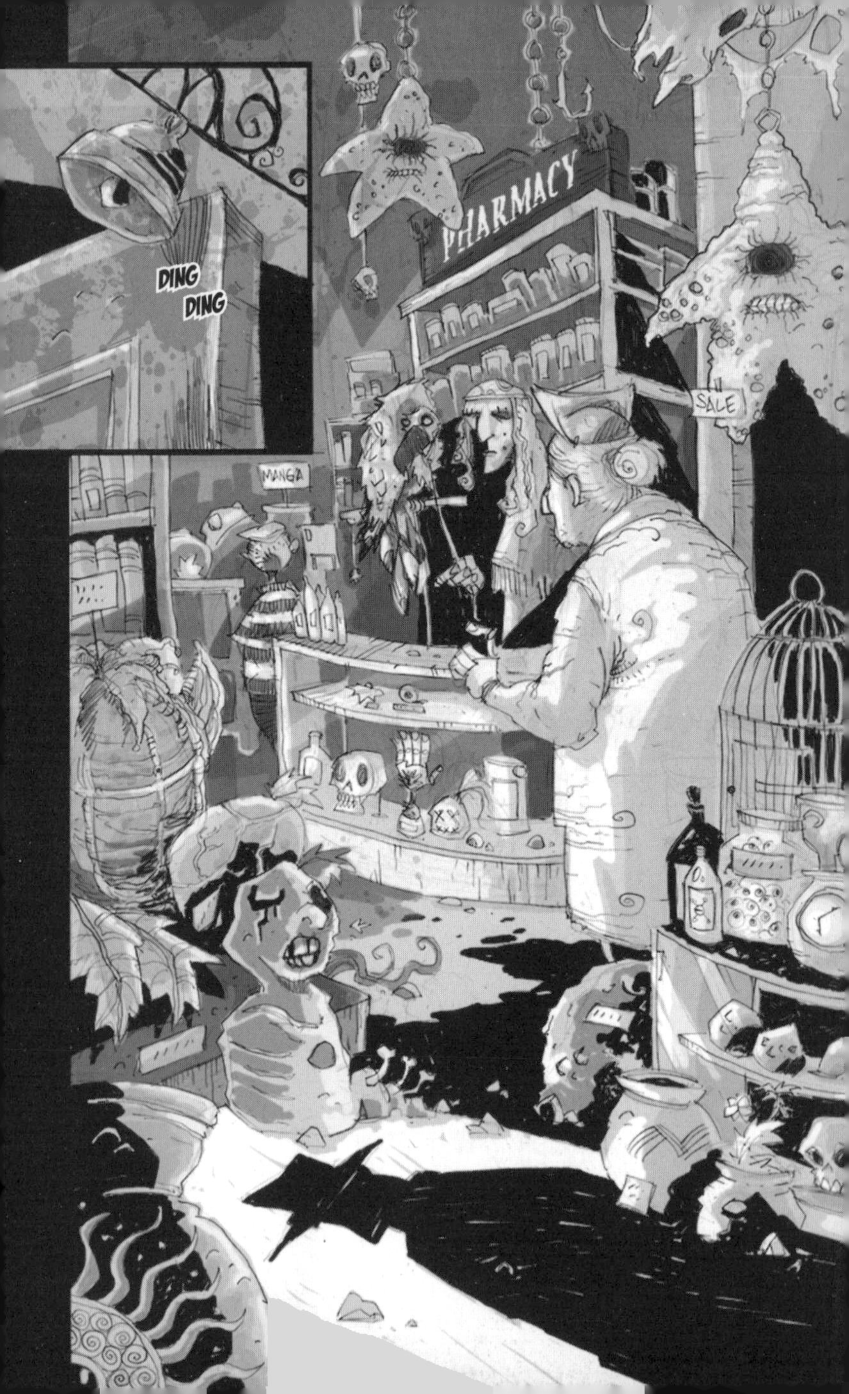
DING
DING
PHARMACY
SALE
MANGA

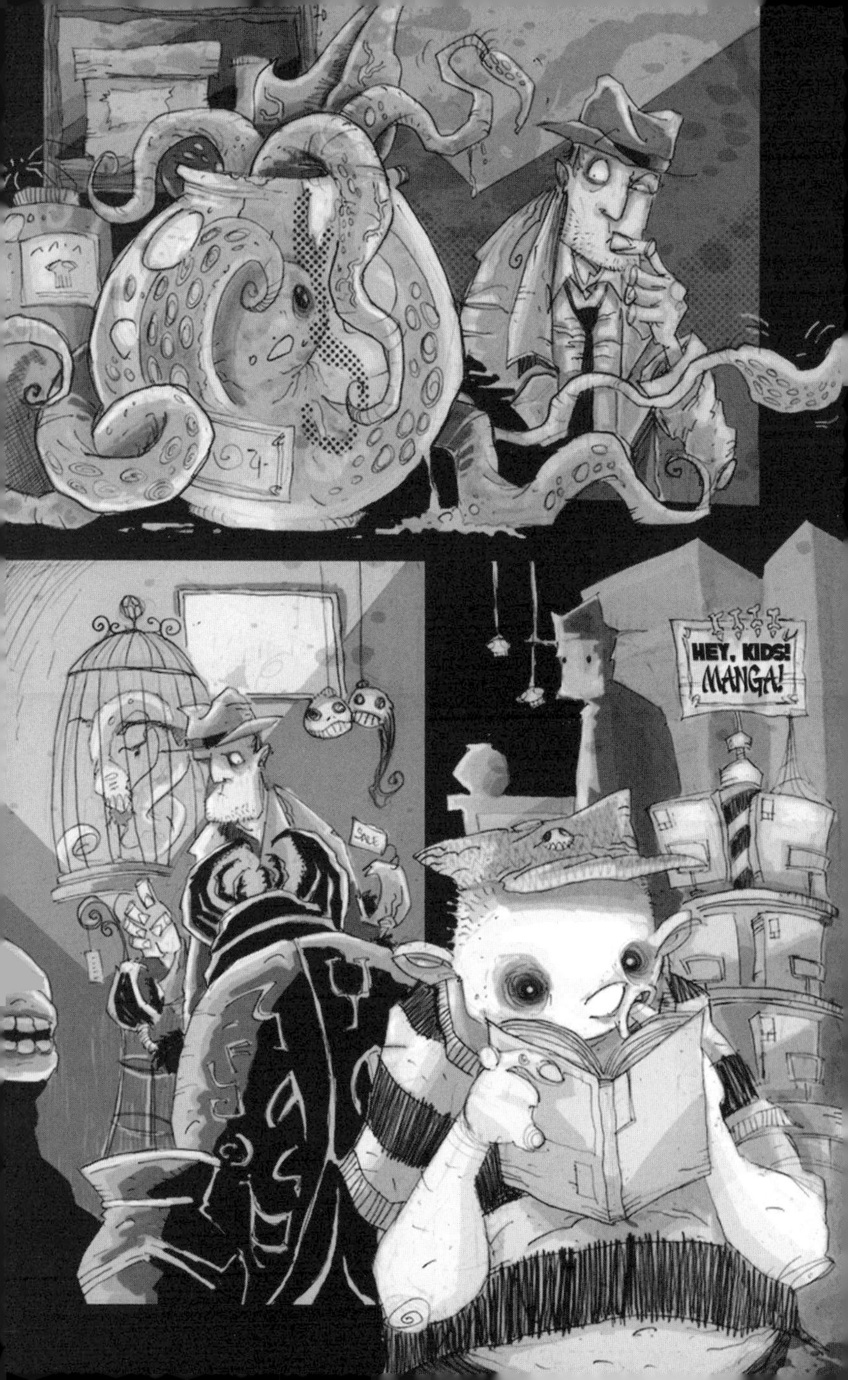
SALE
HEY, KIDS! MANGA!

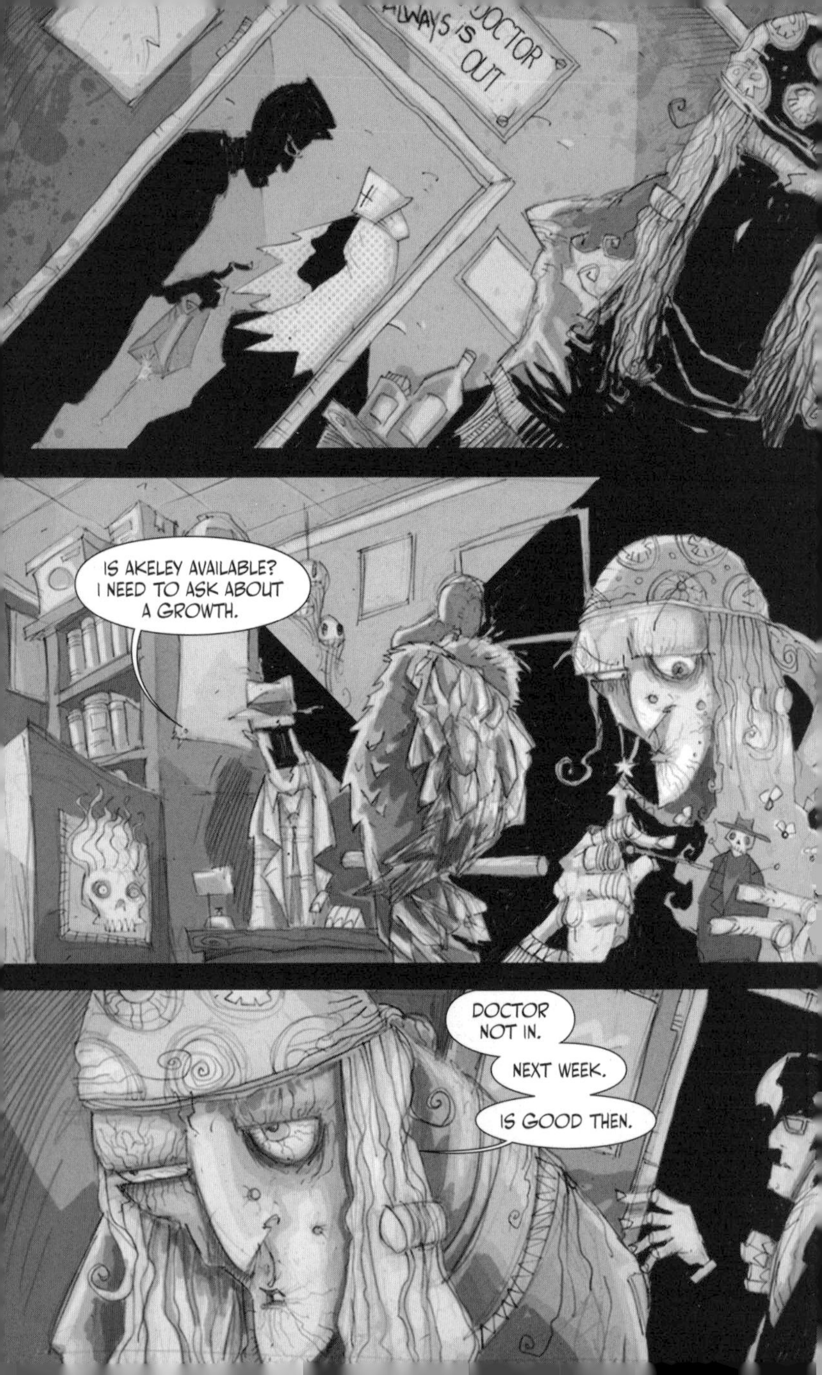

ALWAYS IS DOCTOR OUT
IS AKELEY AVAILABLE? I NEED TO ASK ABOUT A GROWTH.
DOCTOR NOT IN.
NEXT WEEK.
IS GOOD THEN.

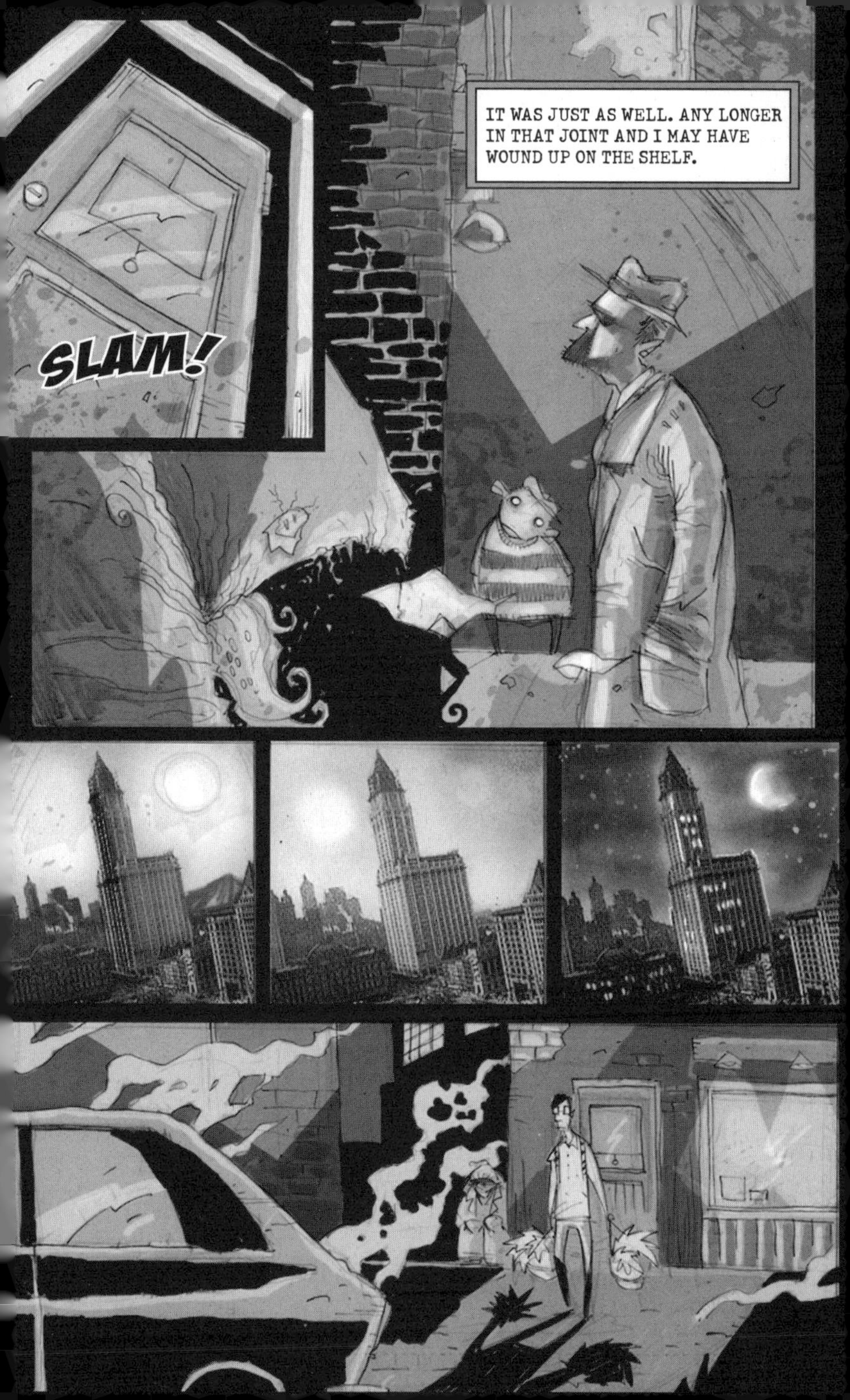
SLAM!
IT WAS JUST AS WELL. ANY LONGER IN THAT JOINT AND I MAY HAVE WOUND UP ON THE SHELF.

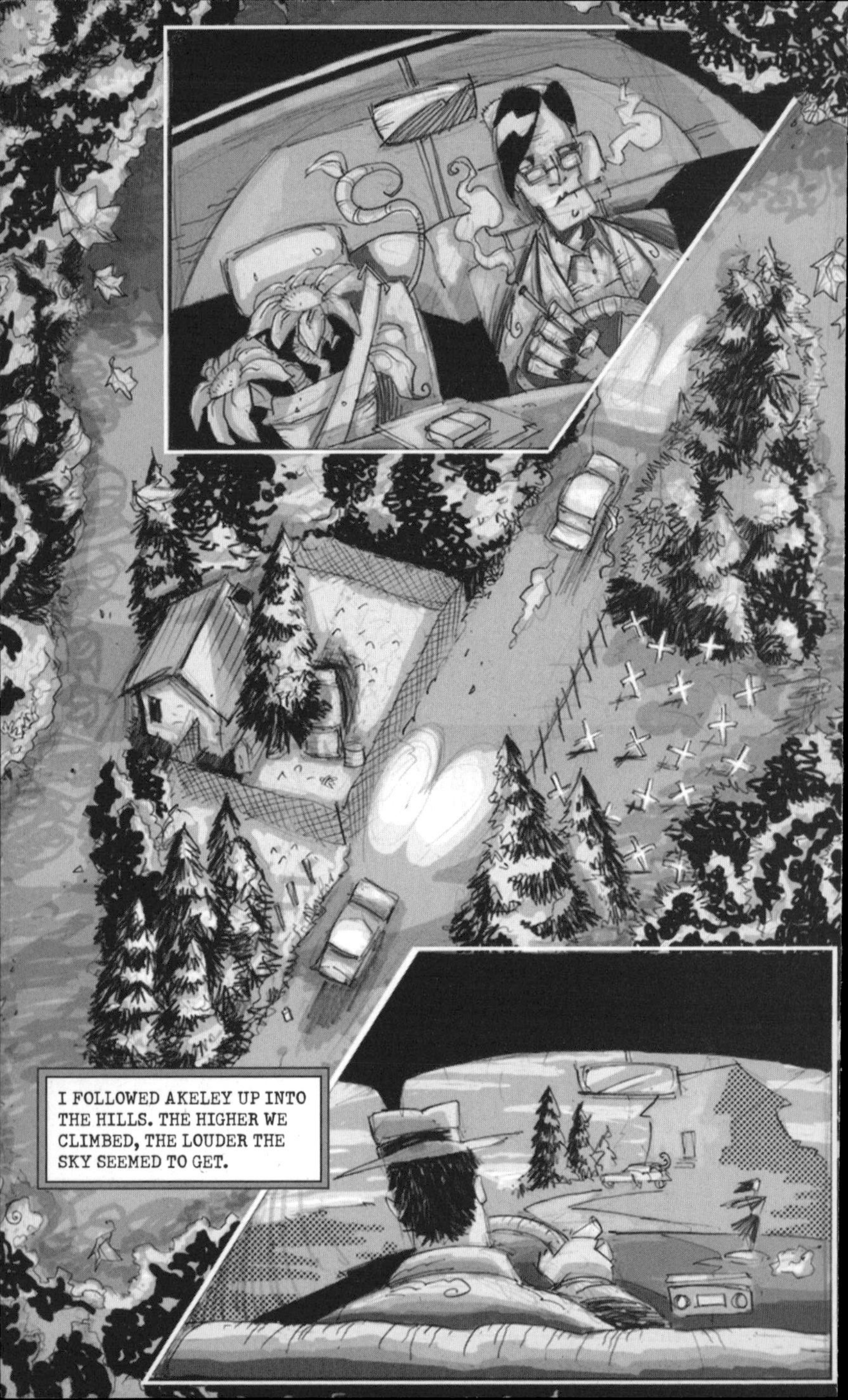
I FOLLOWED AKELEY UP INTO THE HILLS. THE HIGHER WE CLIMBED, THE LOUDER THE SKY SEEMED TO GET.

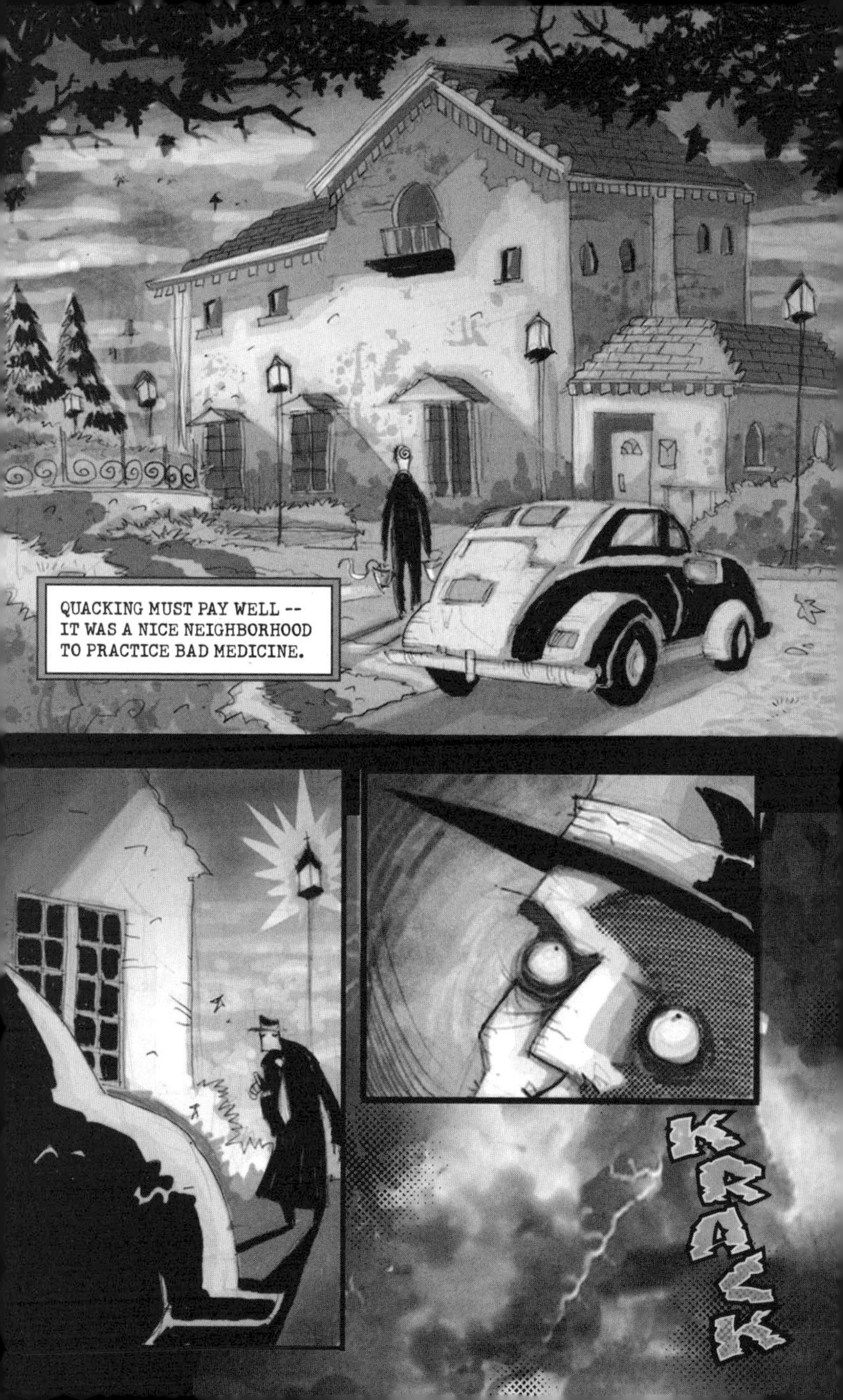
QUACKING MUST PAY WELL -- IT WAS A NICE NEIGHBORHOOD TO PRACTICE BAD MEDICINE.
KRAK

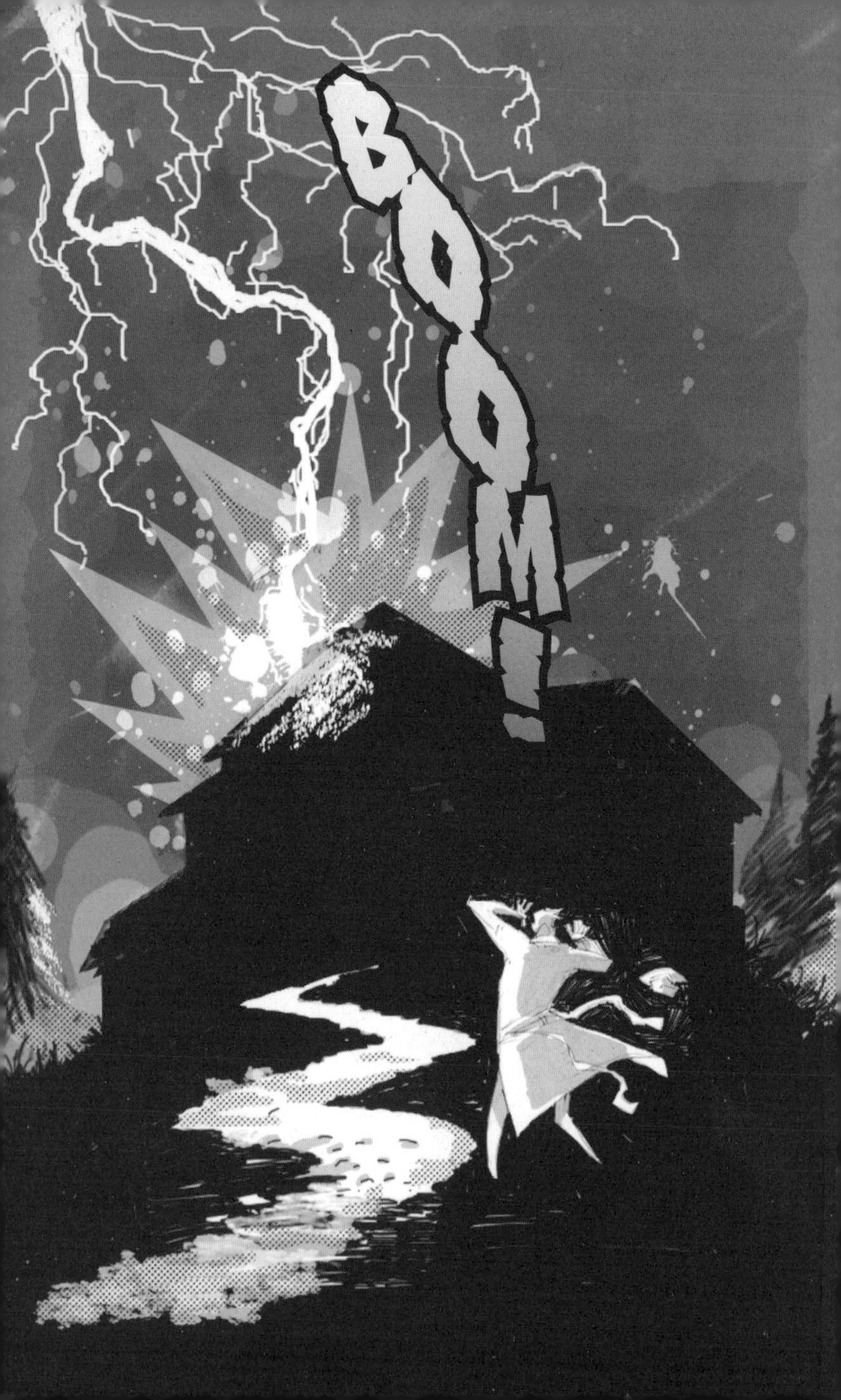
BOOM!

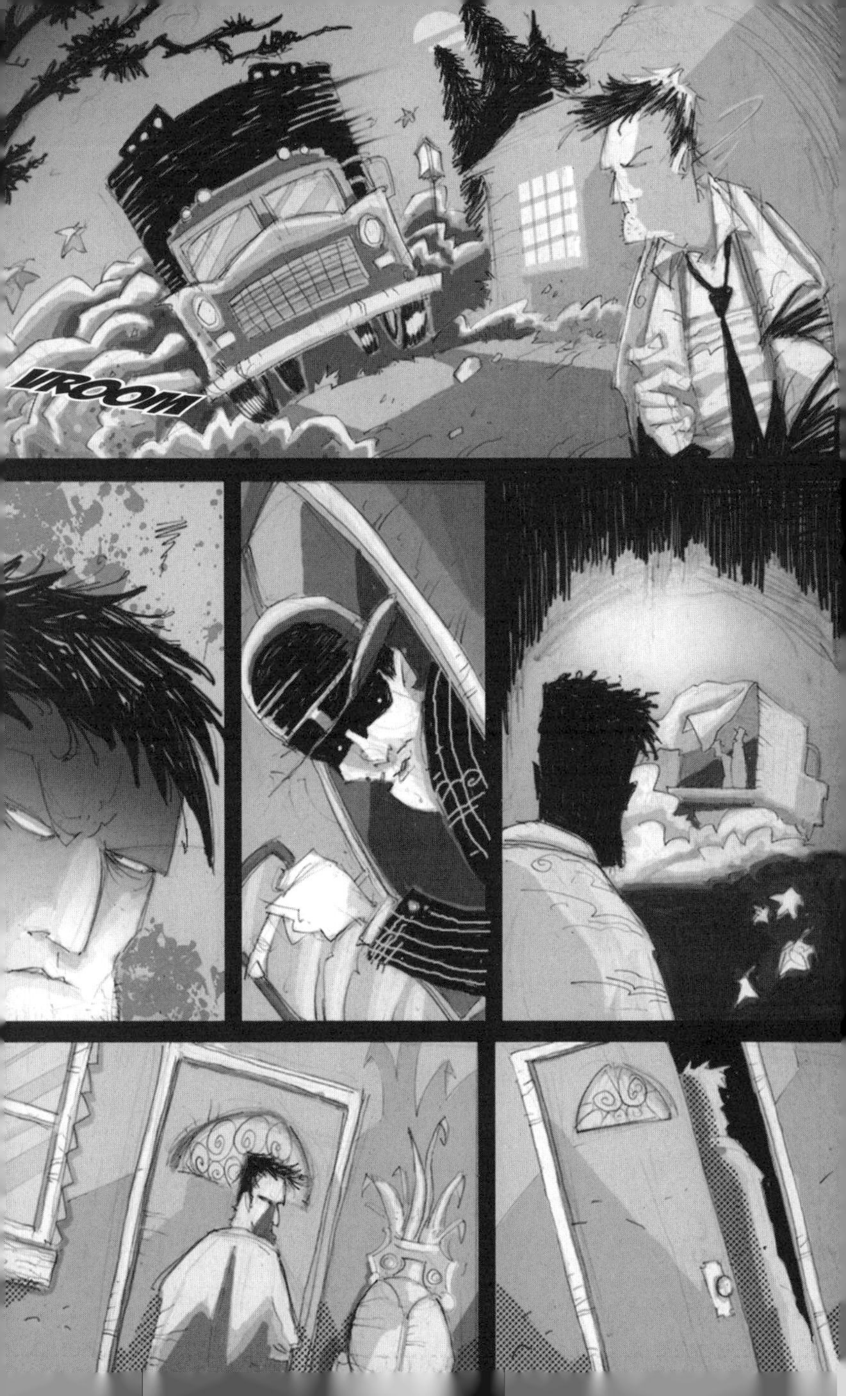
VROOM

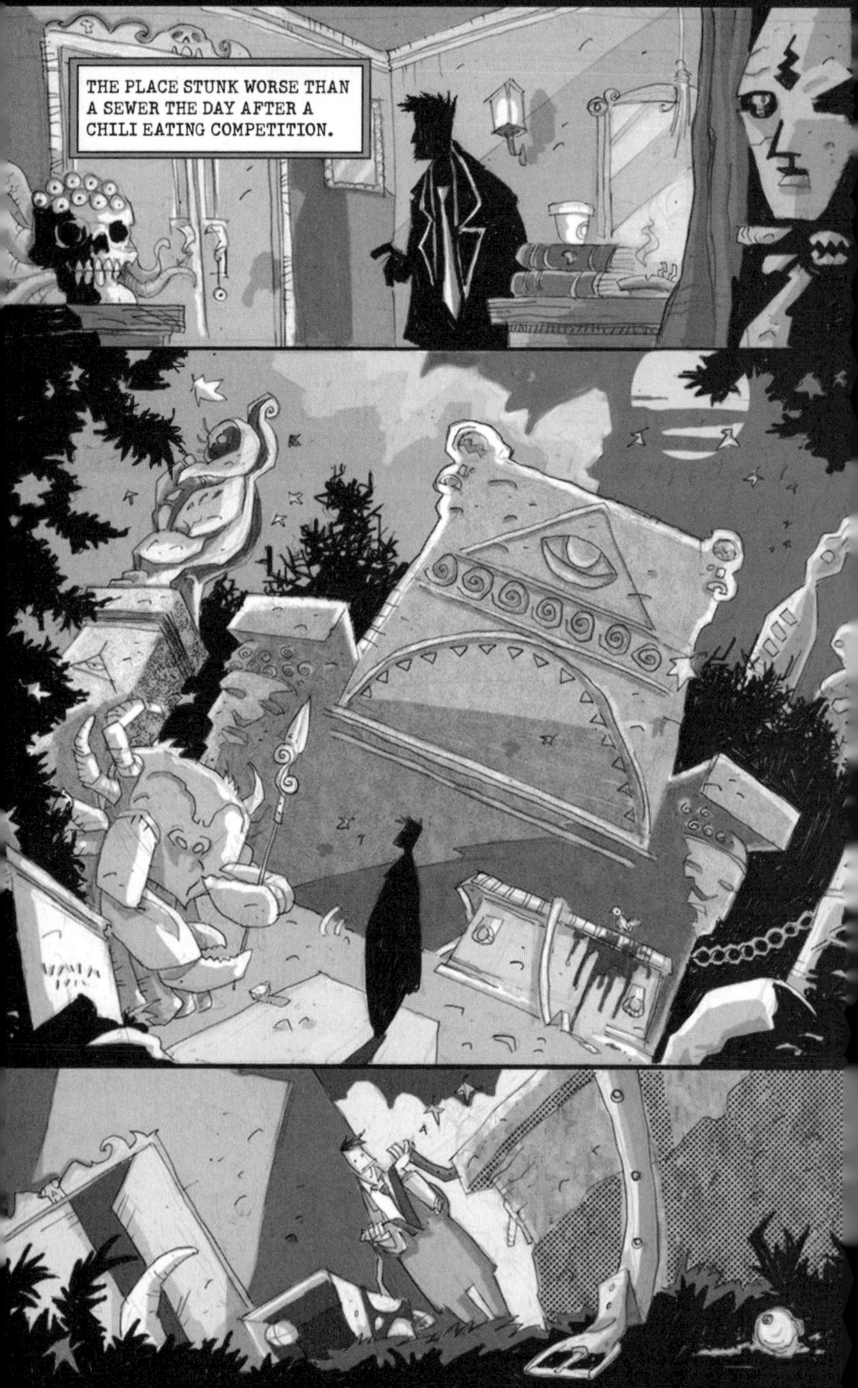
THE PLACE STUNK WORSE THAN A SEWER THE DAY AFTER A CHILI EATING COMPETITION.

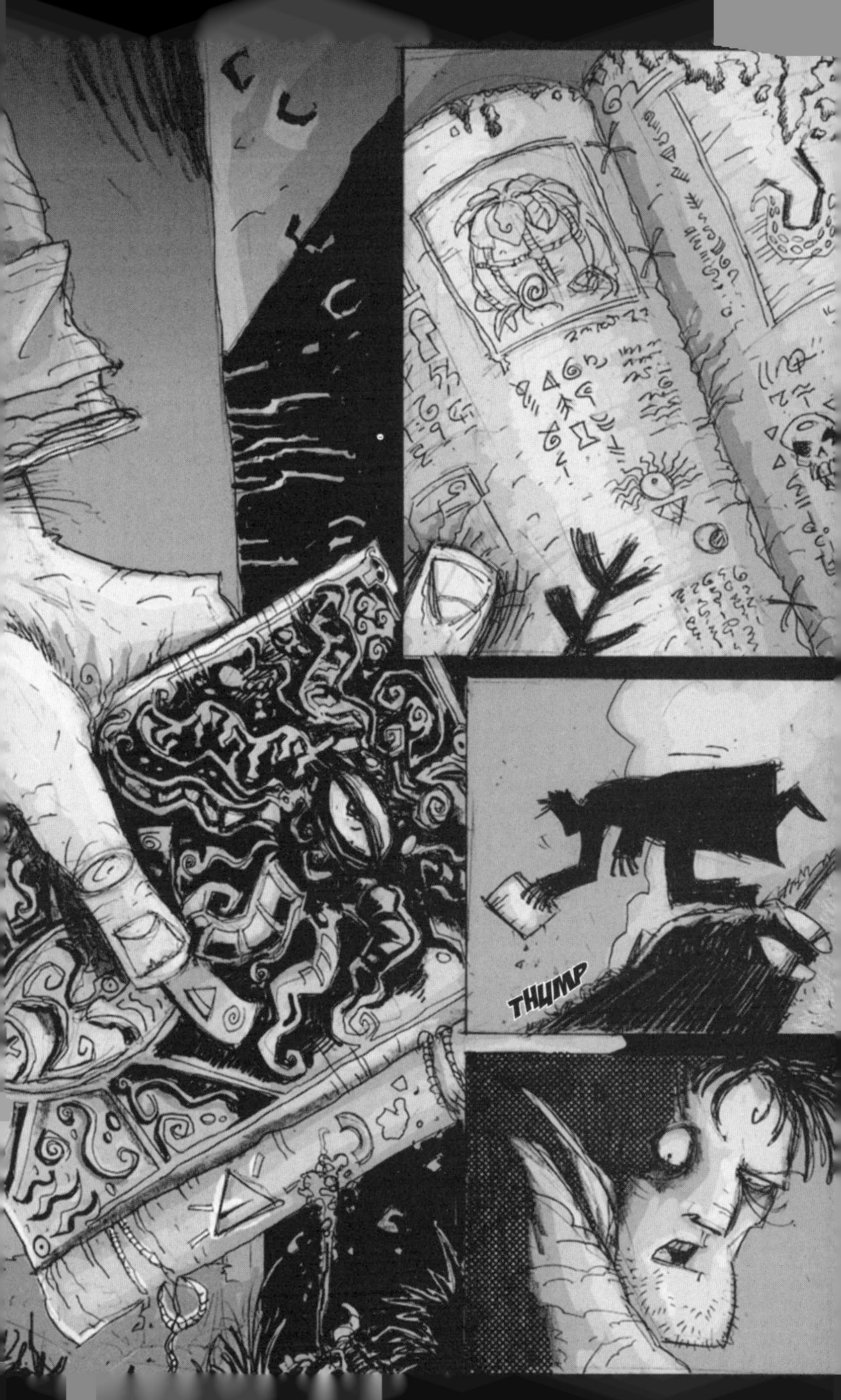
THUMP

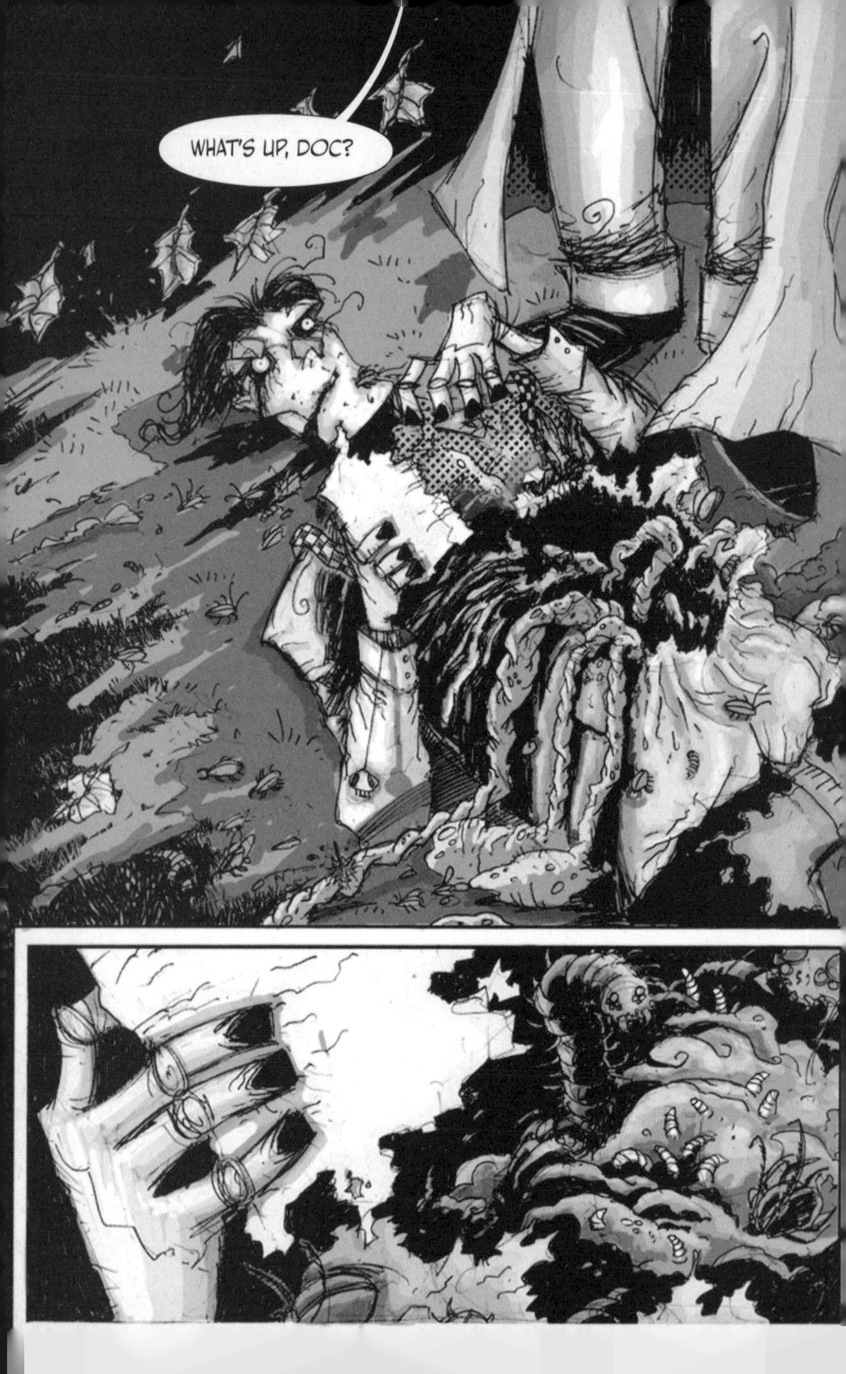
WHAT'S UP, DOC?

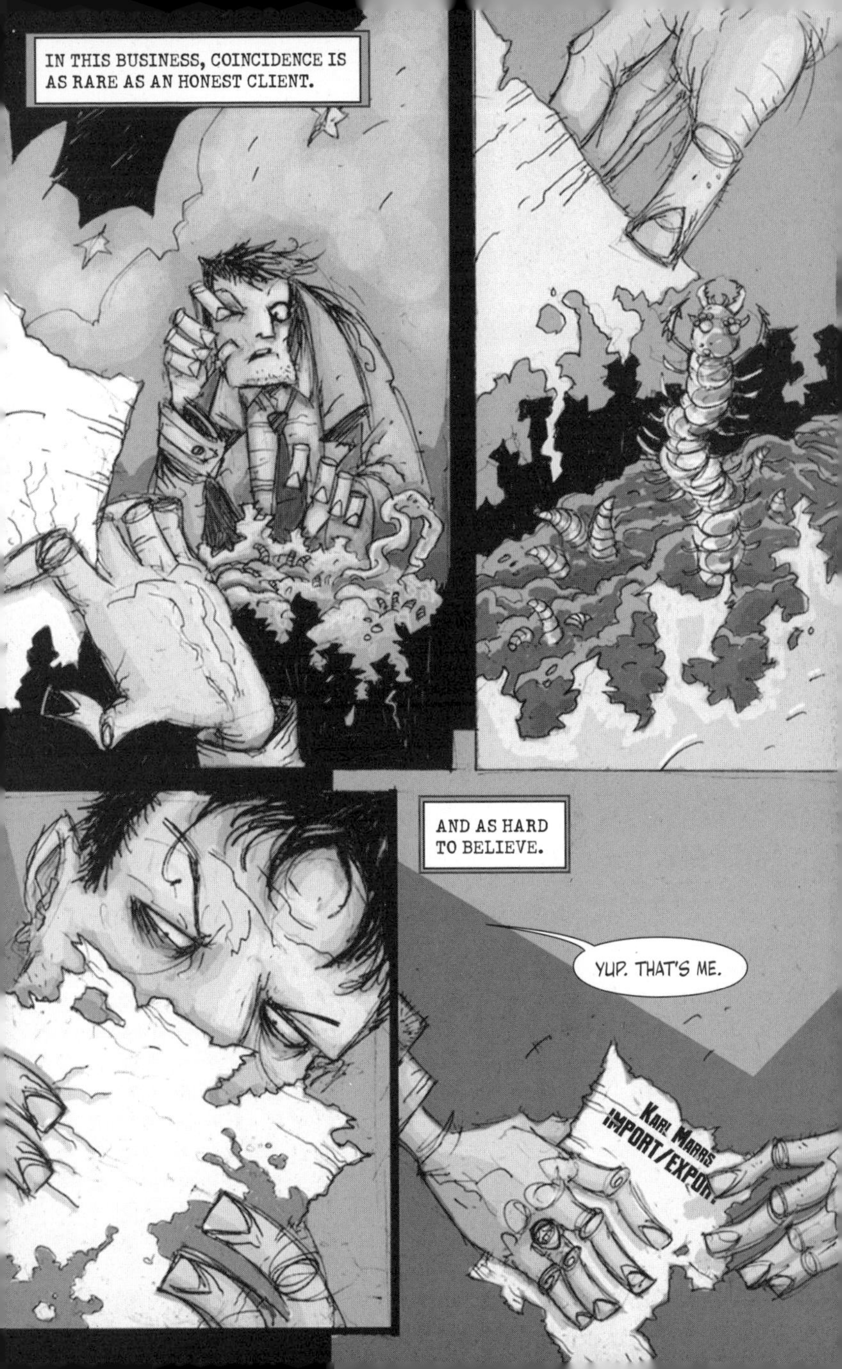
IN THIS BUSINESS, COINCIDENCE IS AS RARE AS AN HONEST CLIENT.
AND AS HARD TO BELIEVE.
YUP. THAT'S ME.
KARL MARRS

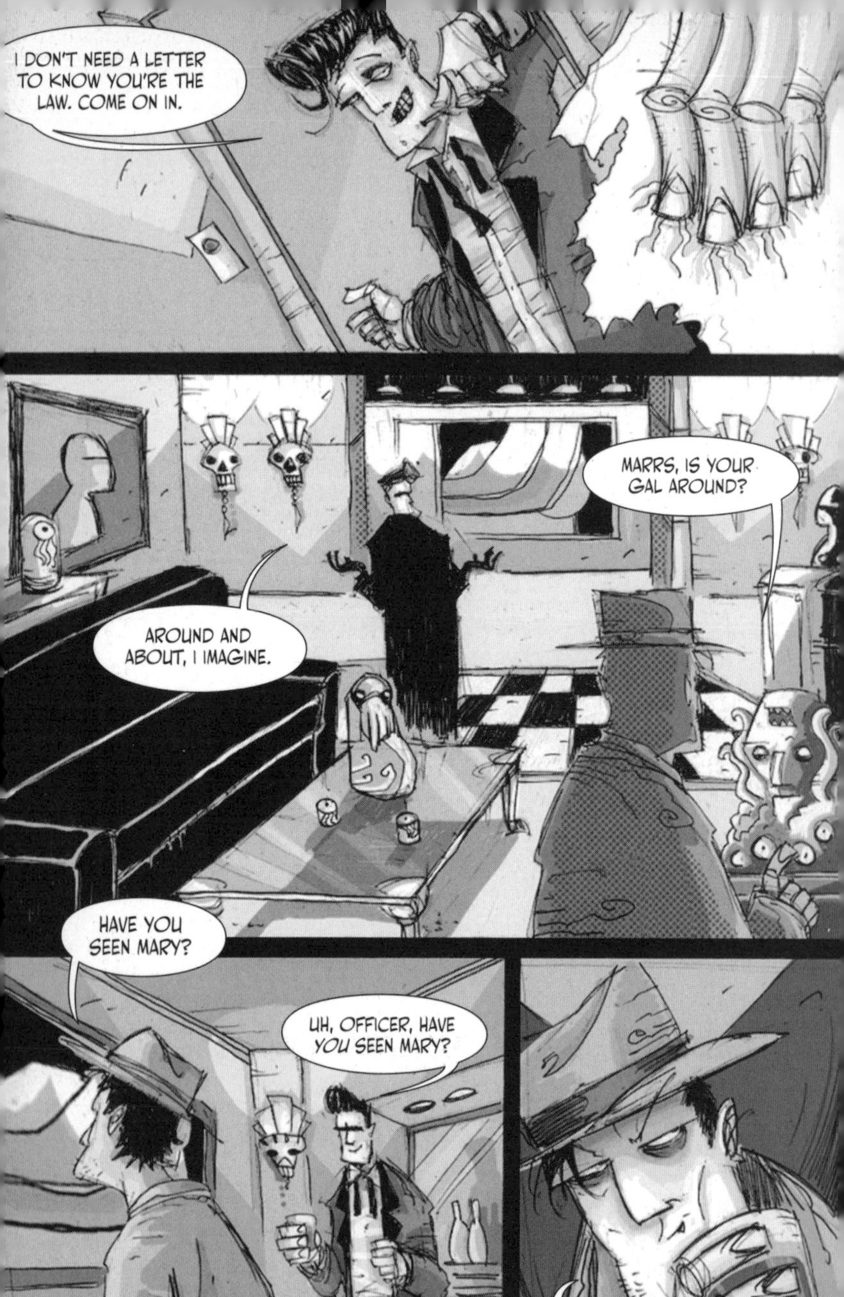
I DON'T NEED A LETTER TO KNOW YOU'RE THE LAW. COME ON IN.
AROUND AND ABOUT, I IMAGINE.
MARRS, IS YOUR GAL AROUND?
HAVE YOU SEEN MARY?
UH, OFFICER, HAVE YOU SEEN MARY?
SHE'S SPECIAL, HUH?

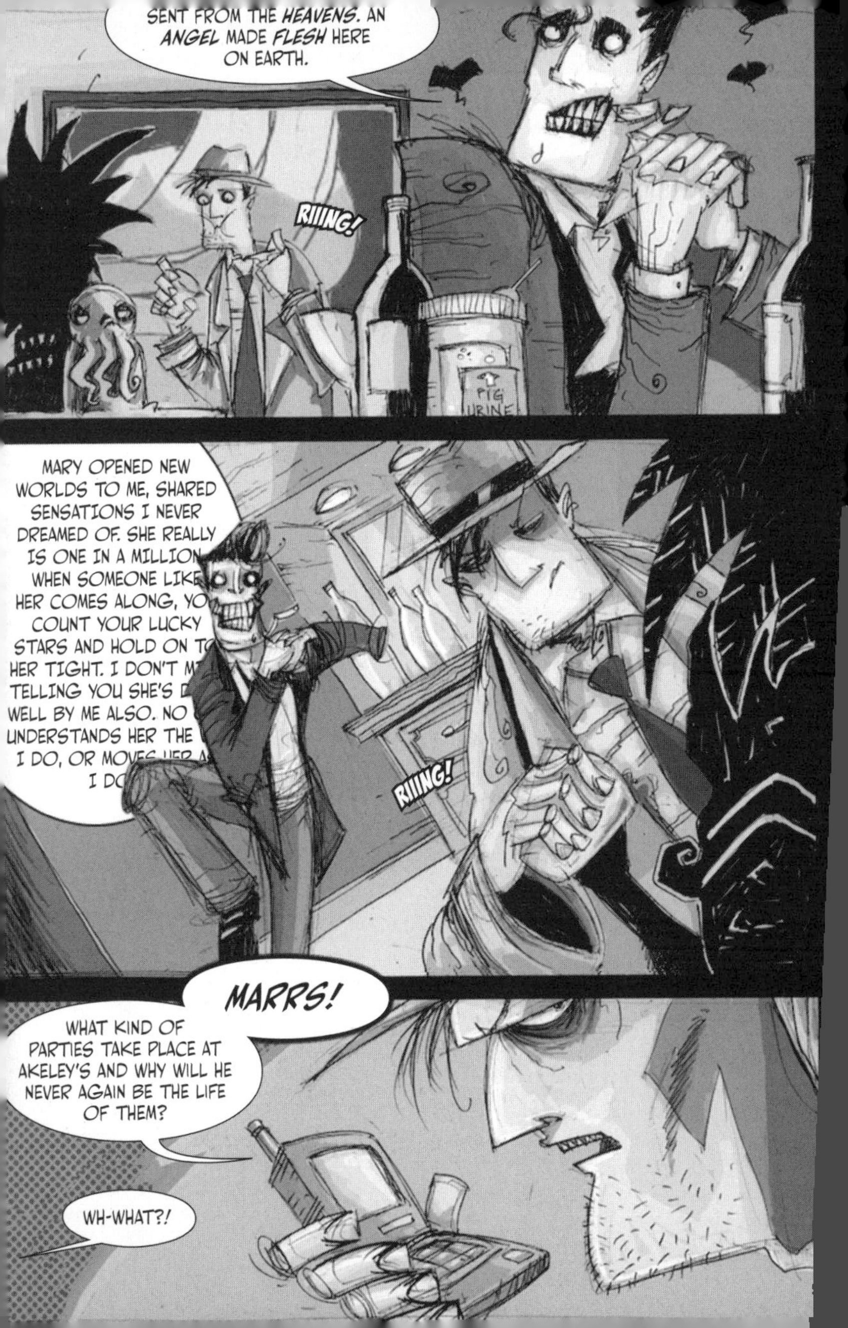
SENT FROM THE *HEAVENS.* AN *ANGEL* MADE *FLESH* HERE ON EARTH.
RIIING!
PIG URINE
MARY OPENED NEW WORLDS TO ME, SHARED SENSATIONS I NEVER DREAMED OF. SHE REALLY IS ONE IN A MILLION WHEN SOMEONE LIKE HER COMES ALONG, YO COUNT YOUR LUCKY STARS AND HOLD ON TO HER TIGHT. I DON'T M TELLING YOU SHE'S D WELL BY ME ALSO. NO UNDERSTANDS HER THE I DO, OR MOVES HER A I DO
RIIING!
MARRS!
WHAT KIND OF PARTIES TAKE PLACE AT AKELEY'S AND WHY WILL HE NEVER AGAIN BE THE LIFE OF THEM?
WH-WHAT?!

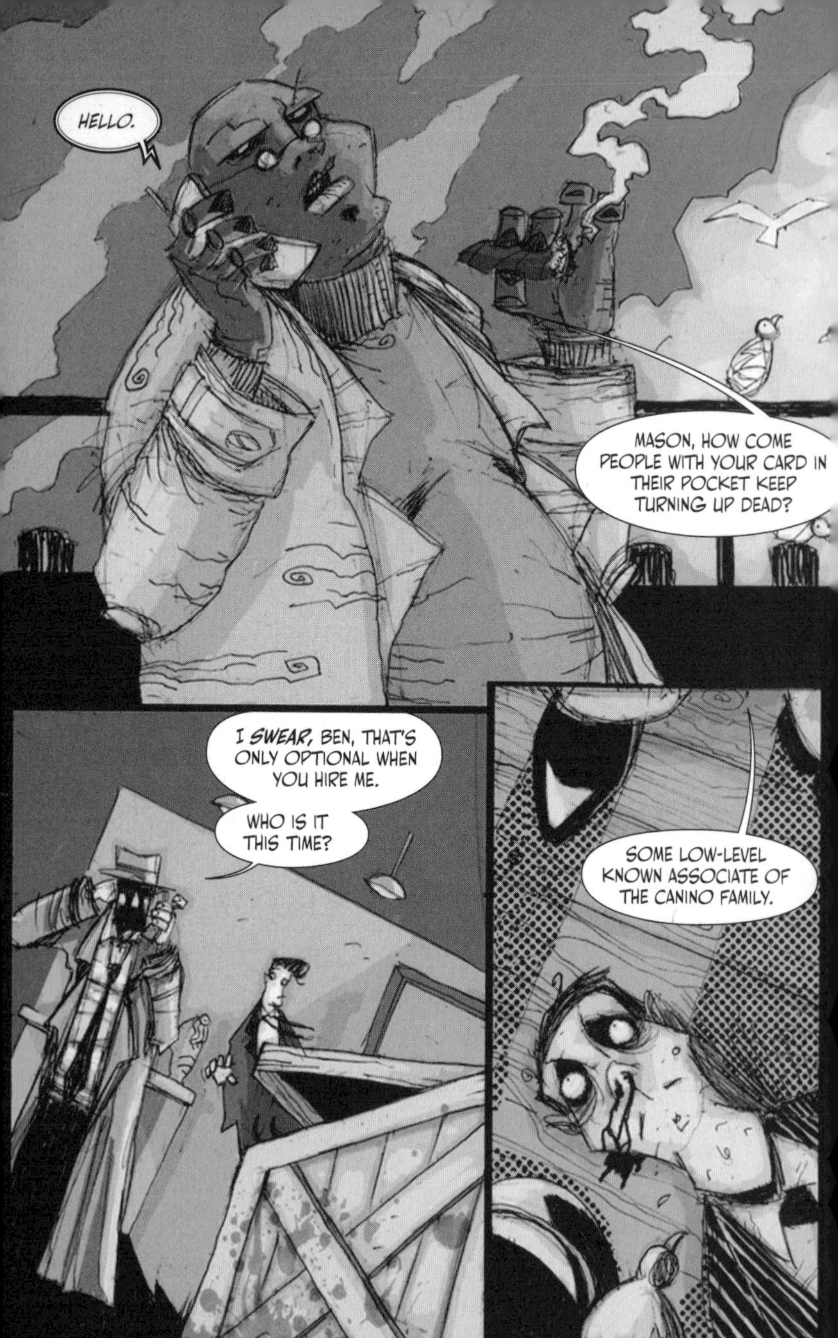
HELLO.
MASON, HOW COME PEOPLE WITH YOUR CARD IN THEIR POCKET KEEP TURNING UP DEAD?
I *SWEAR,* BEN, THAT'S ONLY OPTIONAL WHEN YOU HIRE ME.
WHO IS IT THIS TIME?
SOME LOW-LEVEL KNOWN ASSOCIATE OF THE CANINO FAMILY.

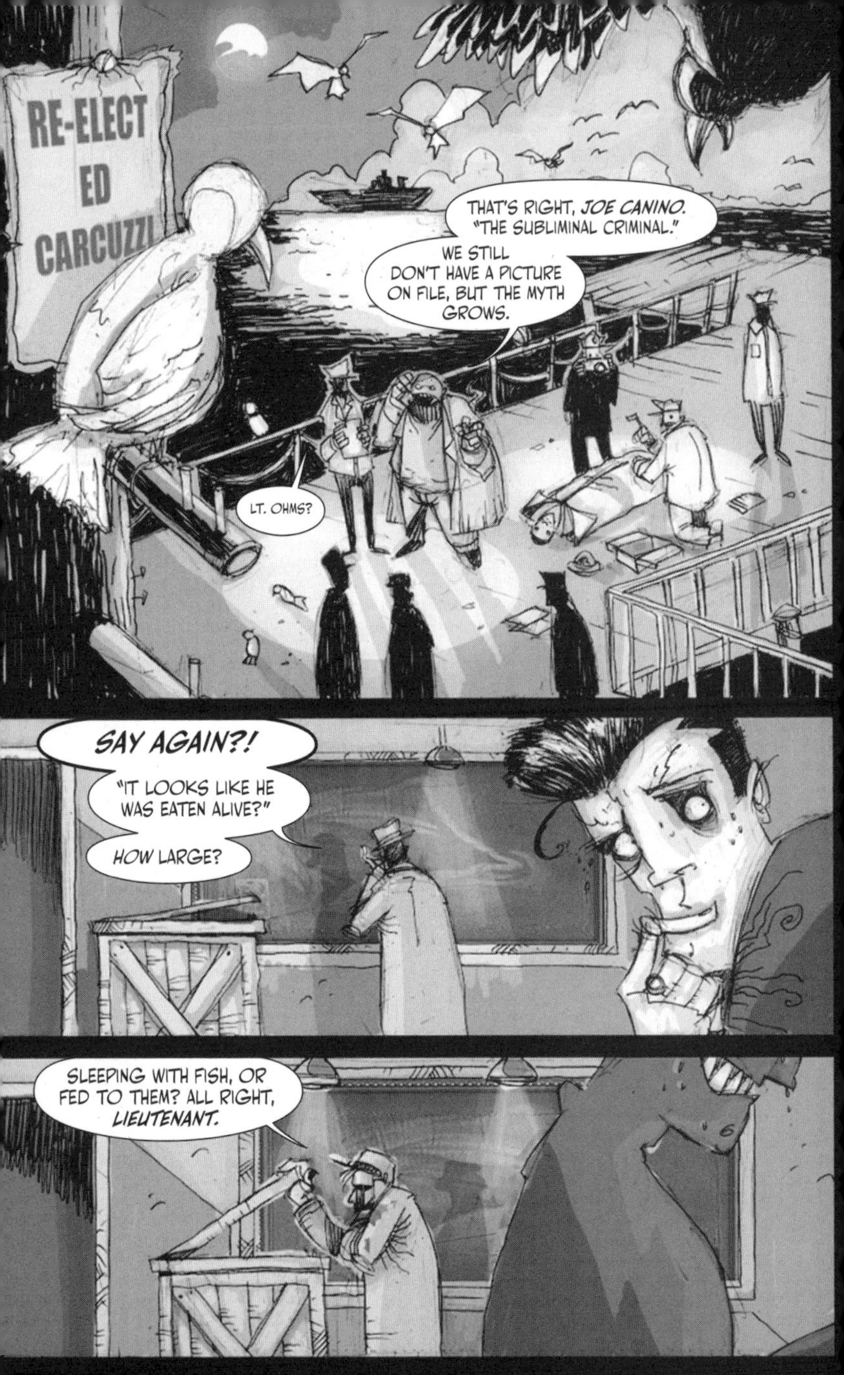
RE-ELECT ED CARCUZZI
THAT'S RIGHT, *JOE CANINO.* "THE SUBLIMINAL CRIMINAL."
WE STILL DON'T HAVE A PICTURE ON FILE, BUT THE MYTH GROWS.
LT. OHMS?
*SAY AGAIN?!*
"IT LOOKS LIKE HE WAS EATEN ALIVE?"
*HOW* LARGE?
SLEEPING WITH FISH, OR FED TO THEM? ALL RIGHT, *LIEUTENANT.*

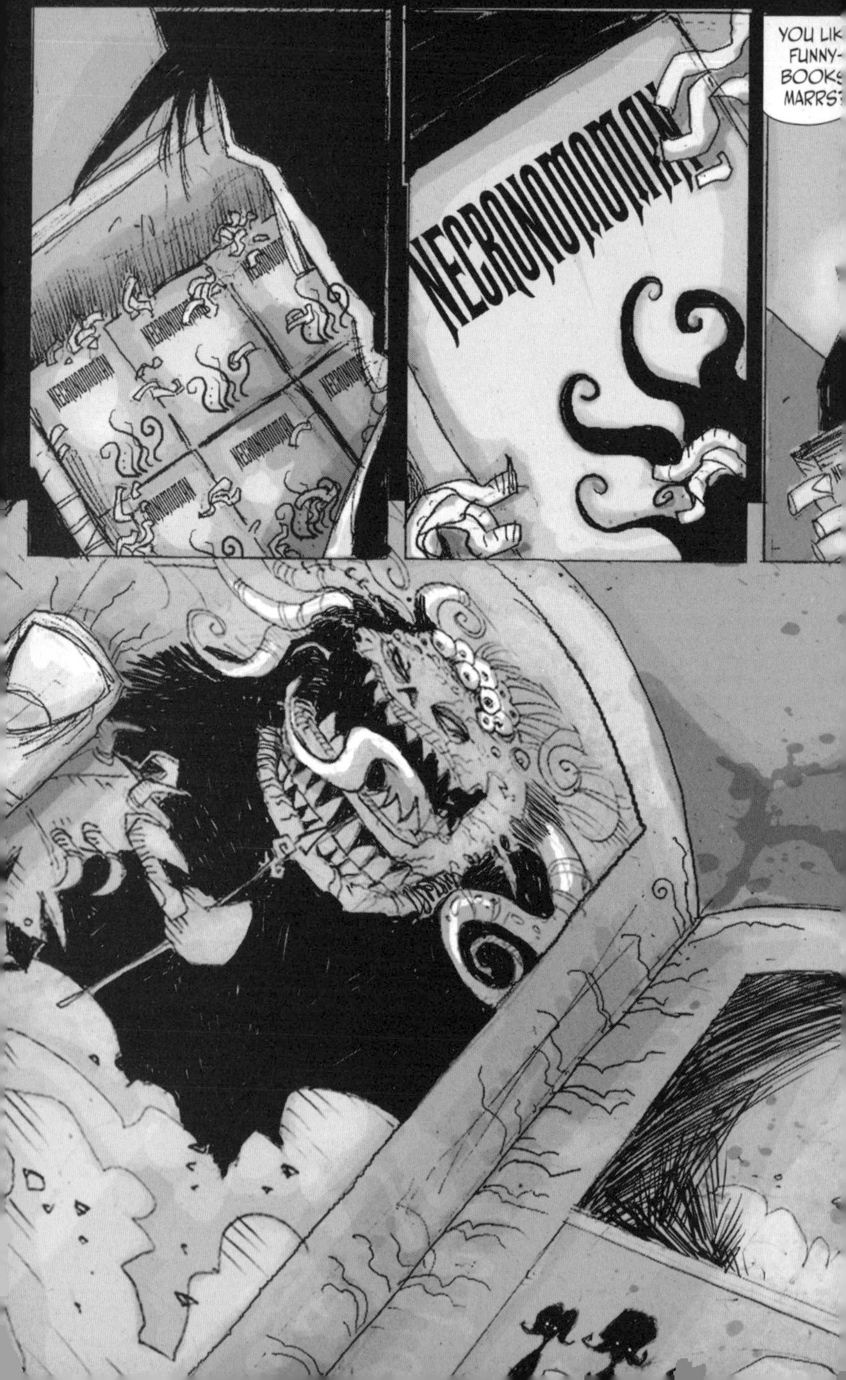
NECRONOMOMAN
YOU LIK FUNNY-BOOKS MARRS?

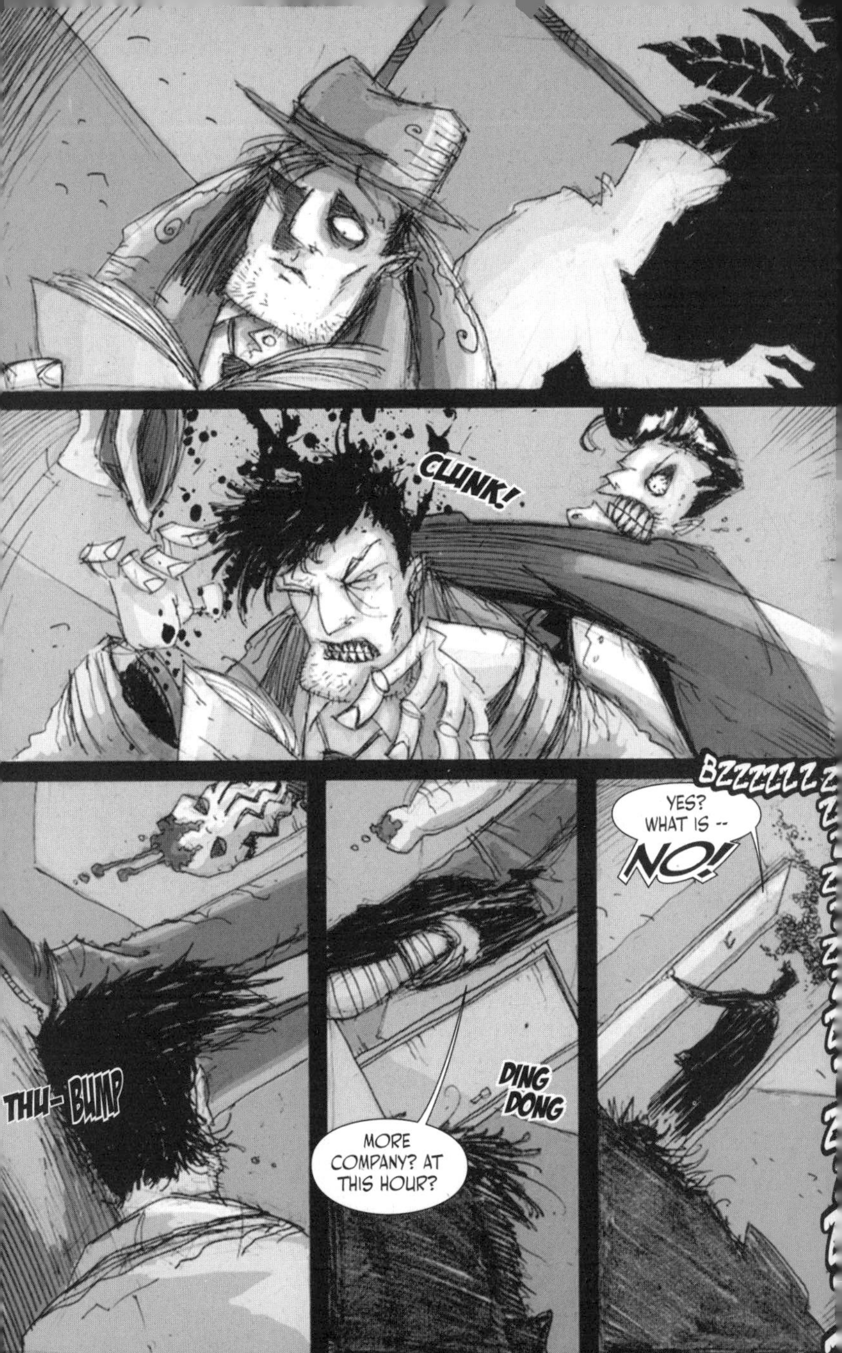
CLUNK!
THU- BUMP
DING DONG
MORE COMPANY? AT THIS HOUR?
BZZZZZZZZ
YES? WHAT IS --
NO!

BZZZZZ ZZZBZZZZZZZZZZZ
DON'T TAKE ME BACK TO GATEMOUTH!
BZZZZZZZZZZZZZZZZZZZBZZZ
HE DOESN'T KNOW!! I DIDN'T SAY A WORD!!
ZZZZZZZZZZZZZZZZZZBZZZZZZZ
NO!! AH!! AHH!! AHGH! ARRRHHGGH!!
AURLGHK

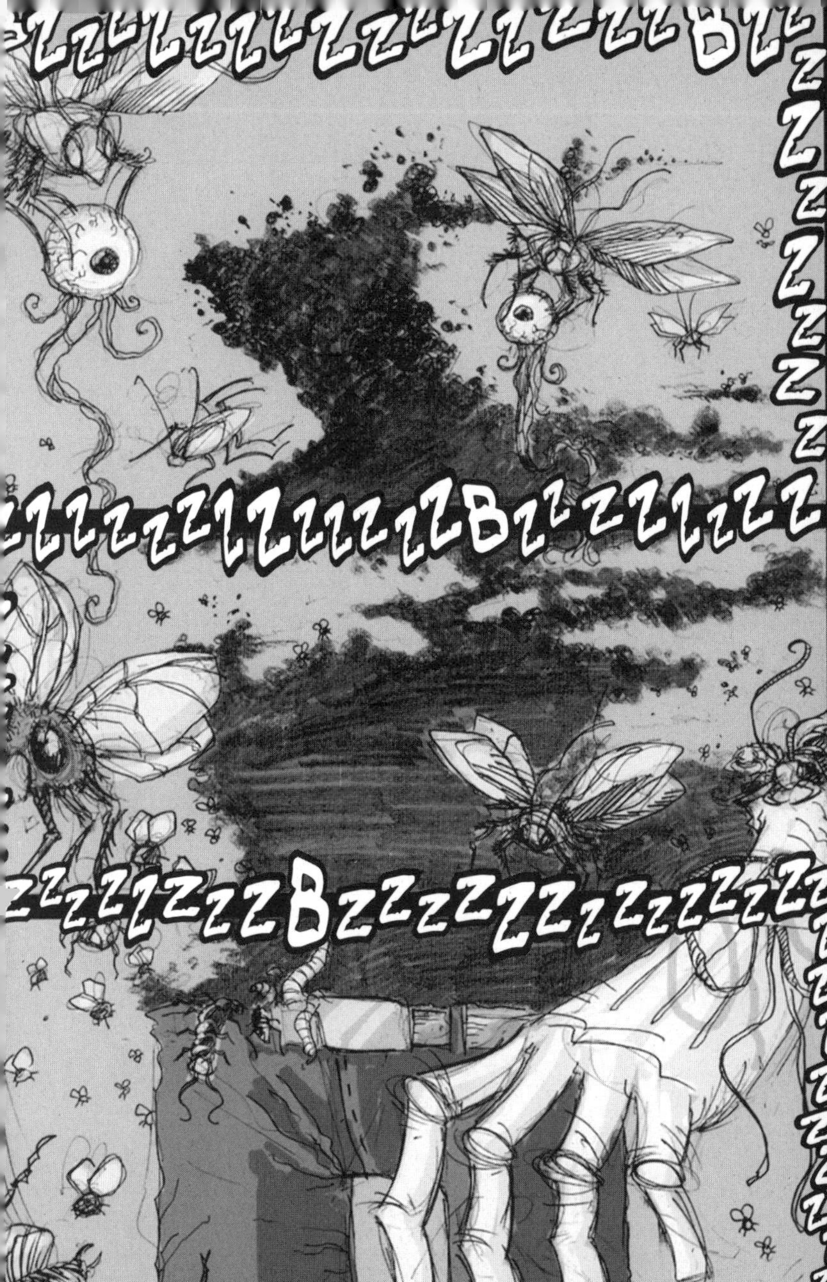

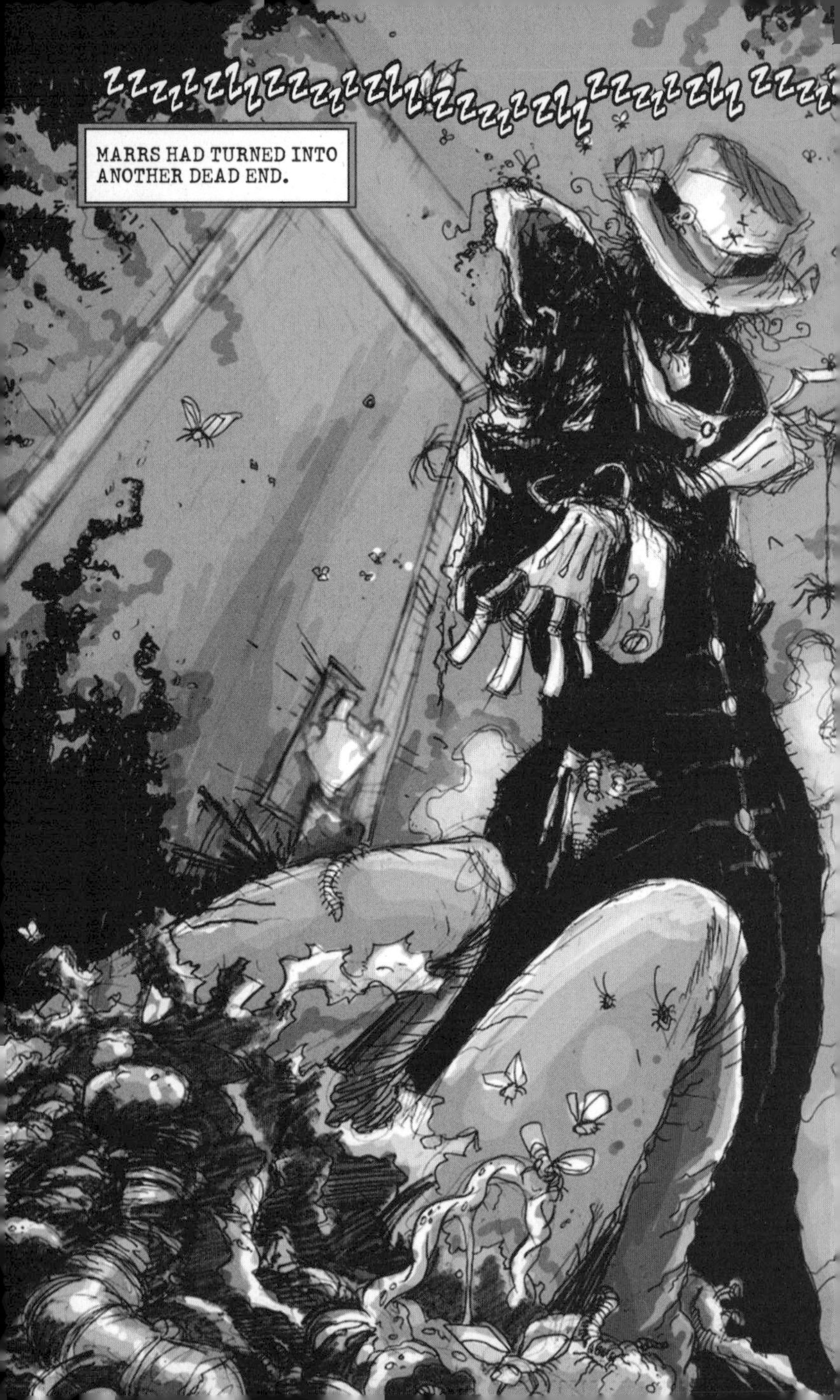
ZZZZZZZZZZZZZZZZZZZZZZZZZZZZZZZZZZZZZZ
MARRS HAD TURNED INTO ANOTHER DEAD END.

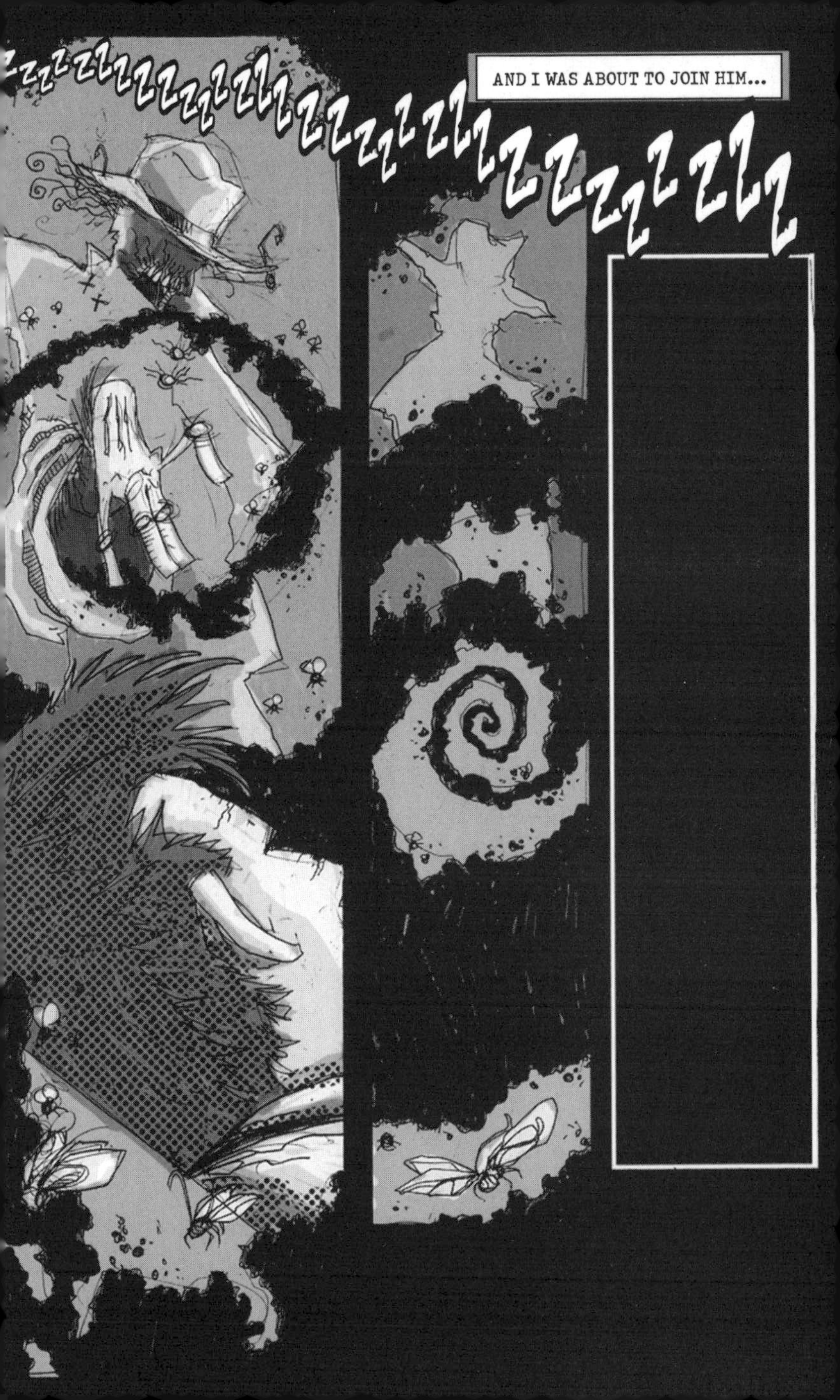
AND I WAS ABOUT TO JOIN HIM...
ZZZZZZZZZZZZZZZZZZZZZZZZZZZ

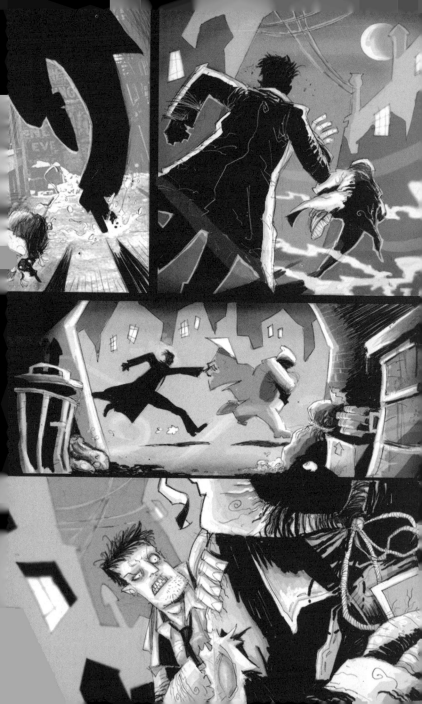

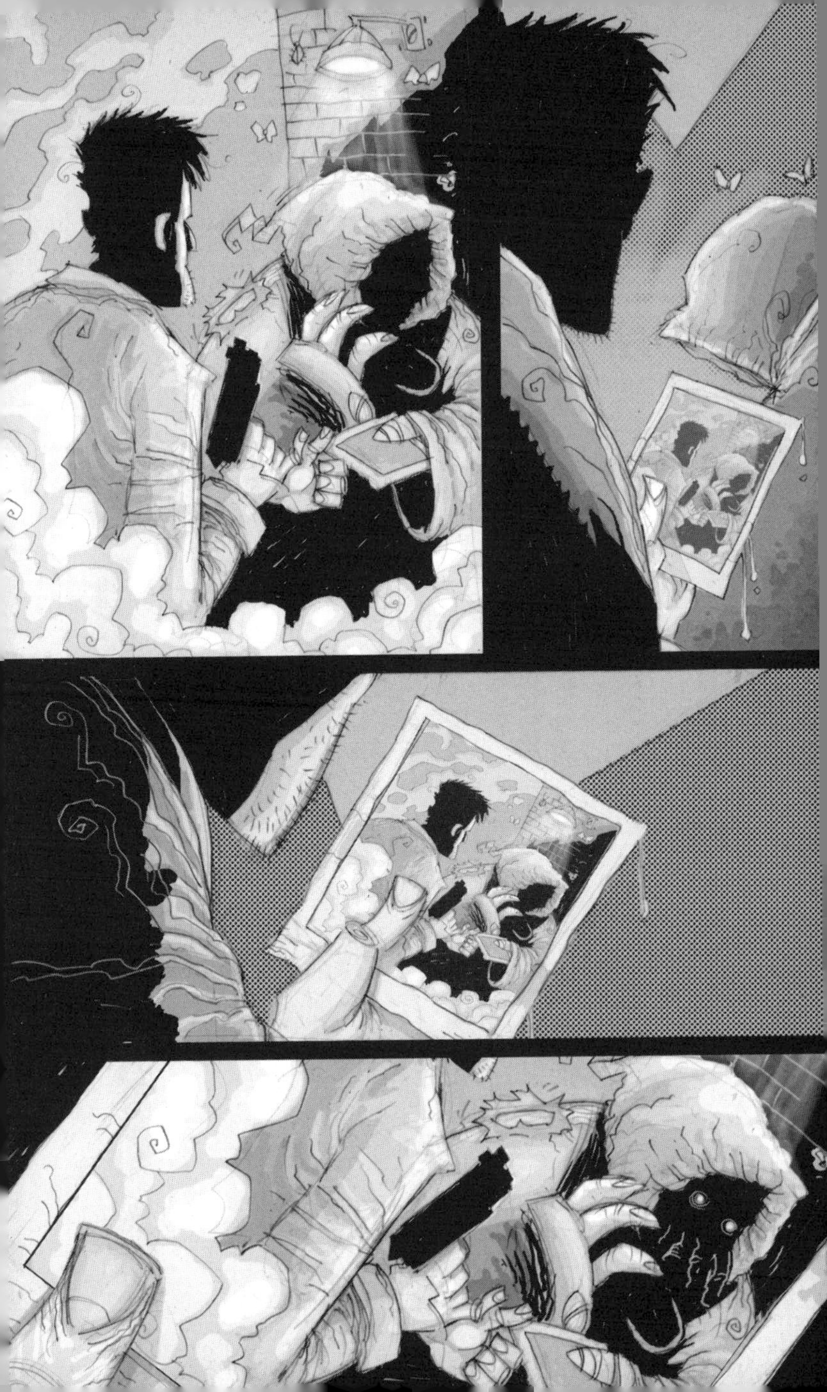

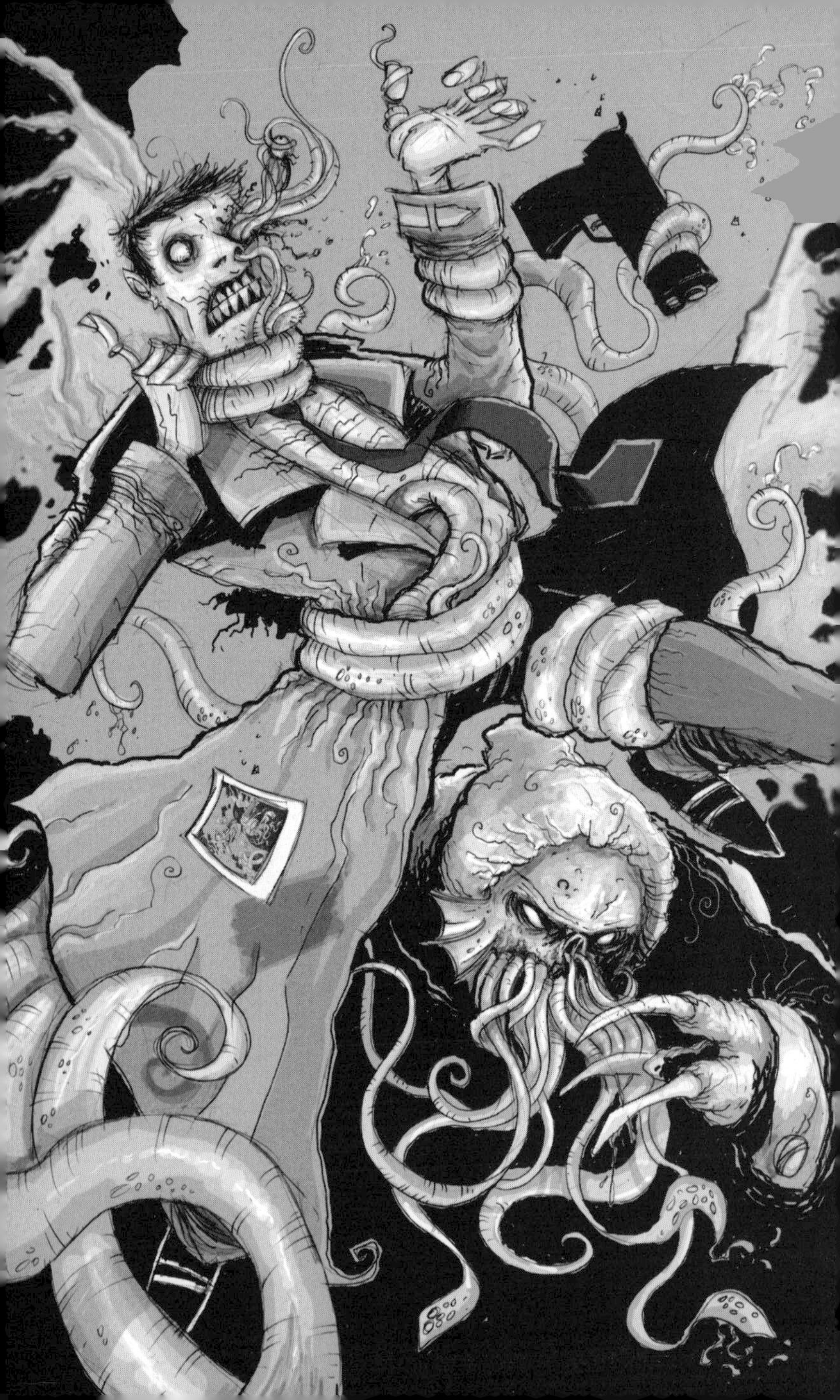

# CHAPTER 2:
## ENTANGLED THREADS

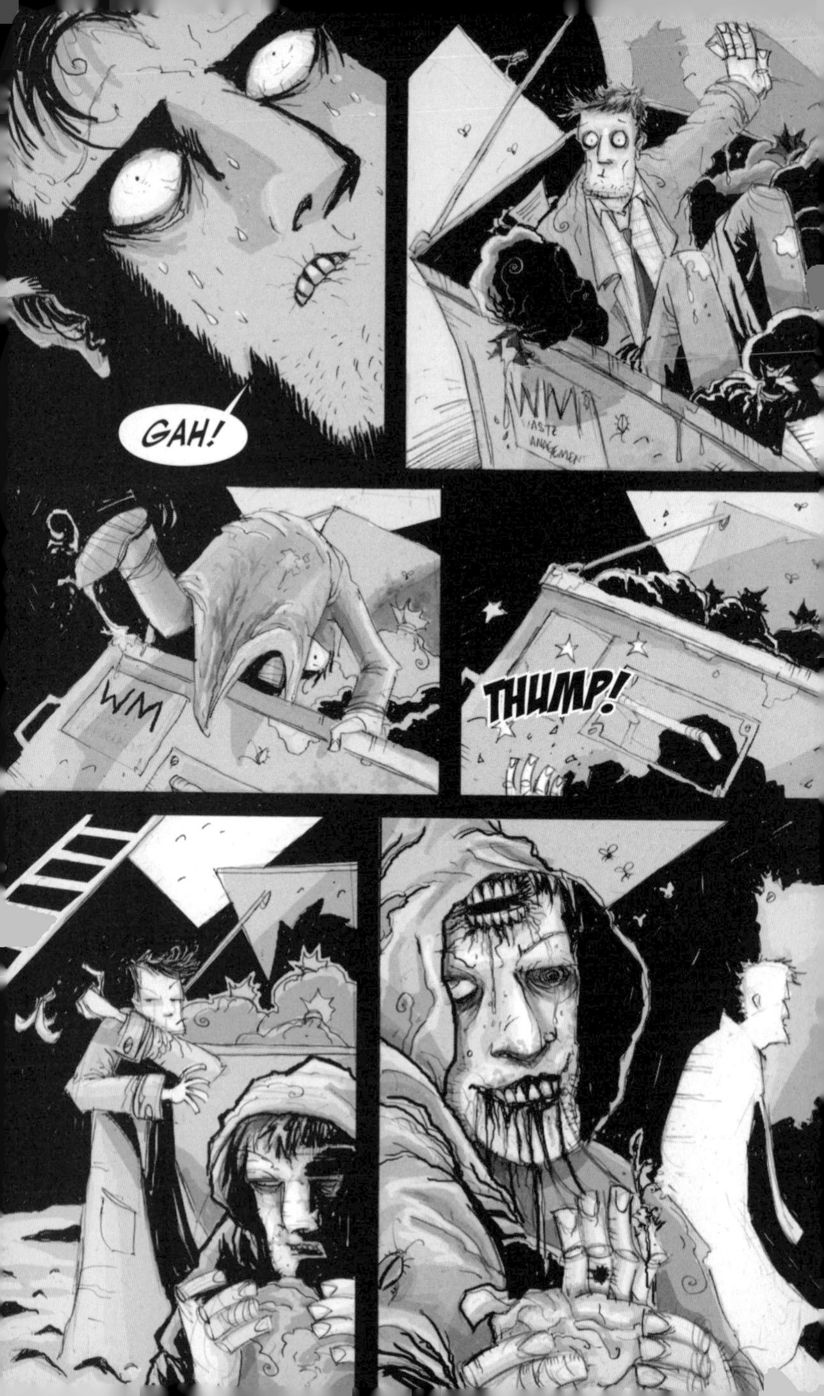
GAH!
WM
WM
THUMP!

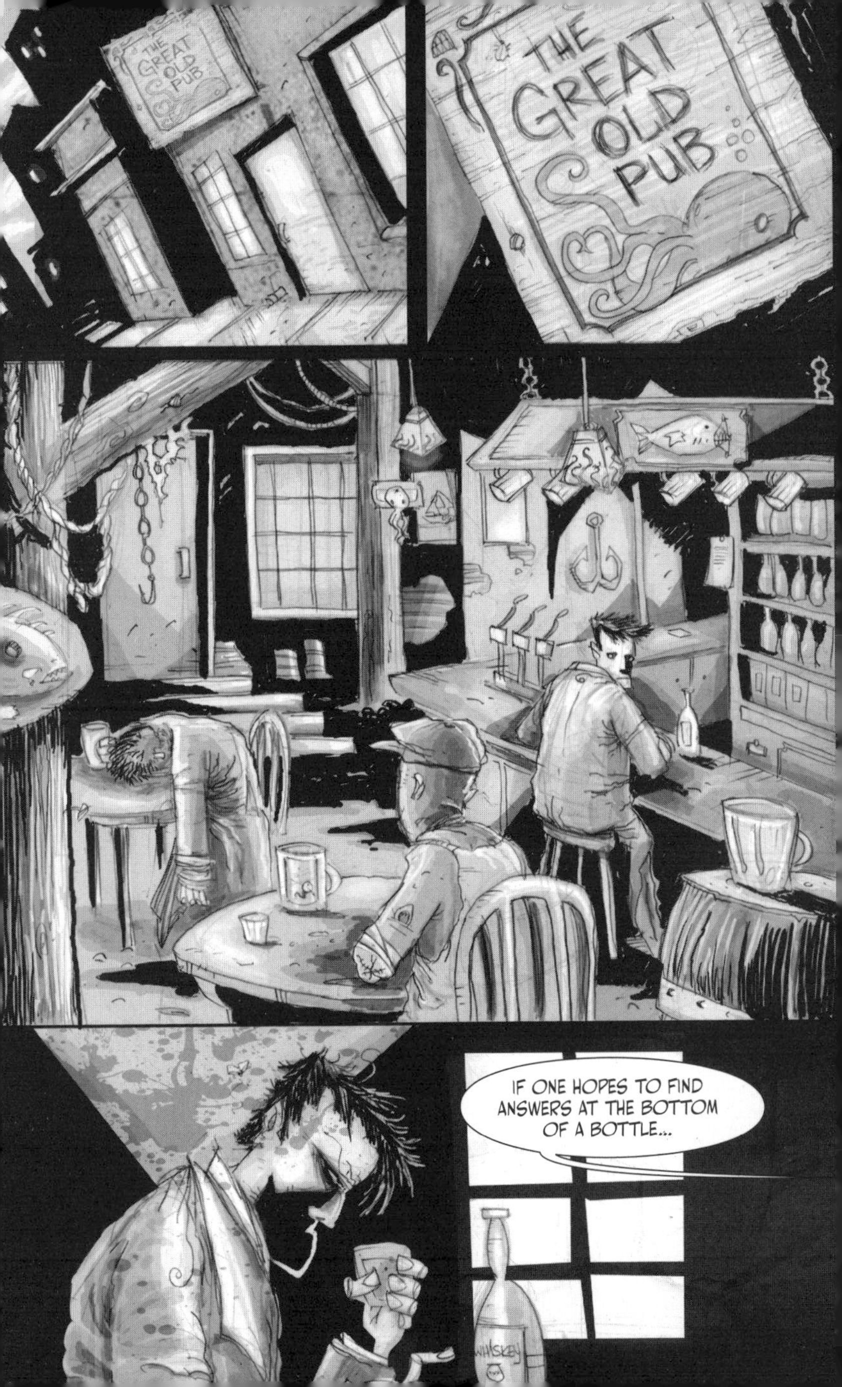
THE GREAT OLD PUB
THE GREAT OLD PUB
IF ONE HOPES TO FIND ANSWERS AT THE BOTTOM OF A BOTTLE...
WHISKEY

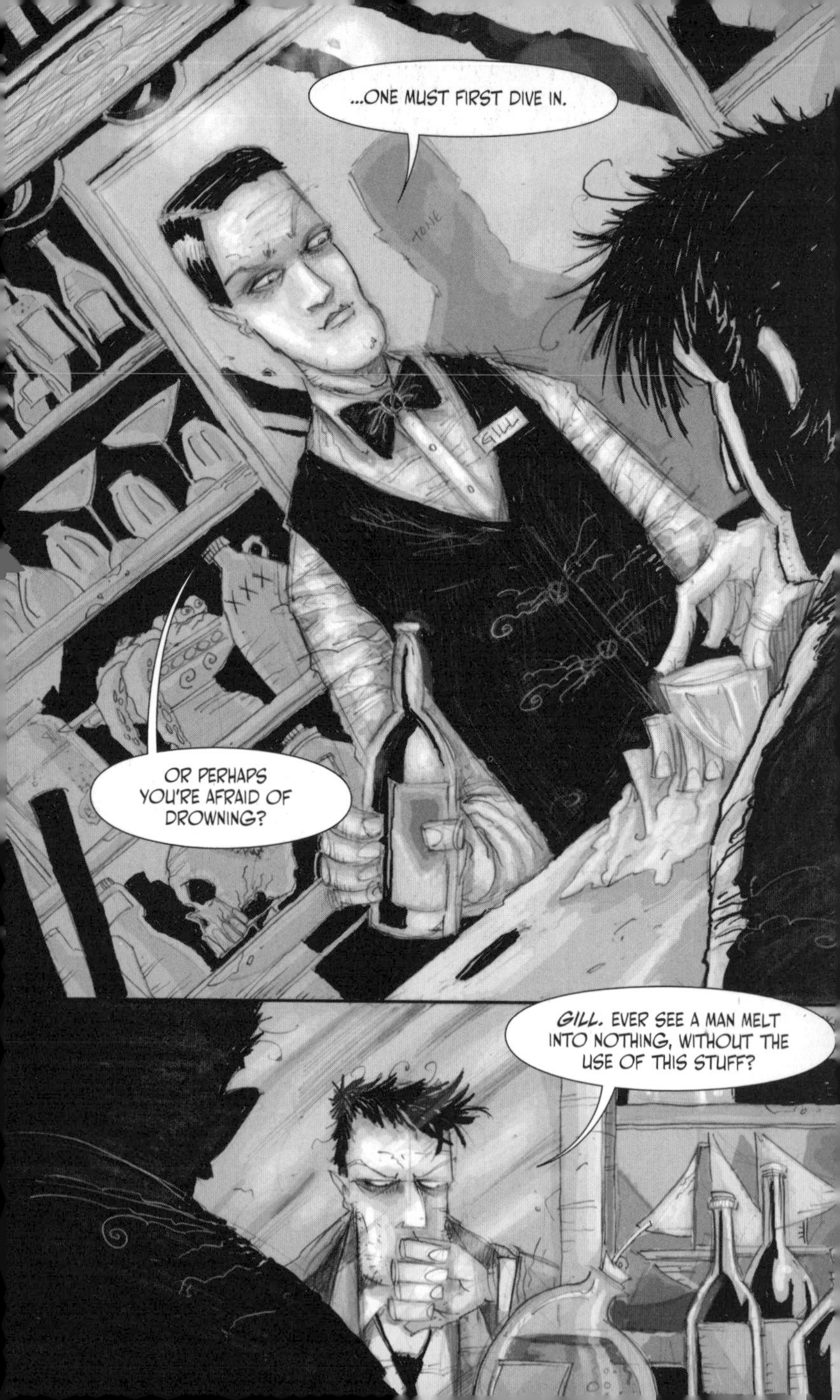
...ONE MUST FIRST DIVE IN.
OR PERHAPS YOU'RE AFRAID OF DROWNING?
*GILL.* EVER SEE A MAN MELT INTO NOTHING, WITHOUT THE USE OF THIS STUFF?

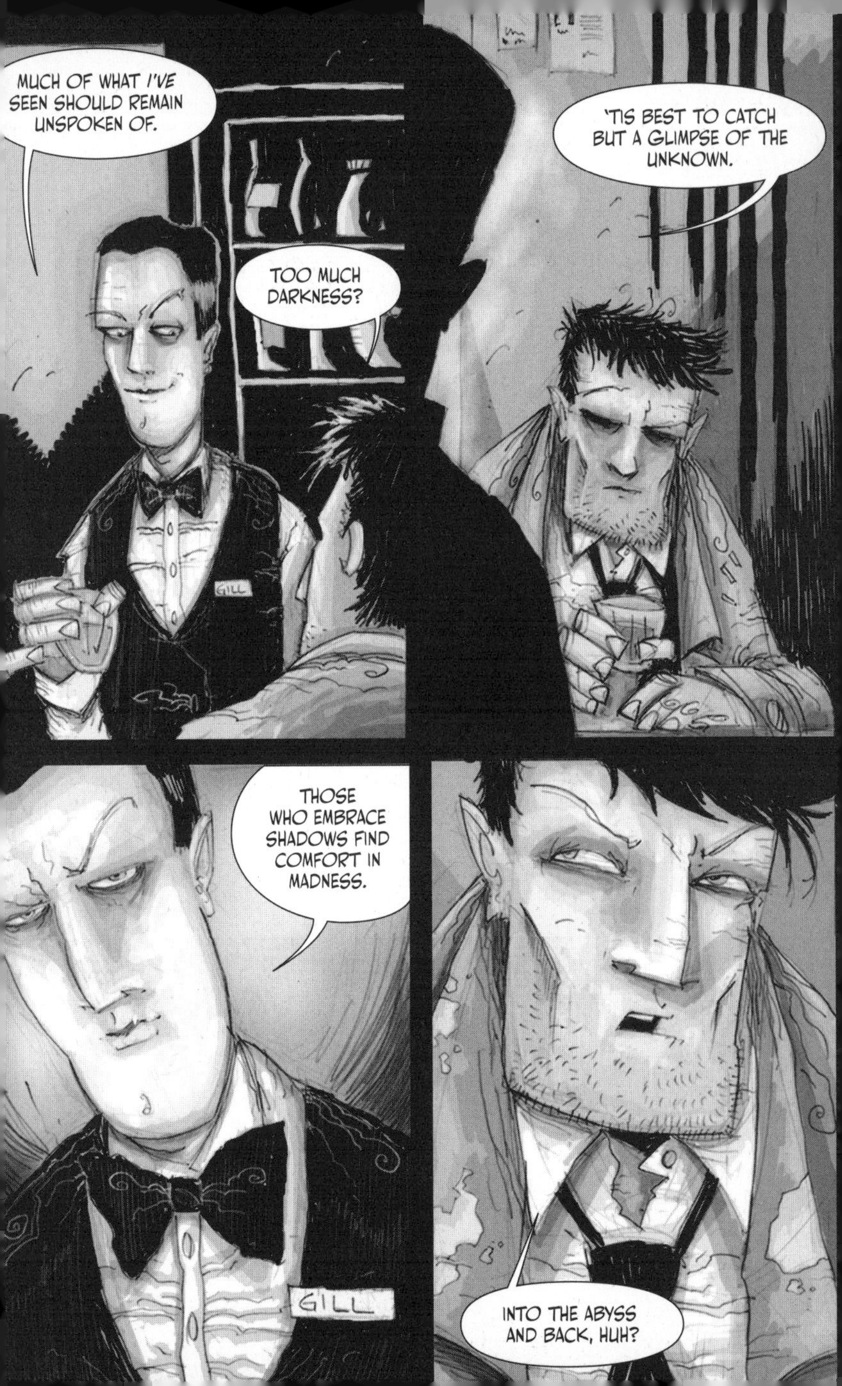
MUCH OF WHAT I'VE SEEN SHOULD REMAIN UNSPOKEN OF.
TOO MUCH DARKNESS?
'TIS BEST TO CATCH BUT A GLIMPSE OF THE UNKNOWN.
GILL
THOSE WHO EMBRACE SHADOWS FIND COMFORT IN MADNESS.
GILL
INTO THE ABYSS AND BACK, HUH?

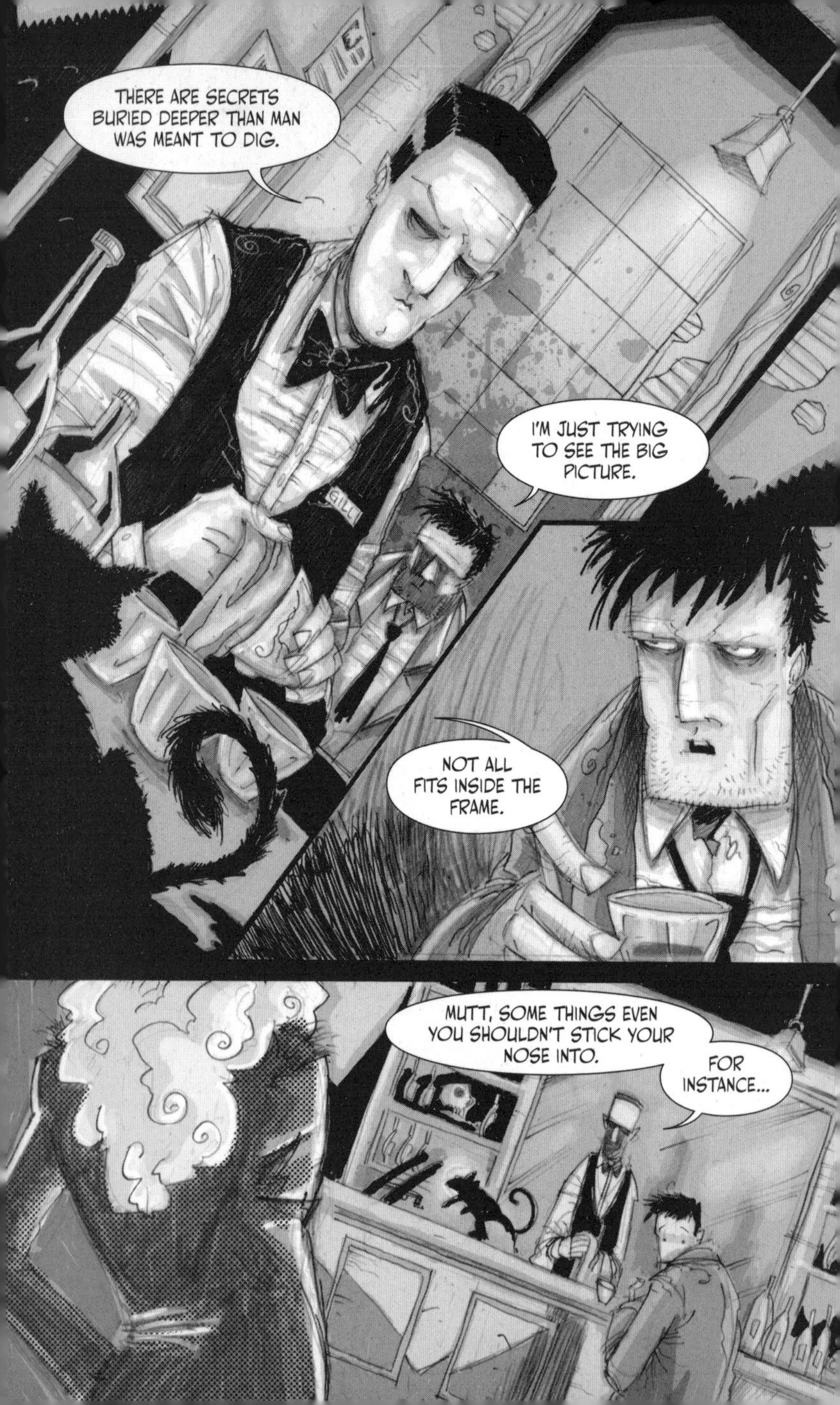
THERE ARE SECRETS BURIED DEEPER THAN MAN WAS MEANT TO DIG.
I'M JUST TRYING TO SEE THE BIG PICTURE.
GILL
NOT ALL FITS INSIDE THE FRAME.
MUTT, SOME THINGS EVEN YOU SHOULDN'T STICK YOUR NOSE INTO.
FOR INSTANCE...

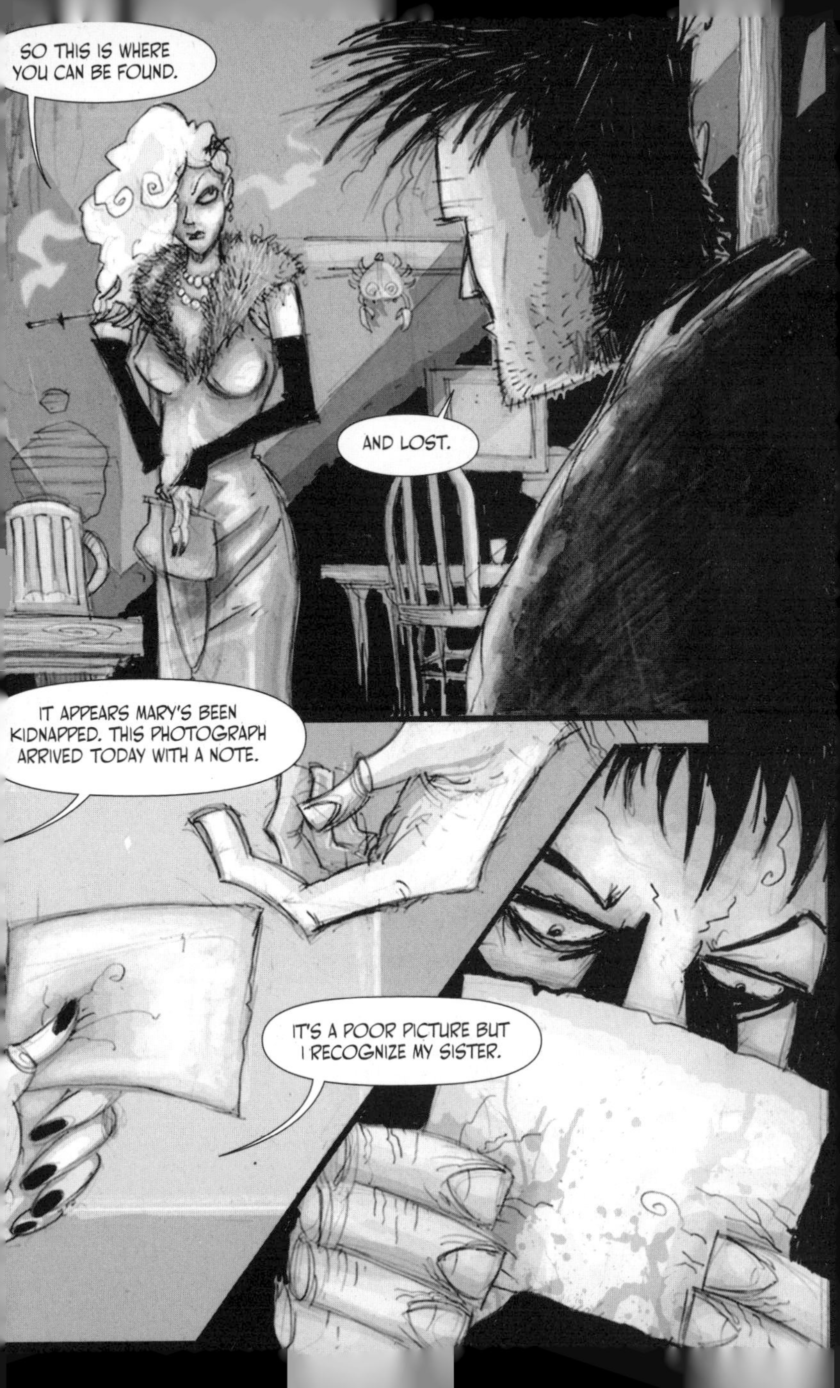
SO THIS IS WHERE YOU CAN BE FOUND.
AND LOST.
IT APPEARS MARY'S BEEN KIDNAPPED. THIS PHOTOGRAPH ARRIVED TODAY WITH A NOTE.
IT'S A POOR PICTURE BUT I RECOGNIZE MY SISTER.

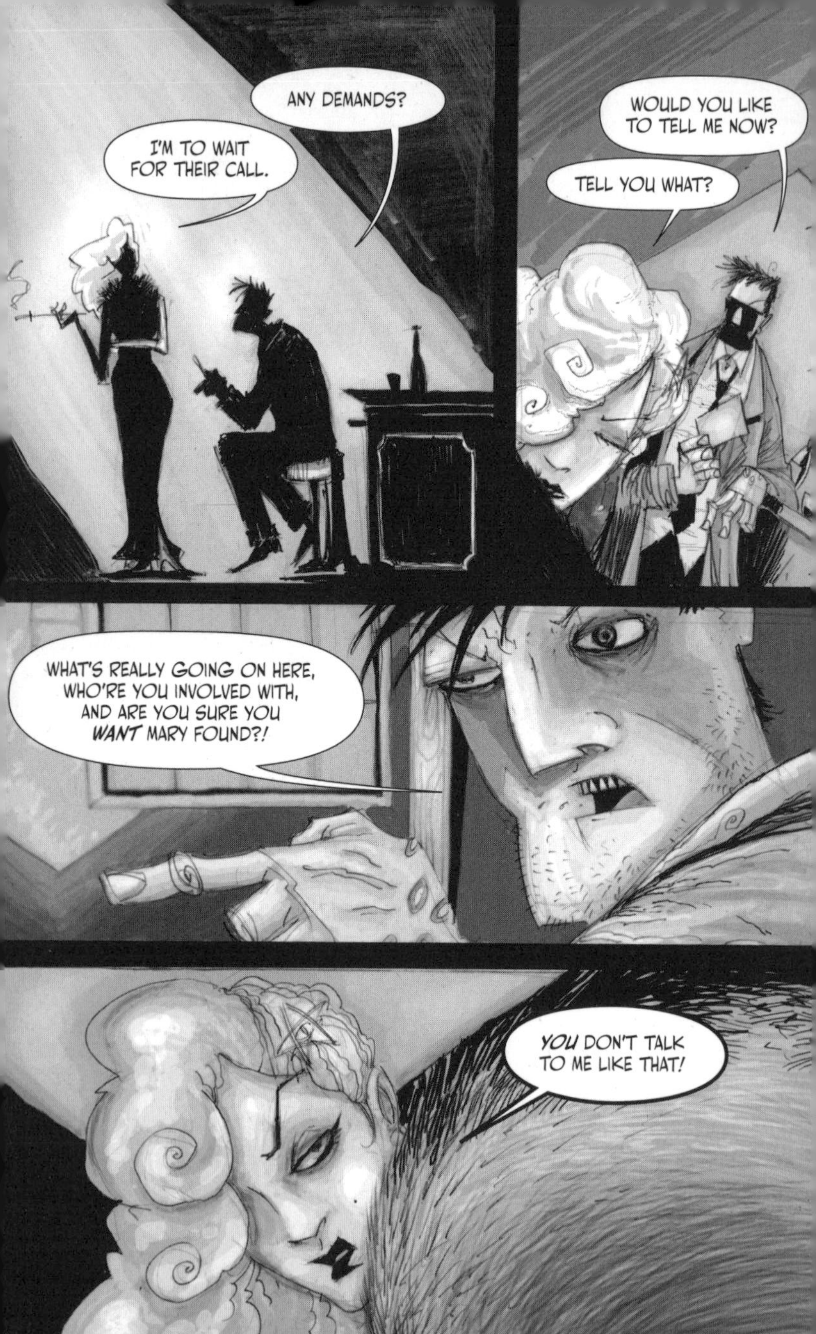
I'M TO WAIT FOR THEIR CALL.
ANY DEMANDS?
WOULD YOU LIKE TO TELL ME NOW?
TELL YOU WHAT?
WHAT'S REALLY GOING ON HERE, WHO'RE YOU INVOLVED WITH, AND ARE YOU SURE YOU *WANT* MARY FOUND?!
*YOU* DON'T TALK TO ME LIKE THAT!

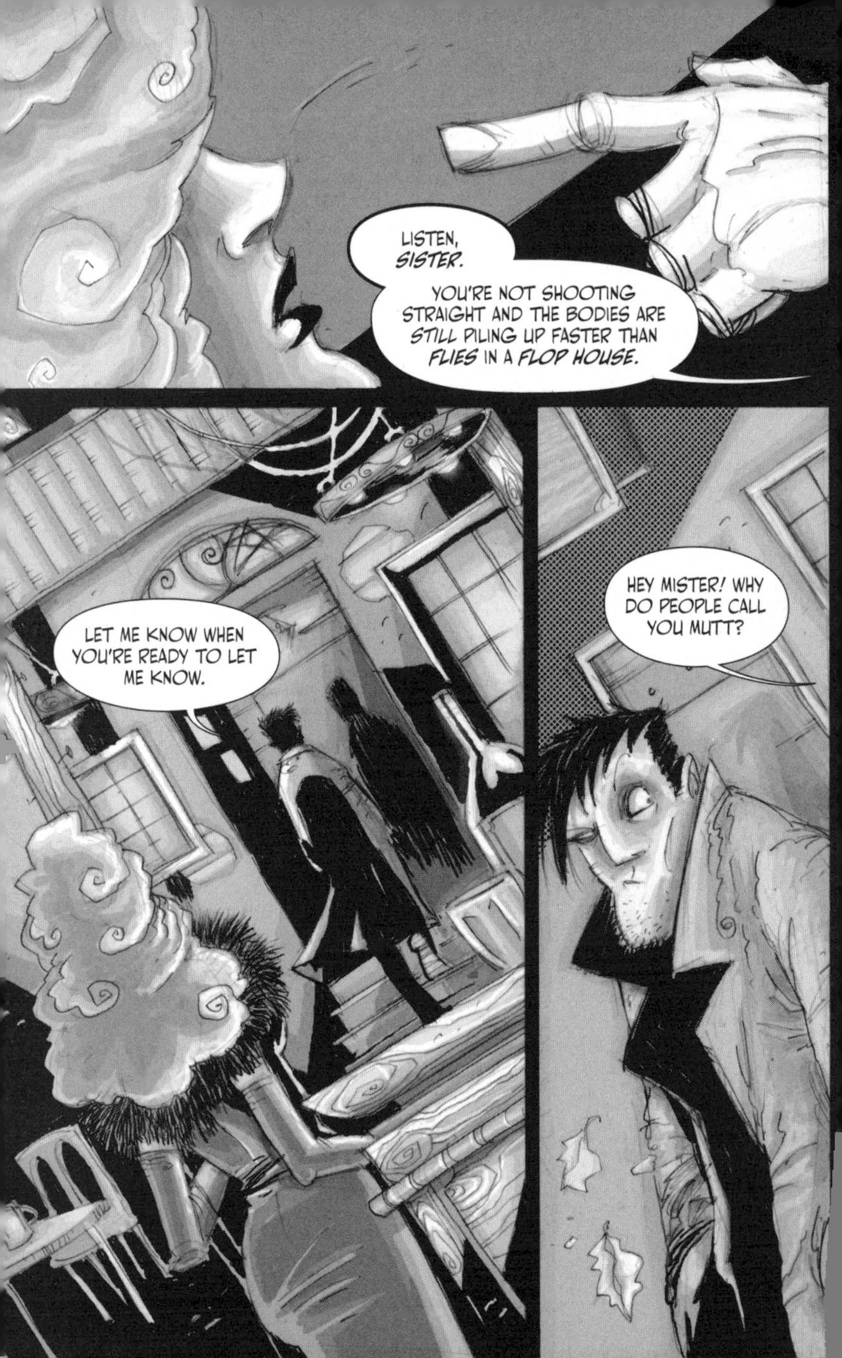
LISTEN, *SISTER.*
YOU'RE NOT SHOOTING STRAIGHT AND THE BODIES ARE *STILL* PILING UP FASTER THAN *FLIES* IN A *FLOP HOUSE.*
LET ME KNOW WHEN YOU'RE READY TO LET ME KNOW.
HEY MISTER! WHY DO PEOPLE CALL YOU MUTT?

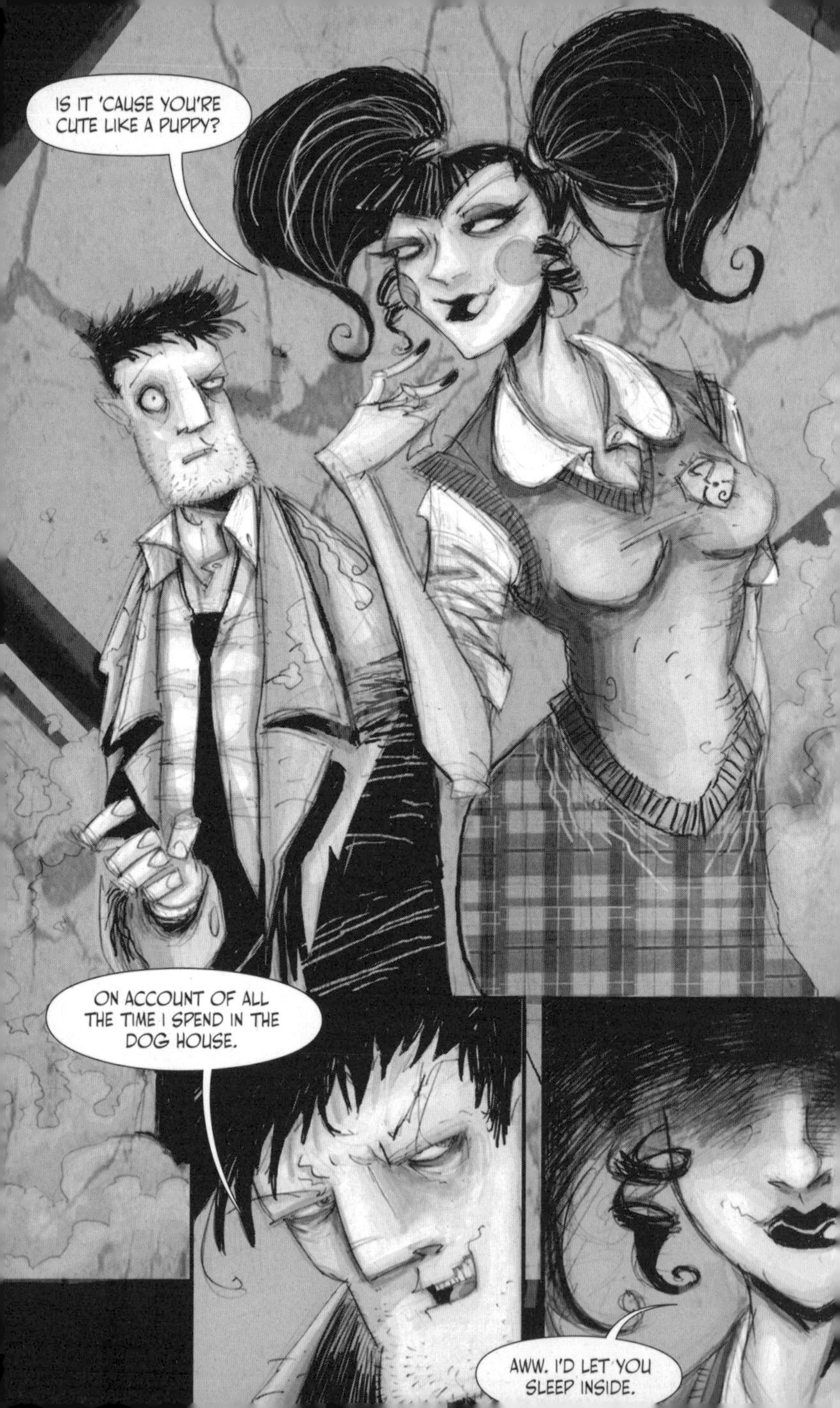
IS IT 'CAUSE YOU'RE CUTE LIKE A PUPPY?
ON ACCOUNT OF ALL THE TIME I SPEND IN THE DOG HOUSE.
AWW. I'D LET YOU SLEEP INSIDE.

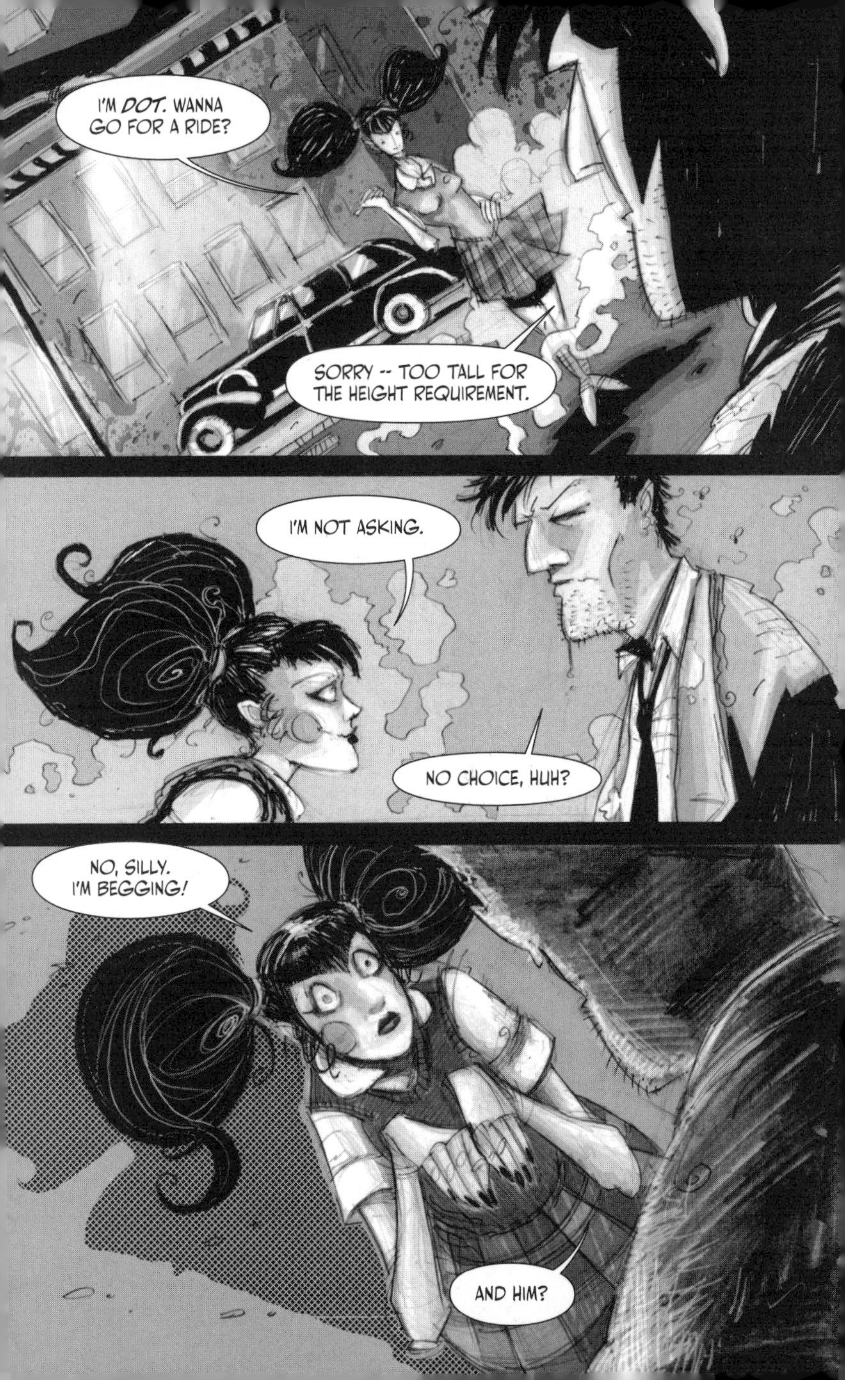
I'M *DOT.* WANNA GO FOR A RIDE?
SORRY -- TOO TALL FOR THE HEIGHT REQUIREMENT.
I'M NOT ASKING.
NO CHOICE, HUH?
NO, SILLY. I'M BEGGING!
AND HIM?

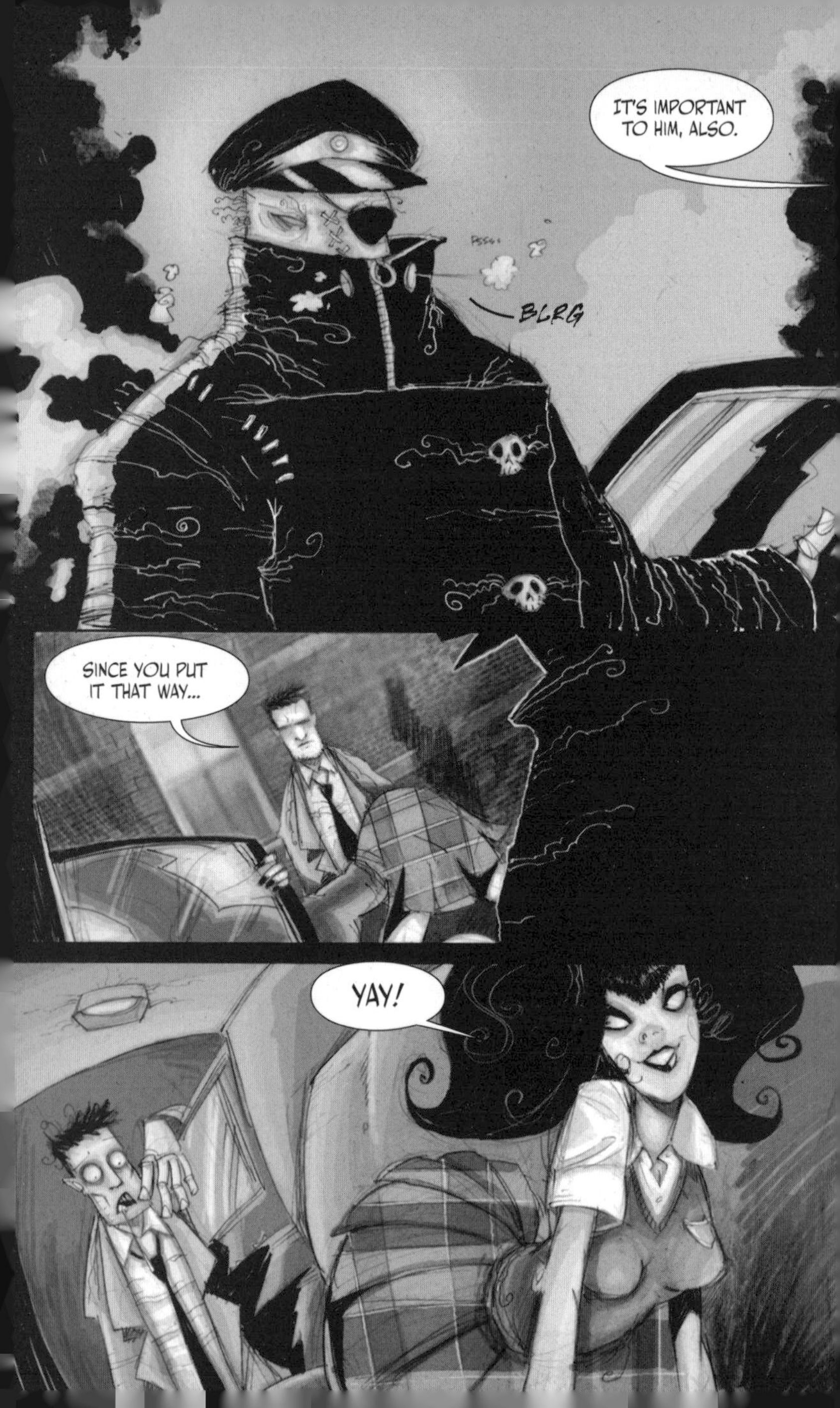
IT'S IMPORTANT TO HIM, ALSO.
BLRG
SINCE YOU PUT IT THAT WAY...
YAY!

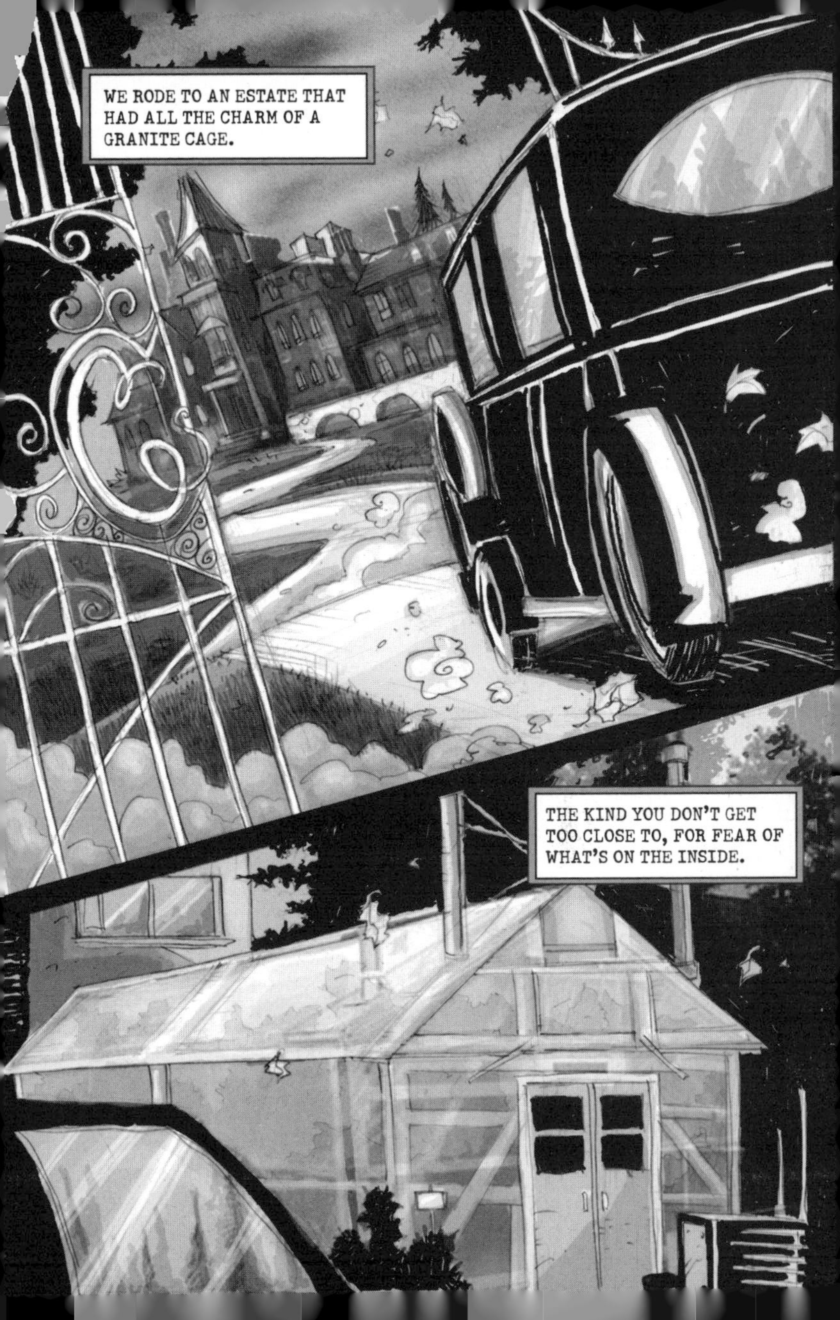
WE RODE TO AN ESTATE THAT HAD ALL THE CHARM OF A GRANITE CAGE.
THE KIND YOU DON'T GET TOO CLOSE TO, FOR FEAR OF WHAT'S ON THE INSIDE.

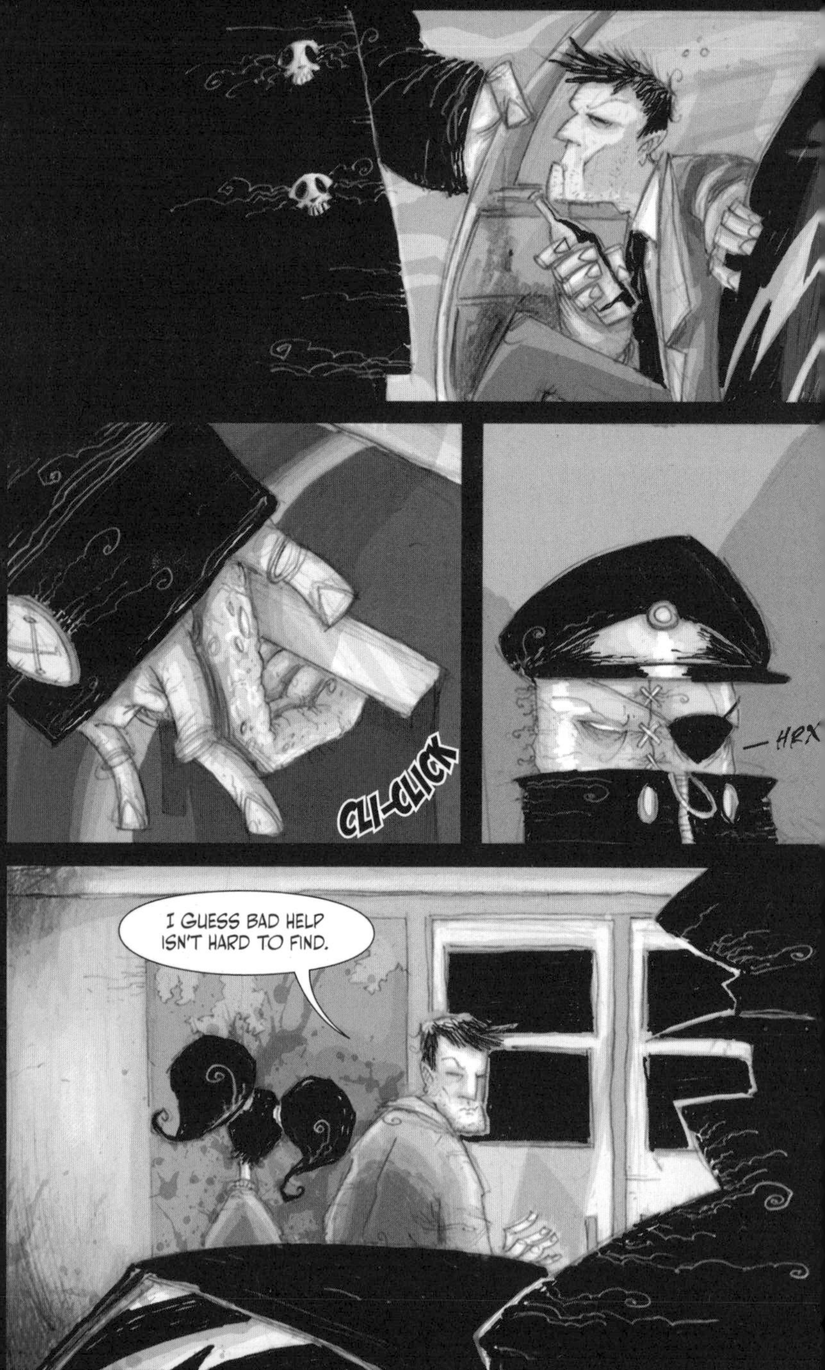
CLI-CLICK
— HRX
I GUESS BAD HELP ISN'T HARD TO FIND.

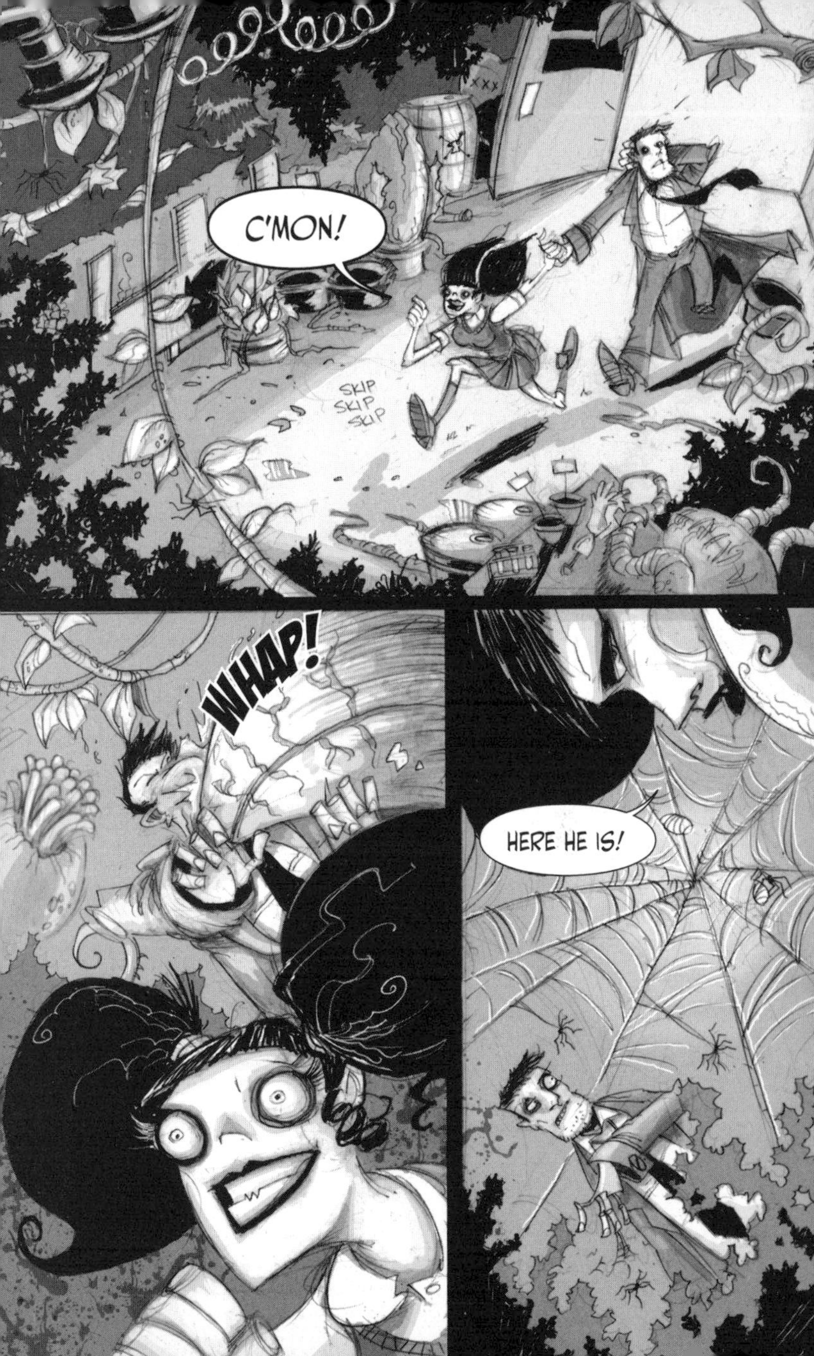
C'MON!
SKIP SKIP SKIP
WHAP!
HERE HE IS!

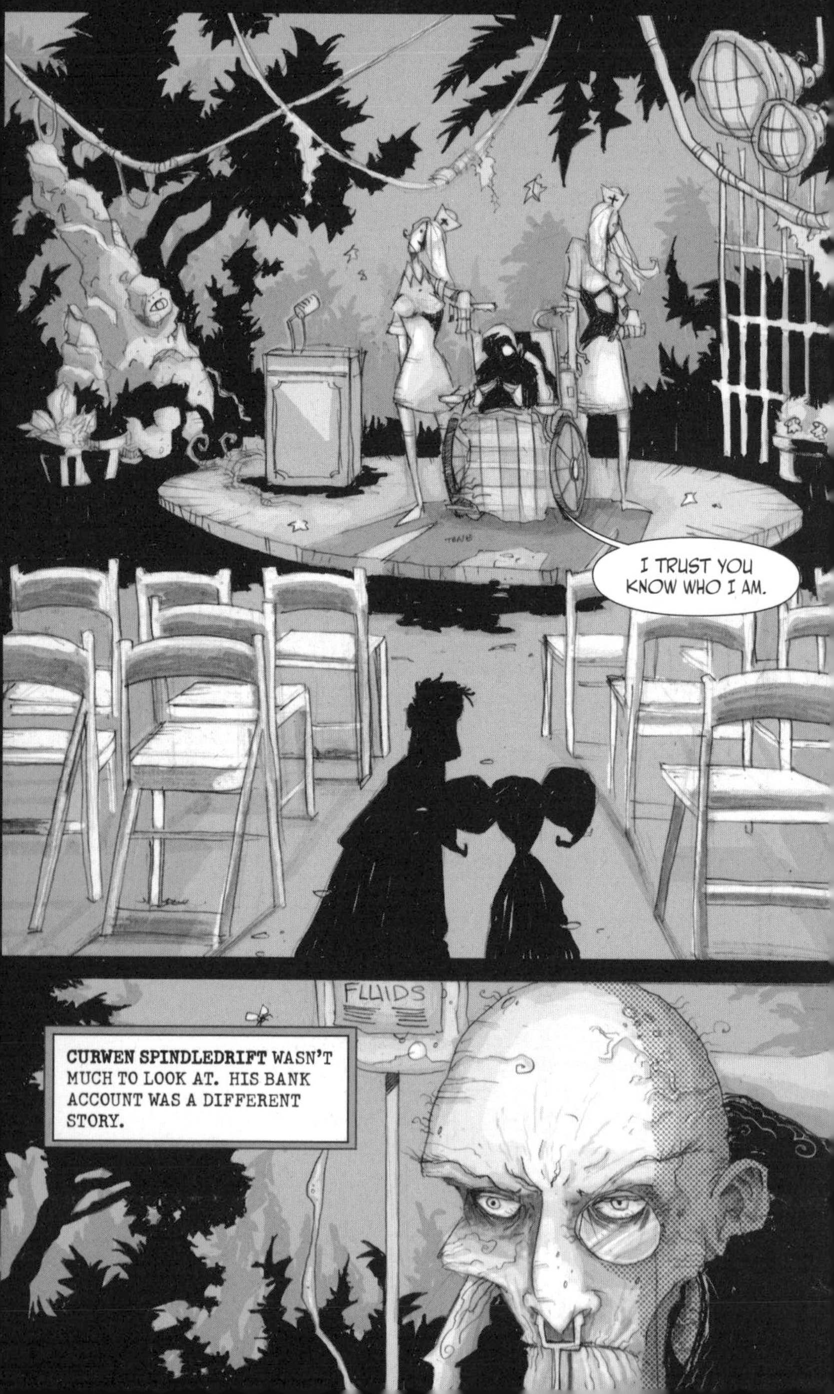
I TRUST YOU KNOW WHO I AM.
FLUIDS
CURWEN SPINDLEDRIFT WASN'T MUCH TO LOOK AT. HIS BANK ACCOUNT WAS A DIFFERENT STORY.

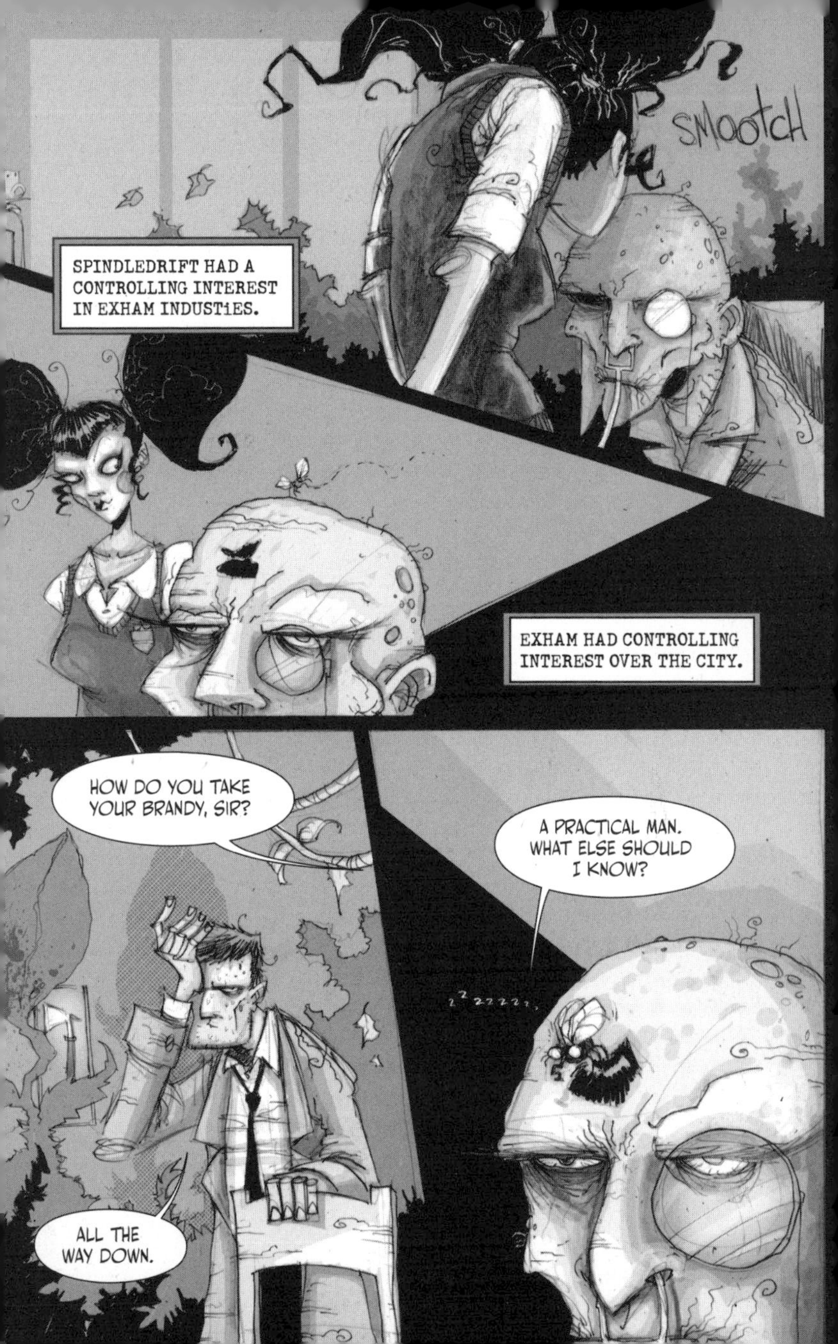
SMOOTCH
SPINDLEDRIFT HAD A CONTROLLING INTEREST IN EXHAM INDUSTiES.
EXHAM HAD CONTROLLING INTEREST OVER THE CITY.
HOW DO YOU TAKE YOUR BRANDY, SIR?
ALL THE WAY DOWN.
A PRACTICAL MAN. WHAT ELSE SHOULD I KNOW?
zzzzzzz

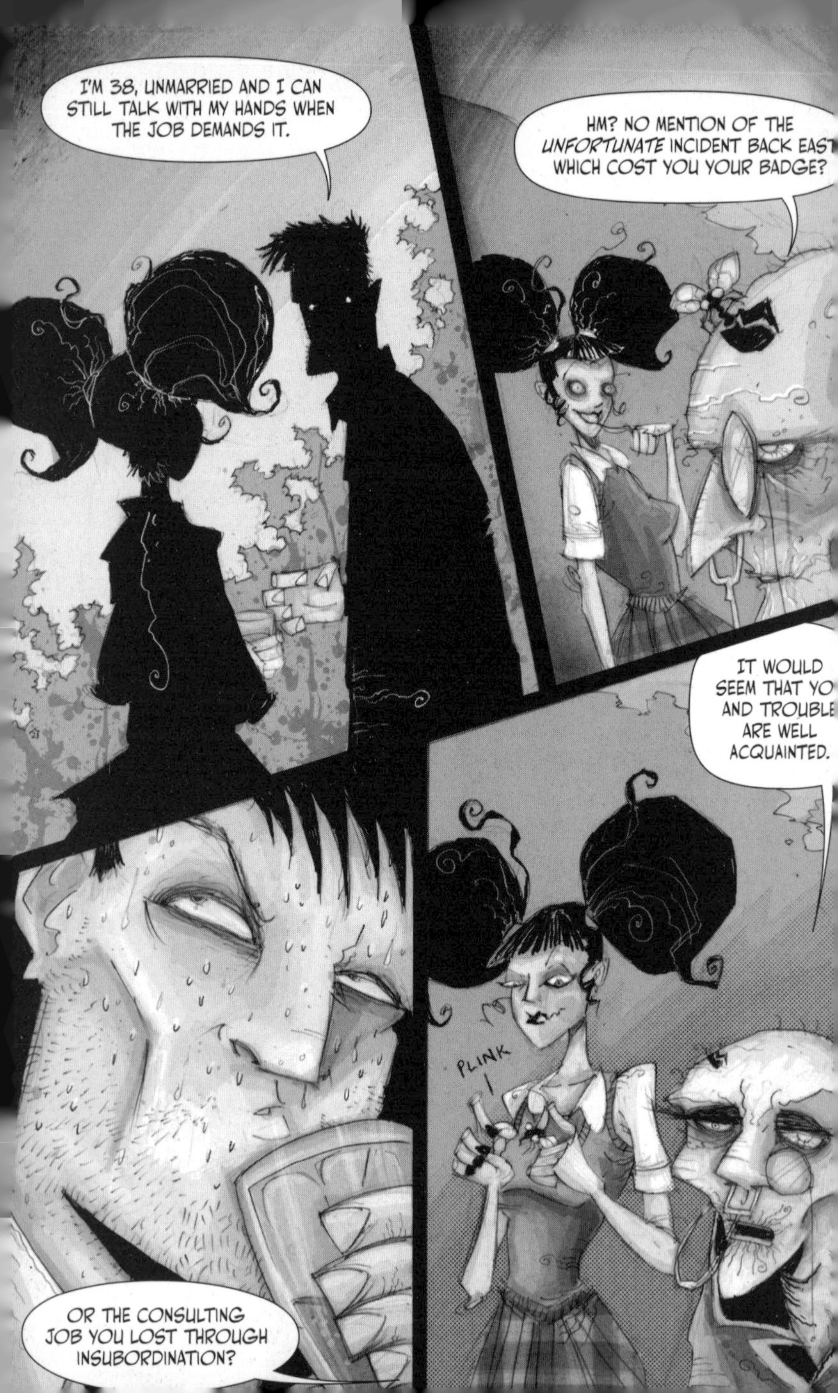
I'M 38, UNMARRIED AND I CAN STILL TALK WITH MY HANDS WHEN THE JOB DEMANDS IT.
HM? NO MENTION OF THE *UNFORTUNATE* INCIDENT BACK EAST WHICH COST YOU YOUR BADGE?
OR THE CONSULTING JOB YOU LOST THROUGH INSUBORDINATION?
IT WOULD SEEM THAT YO AND TROUBLE ARE WELL ACQUAINTED.
PLINK

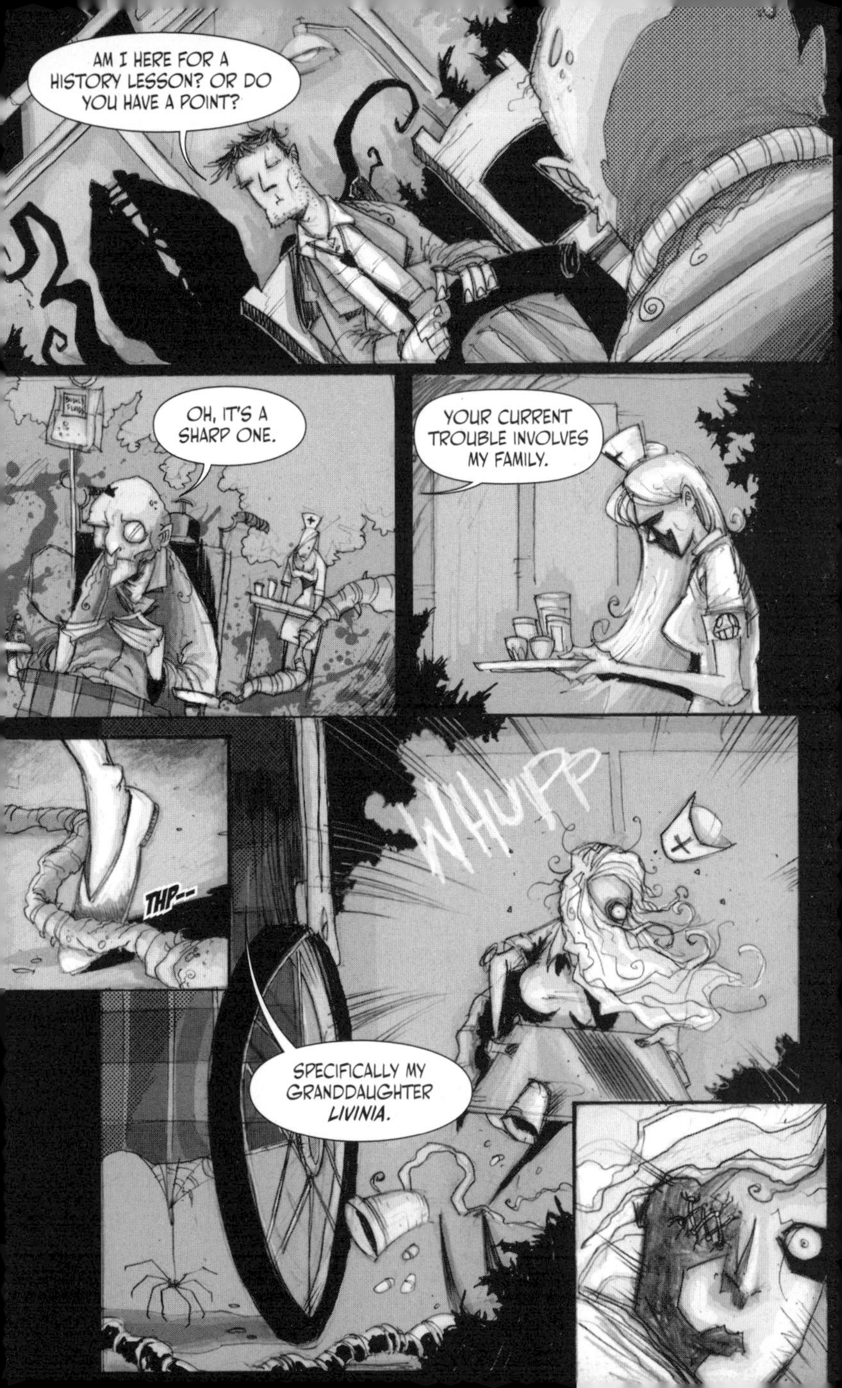
AM I HERE FOR A HISTORY LESSON? OR DO YOU HAVE A POINT?
OH, IT'S A SHARP ONE.
YOUR CURRENT TROUBLE INVOLVES MY FAMILY.
THP--
WHUPP
SPECIFICALLY MY GRANDDAUGHTER *LIVINIA*.

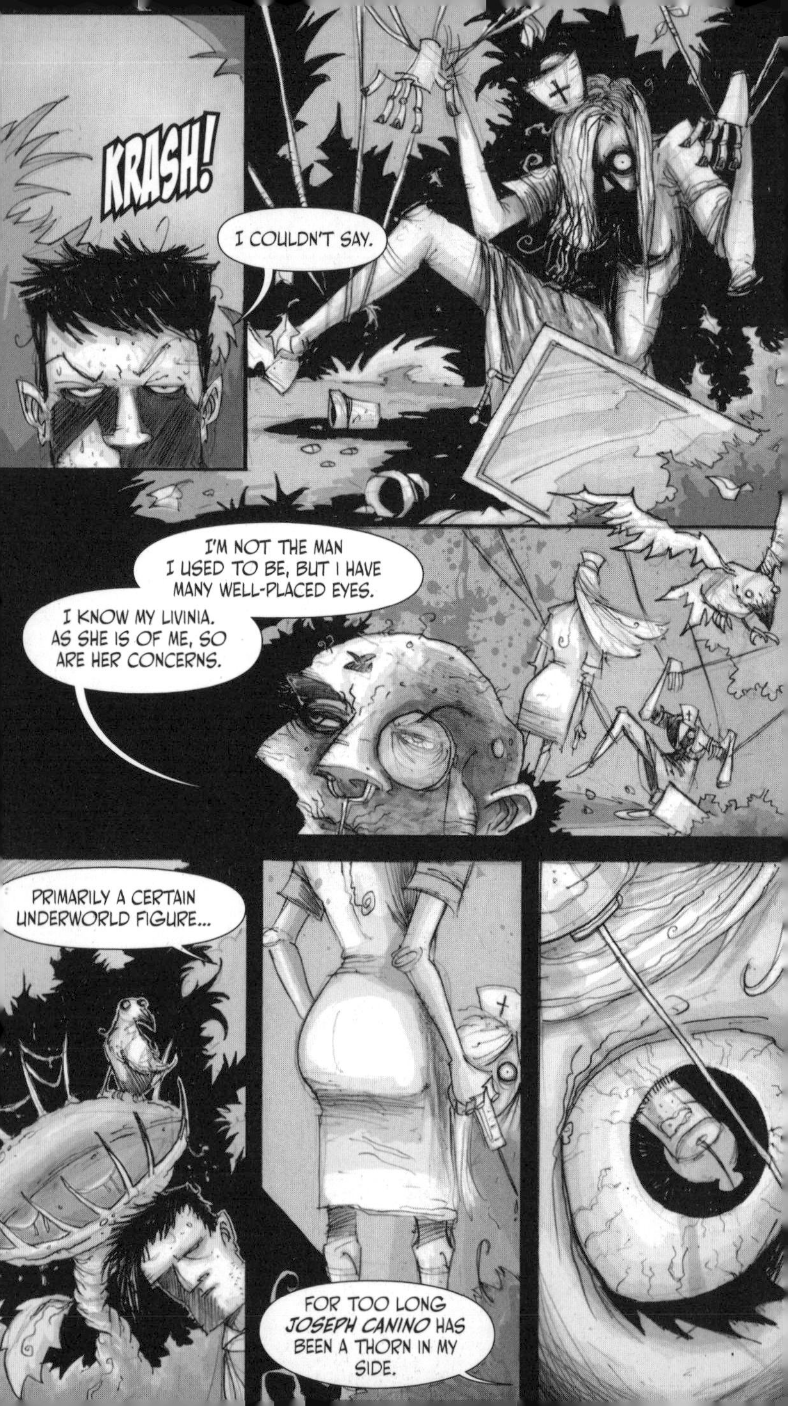
KRASH!
I COULDN'T SAY.
I'M NOT THE MAN I USED TO BE, BUT I HAVE MANY WELL-PLACED EYES.
I KNOW MY LIVINIA. AS SHE IS OF ME, SO ARE HER CONCERNS.
PRIMARILY A CERTAIN UNDERWORLD FIGURE...
FOR TOO LONG *JOSEPH CANINO* HAS BEEN A THORN IN MY SIDE.

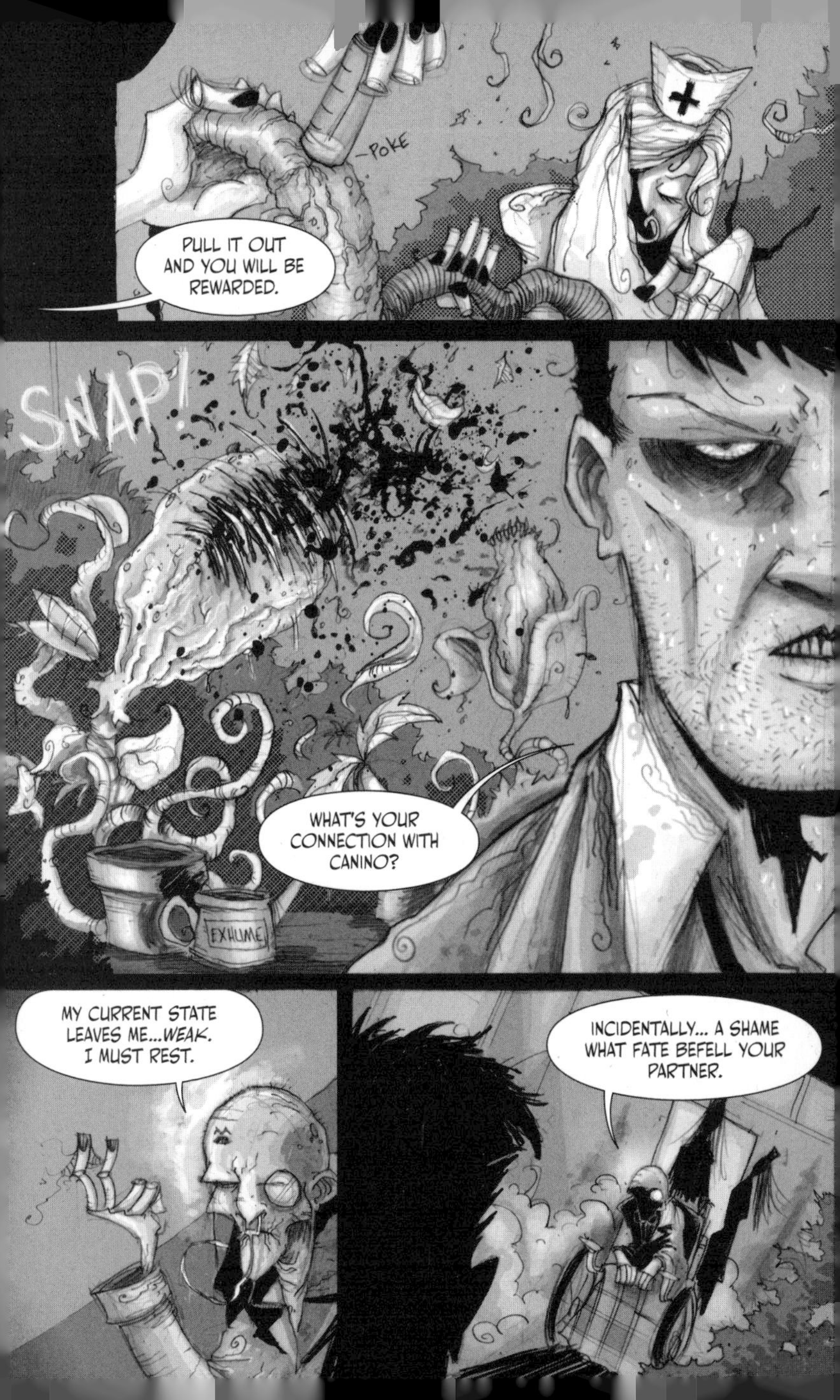
-POKE
PULL IT OUT AND YOU WILL BE REWARDED.
SNAP!
WHAT'S YOUR CONNECTION WITH CANINO?
EXHUME
MY CURRENT STATE LEAVES ME...WEAK. I MUST REST.
INCIDENTALLY... A SHAME WHAT FATE BEFELL YOUR PARTNER.

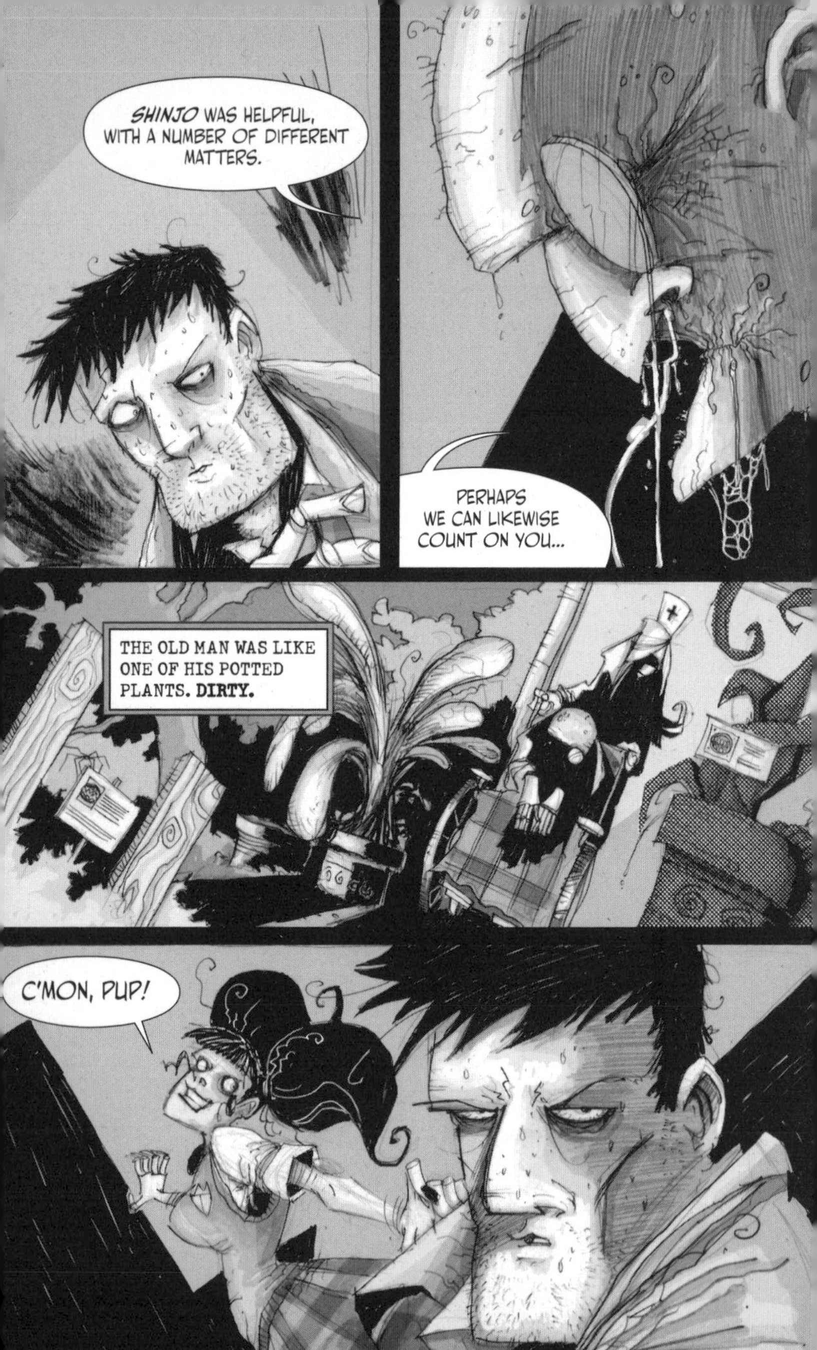
SHINJO WAS HELPFUL, WITH A NUMBER OF DIFFERENT MATTERS.
PERHAPS WE CAN LIKEWISE COUNT ON YOU...
THE OLD MAN WAS LIKE ONE OF HIS POTTED PLANTS. DIRTY.
C'MON, PUP!

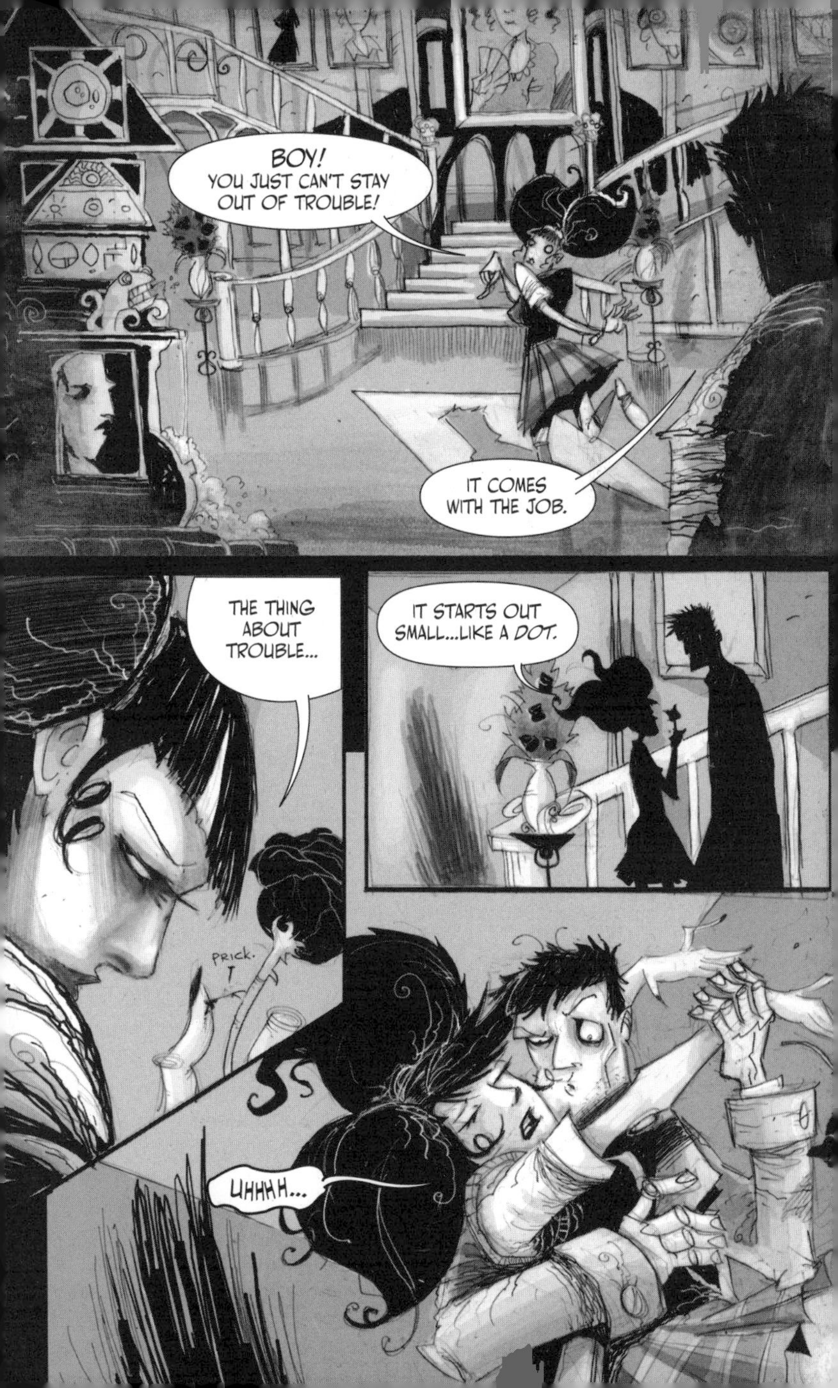
BOY! YOU JUST CAN'T STAY OUT OF TROUBLE!
IT COMES WITH THE JOB.
THE THING ABOUT TROUBLE...
IT STARTS OUT SMALL...LIKE A *DOT.*
PRICK.
UHHHH...

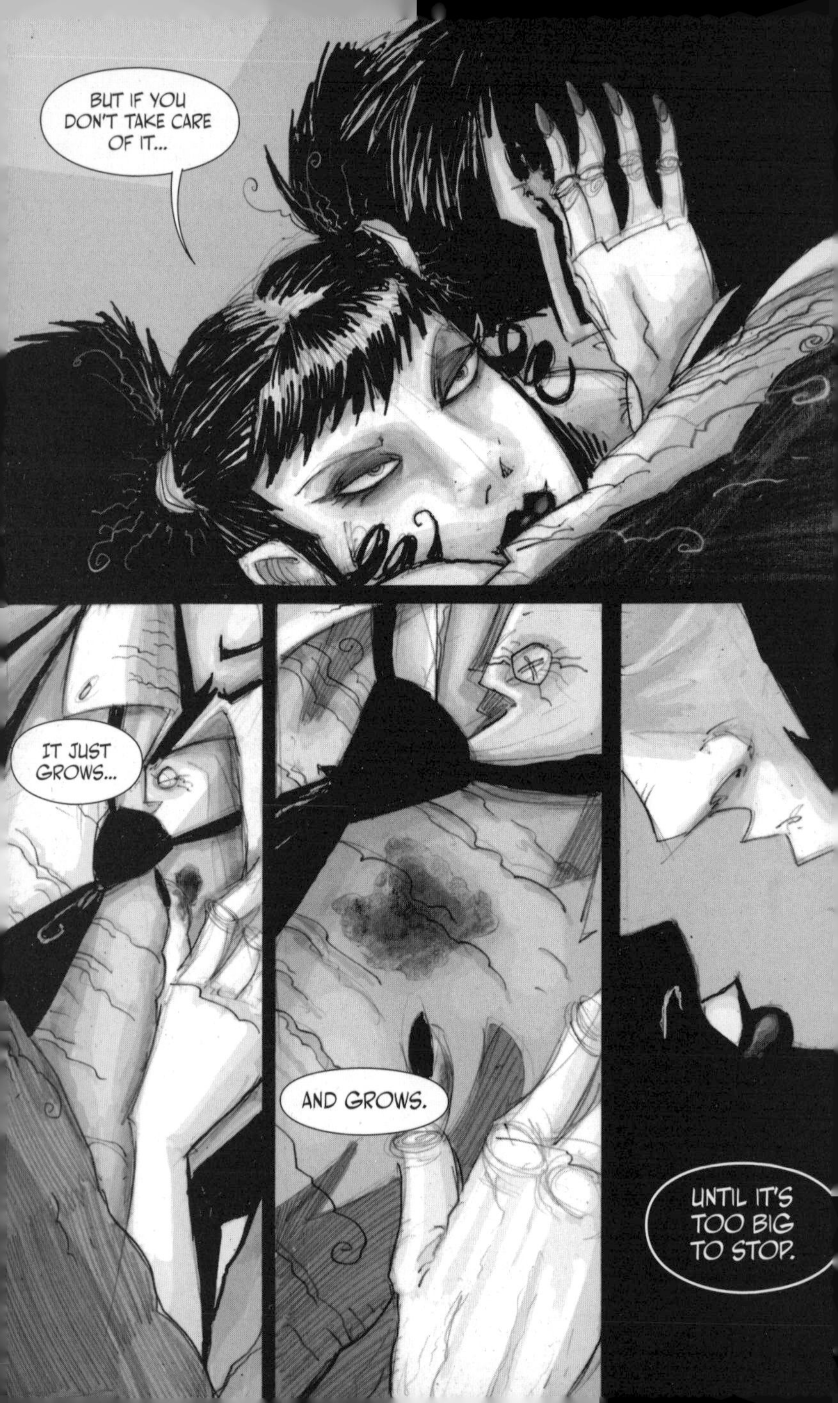
BUT IF YOU DON'T TAKE CARE OF IT...
IT JUST GROWS...
AND GROWS.
UNTIL IT'S TOO BIG TO STOP.

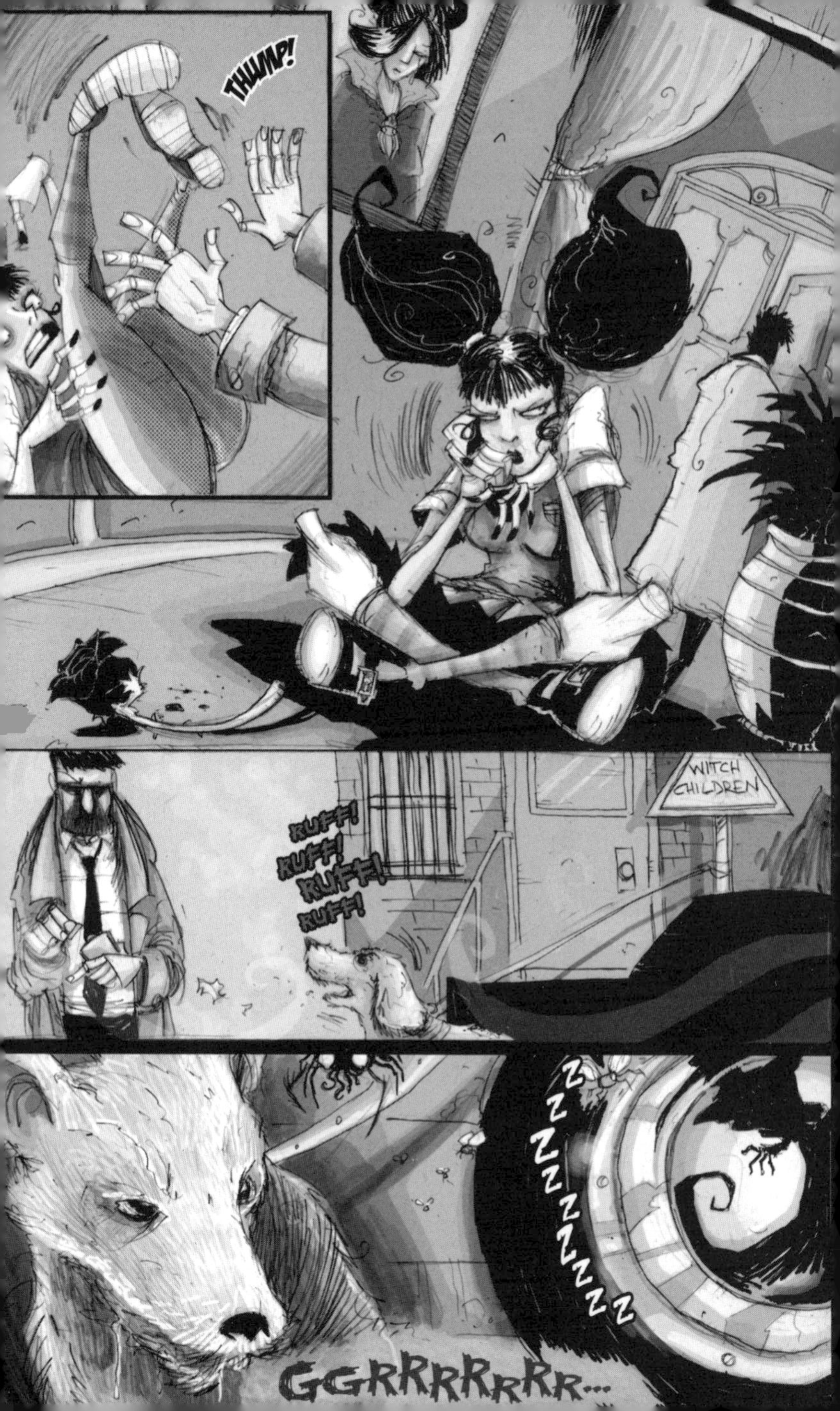
THUMP!
RUFF!
RUFF!
RUFF!
RUFF!
WITCH CHILDREN
Z Z Z Z Z Z Z Z Z Z
GGRRRRRRRR...

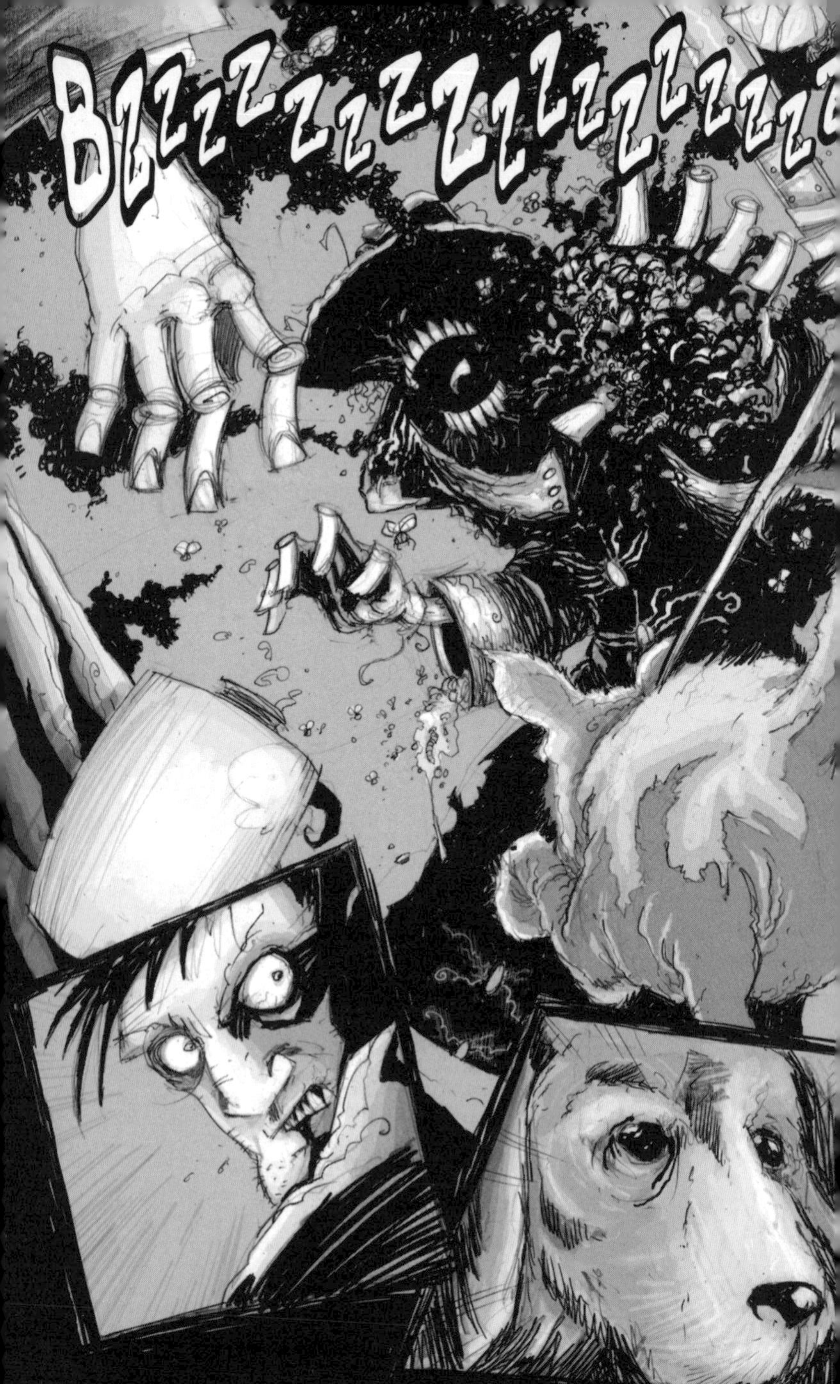
BZZZZZZZZZZZZZZZZZ

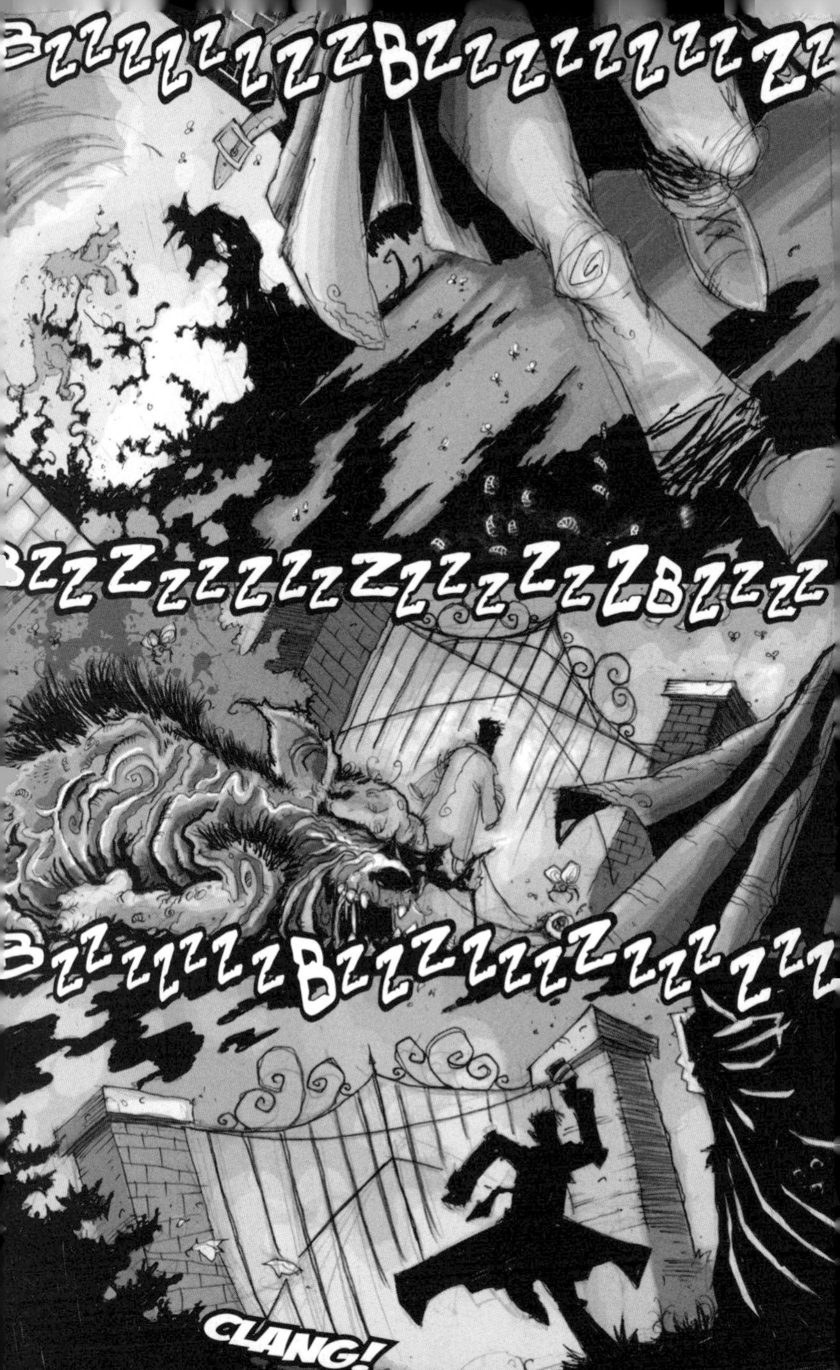
BZZZZZZZZBZZZZZZZZZZ
BZZZZZZZZZZZZZZZZBZZZZ
BZZZZZZZZBZZZZZZZZZZZZZZZ
CLANG!

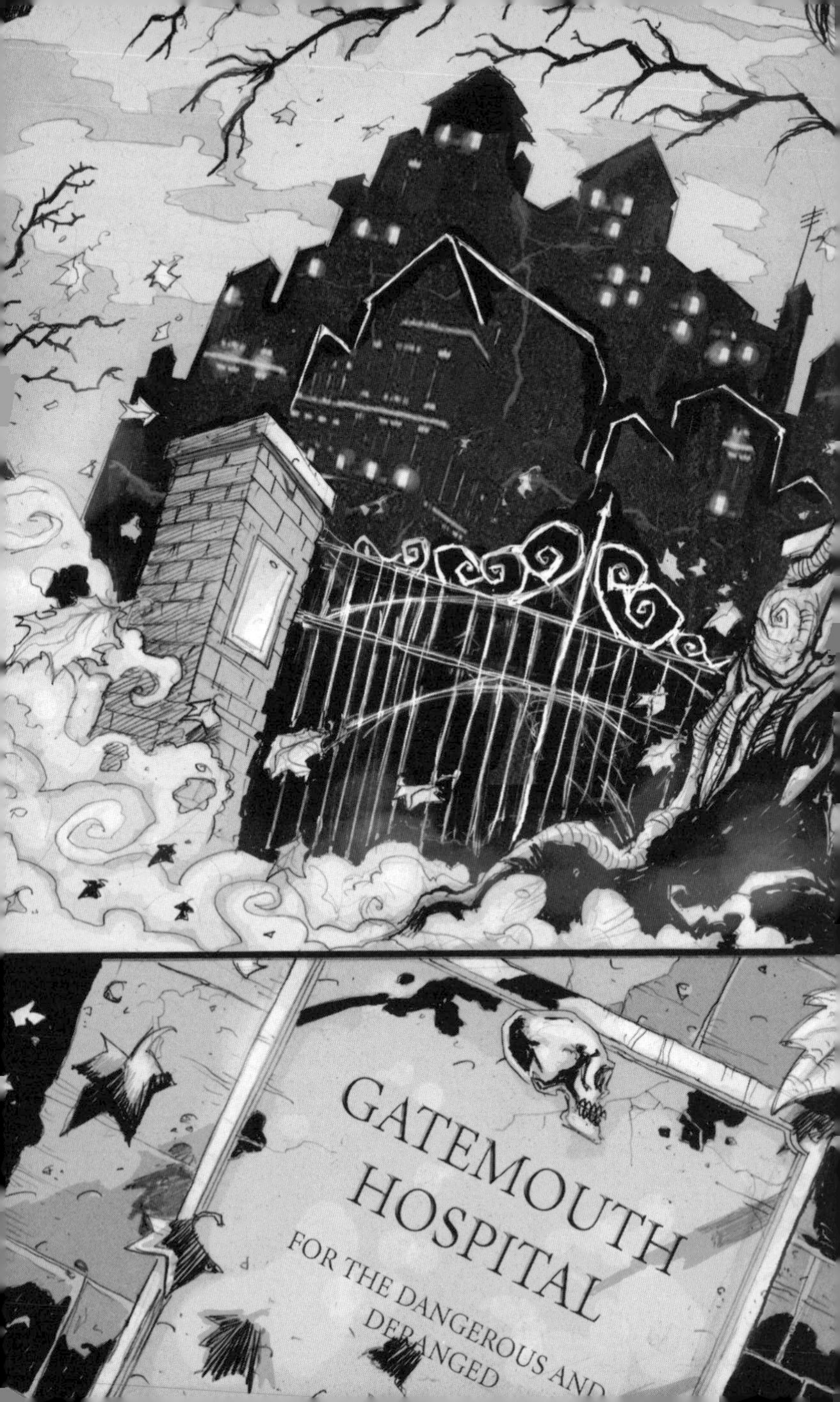
GATEMOUTH
HOSPITAL
FOR THE DANGEROUS AND
DERANGED

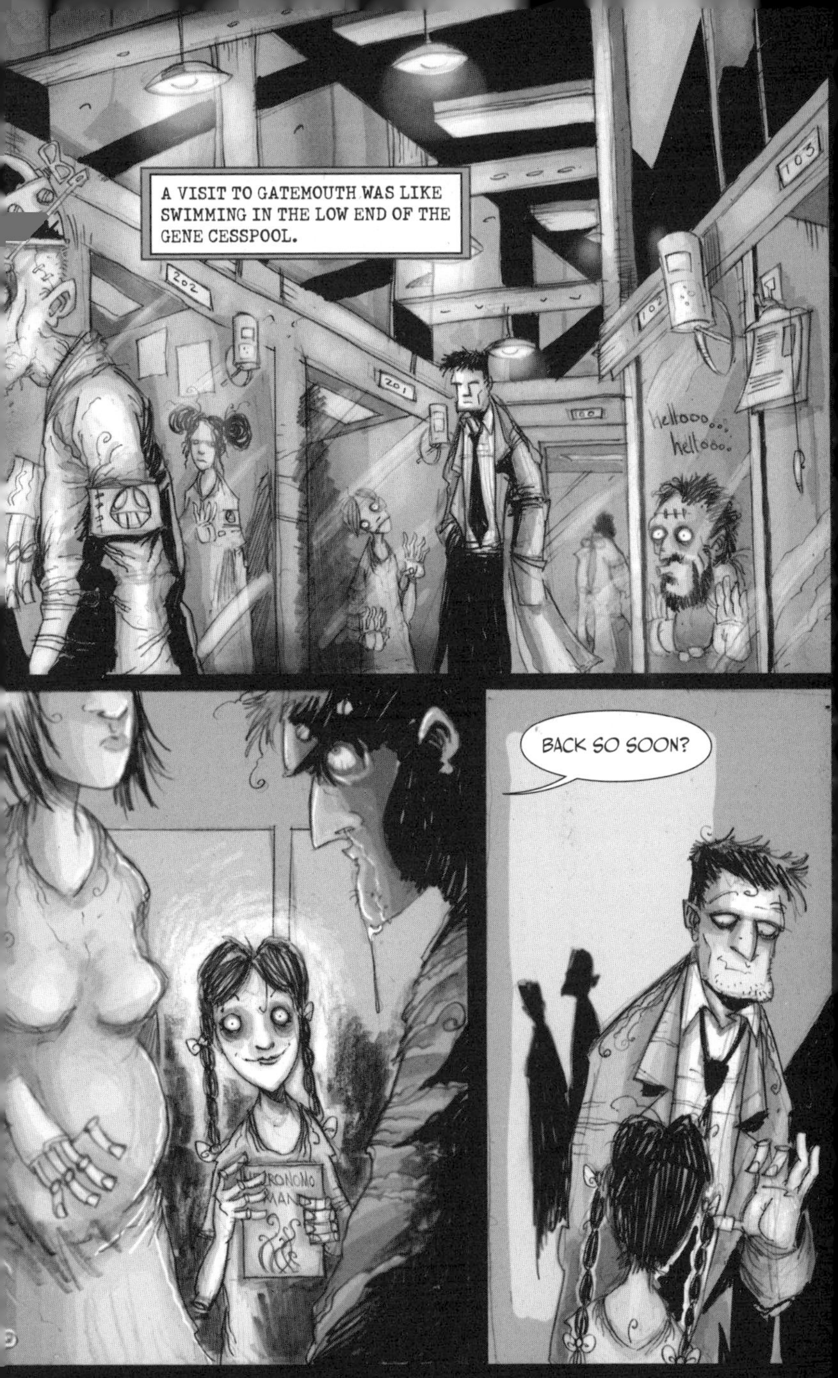
A VISIT TO GATEMOUTH WAS LIKE SWIMMING IN THE LOW END OF THE GENE CESSPOOL.
103
202
102
201
hellooo...
hellooo.
BACK SO SOON?

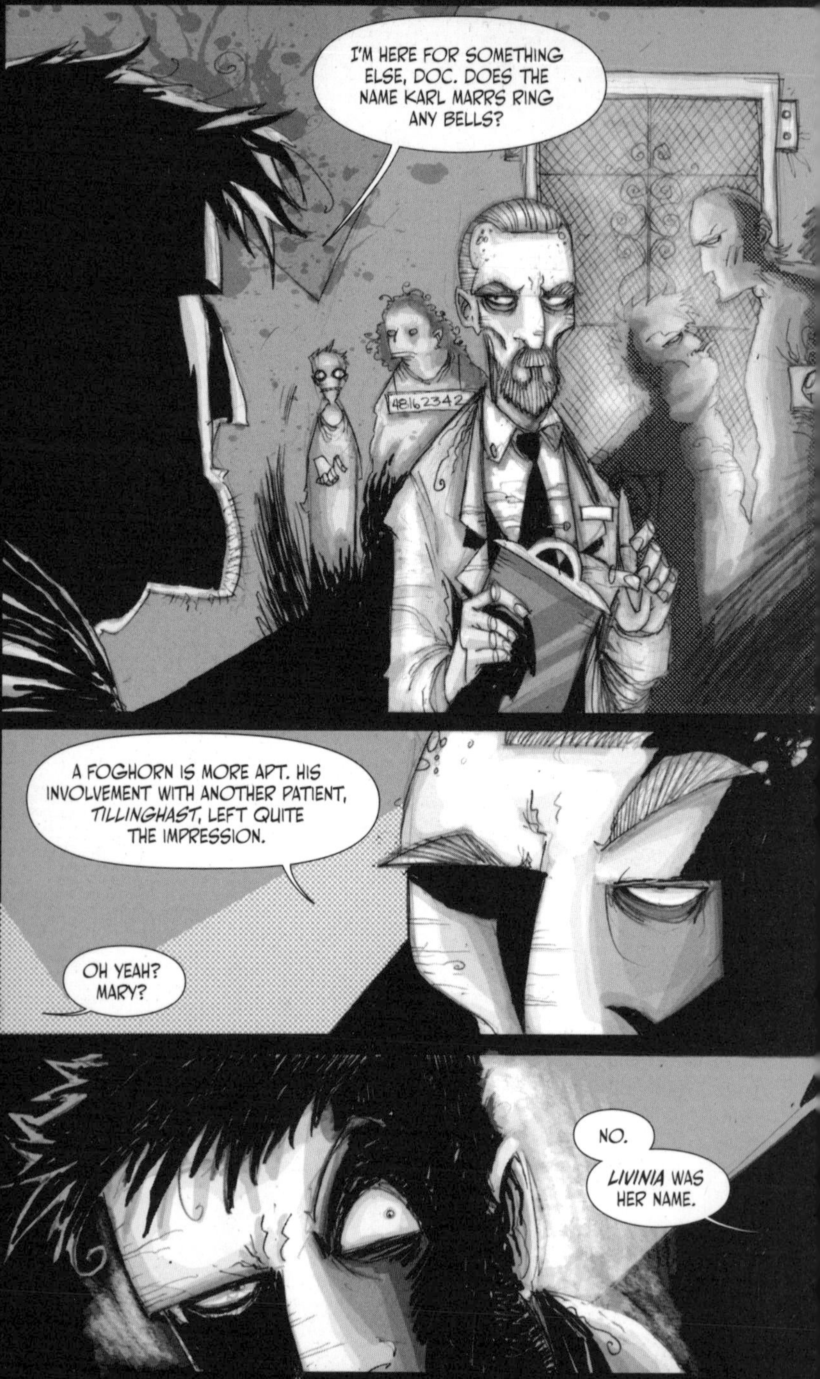
I'M HERE FOR SOMETHING ELSE, DOC. DOES THE NAME KARL MARRS RING ANY BELLS?
48162342
A FOGHORN IS MORE APT. HIS INVOLVEMENT WITH ANOTHER PATIENT, *TILLINGHAST*, LEFT QUITE THE IMPRESSION.
OH YEAH? MARY?
NO.
*LIVINIA* WAS HER NAME.

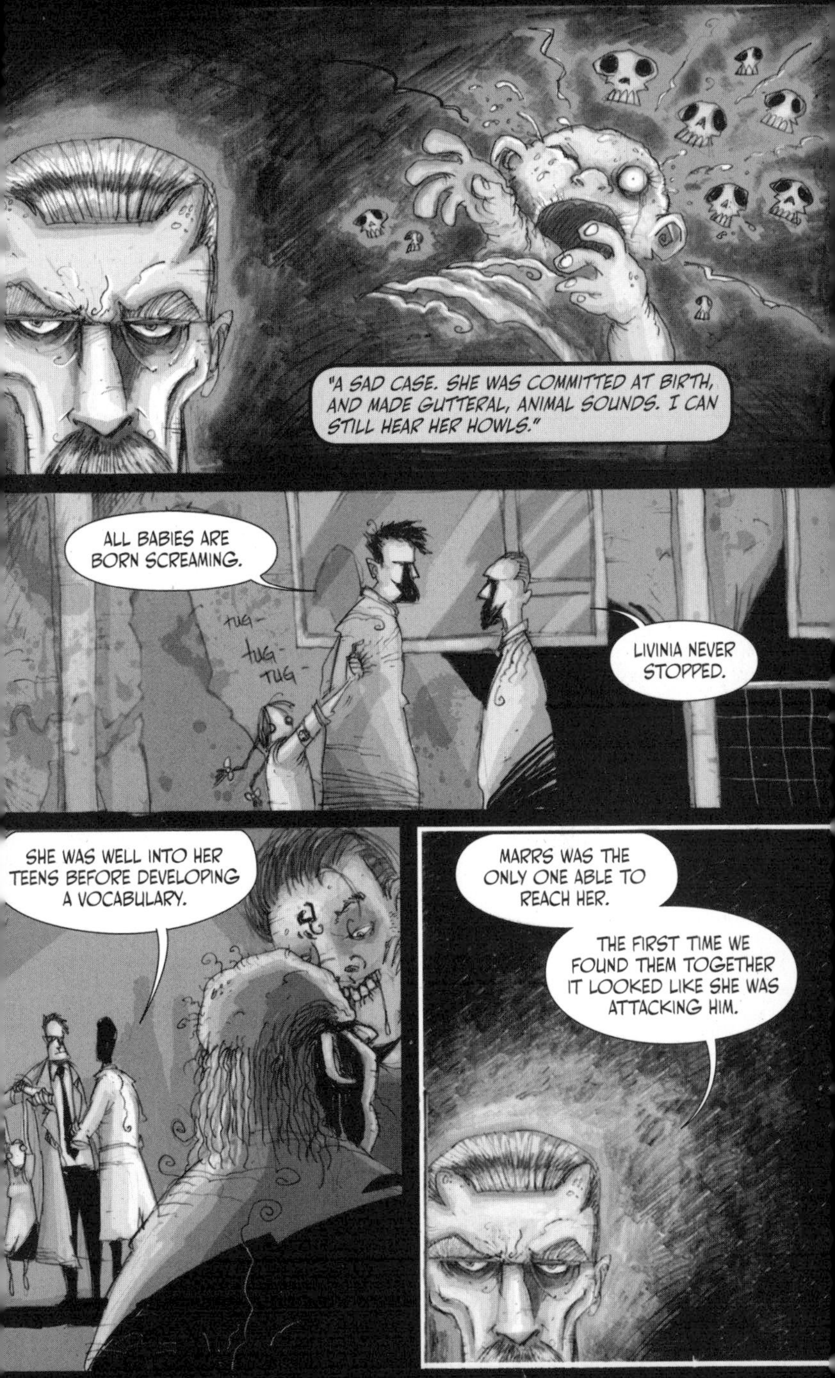
"A SAD CASE. SHE WAS COMMITTED AT BIRTH, AND MADE GUTTERAL, ANIMAL SOUNDS. I CAN STILL HEAR HER HOWLS."
ALL BABIES ARE BORN SCREAMING.
TUG- TUG- TUG
LIVINIA NEVER STOPPED.
SHE WAS WELL INTO HER TEENS BEFORE DEVELOPING A VOCABULARY.
MARRS WAS THE ONLY ONE ABLE TO REACH HER.
THE FIRST TIME WE FOUND THEM TOGETHER IT LOOKED LIKE SHE WAS ATTACKING HIM.

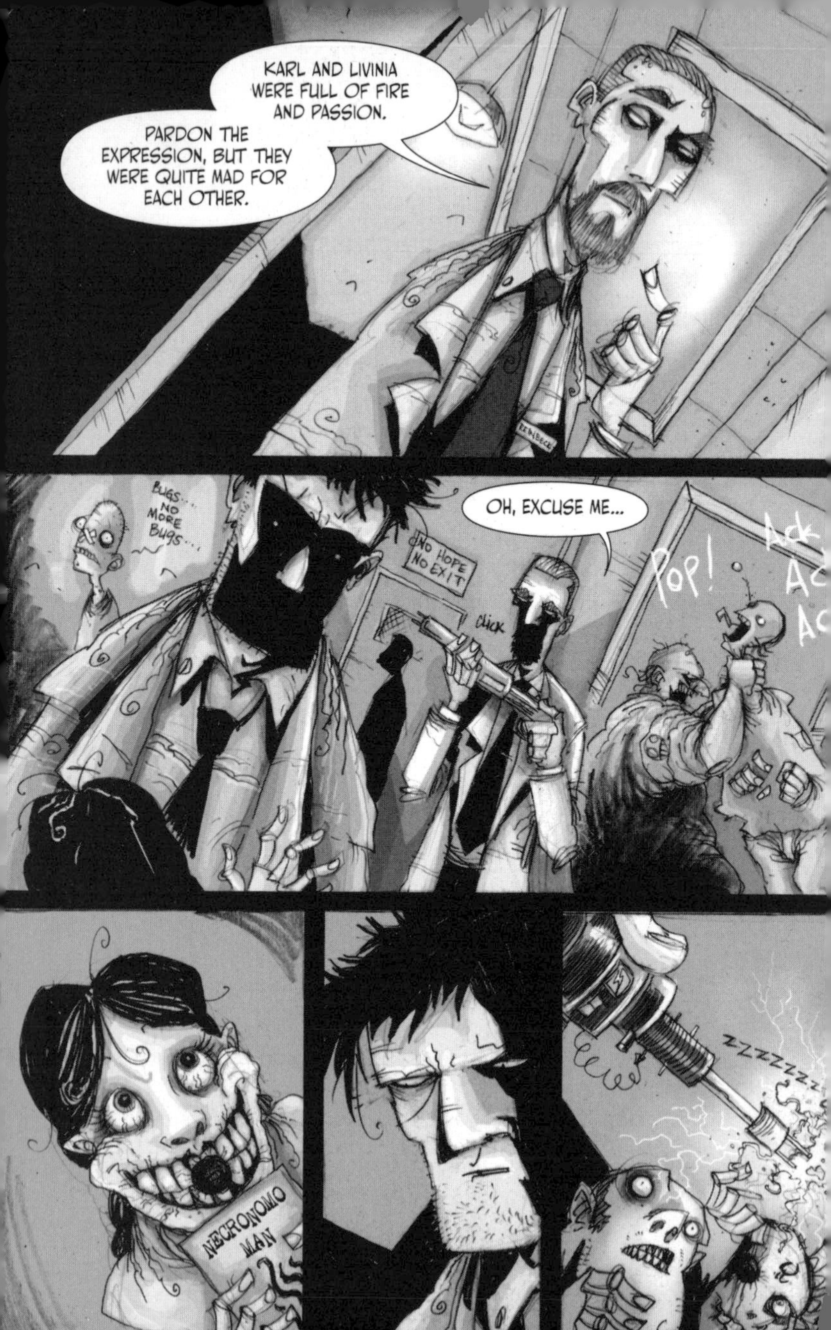
KARL AND LIVINIA WERE FULL OF FIRE AND PASSION.
PARDON THE EXPRESSION, BUT THEY WERE QUITE MAD FOR EACH OTHER.
BUGS... NO MORE BUGS...
NO HOPE NO EXIT
OH, EXCUSE ME...
CLICK
POP!
Ack
NECRONOMO MAN
ZZZZZZZ

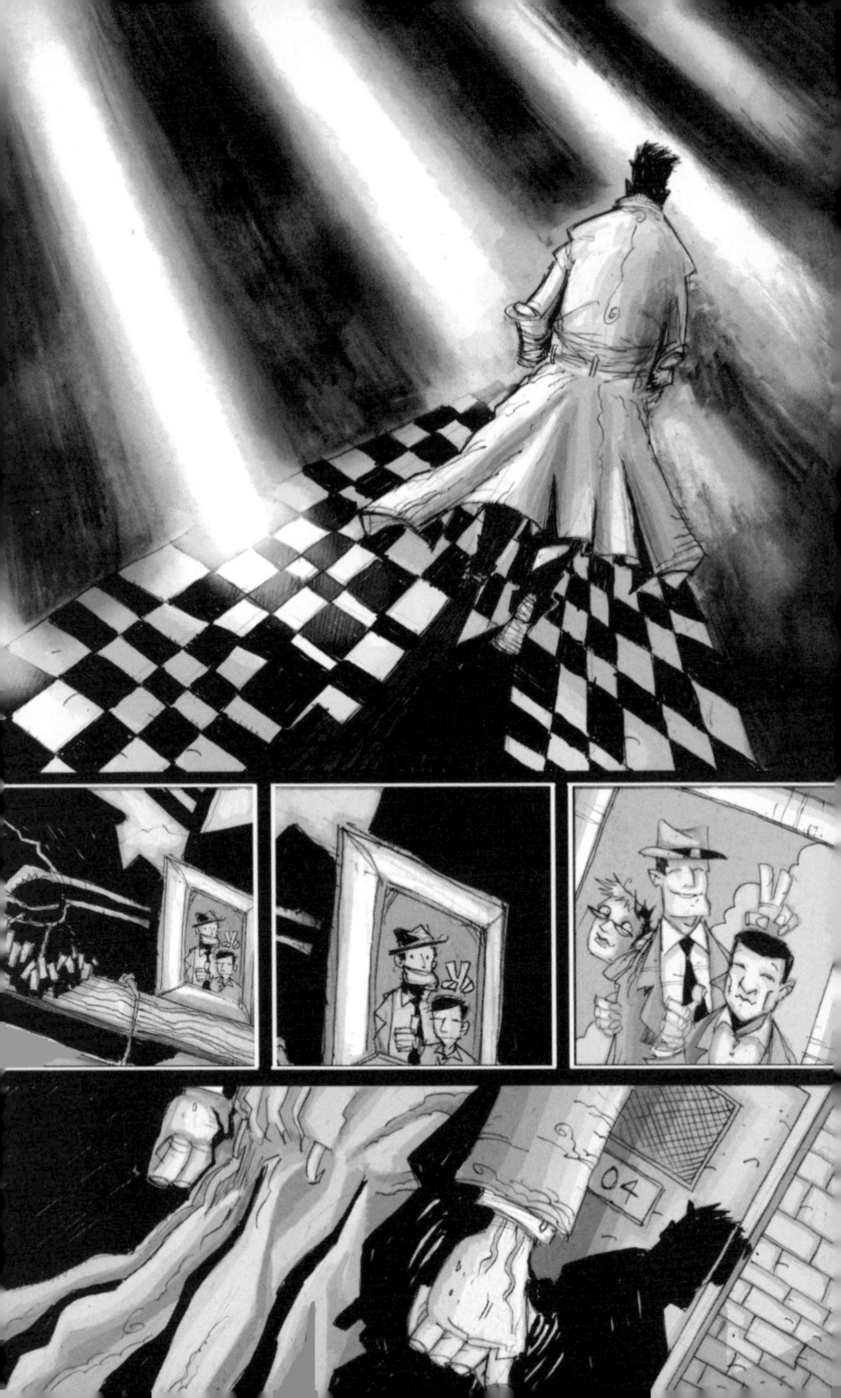
04

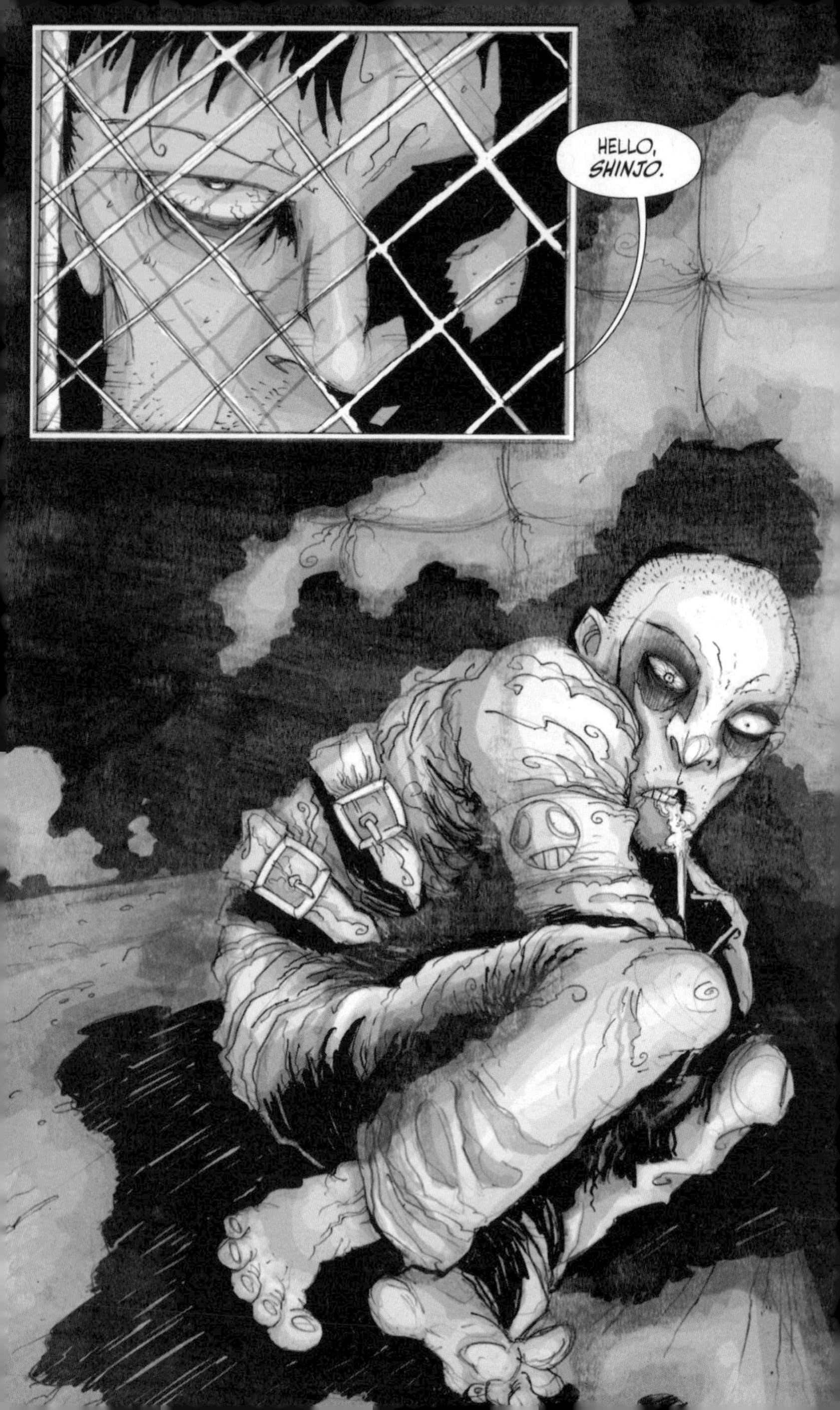
HELLO, SHINJO.

# CHAPTER 3:
## In Too Deep

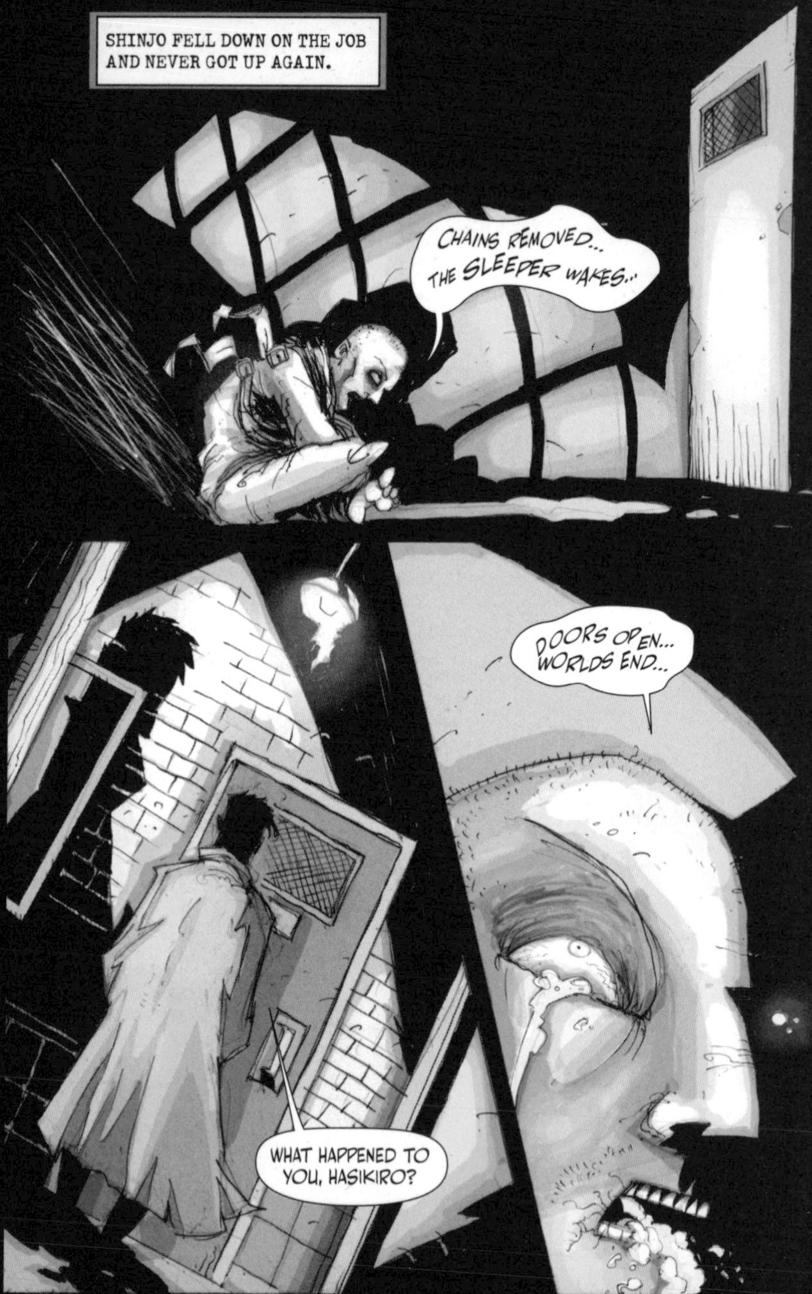
SHINJO FELL DOWN ON THE JOB AND NEVER GOT UP AGAIN.
CHAINS REMOVED... THE SLEEPER WAKES...
DOORS OPEN... WORLDS END...
WHAT HAPPENED TO YOU, HASIKIRO?

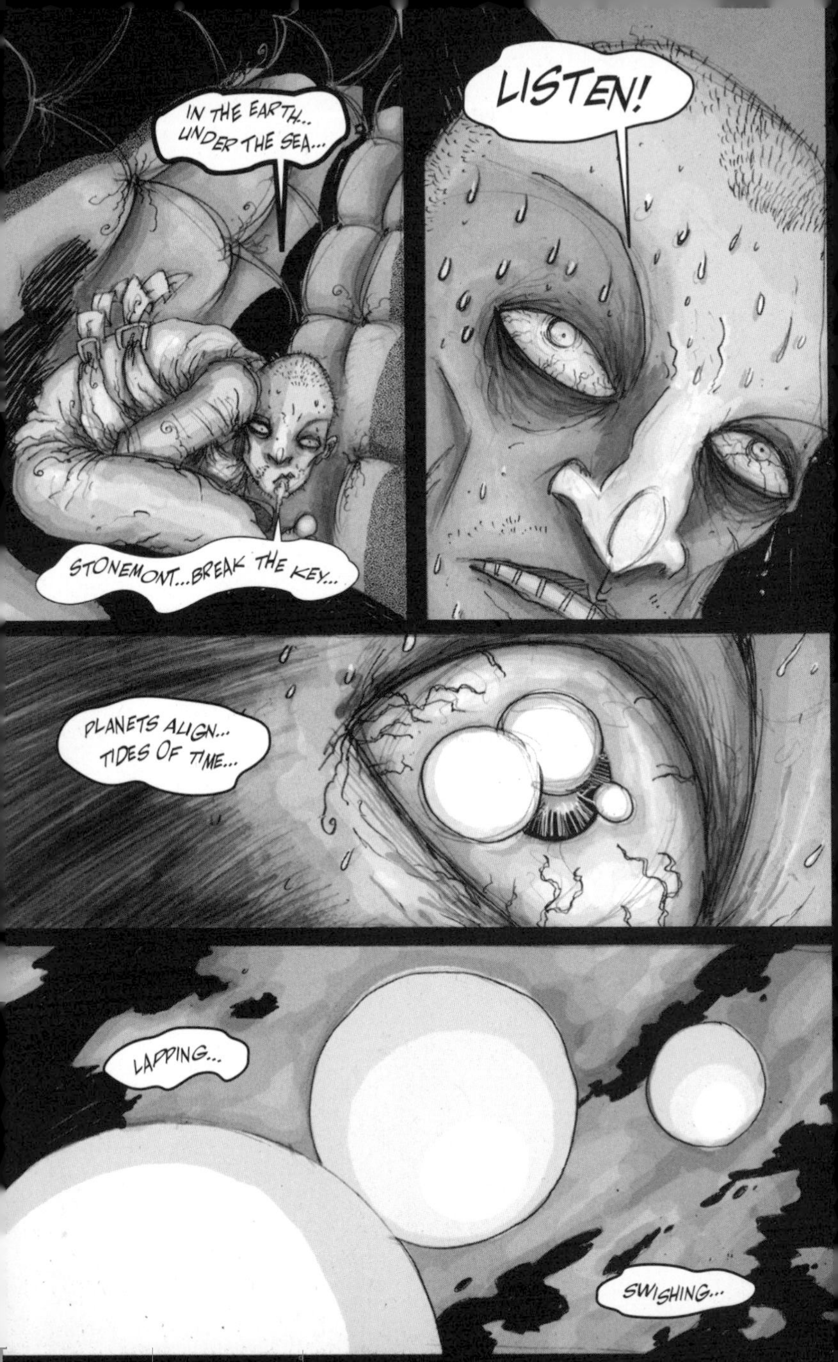
IN THE EARTH... UNDER THE SEA...
STONEMONT...BREAK THE KEY...
LISTEN!
PLANETS ALIGN... TIDES OF TIME...
LAPPING...
SWISHING...

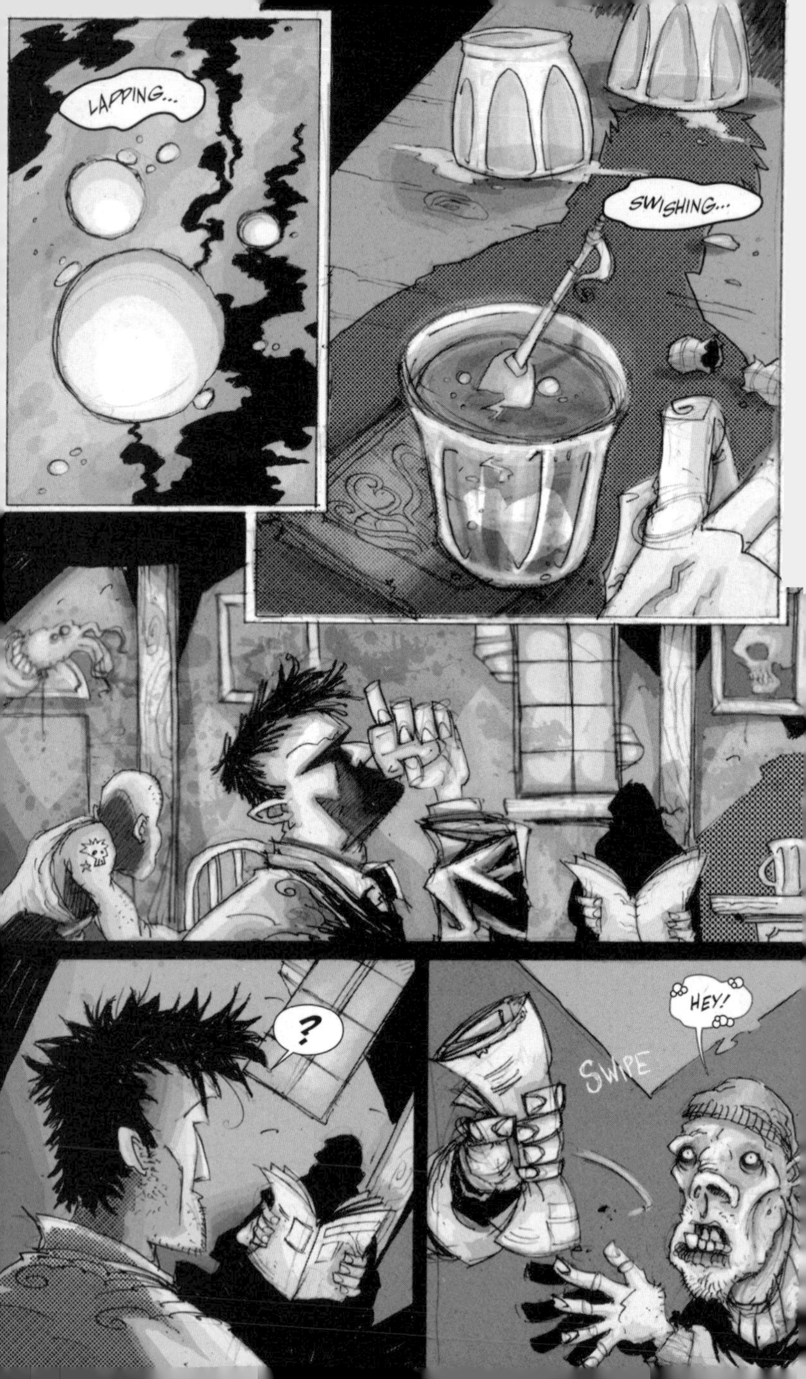
LAPPING...
SWISHING...
?
SWIPE
HEY!

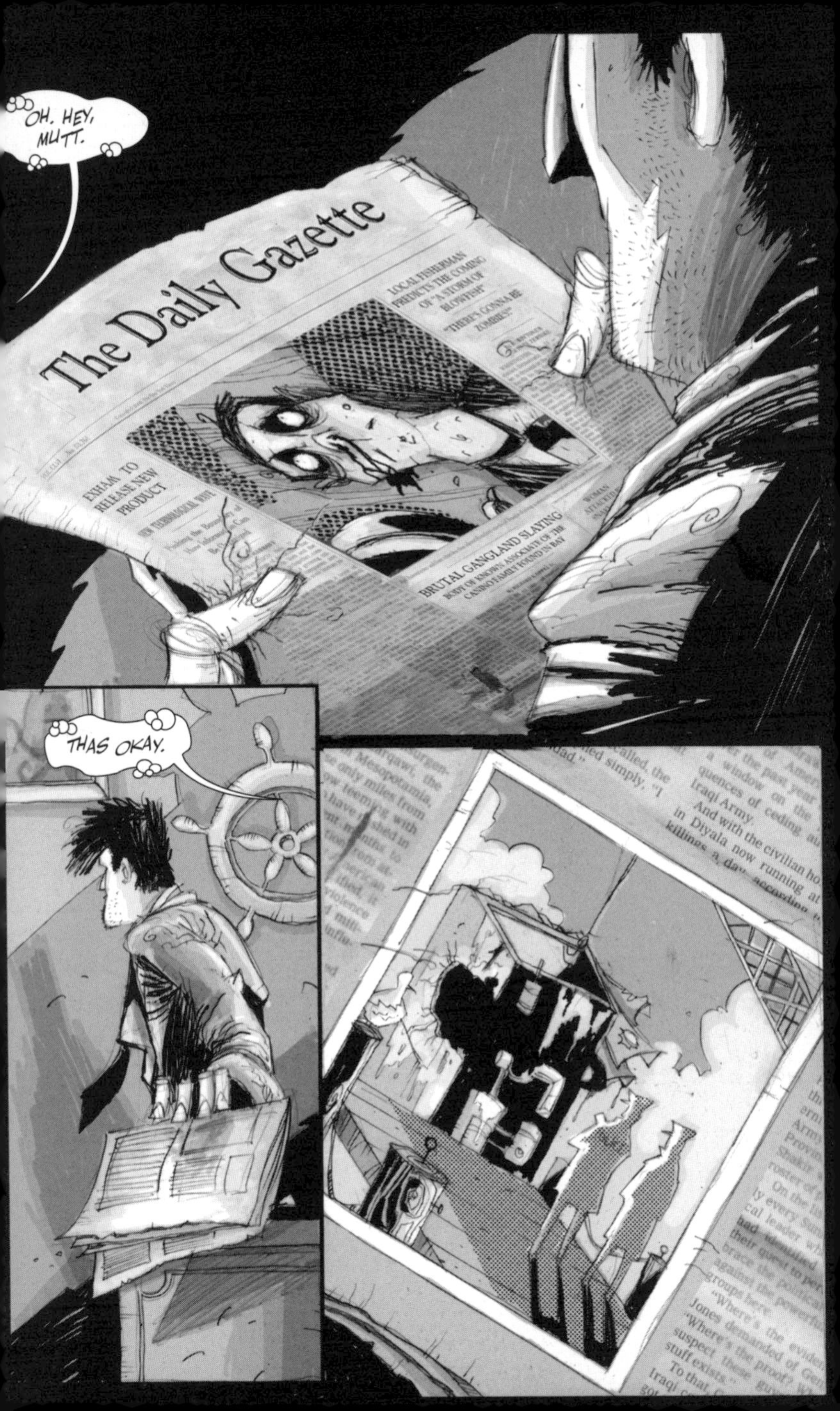
OH. HEY, MUTT.
The Daily Gazette
LOCAL FISHERMAN PREDICTS THE COMING OF "A STORM OF BLOWFISH"
"THERE'S GONNA BE ZOMBIES!"
EXHAM TO RELEASE NEW PRODUCT
BRUTAL GANGLAND SLAYING
BODY OF KNOWN ASSOCIATE OF THE CASINO FAMILY FOUND IN BAY
THAS OKAY.

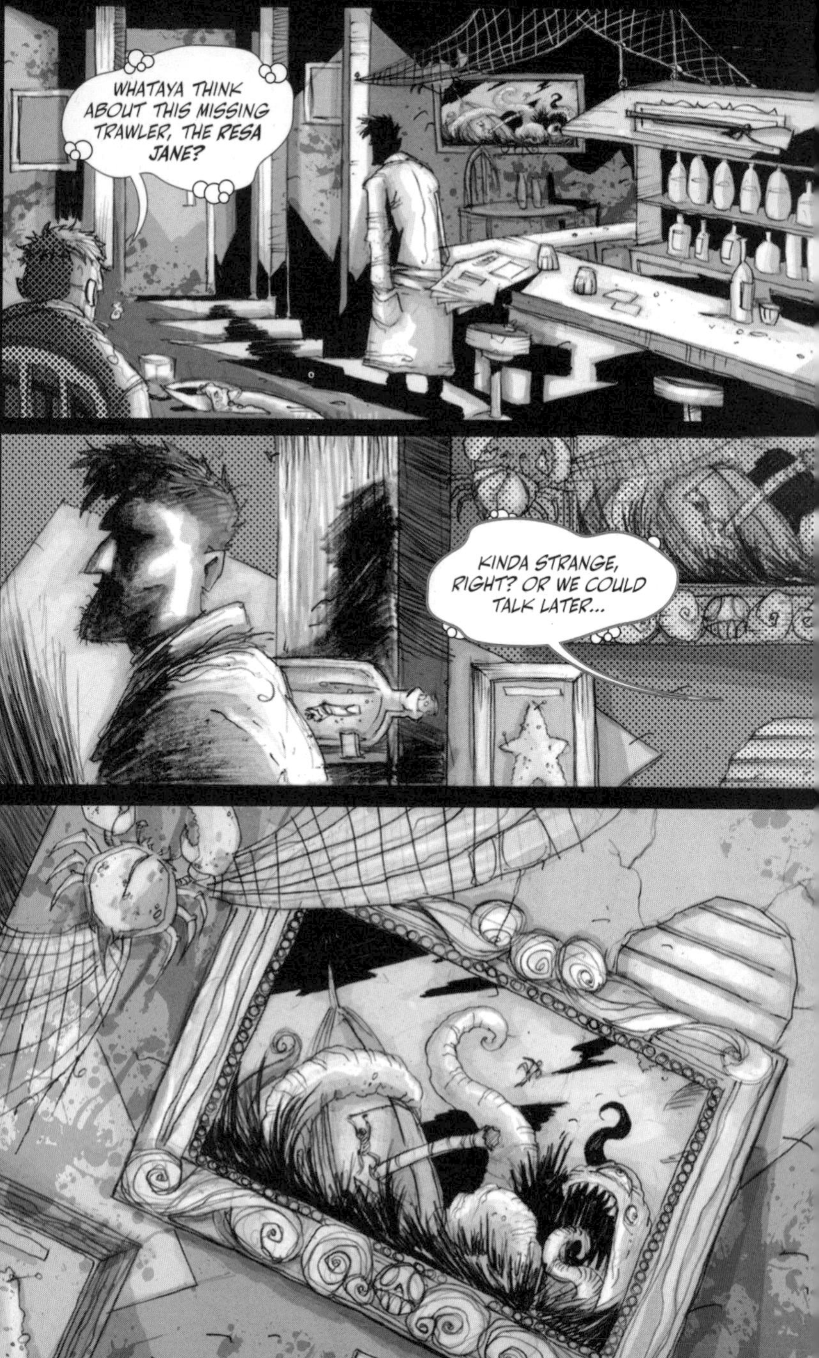
WHATAYA THINK ABOUT THIS MISSING TRAWLER, THE RESA JANE?
KINDA STRANGE, RIGHT? OR WE COULD TALK LATER...

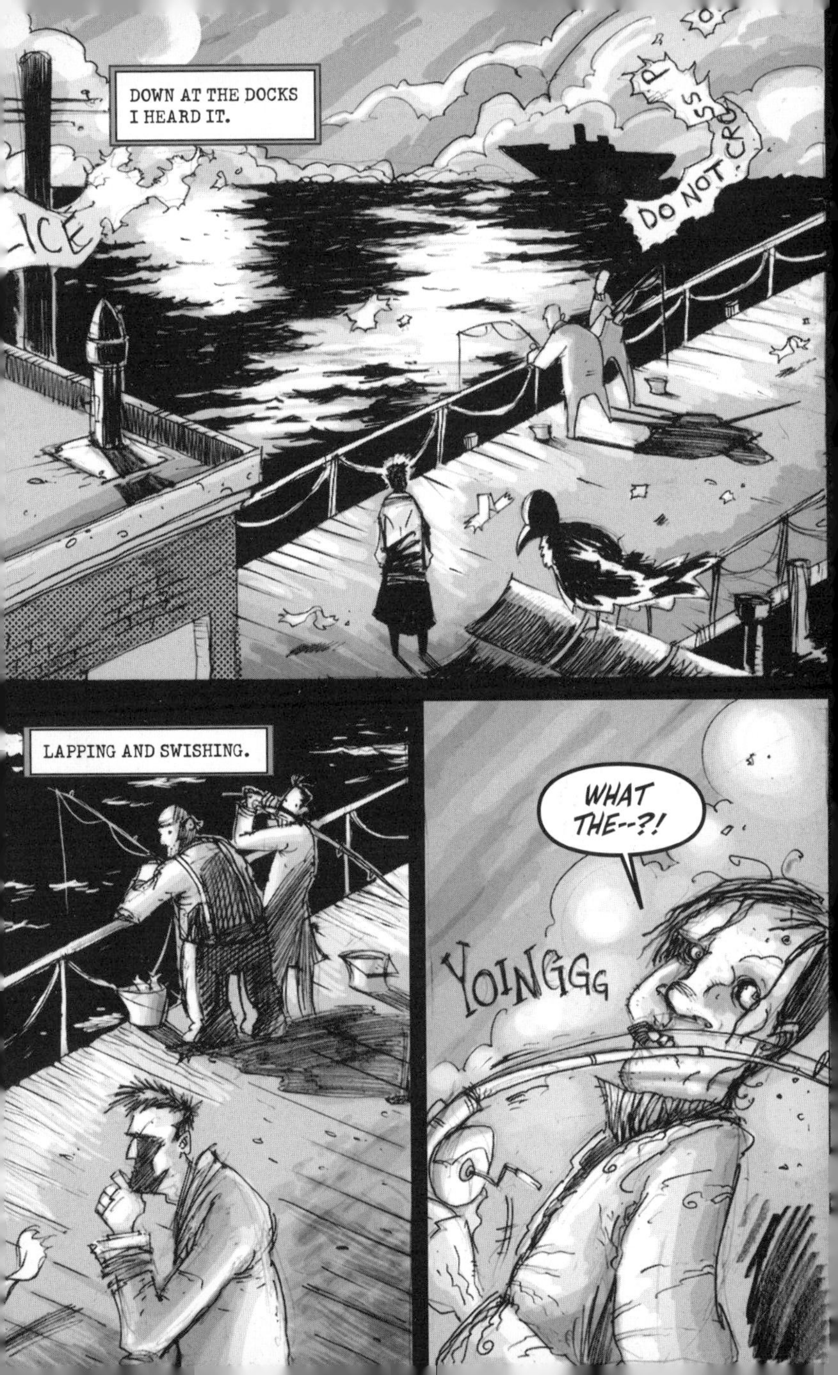
DOWN AT THE DOCKS I HEARD IT.
ICE
DO NOT CROSS
LAPPING AND SWISHING.
WHAT THE--?!
YOINGGG

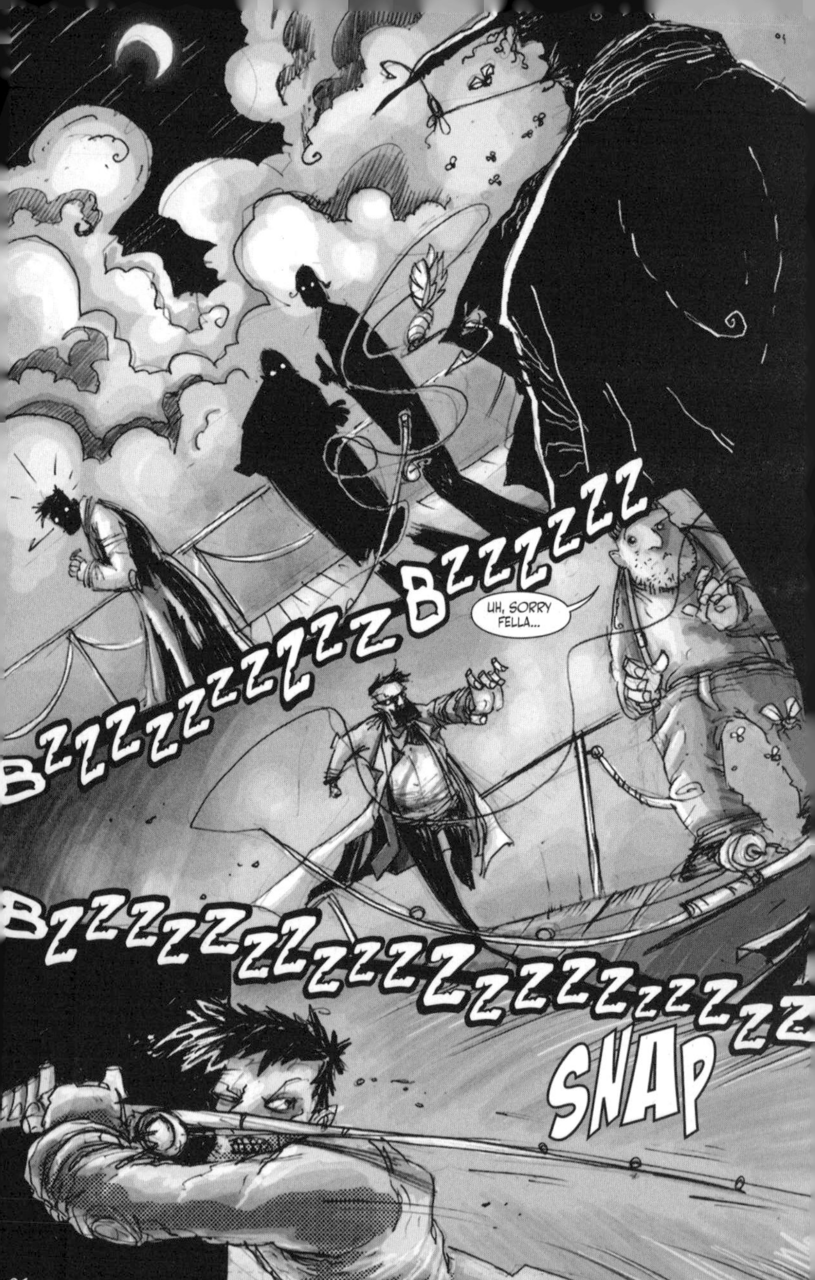

BZZZZZZZZZZZZ
BZZZZZZZZ
UH, SORRY FELLA...
BZZZZZZZZZZZZZZZZZZZZ
SNAP

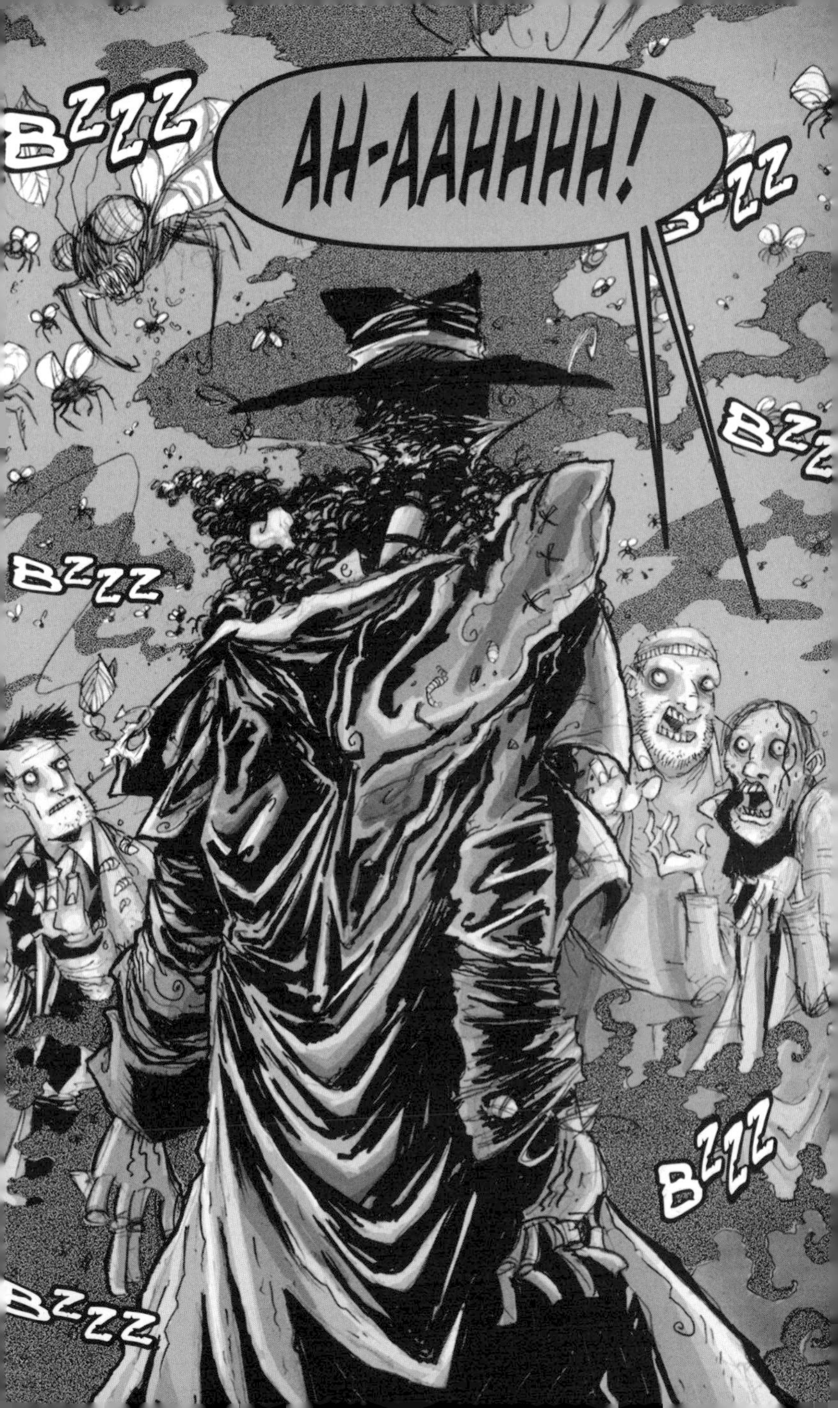
BZZZ
AH-AAHHHH!
BZZ
BZZZ
BZZZ
BZZZ

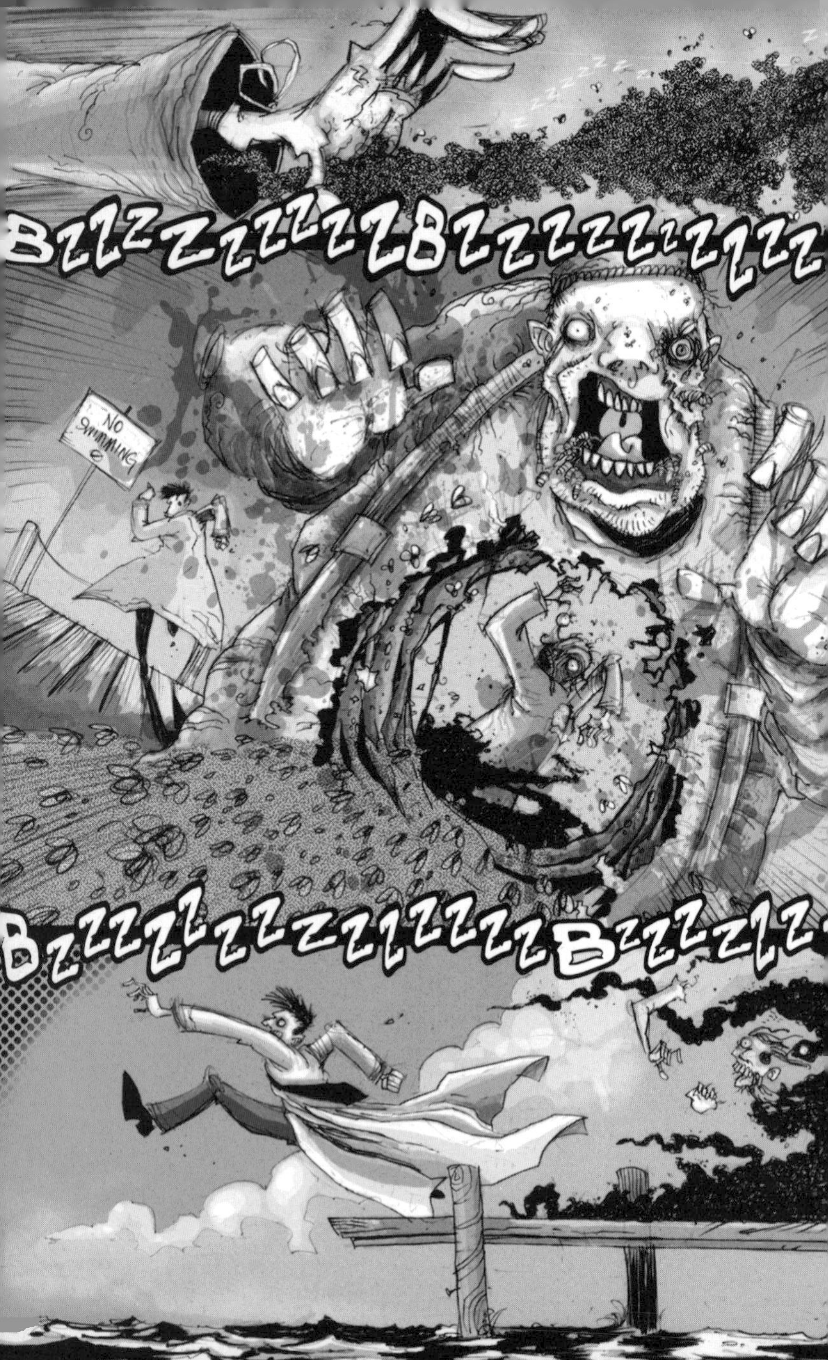
BZZZZZZZZZZZBZZZZZZZZZZZ
NO SWIMMING
BZZZZZZZZZZZZZZZZBZZZZZZ

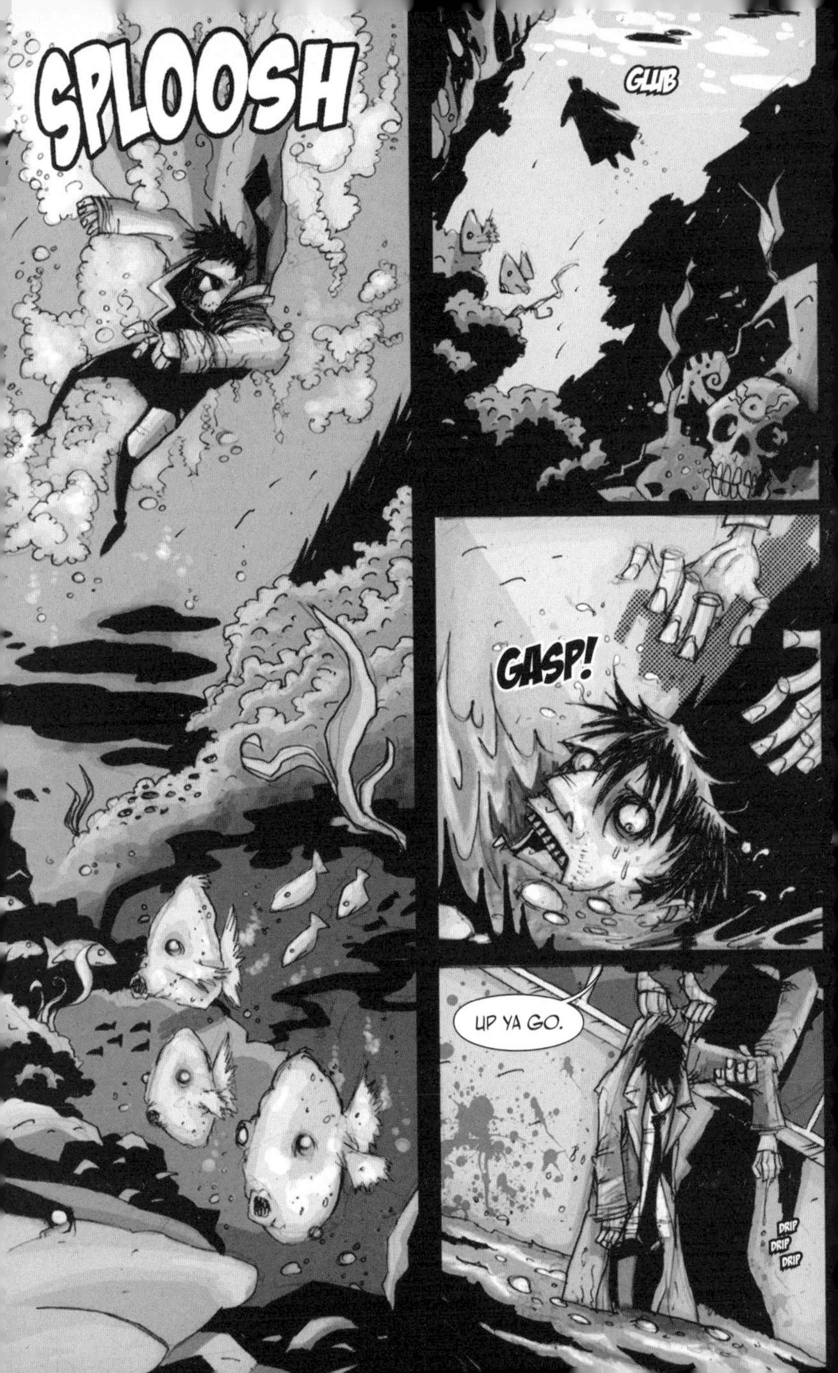
SPLOOSH
GLUB
GASP!
UP YA GO.
DRIP
DRIP
DRIP

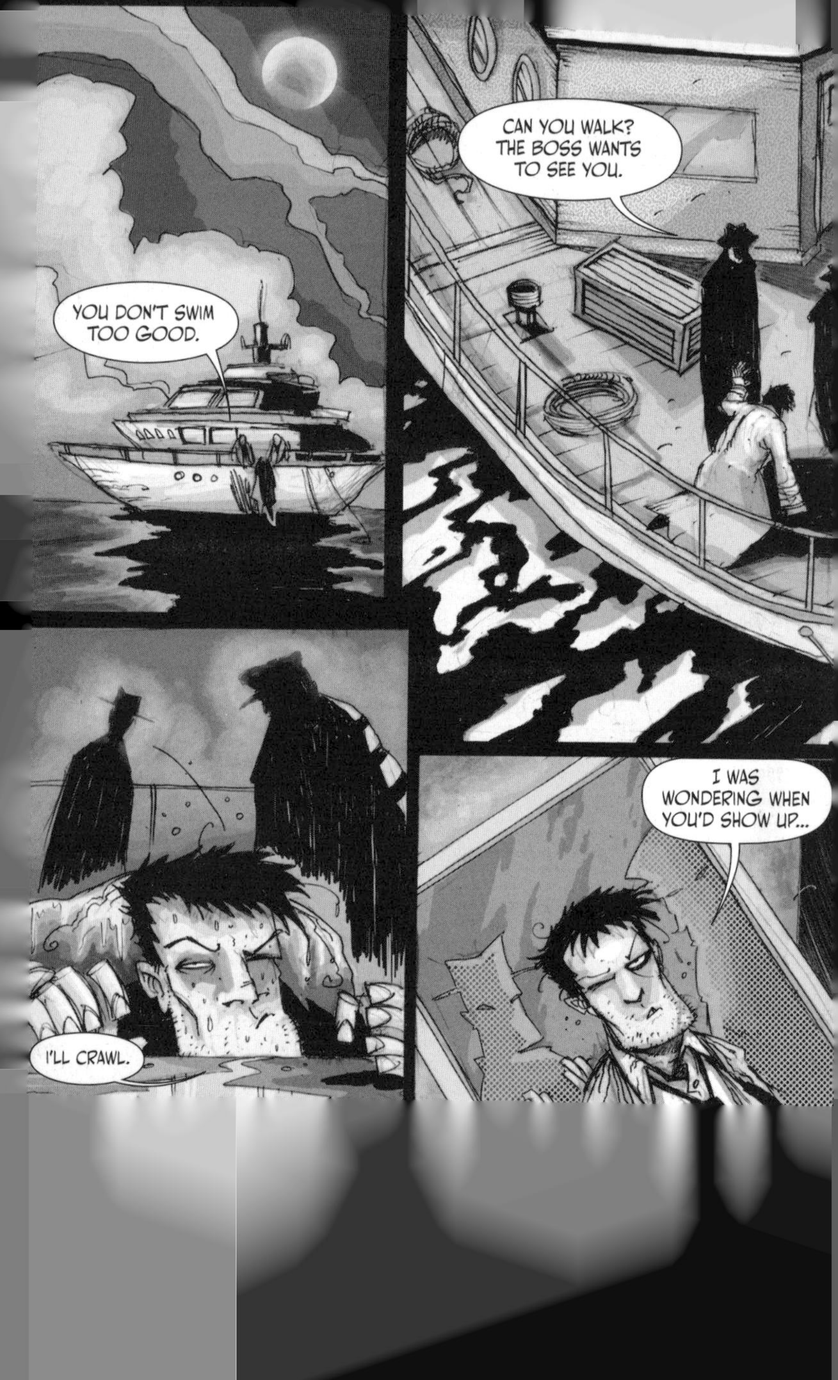
YOU DON'T SWIM TOO GOOD.
CAN YOU WALK? THE BOSS WANTS TO SEE YOU.
I'LL CRAWL.
I WAS WONDERING WHEN YOU'D SHOW UP...

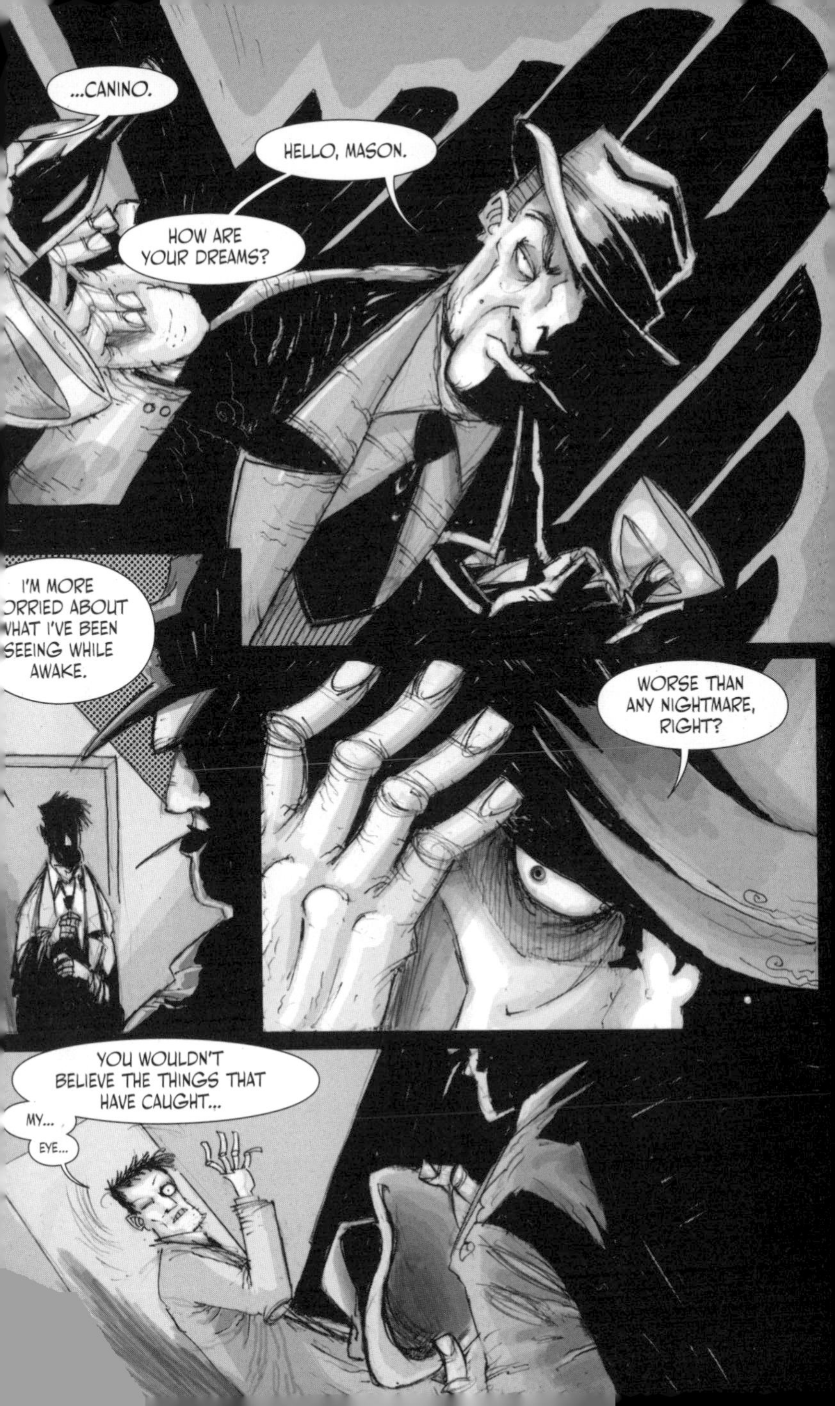
...CANINO.
HELLO, MASON.
HOW ARE YOUR DREAMS?
I'M MORE ORRIED ABOUT VHAT I'VE BEEN SEEING WHILE AWAKE.
WORSE THAN ANY NIGHTMARE, RIGHT?
YOU WOULDN'T BELIEVE THE THINGS THAT HAVE CAUGHT...
MY...
EYE...

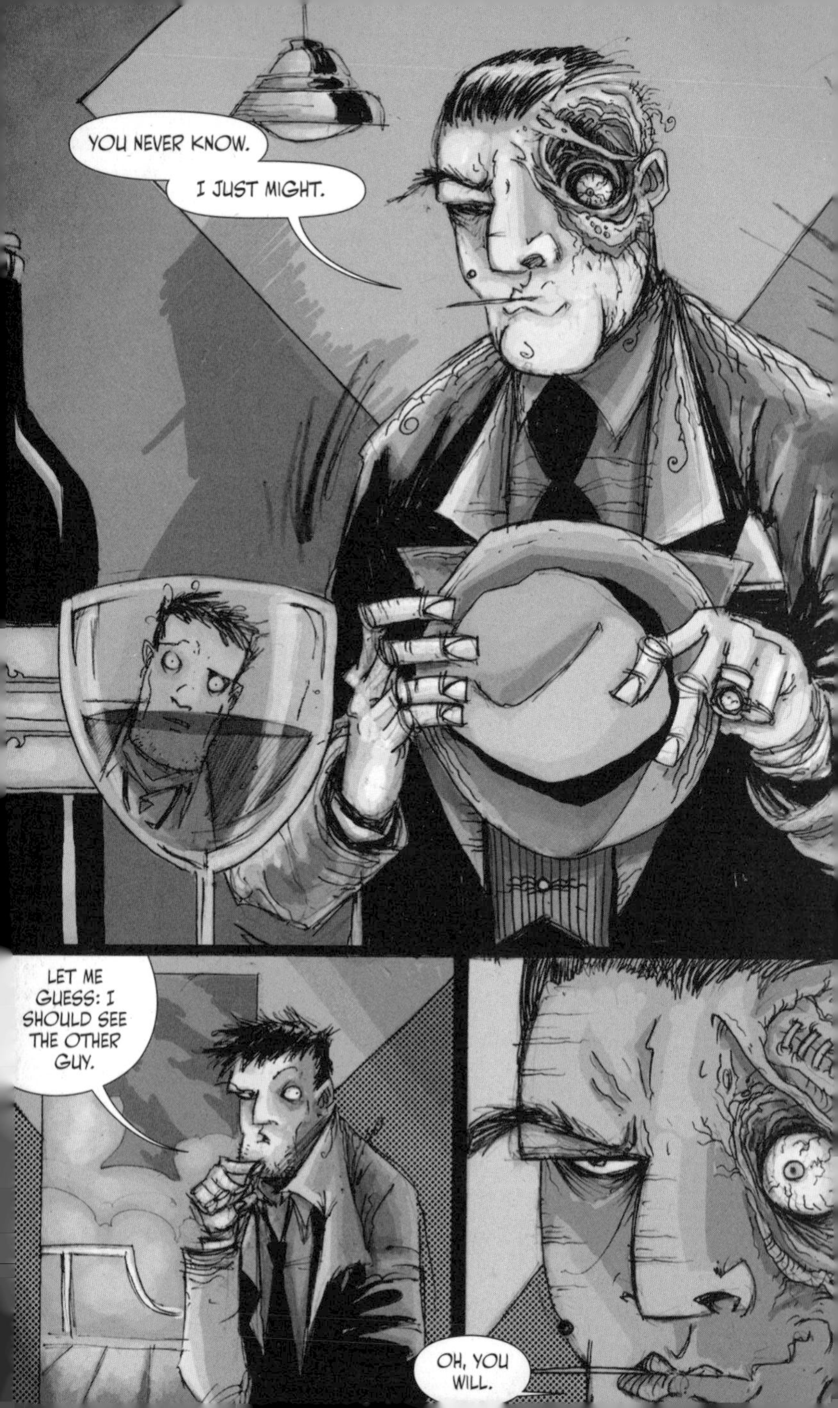
YOU NEVER KNOW.
I JUST MIGHT.
LET ME GUESS: I SHOULD SEE THE OTHER GUY.
OH, YOU WILL.

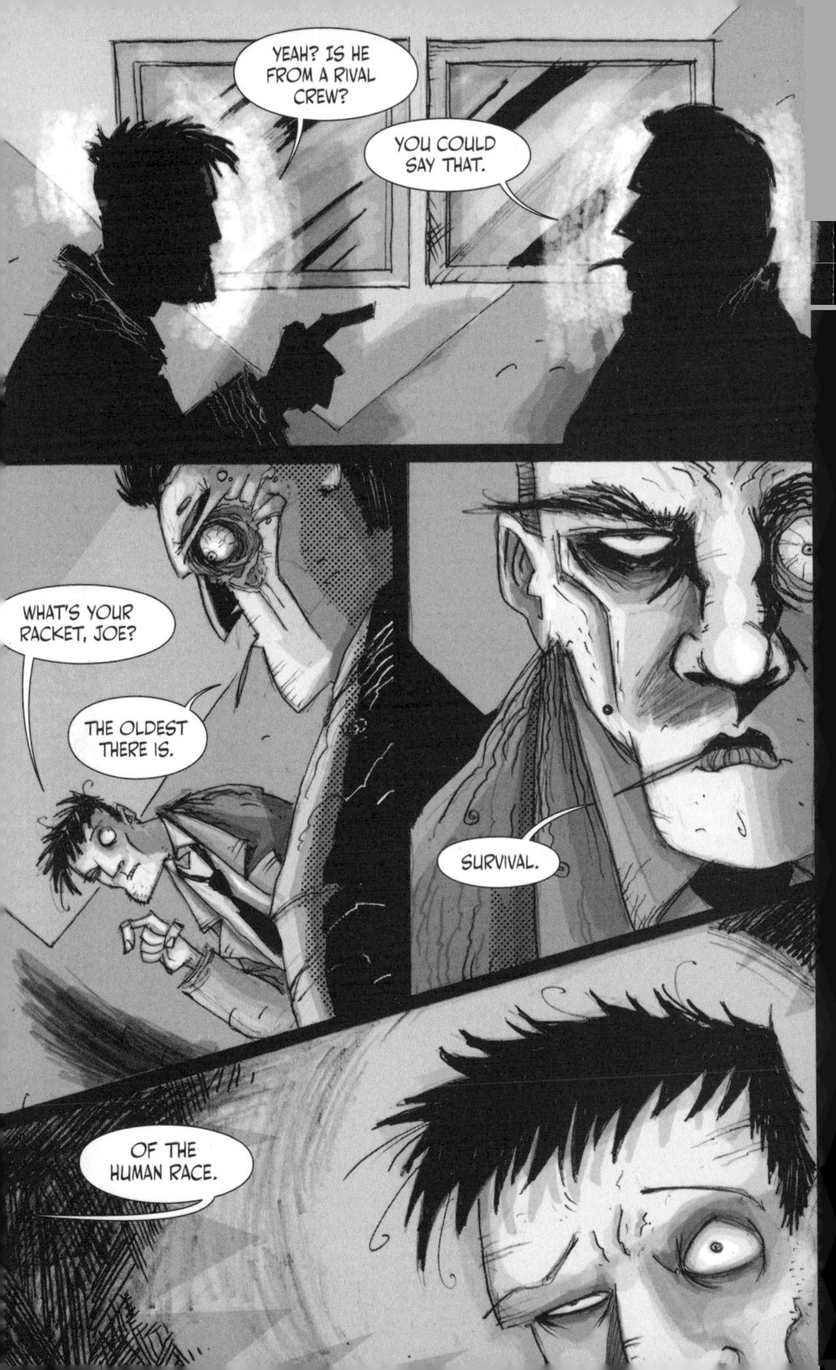
YEAH? IS HE FROM A RIVAL CREW?
YOU COULD SAY THAT.
WHAT'S YOUR RACKET, JOE?
THE OLDEST THERE IS.
SURVIVAL.
OF THE HUMAN RACE.

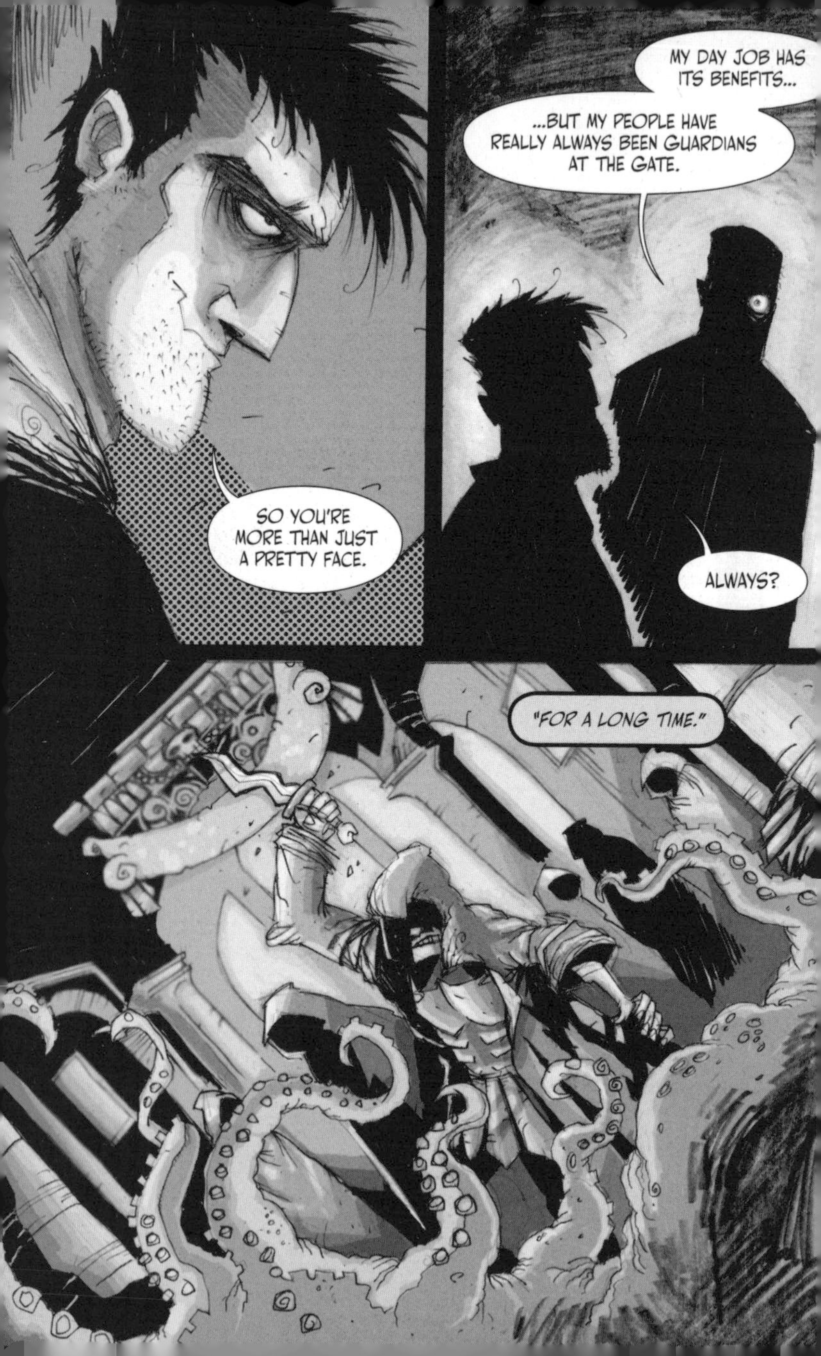
SO YOU'RE MORE THAN JUST A PRETTY FACE.
MY DAY JOB HAS ITS BENEFITS...
...BUT MY PEOPLE HAVE REALLY ALWAYS BEEN GUARDIANS AT THE GATE.
ALWAYS?
"FOR A LONG TIME."

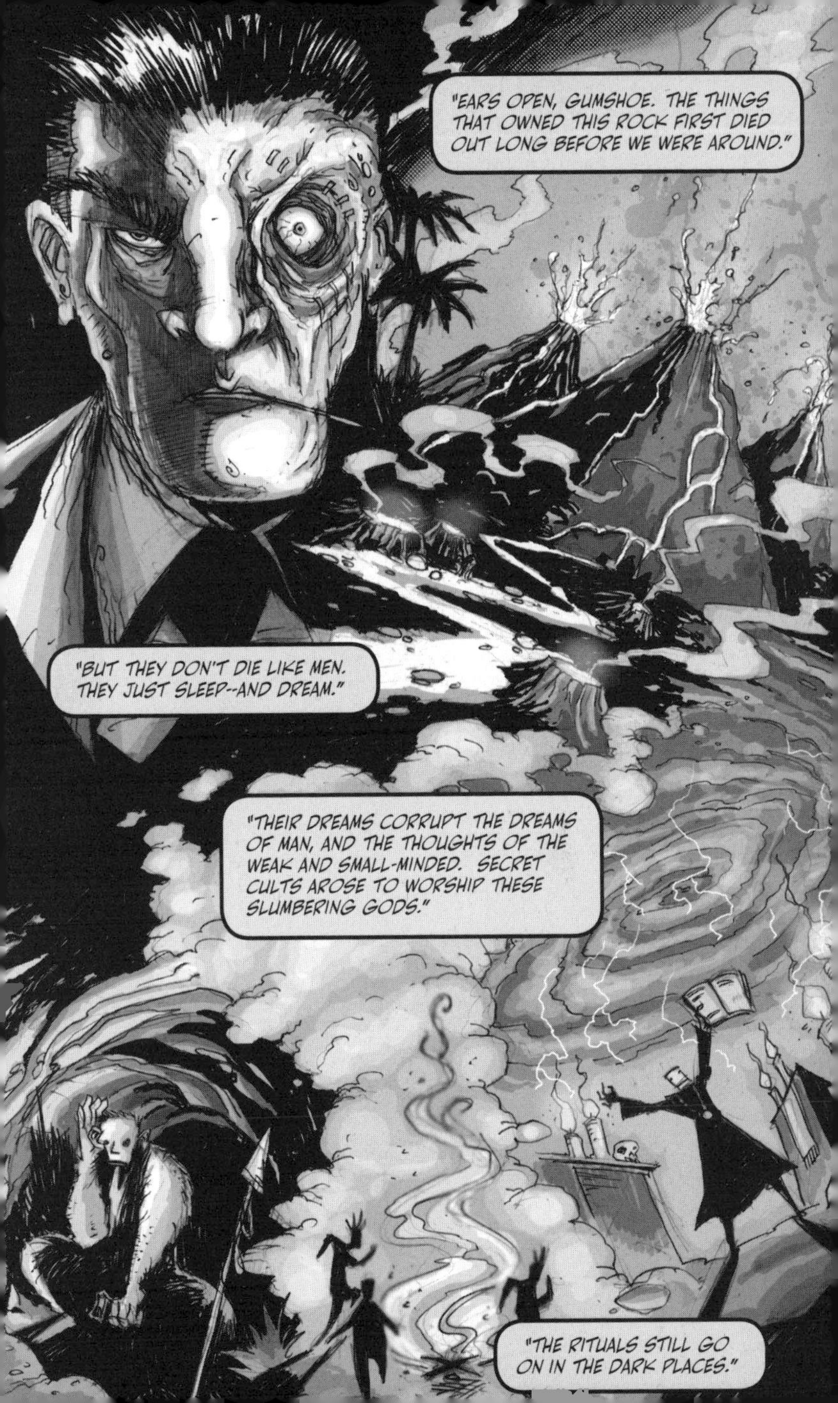
"EARS OPEN, GUMSHOE. THE THINGS THAT OWNED THIS ROCK FIRST DIED OUT LONG BEFORE WE WERE AROUND."
"BUT THEY DON'T DIE LIKE MEN. THEY JUST SLEEP--AND DREAM."
"THEIR DREAMS CORRUPT THE DREAMS OF MAN, AND THE THOUGHTS OF THE WEAK AND SMALL-MINDED. SECRET CULTS AROSE TO WORSHIP THESE SLUMBERING GODS."
"THE RITUALS STILL GO ON IN THE DARK PLACES."

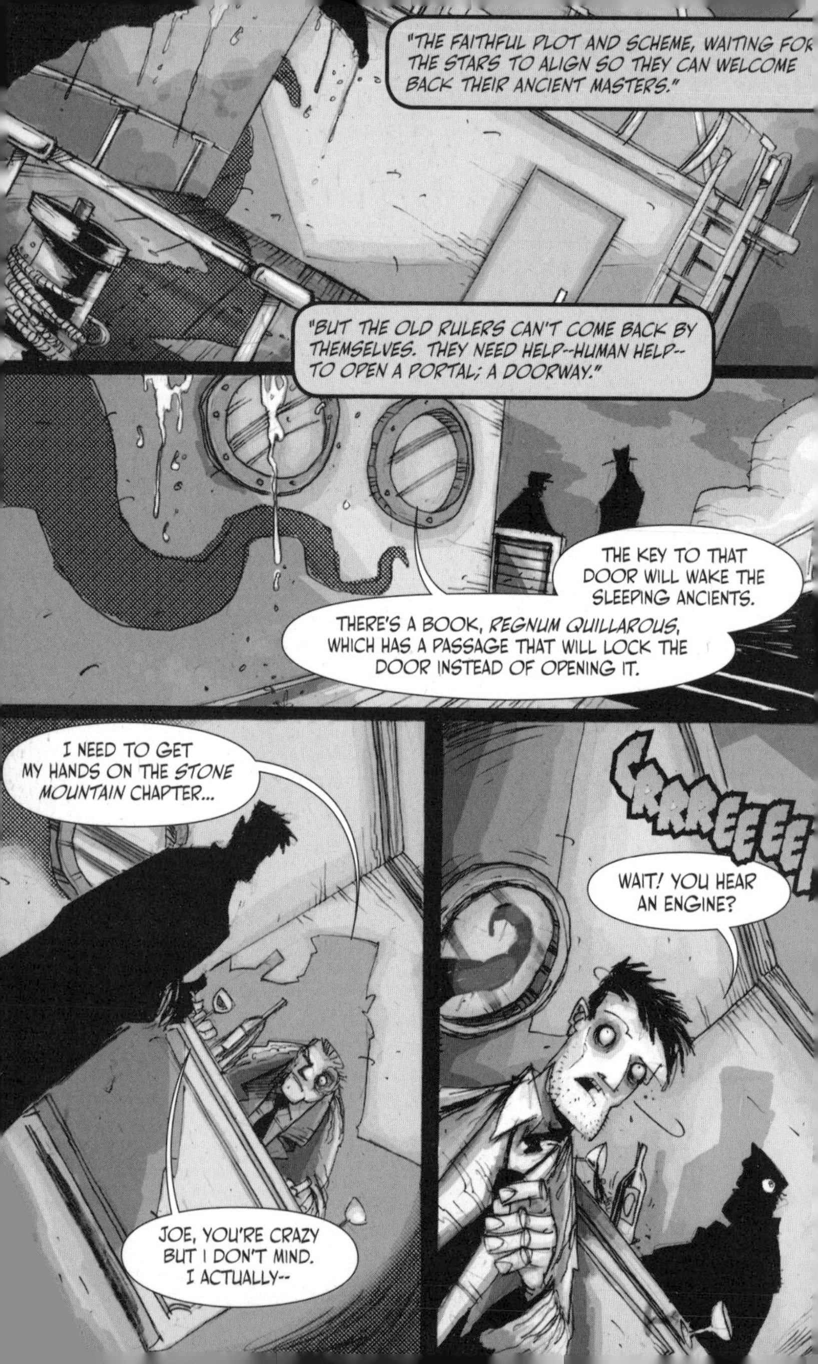
"THE FAITHFUL PLOT AND SCHEME, WAITING FOR THE STARS TO ALIGN SO THEY CAN WELCOME BACK THEIR ANCIENT MASTERS."
"BUT THE OLD RULERS CAN'T COME BACK BY THEMSELVES. THEY NEED HELP--HUMAN HELP--TO OPEN A PORTAL; A DOORWAY."
THE KEY TO THAT DOOR WILL WAKE THE SLEEPING ANCIENTS.
THERE'S A BOOK, *REGNUM QUILLAROUS*, WHICH HAS A PASSAGE THAT WILL LOCK THE DOOR INSTEAD OF OPENING IT.
I NEED TO GET MY HANDS ON THE *STONE MOUNTAIN* CHAPTER...
JOE, YOU'RE CRAZY BUT I DON'T MIND. I ACTUALLY--
CRRREEEEE
WAIT! YOU HEAR AN ENGINE?

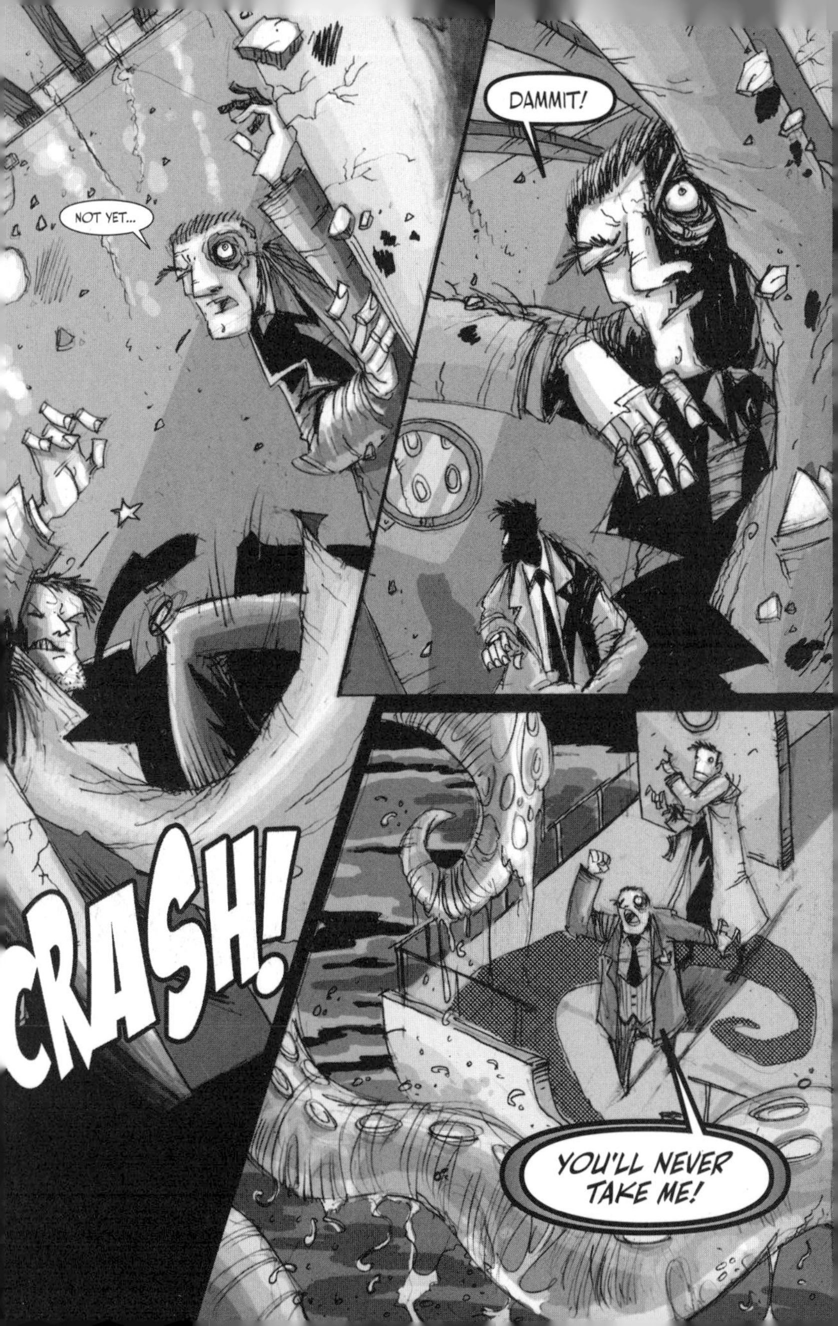
NOT YET...
CRASH!
DAMMIT!
YOU'LL NEVER TAKE ME!

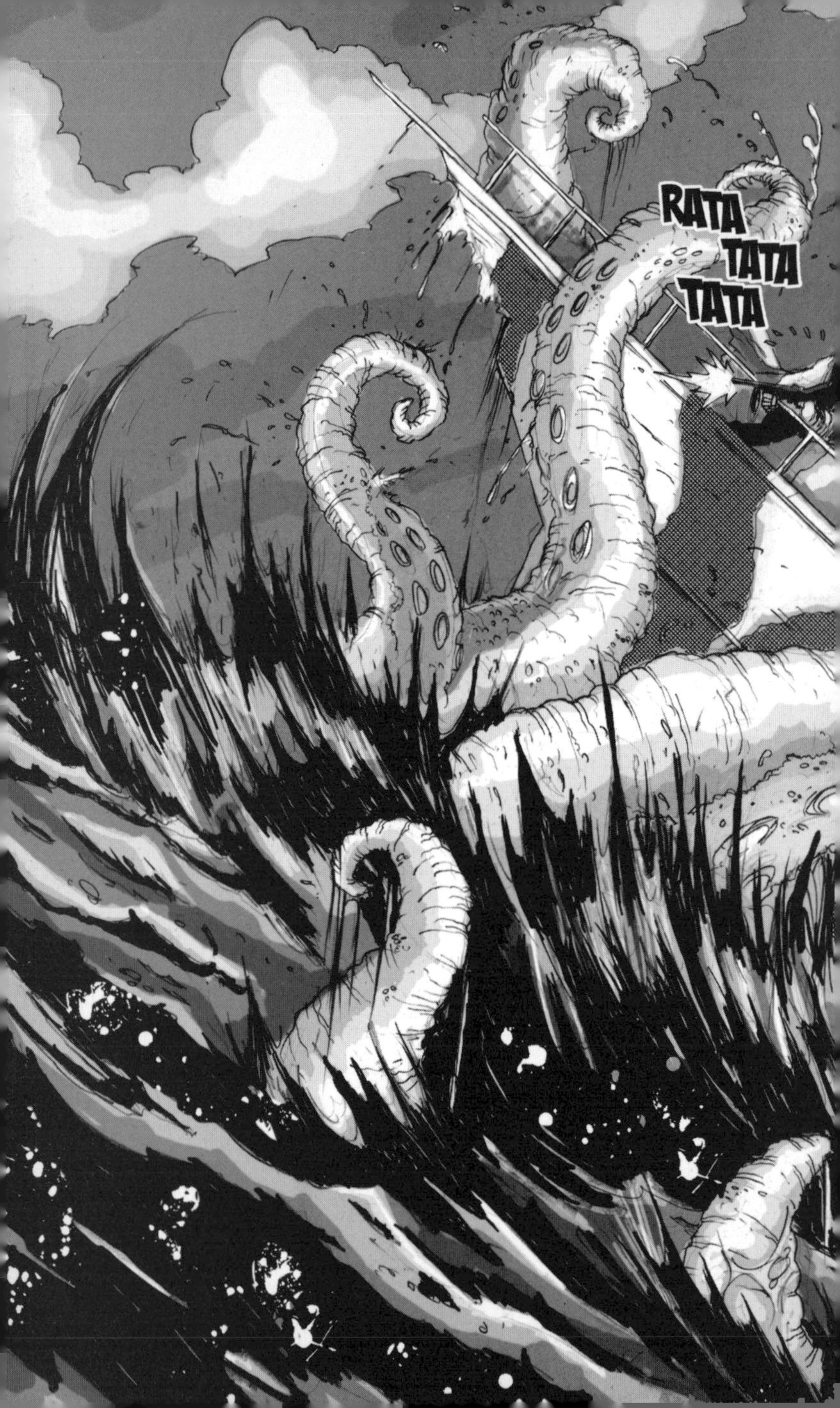
RATA
TATA
TATA

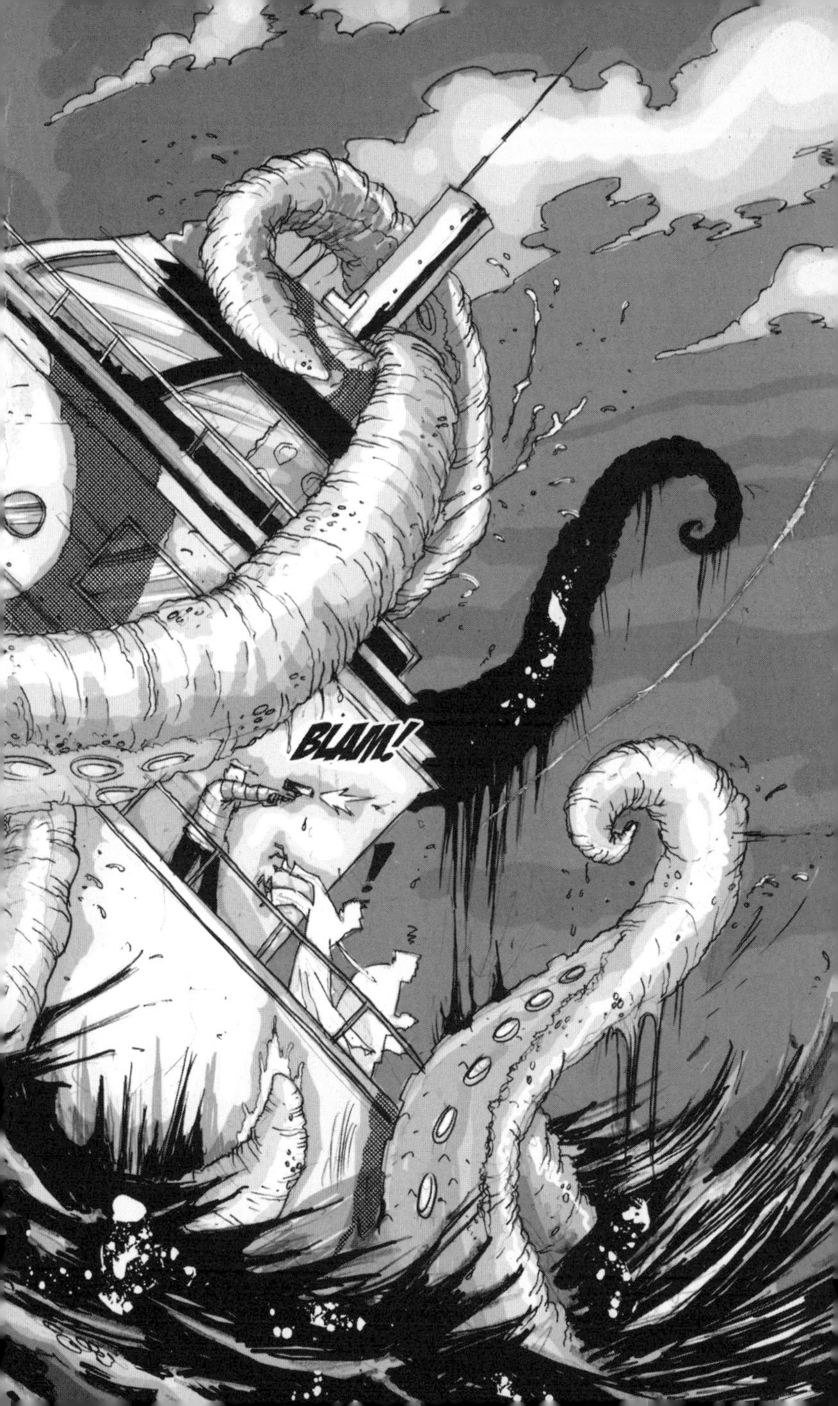
BLAM!
!

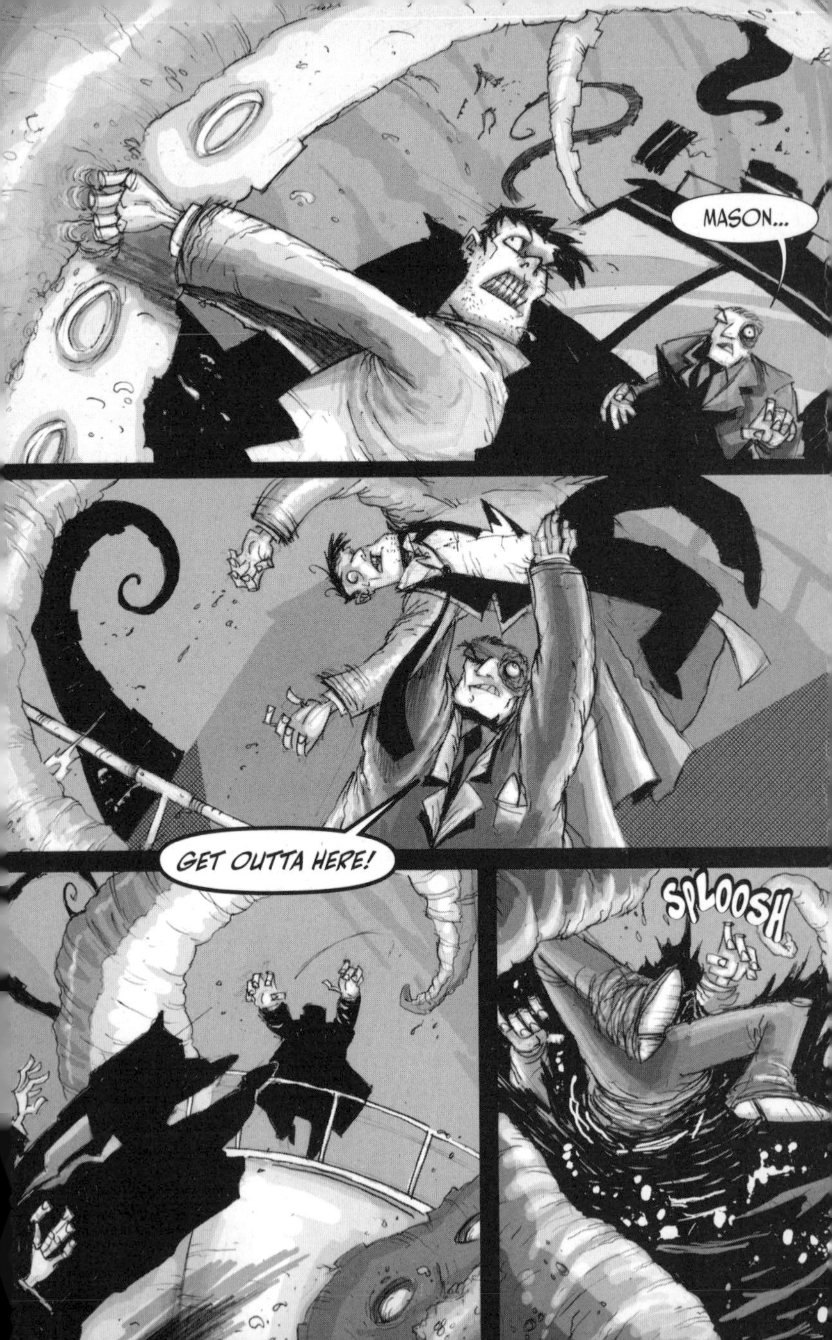
MASON...
GET OUTTA HERE!
SPLOOSH

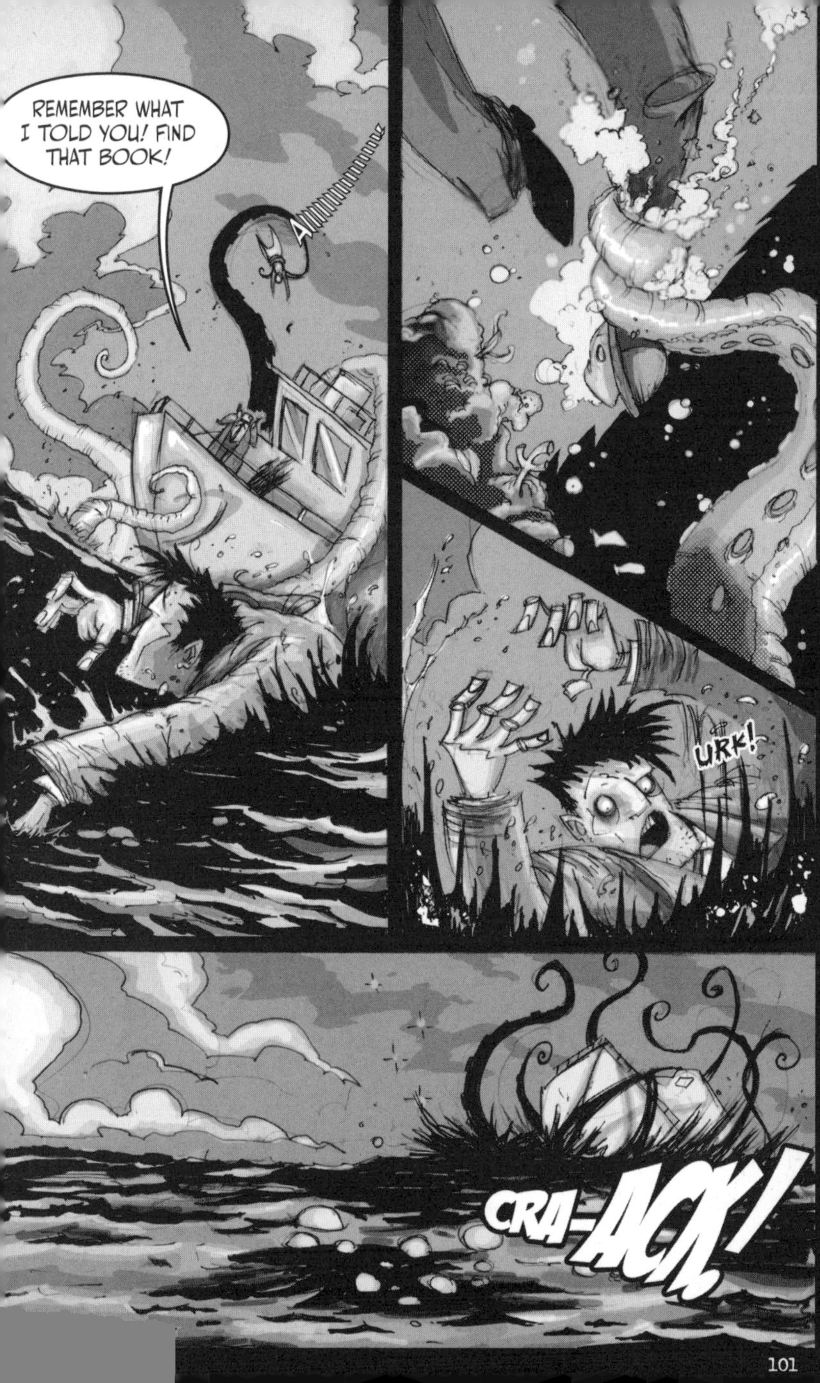
REMEMBER WHAT I TOLD YOU! FIND THAT BOOK!
URK!
CRA-ACK!

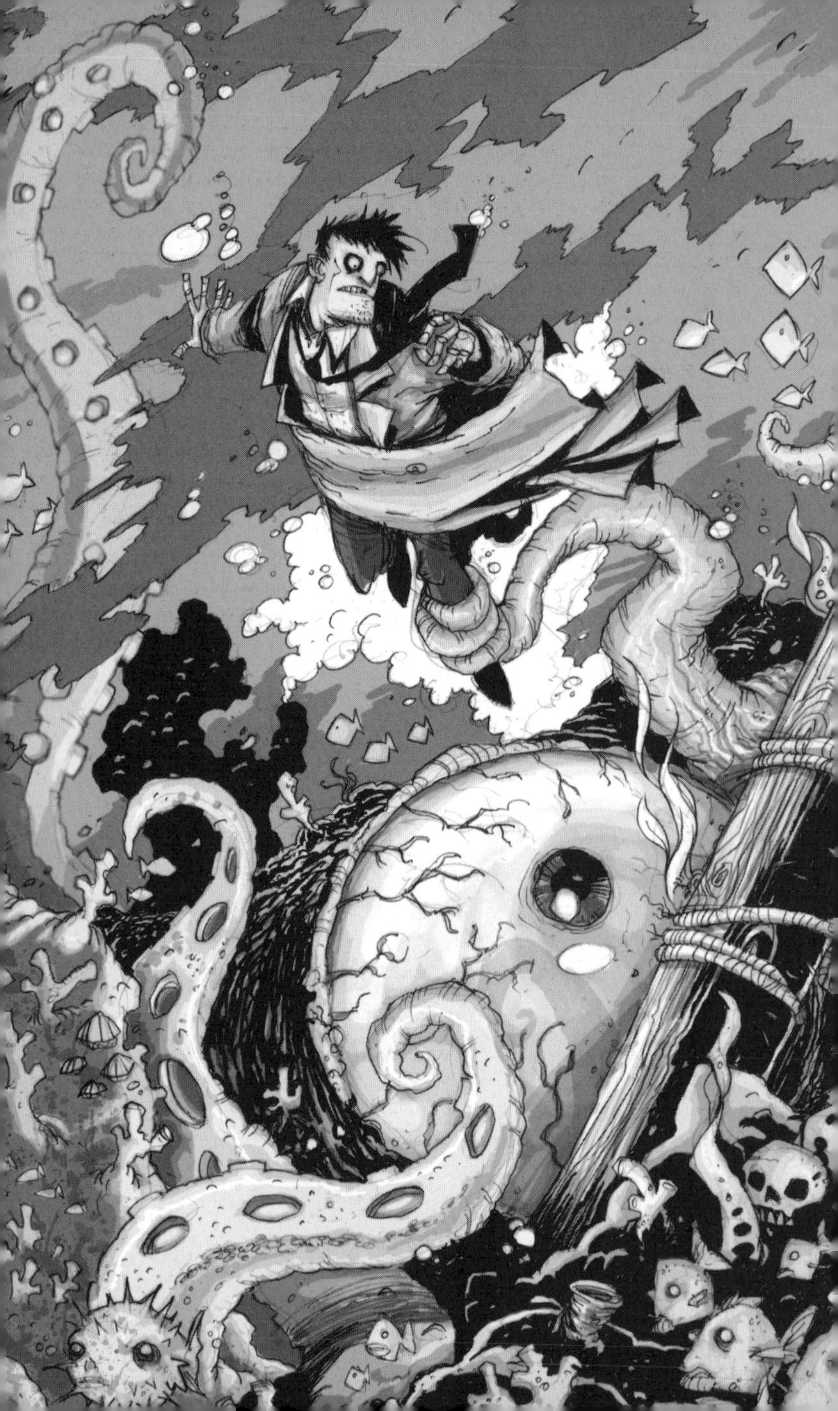

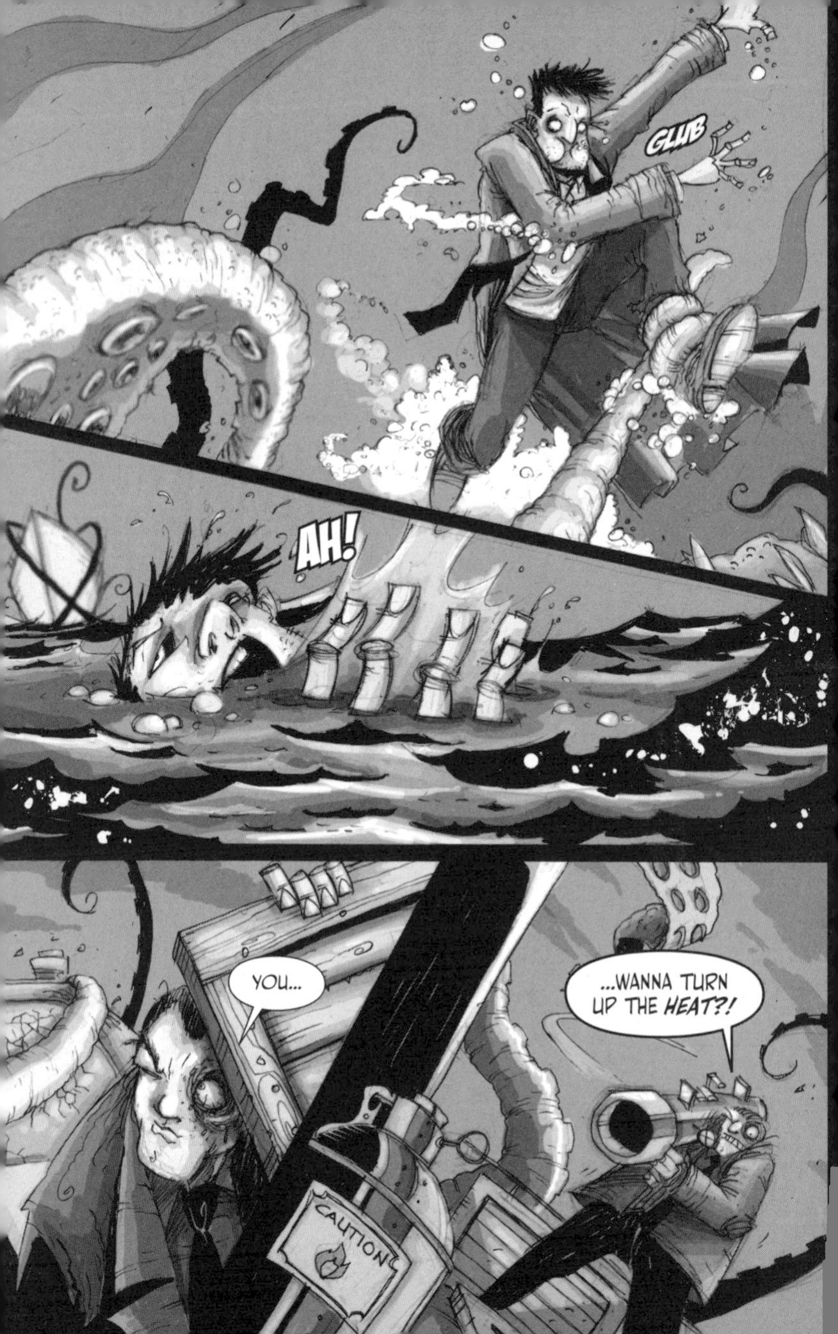
GLUB
AH!
YOU...
...WANNA TURN UP THE HEAT?!
CAUTION

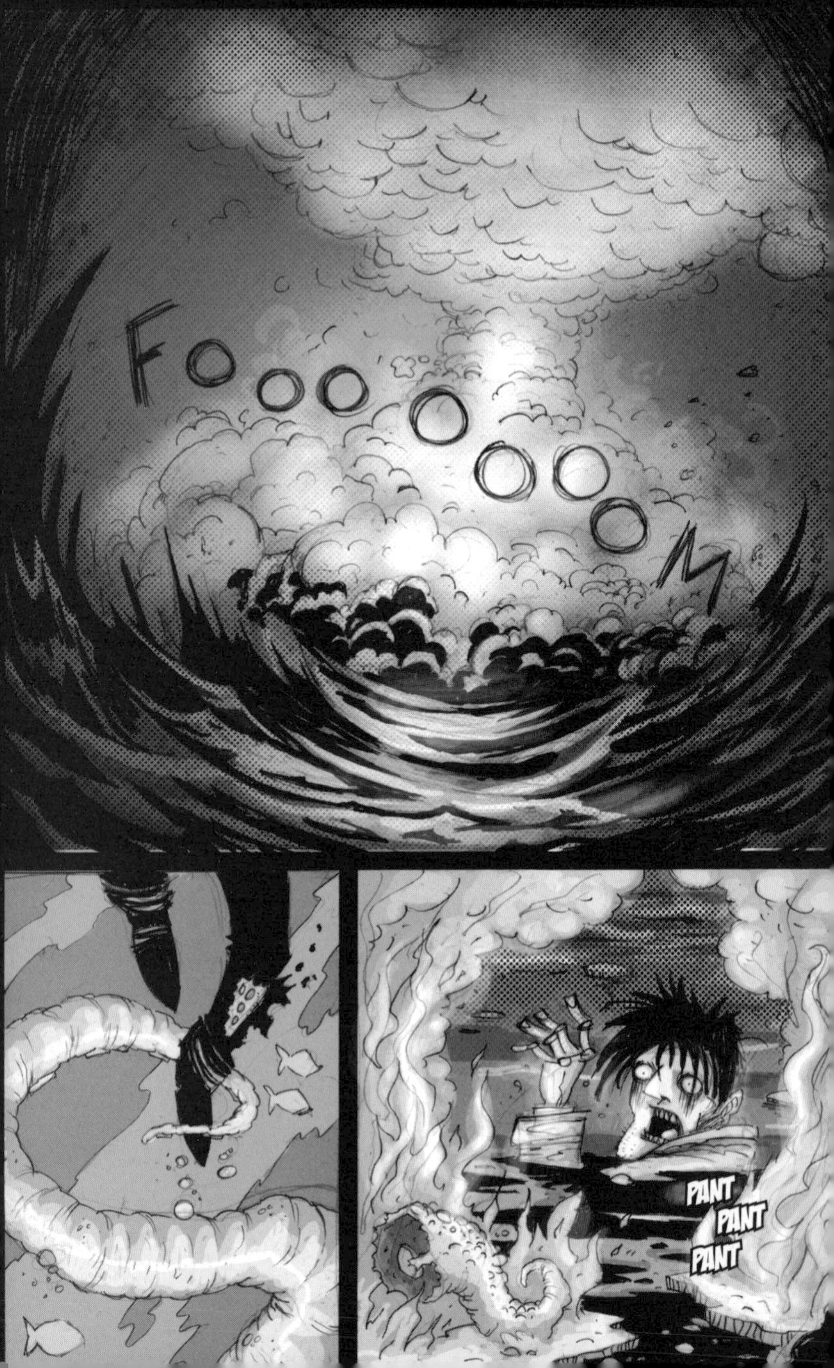
FOOOOOOOOM
PANT
PANT
PANT

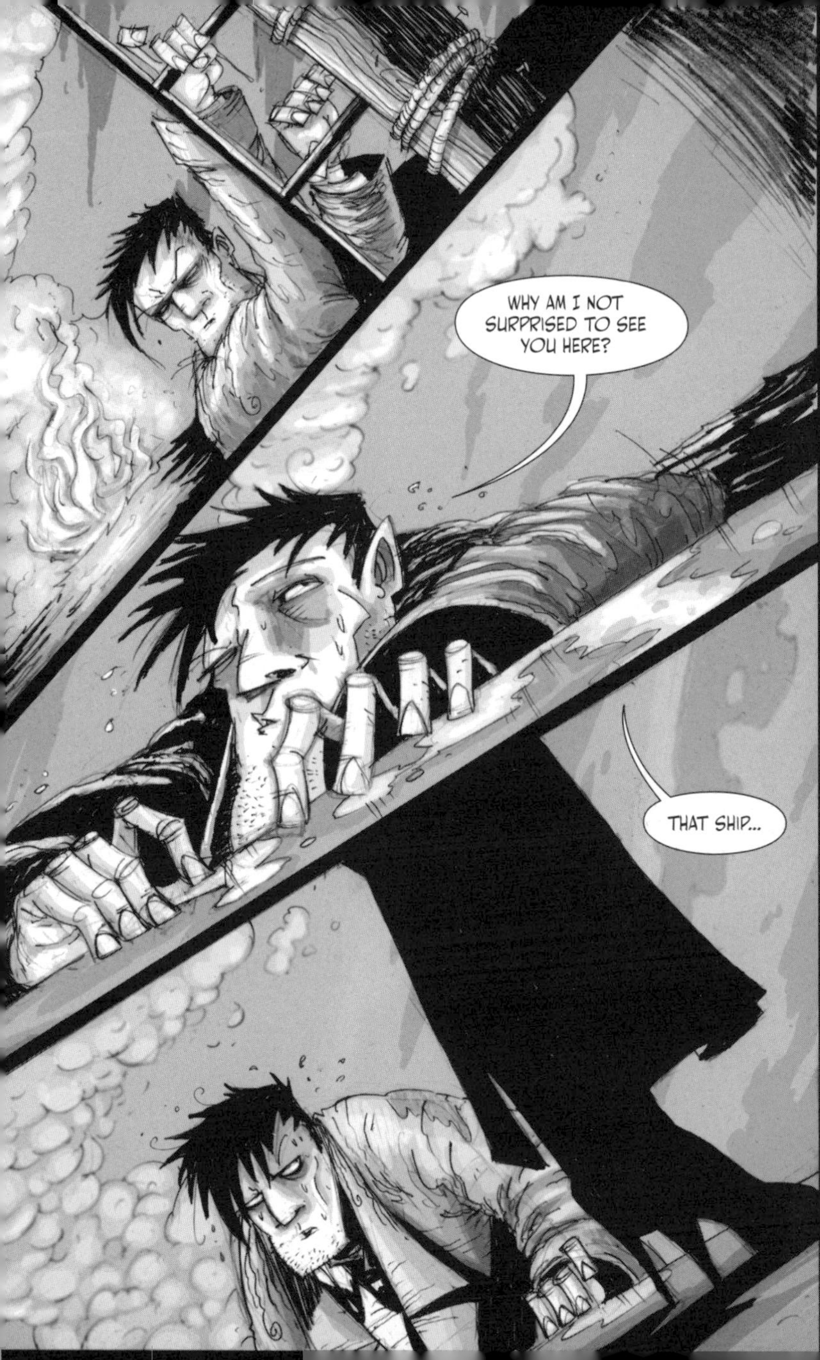
WHY AM I NOT SURPRISED TO SEE YOU HERE?
THAT SHIP...

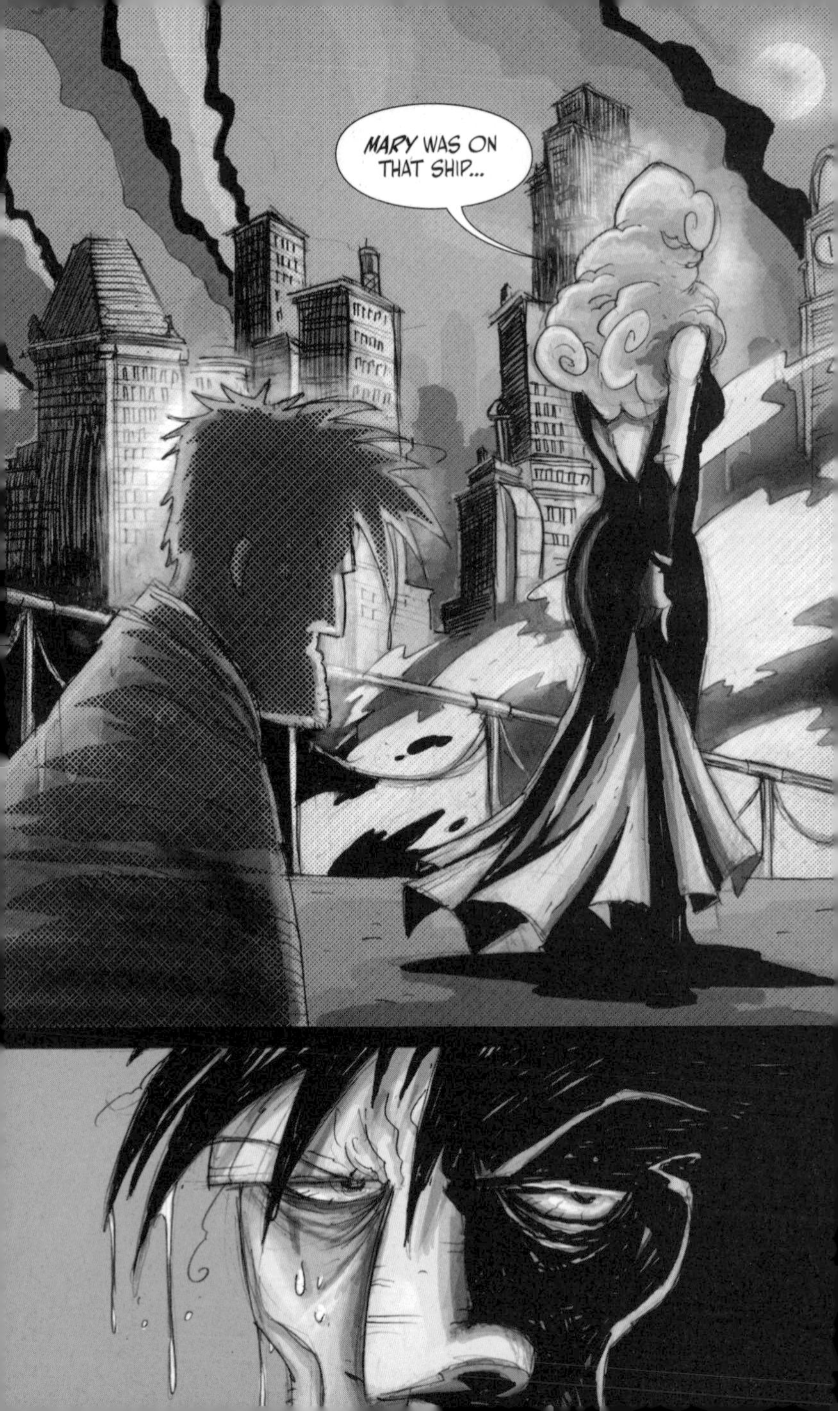
MARY WAS ON THAT SHIP...

# CHAPTER 4:
## The Hot House

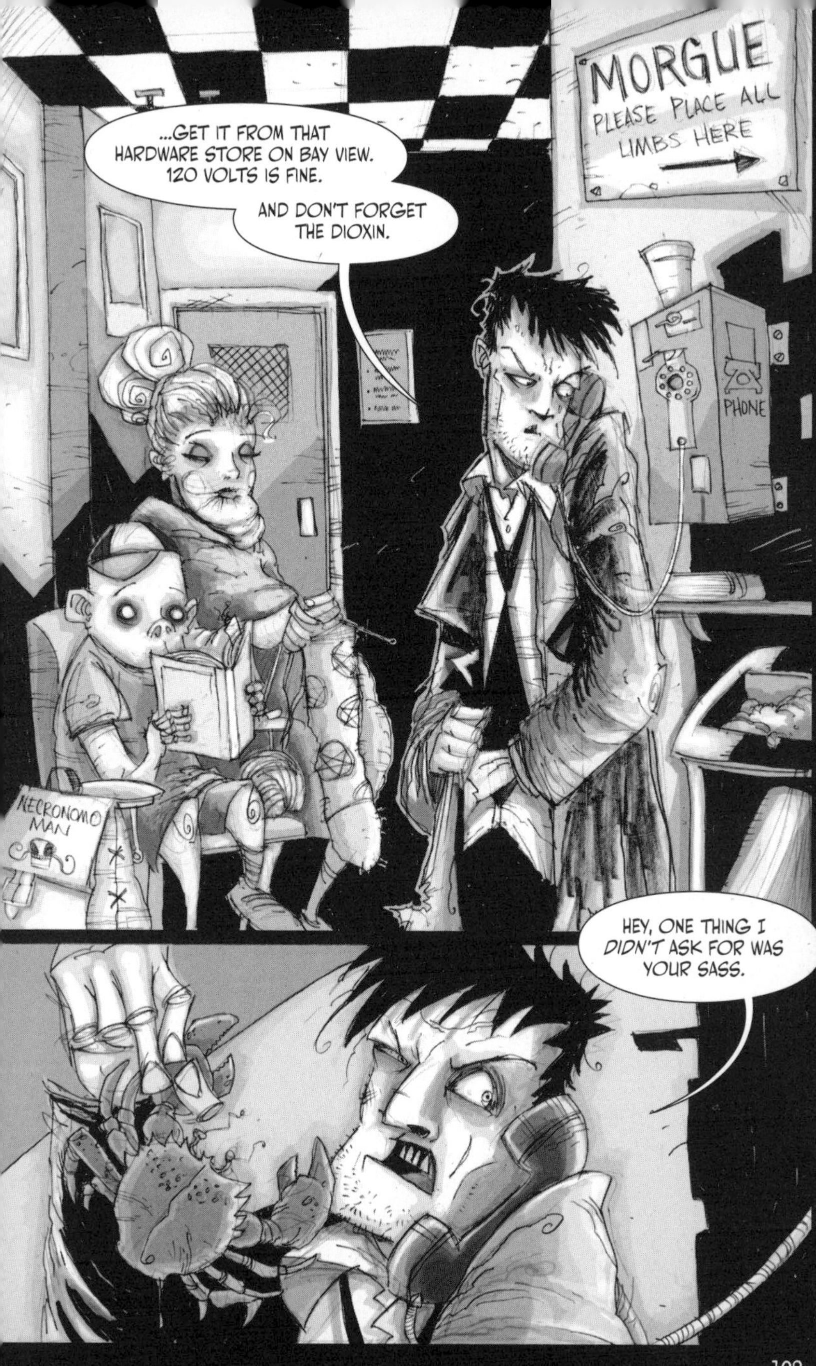
...GET IT FROM THAT HARDWARE STORE ON BAY VIEW. 120 VOLTS IS FINE.
AND DON'T FORGET THE DIOXIN.
MORGUE
PLEASE PLACE ALL LIMBS HERE
PHONE
NECRONOMO MAN
HEY, ONE THING I *DIDN'T* ASK FOR WAS YOUR SASS.

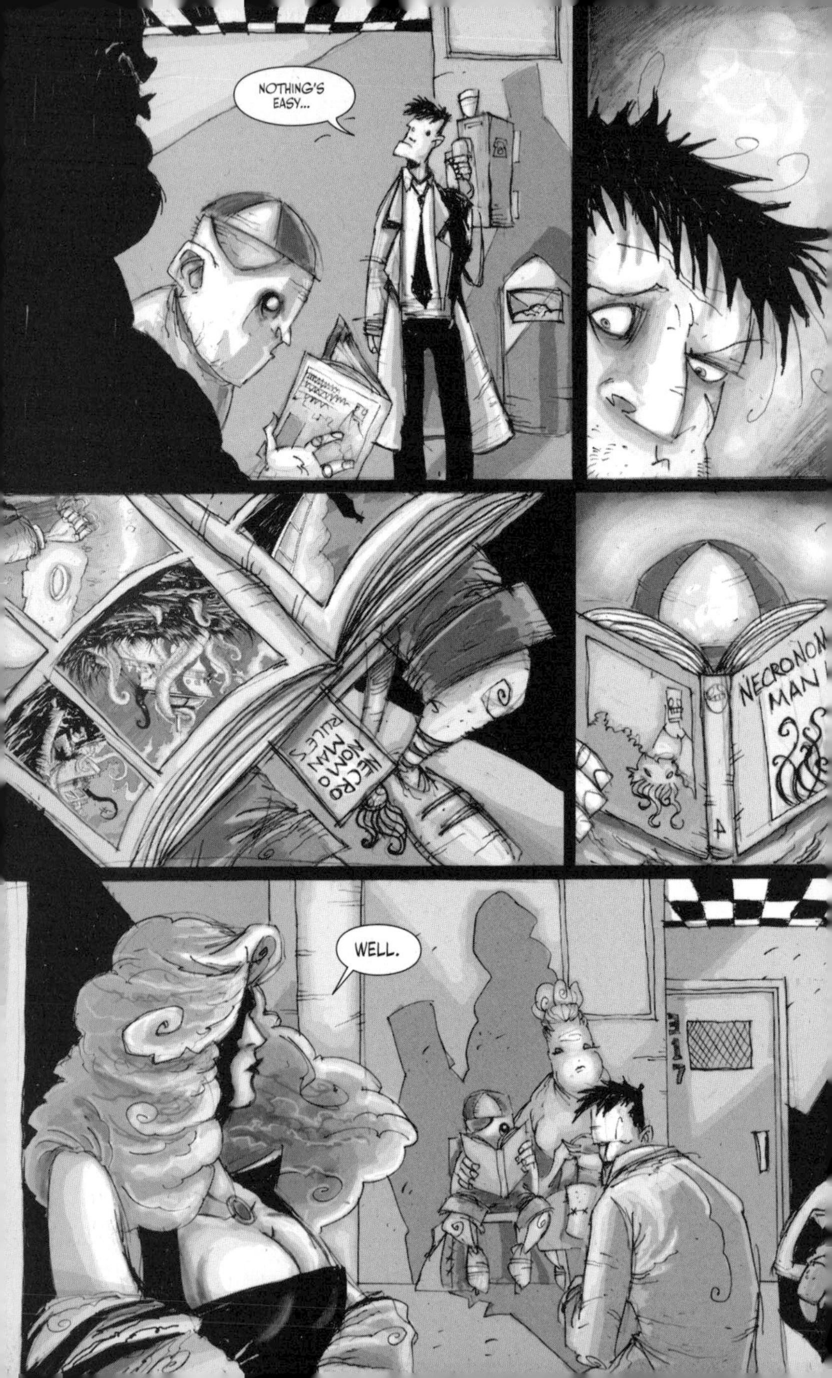
NOTHING'S EASY...
NECRONOM
MAN
WELL.

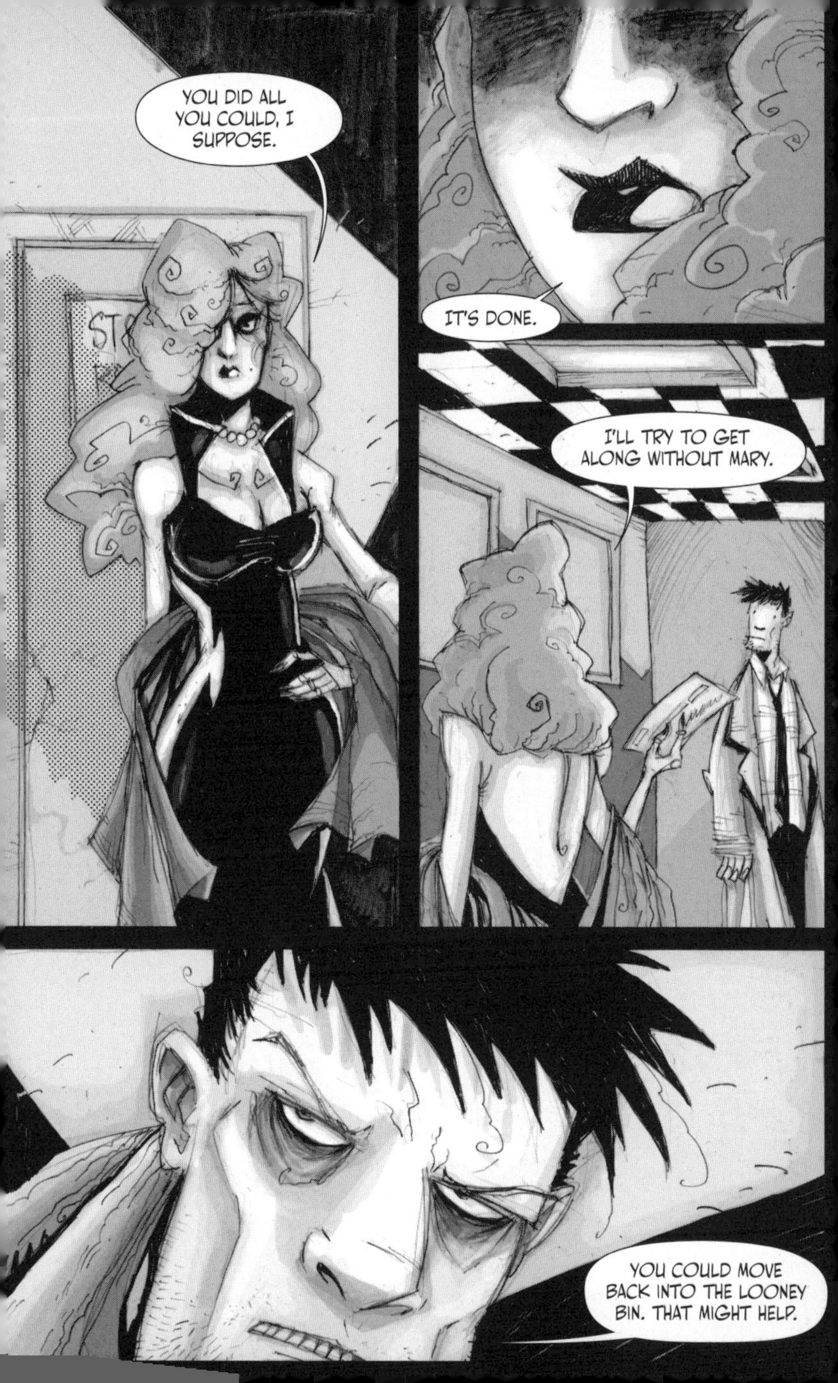
YOU DID ALL YOU COULD, I SUPPOSE.
IT'S DONE.
I'LL TRY TO GET ALONG WITHOUT MARY.
YOU COULD MOVE BACK INTO THE LOONEY BIN. THAT MIGHT HELP.

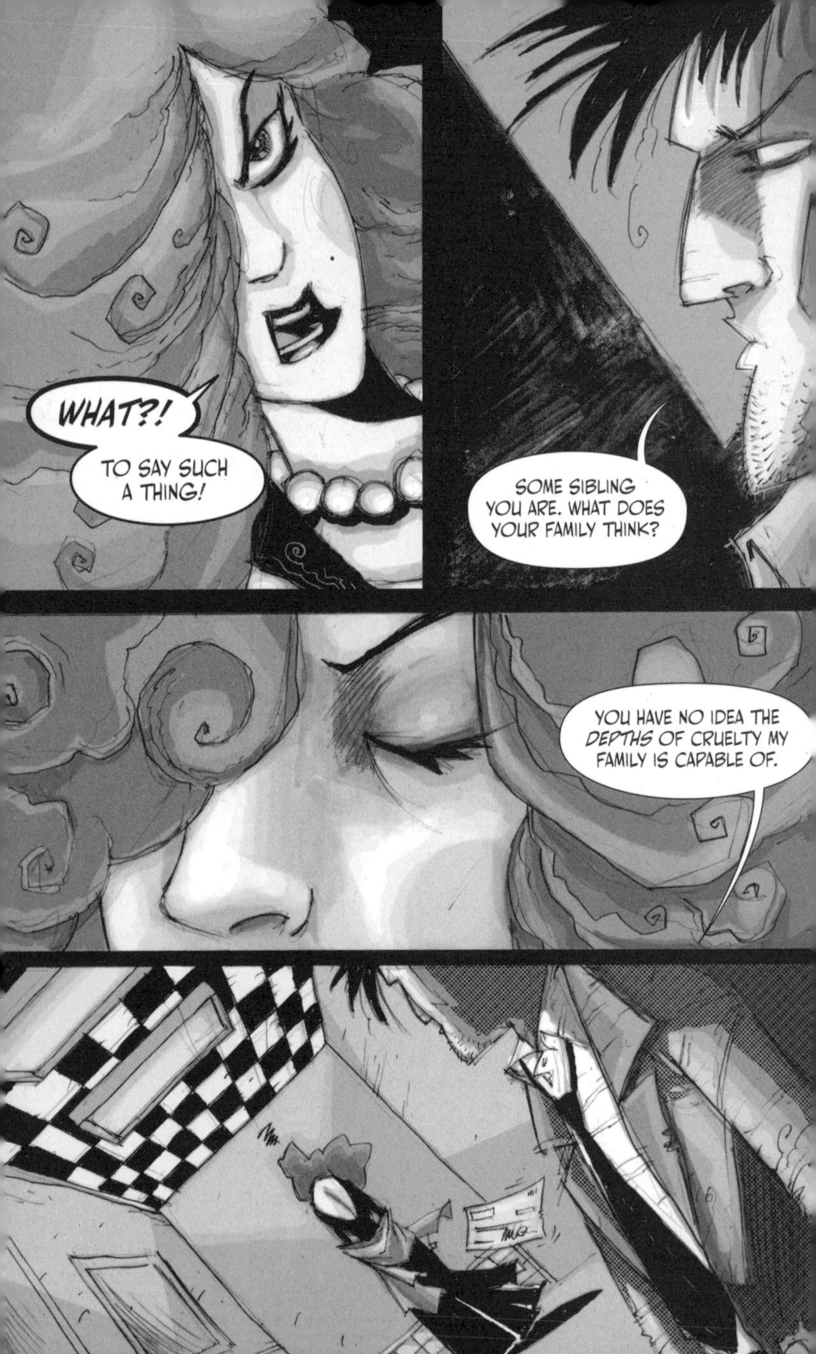
WHAT?!
TO SAY SUCH A THING!
SOME SIBLING YOU ARE. WHAT DOES YOUR FAMILY THINK?
YOU HAVE NO IDEA THE *DEPTHS* OF CRUELTY MY FAMILY IS CAPABLE OF.

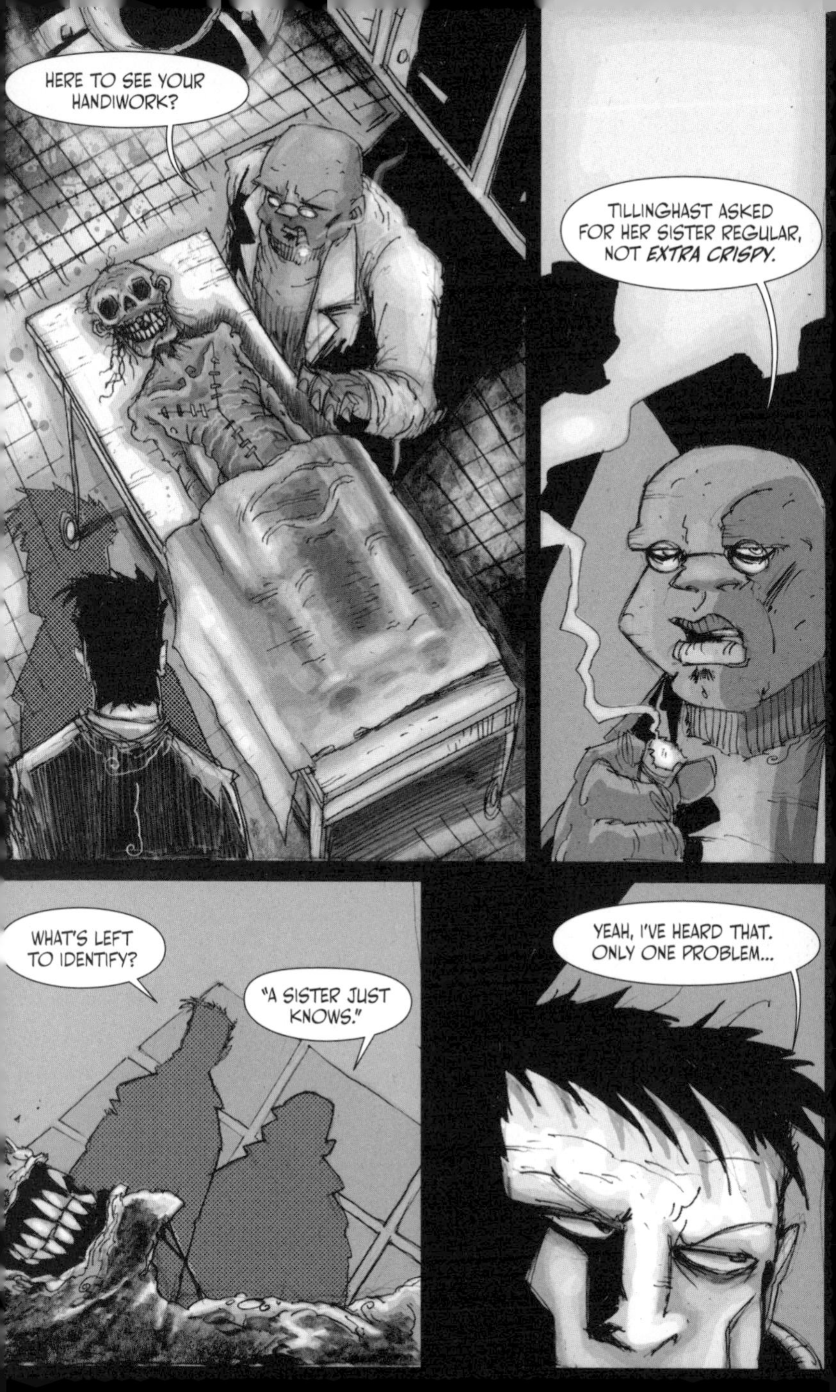
HERE TO SEE YOUR HANDIWORK?
TILLINGHAST ASKED FOR HER SISTER REGULAR, NOT *EXTRA CRISPY.*
WHAT'S LEFT TO IDENTIFY?
"A SISTER JUST KNOWS."
YEAH, I'VE HEARD THAT. ONLY ONE PROBLEM...

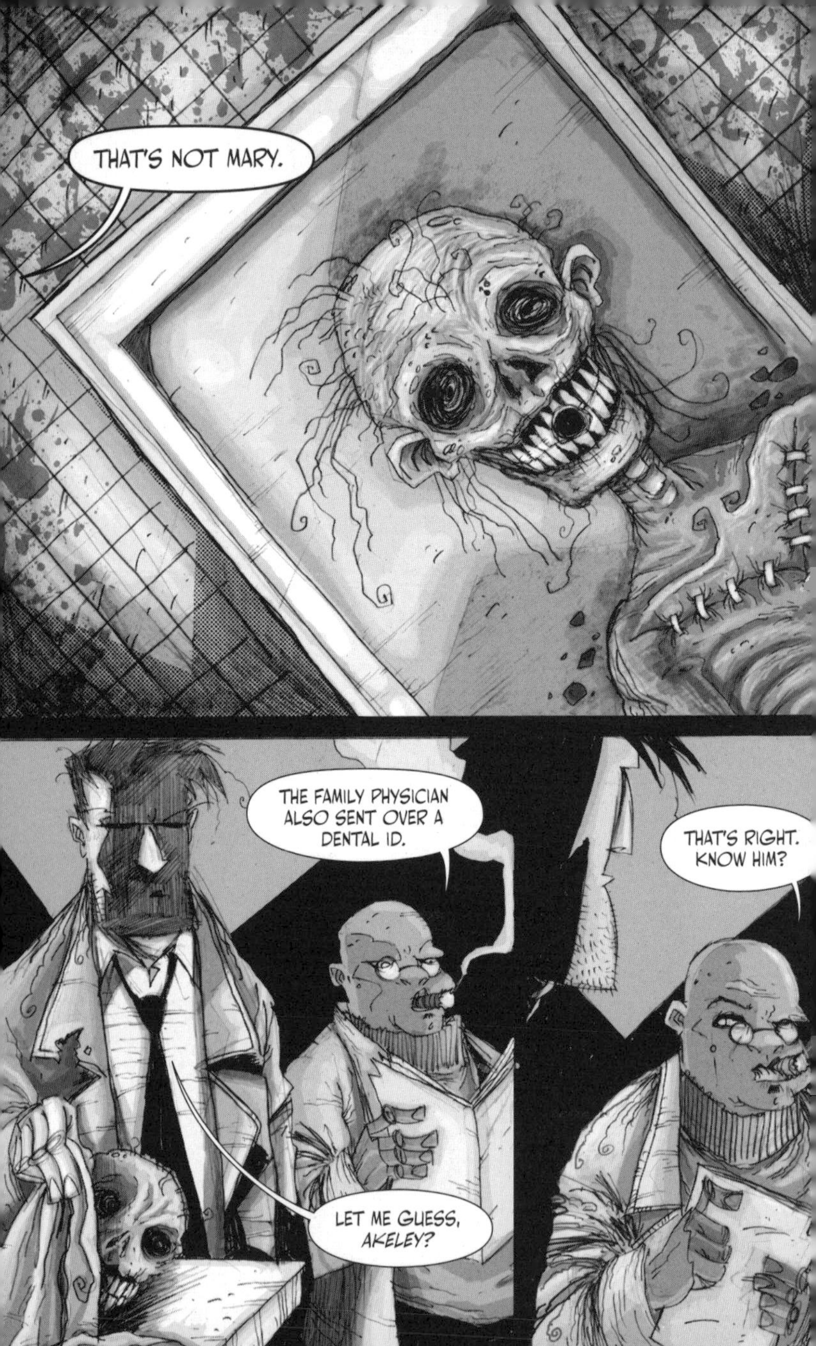
THAT'S NOT MARY.
THE FAMILY PHYSICIAN ALSO SENT OVER A DENTAL ID.
LET ME GUESS, AKELEY?
THAT'S RIGHT. KNOW HIM?

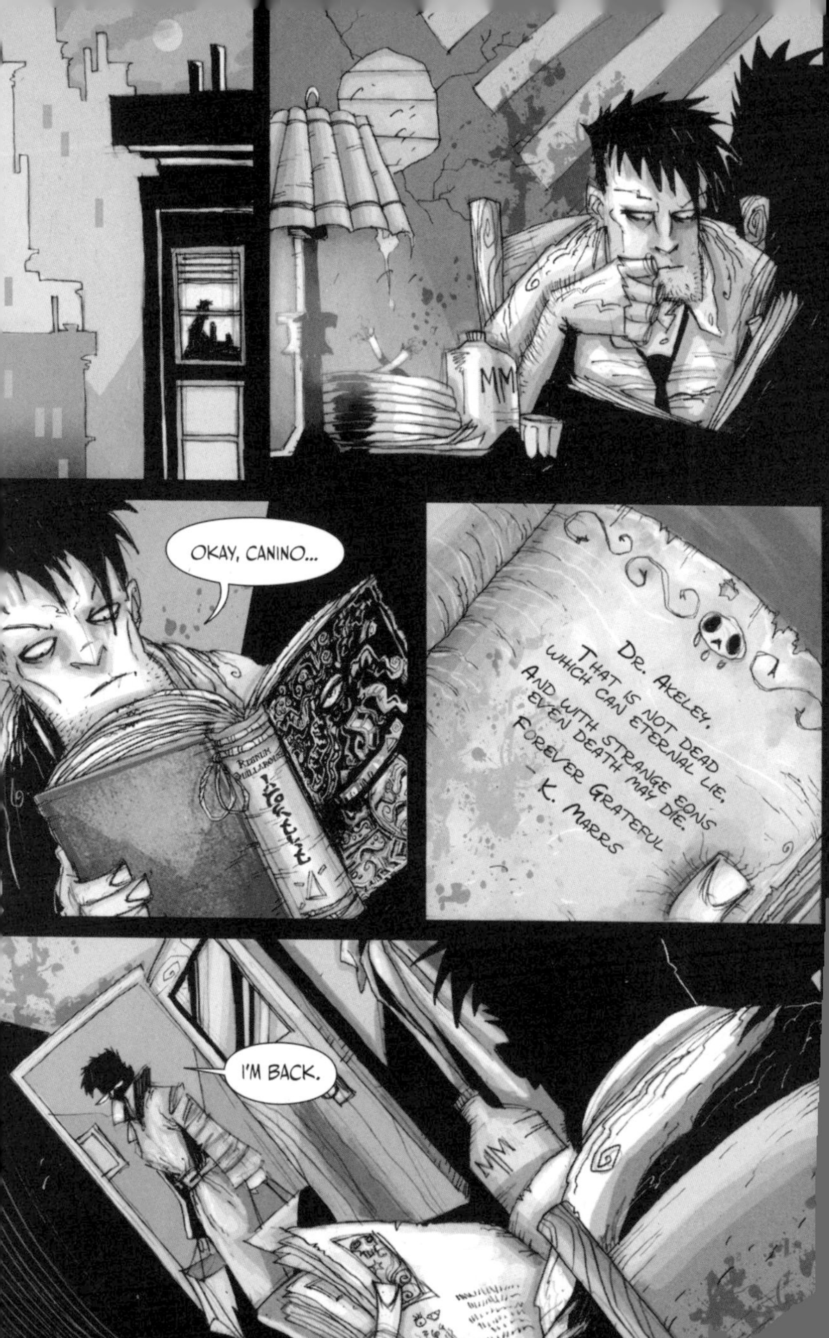
OKAY, CANINO...
DR. AKELEY,
THAT IS NOT DEAD
WHICH CAN ETERNAL LIE,
AND WITH STRANGE EONS
EVEN DEATH MAY DIE.
FOREVER GRATEFUL
K. MARRS
I'M BACK.

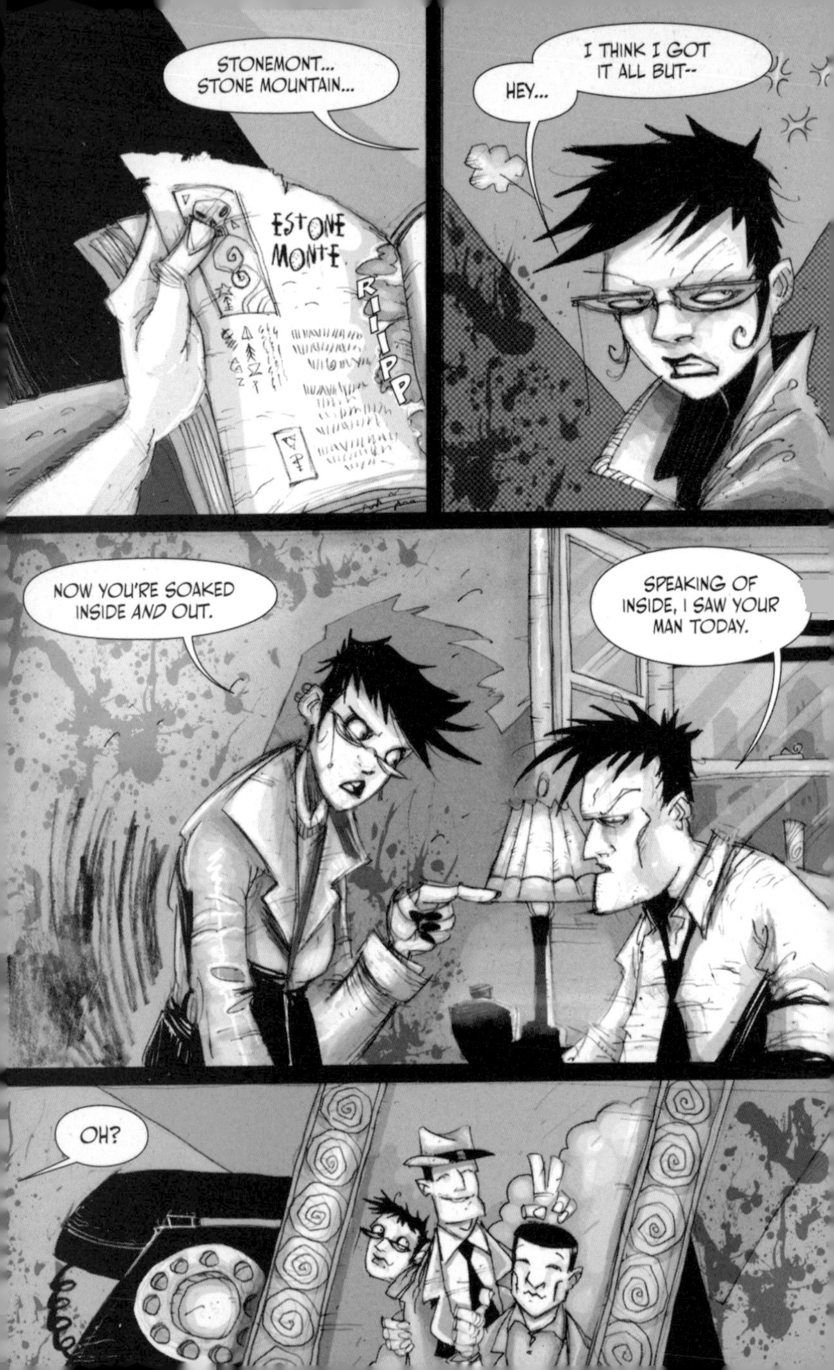
STONEMONT...
STONE MOUNTAIN...
ESTONE MONTE
RIIIPP
I THINK I GOT IT ALL BUT--
HEY...
NOW YOU'RE SOAKED INSIDE *AND* OUT.
SPEAKING OF INSIDE, I SAW YOUR MAN TODAY.
OH?

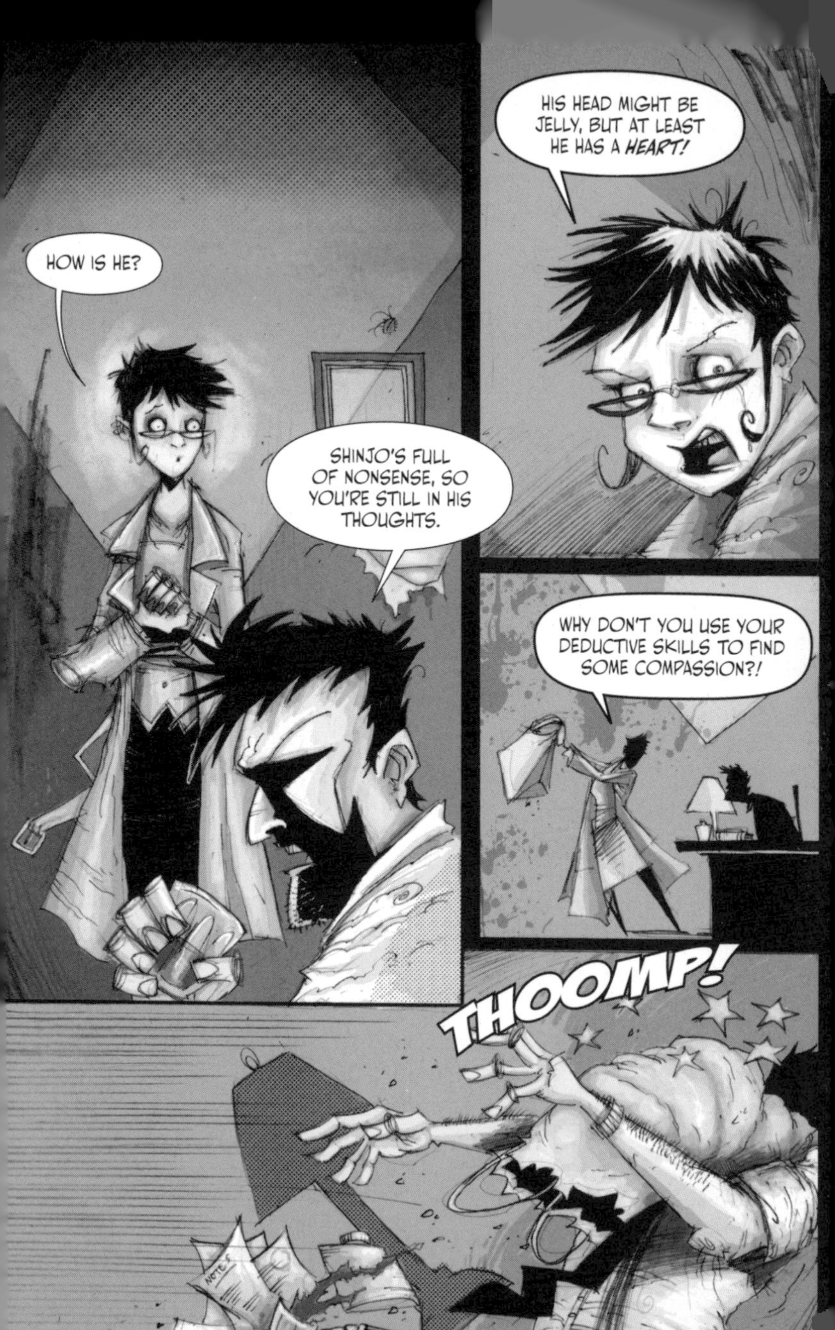
HOW IS HE?
SHINJO'S FULL OF NONSENSE, SO YOU'RE STILL IN HIS THOUGHTS.
HIS HEAD MIGHT BE JELLY, BUT AT LEAST HE HAS A *HEART!*
WHY DON'T YOU USE YOUR DEDUCTIVE SKILLS TO FIND SOME COMPASSION?!
THOOMP!
NOTES

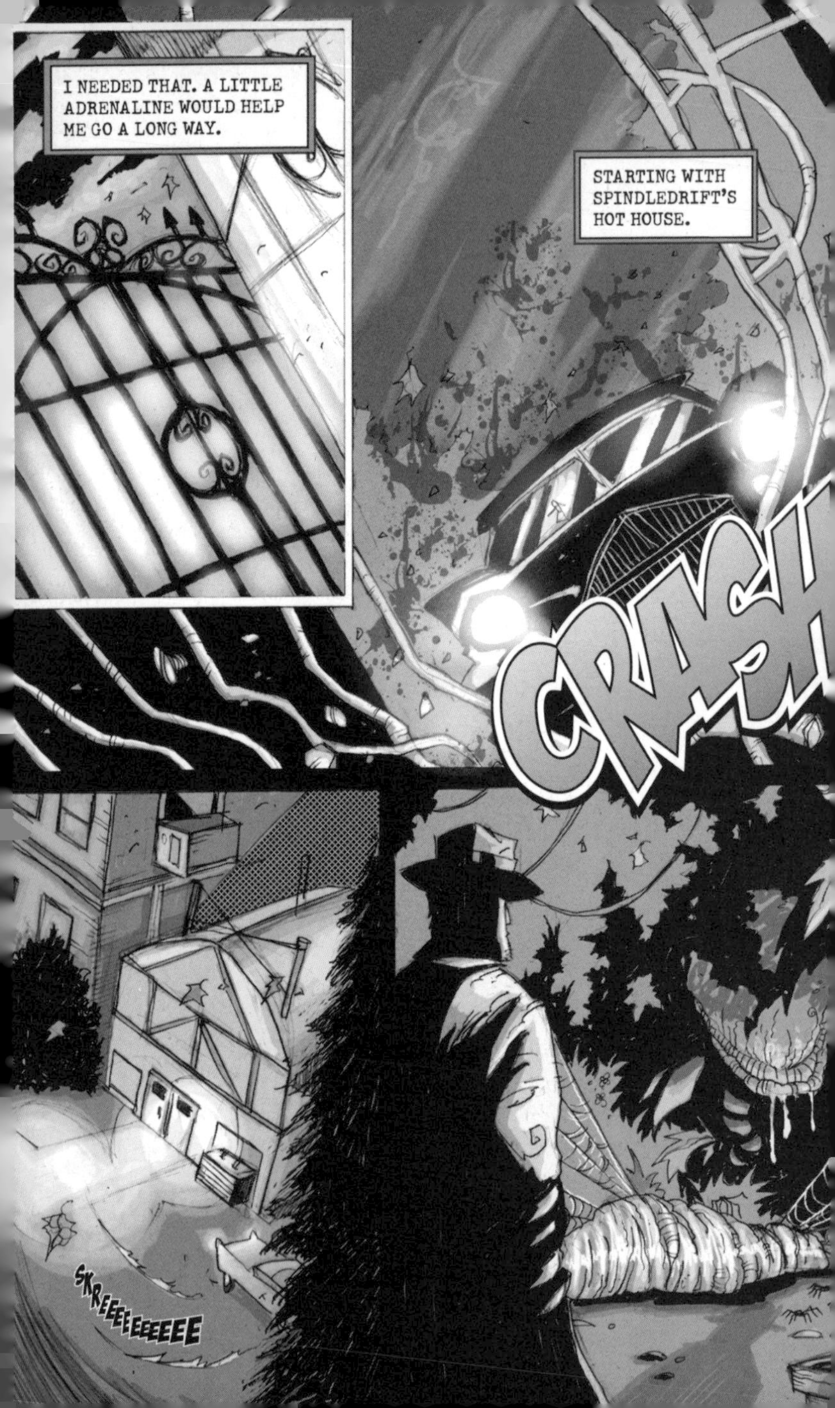
I NEEDED THAT. A LITTLE ADRENALINE WOULD HELP ME GO A LONG WAY.
STARTING WITH SPINDLEDRIFT'S HOT HOUSE.
CRASH
SKREEEEEEEEEE

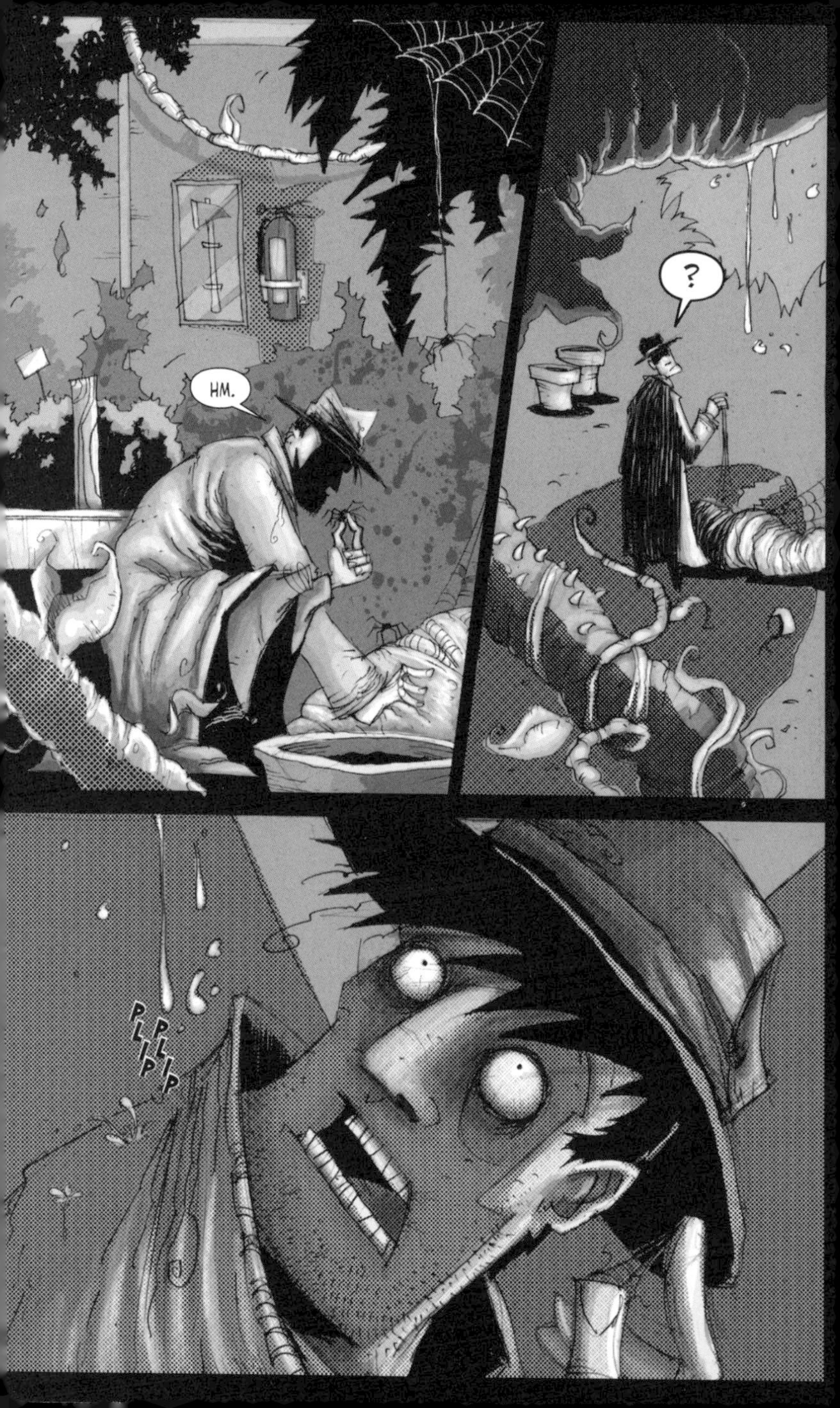
HM.
?
PLIP
PLIP

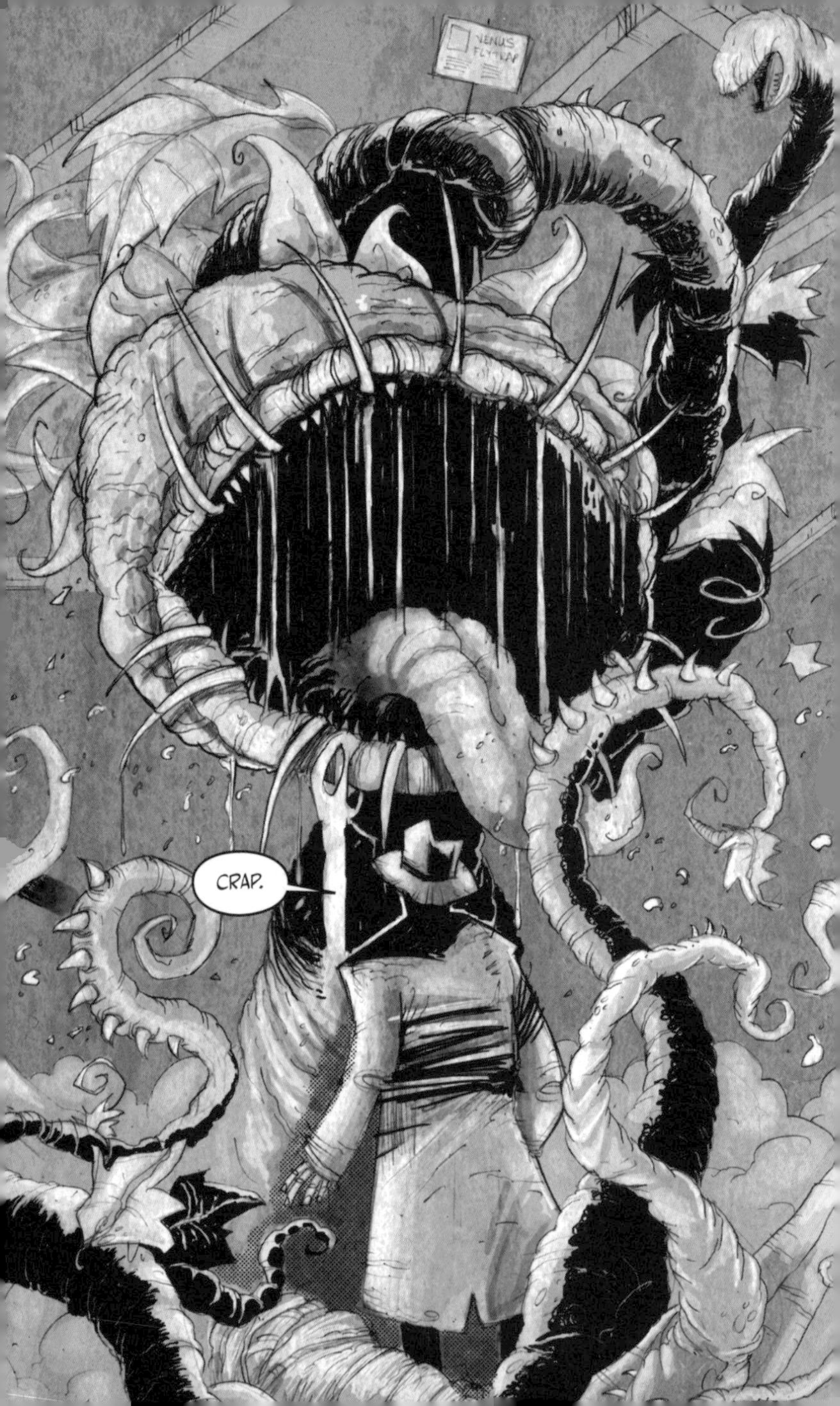
VENUS FLYTRAP
CRAP.

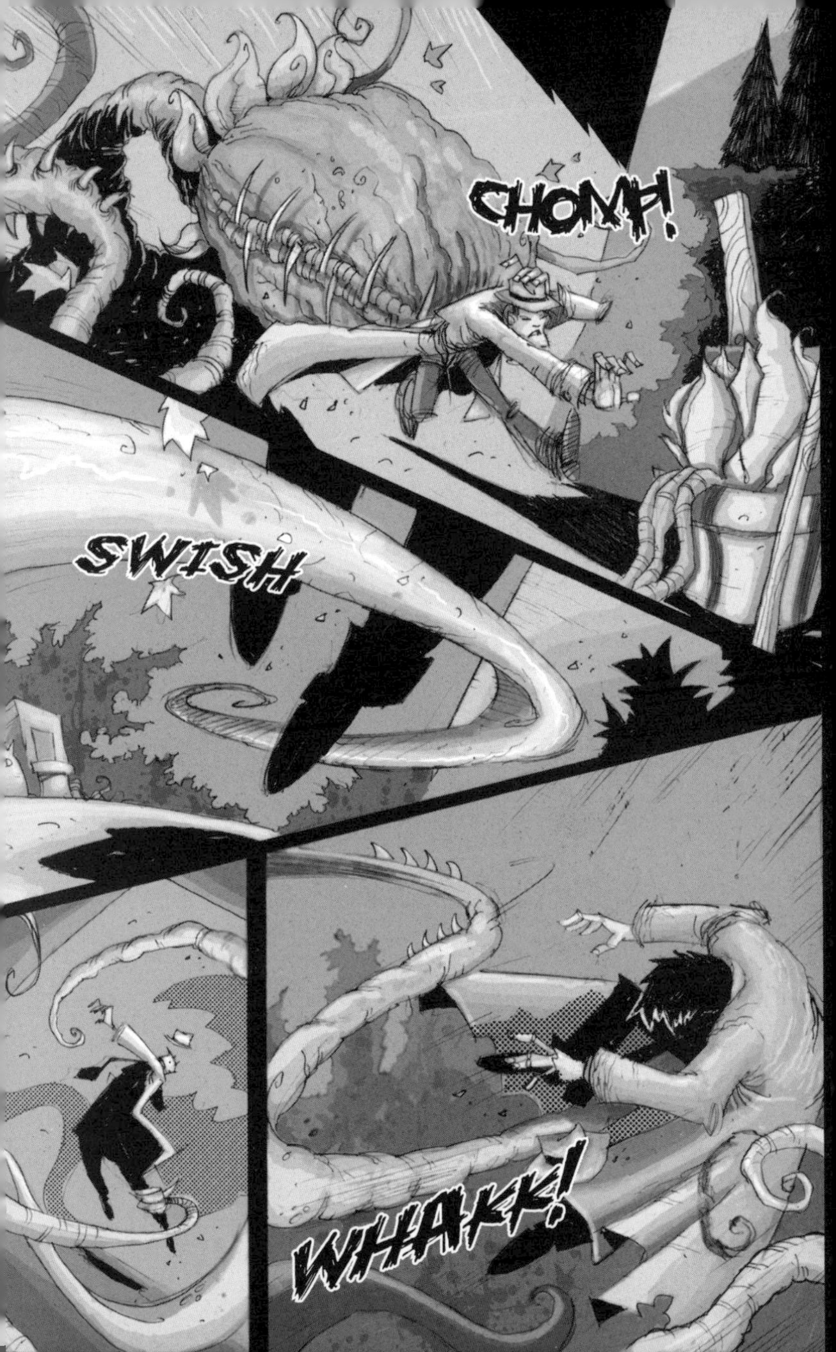
CHOMP!
SWISH
WHAKK!

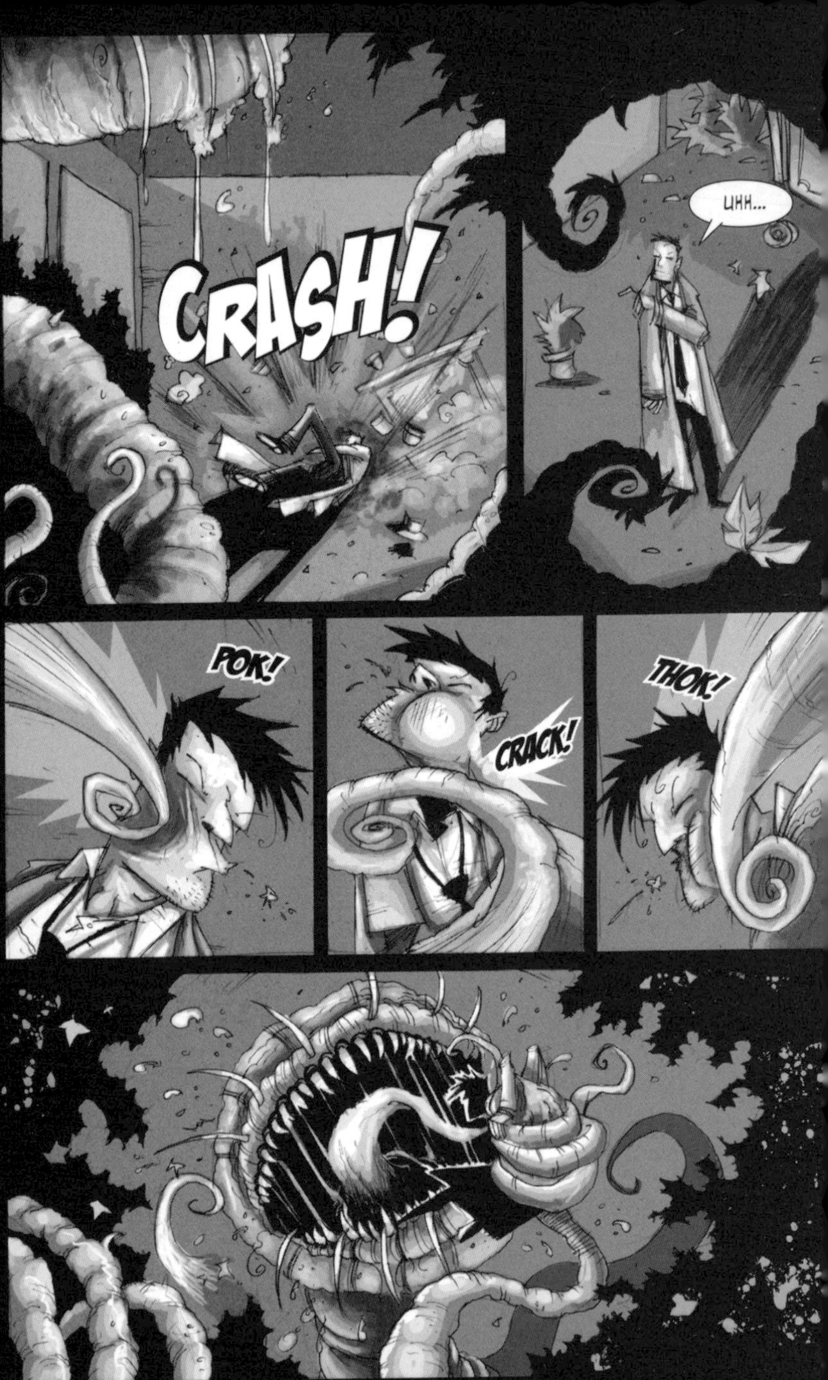
CRASH!
UHH...
POK!
CRACK!
THOK!

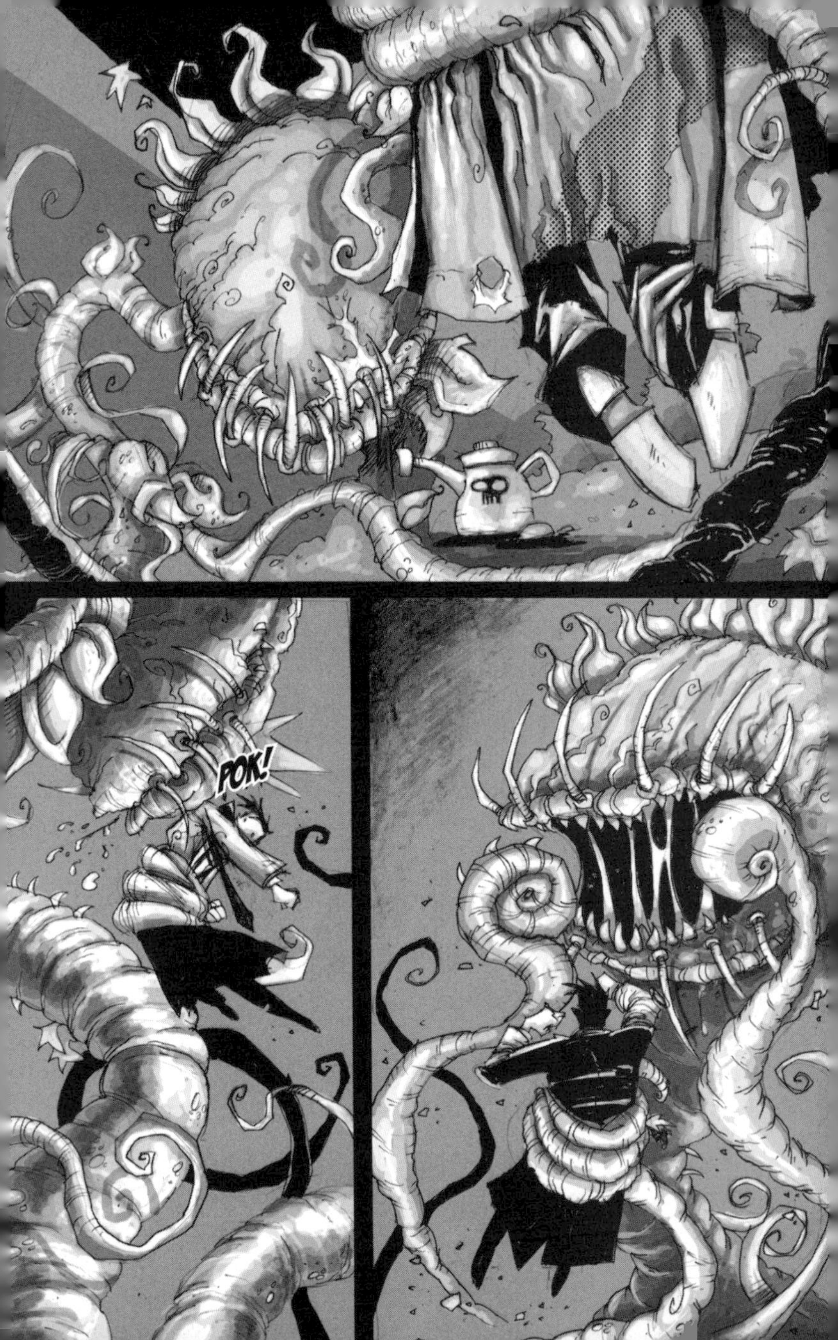
POK!

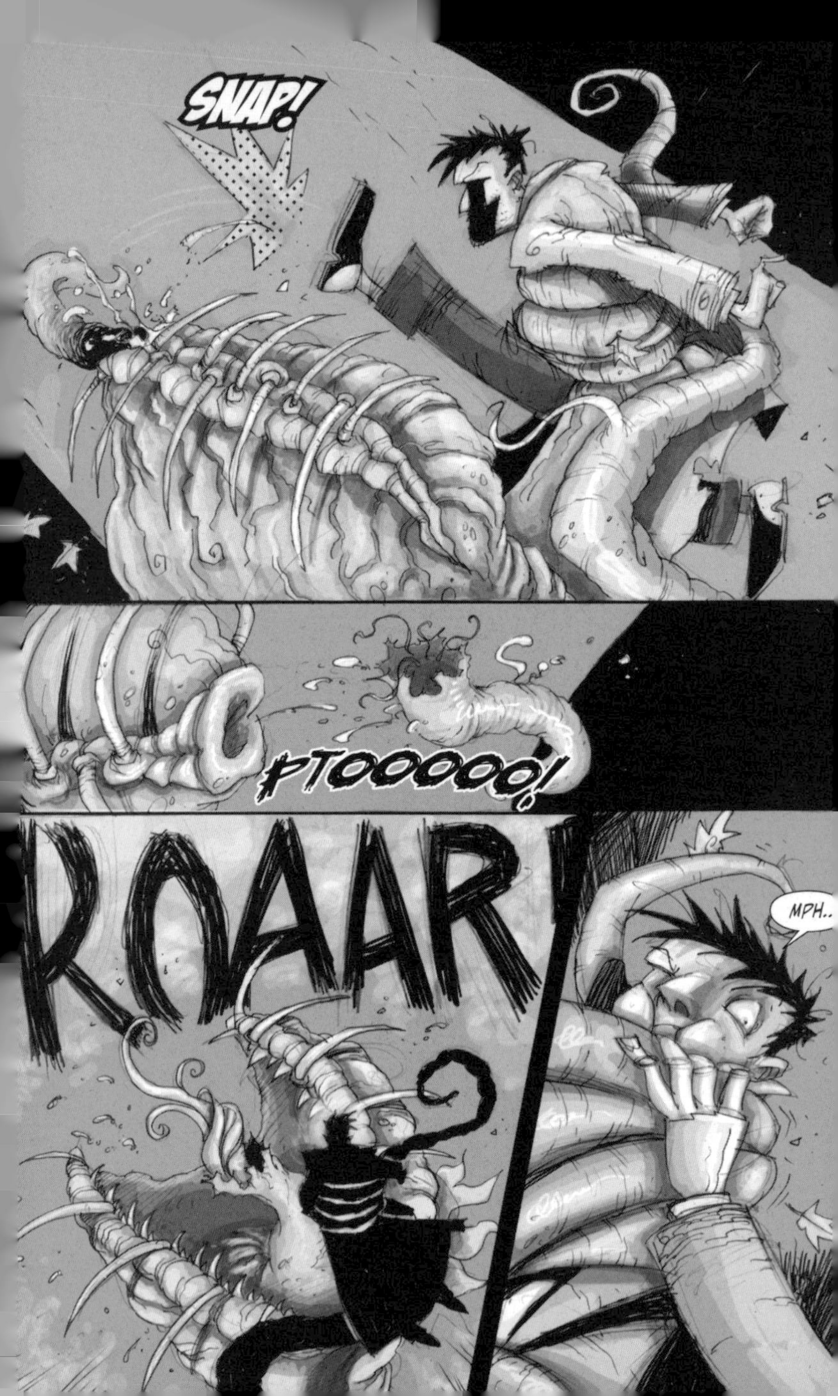
SNAP!
PTOOOOO!
ROAAR!
MPH..

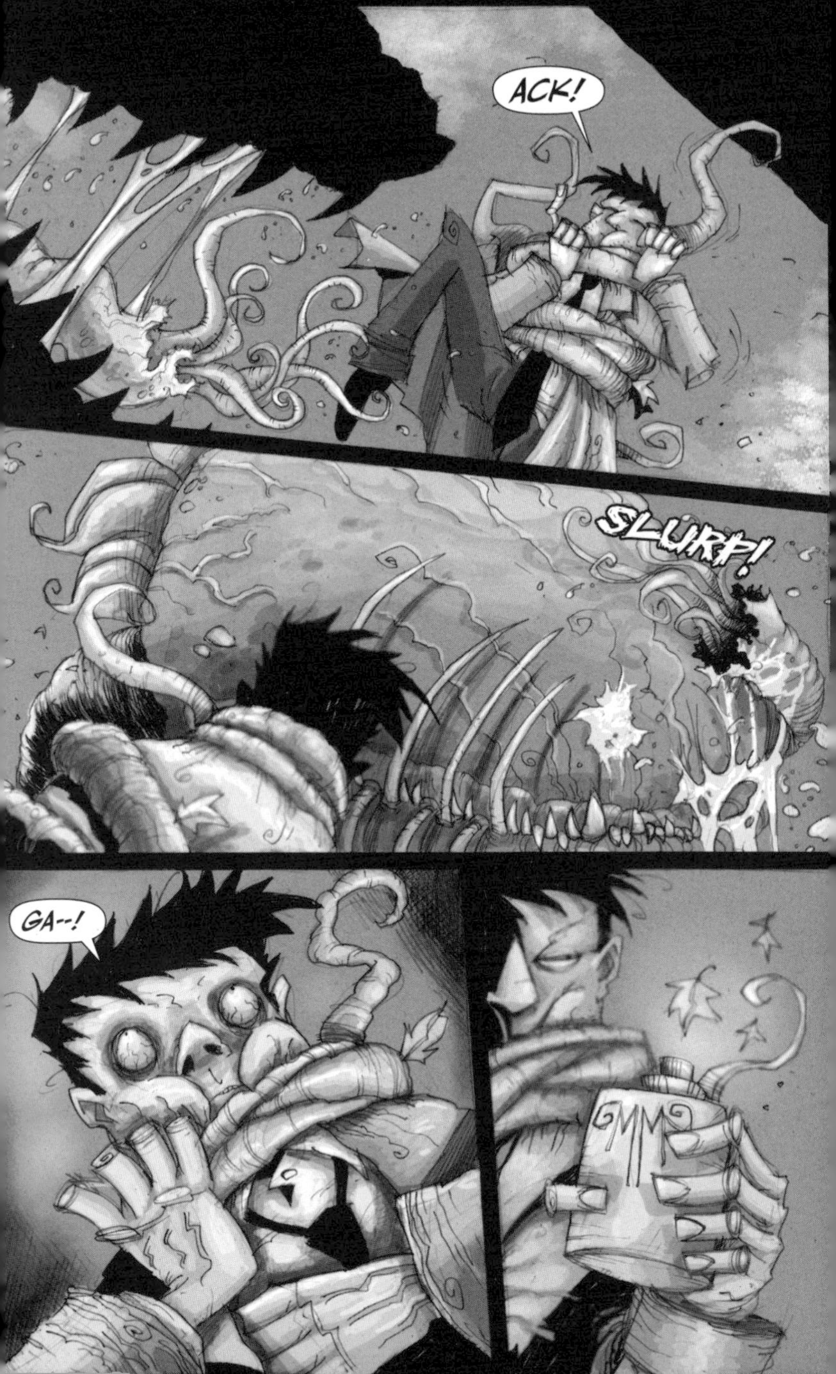
ACK!
SLURP!
GA--!
GMM

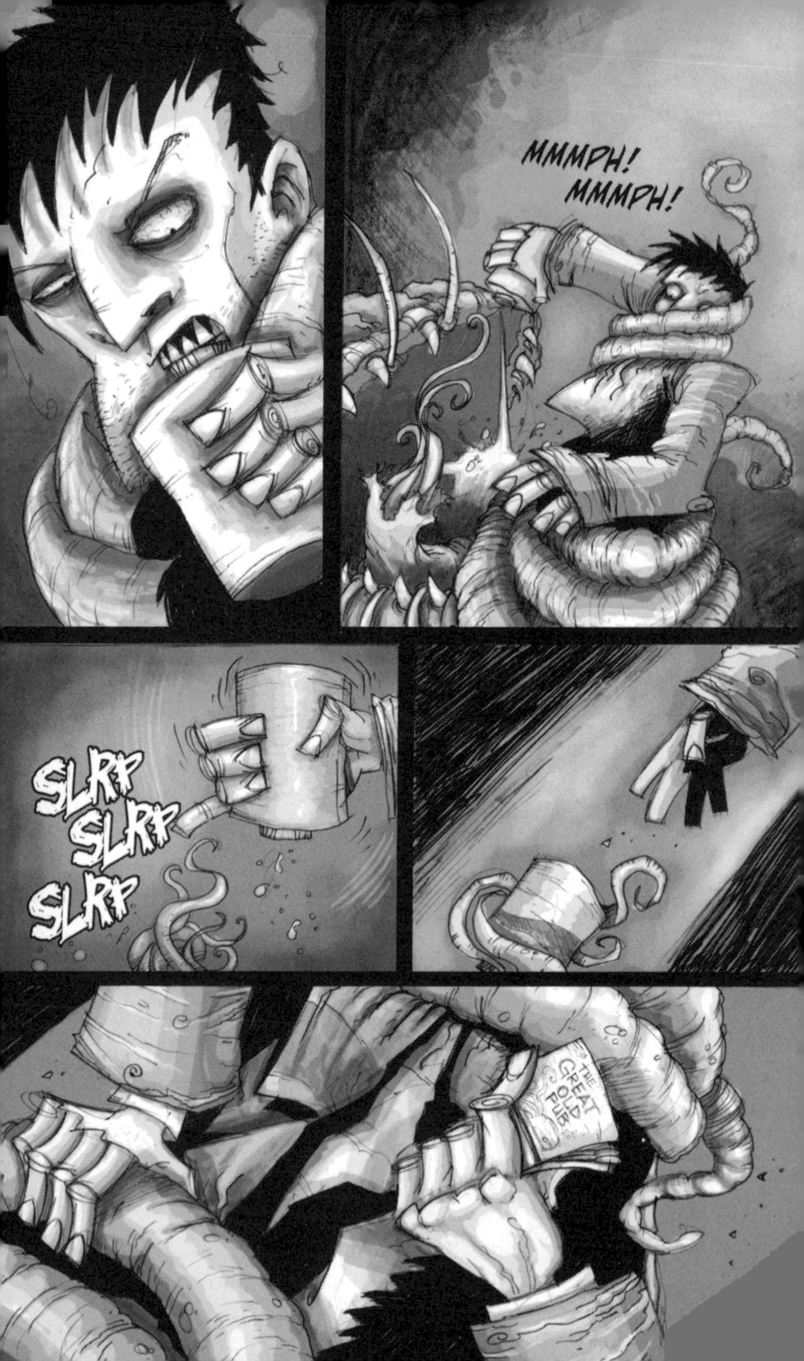
MMMPH! MMMPH!
SLRP SLRP SLRP
THE GREAT OLD PUB

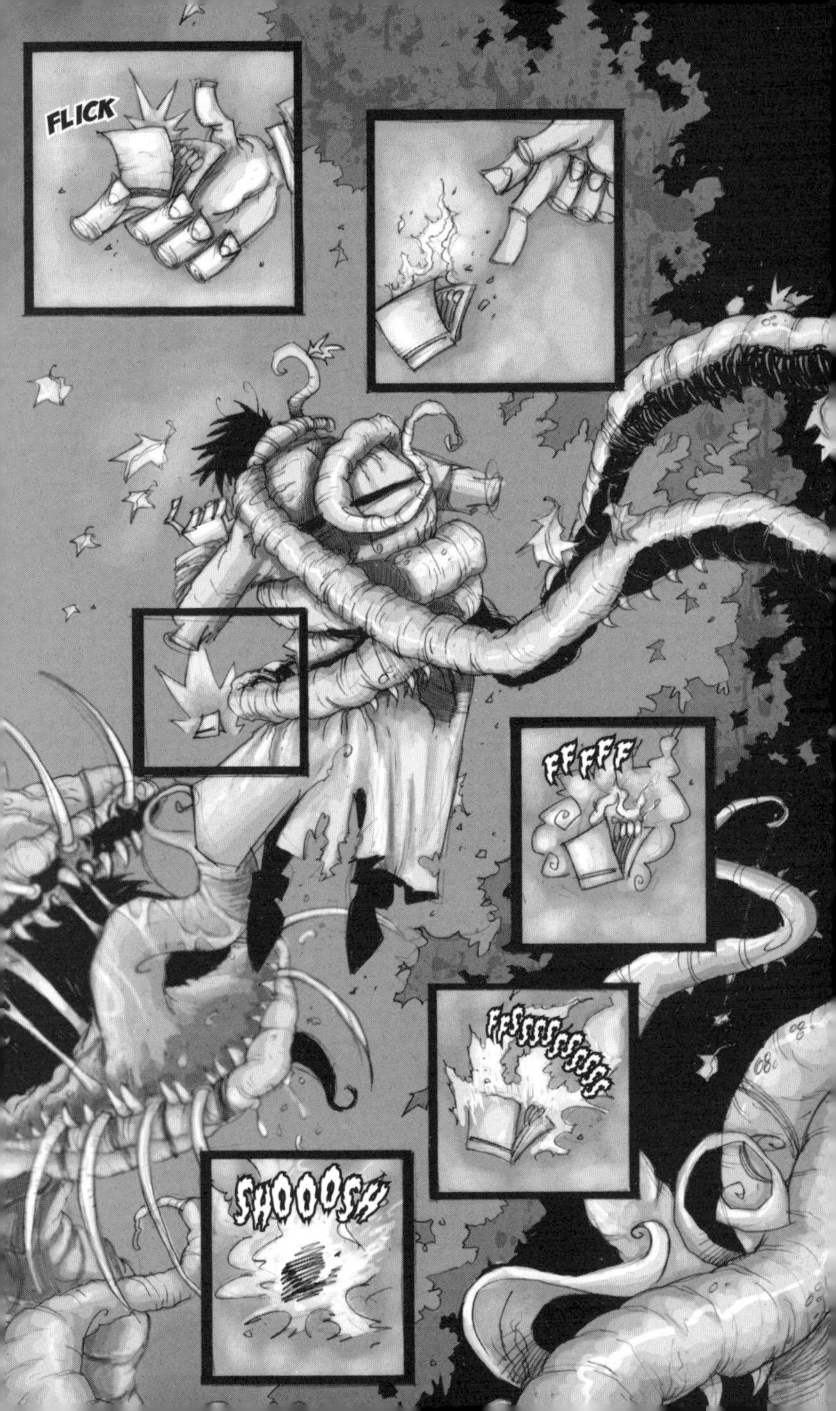
FLICK
FFFFF
FFSSSSSSSSSS
SHOOOSH

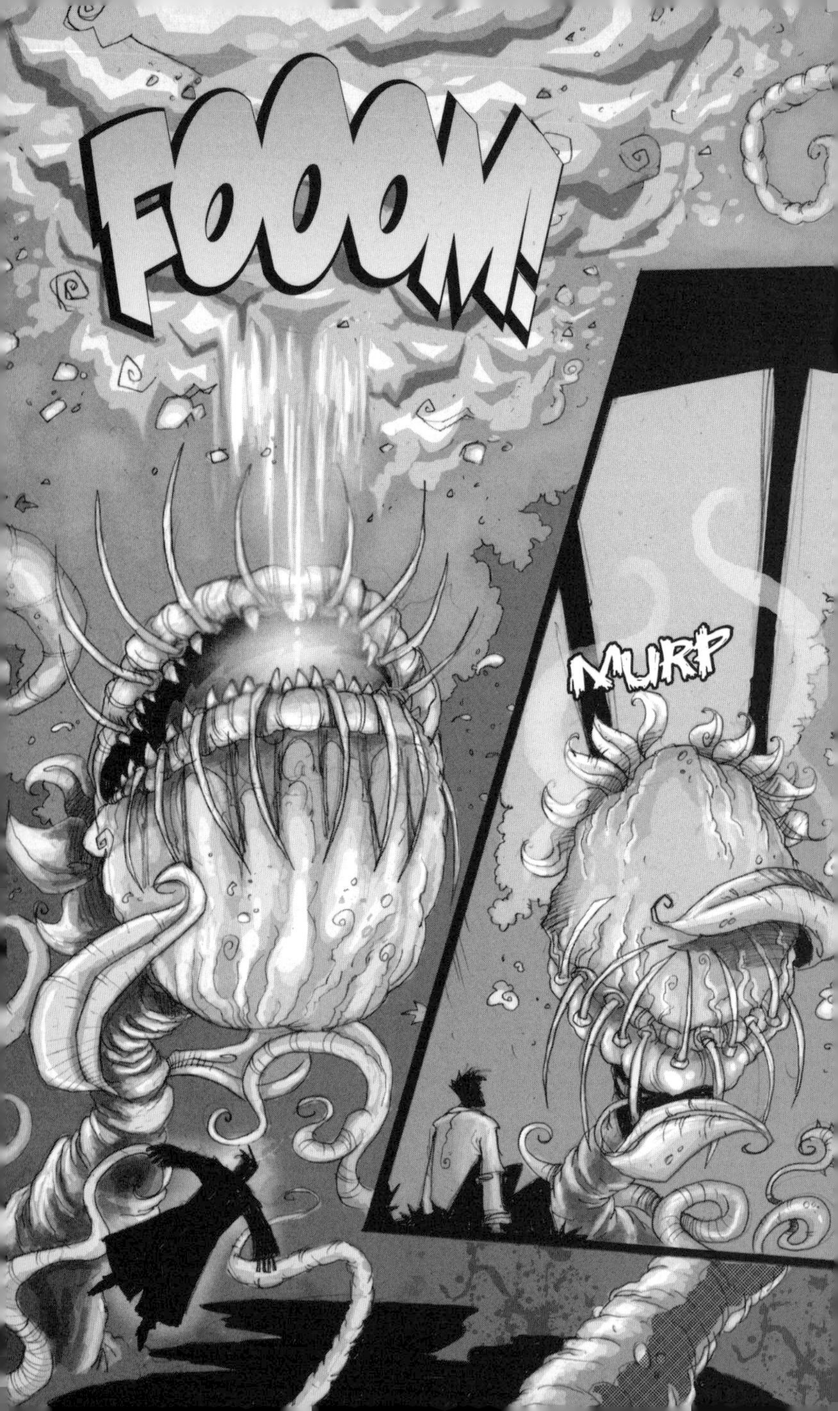
FOOOM!
MURP

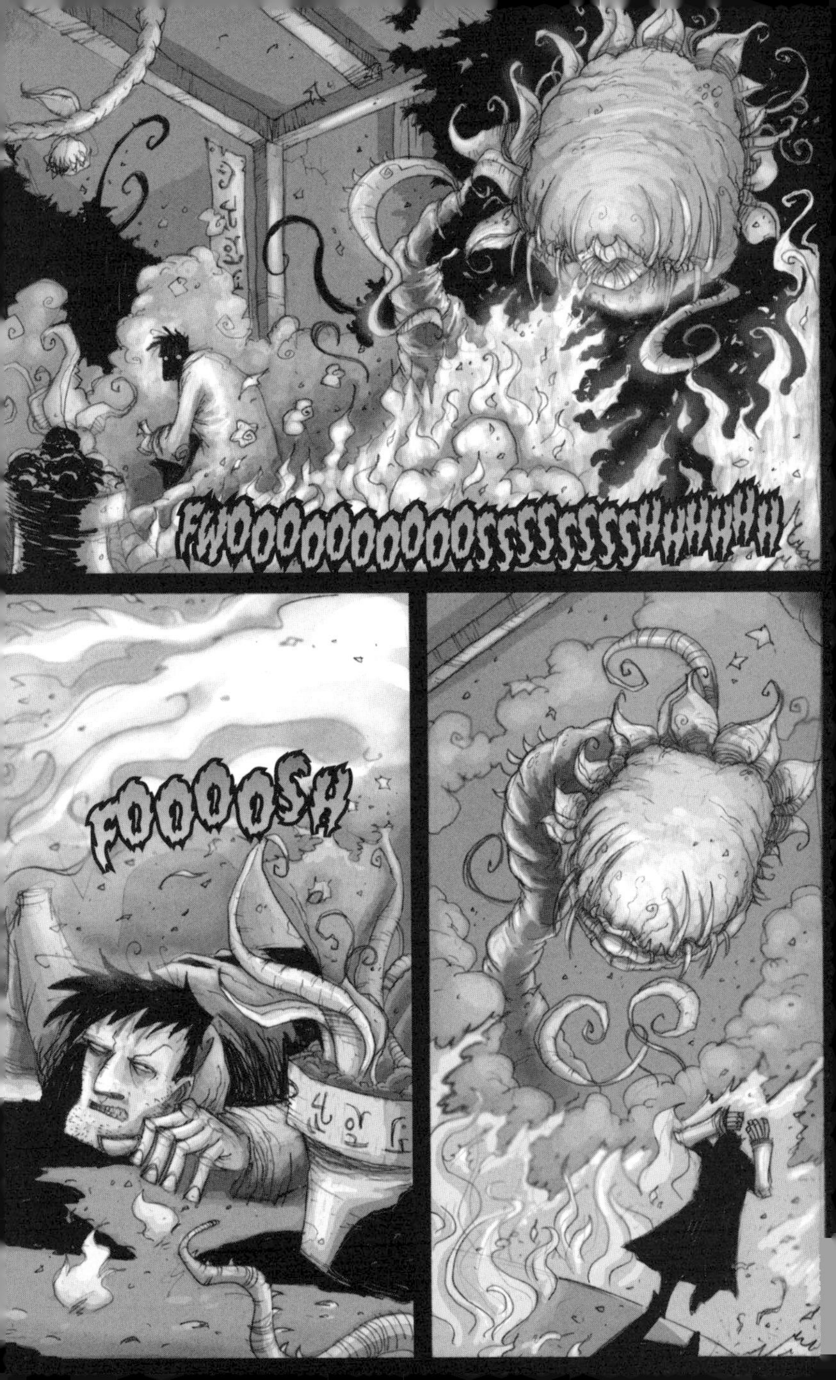
FWOOOOOOOOOOSSSSSSSHHHHHH
FOOOOSH

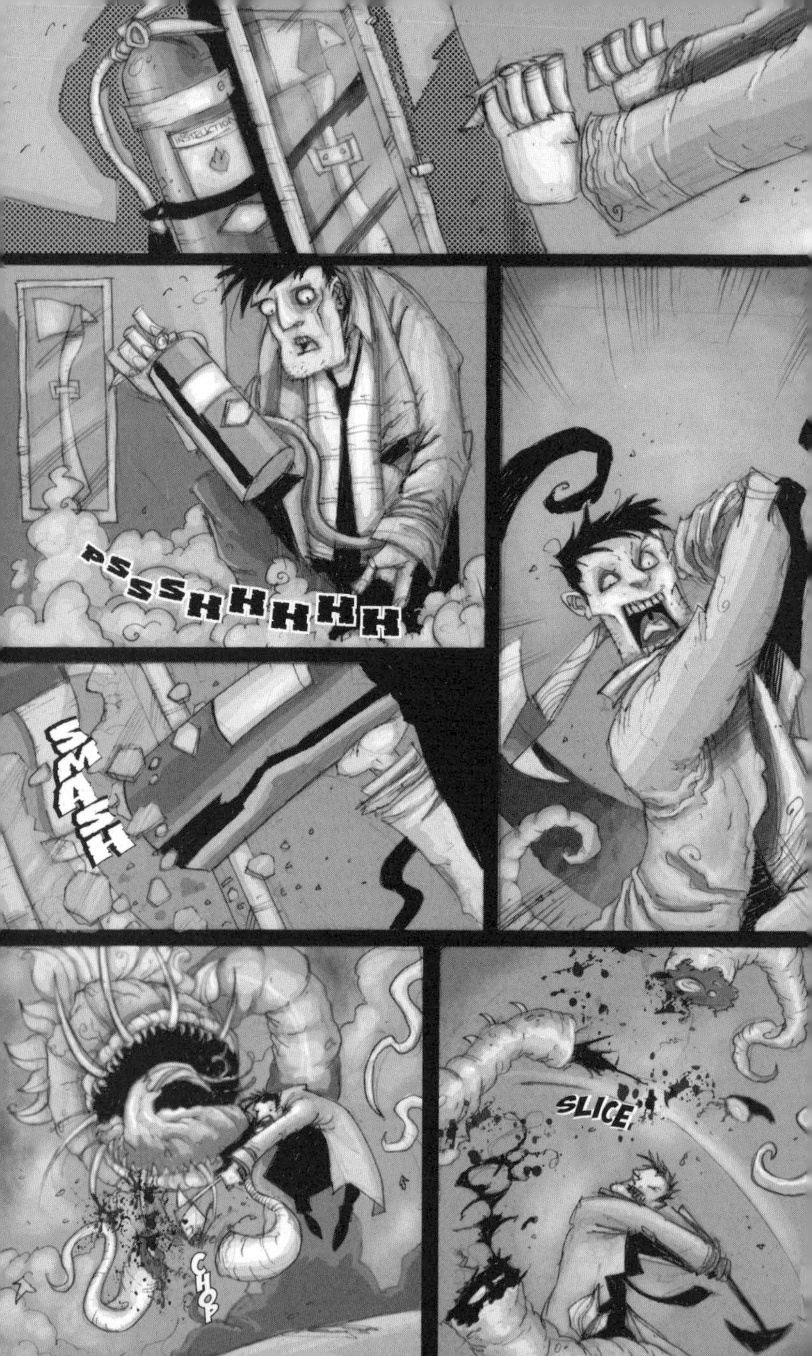
PSSSHHHHHH
SMASH
CHOP
SLICE

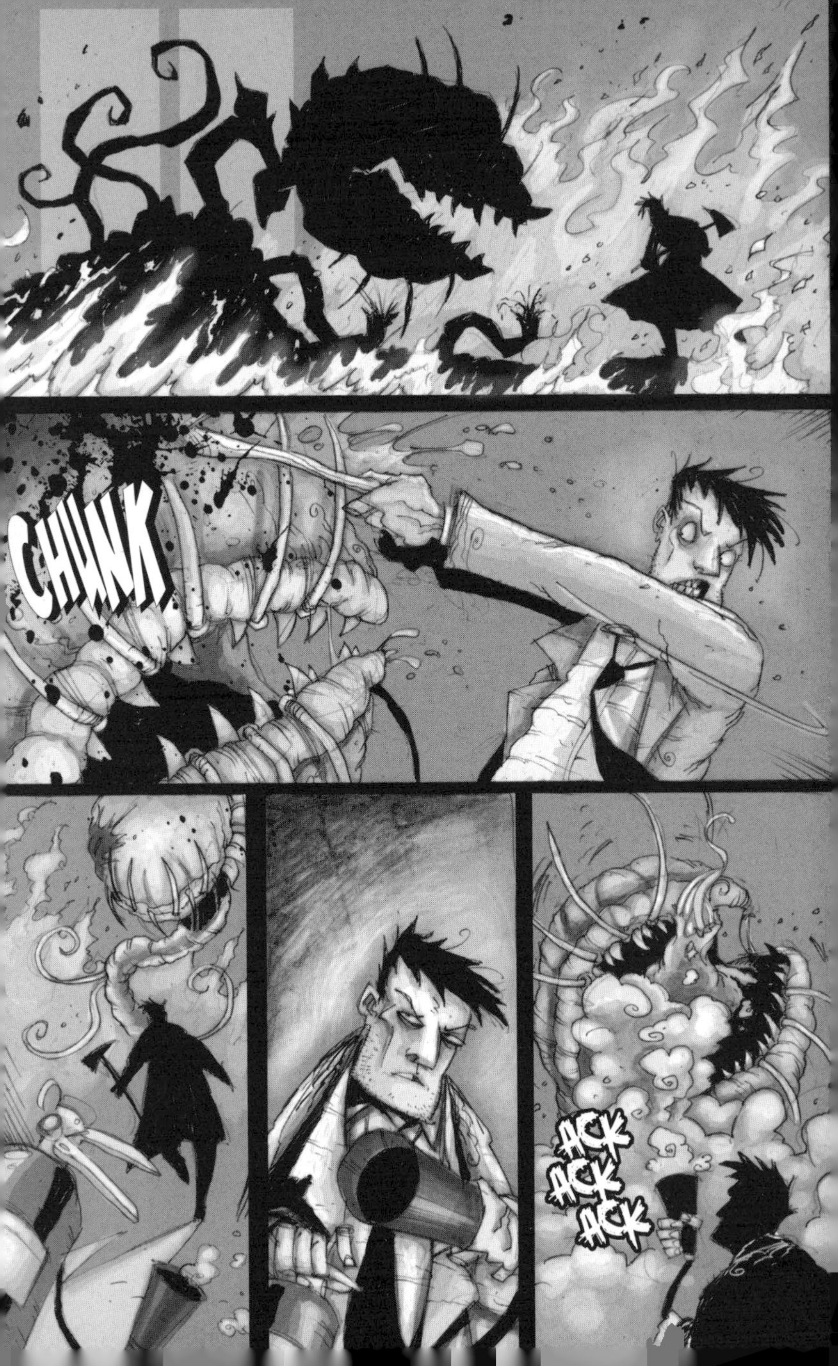
CHUNK
ACK
ACK
ACK

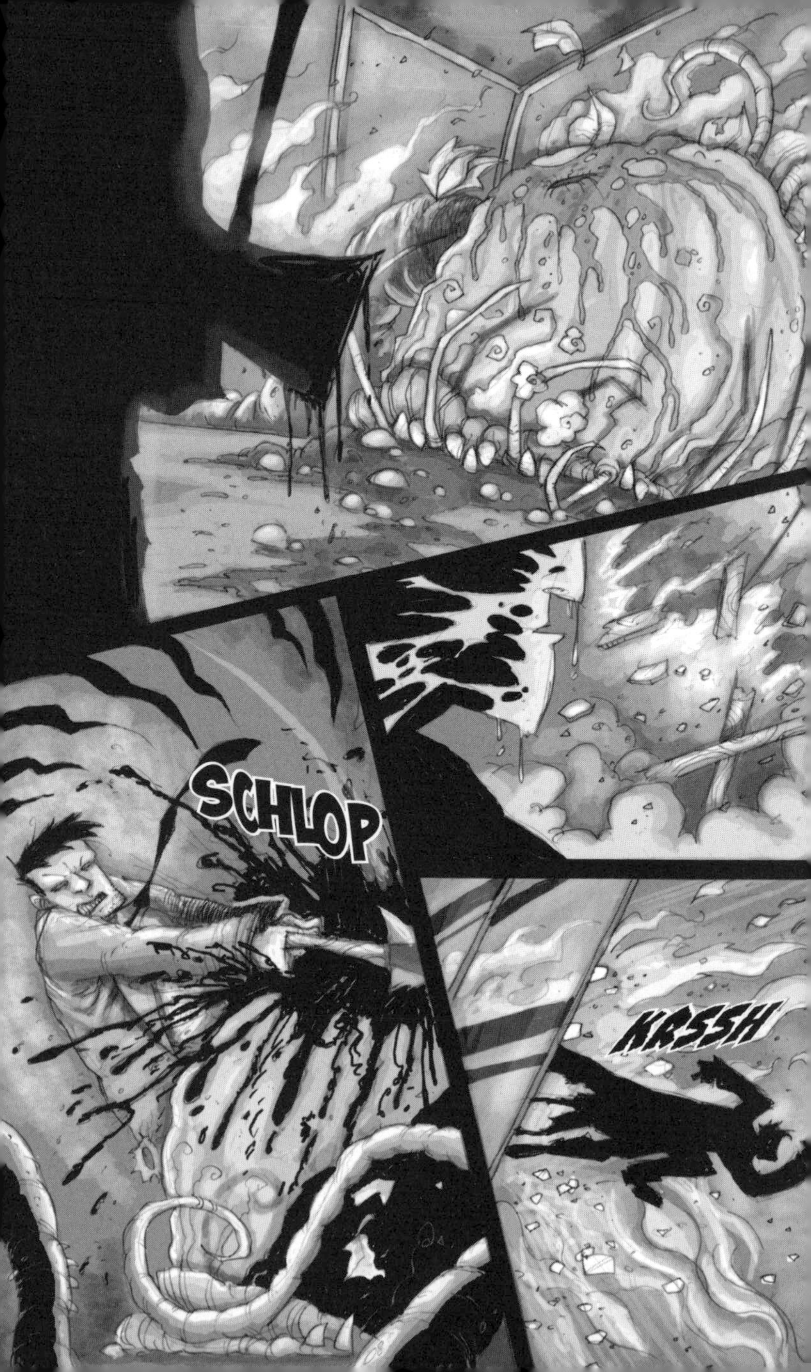
SCHLOP
KRSSH

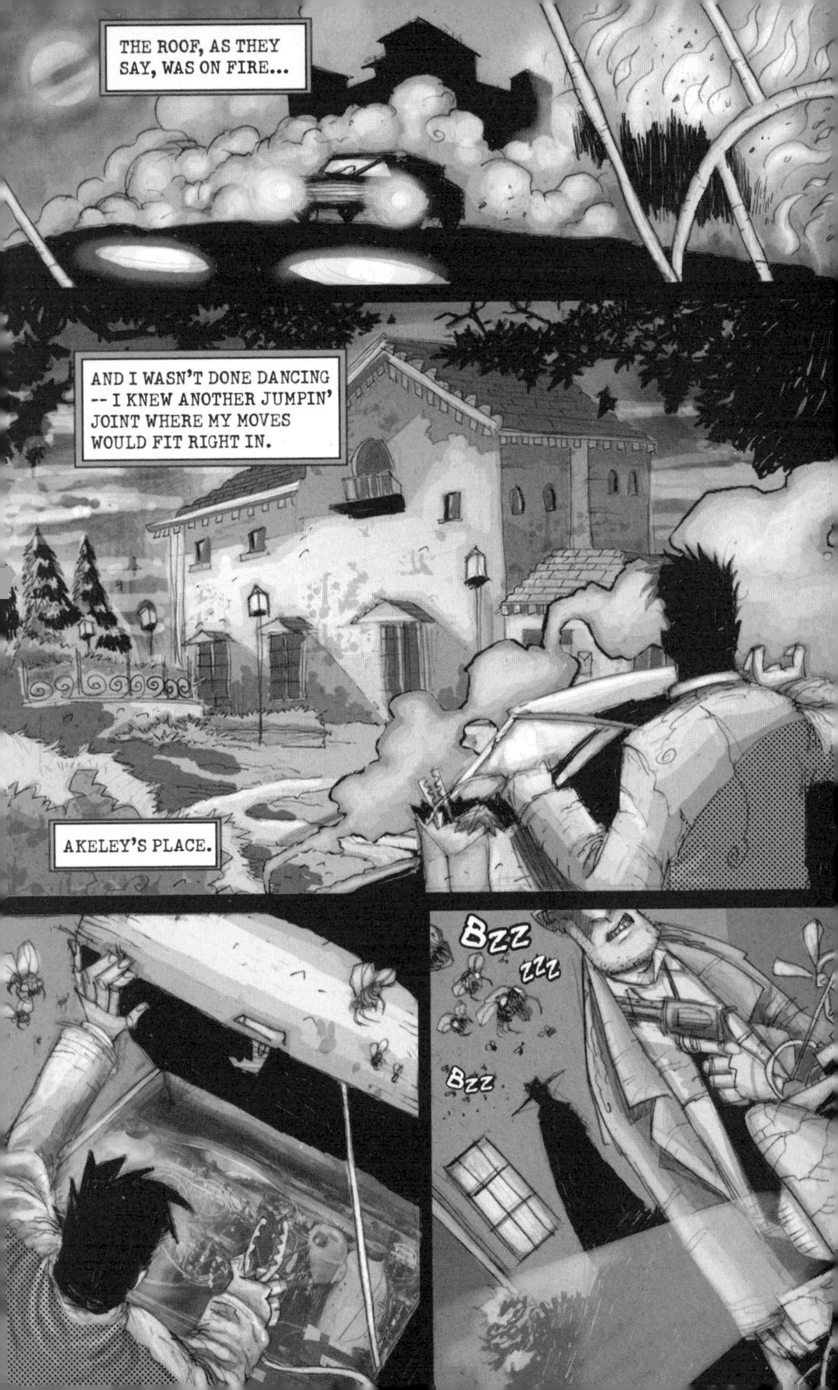
THE ROOF, AS THEY SAY, WAS ON FIRE...
AND I WASN'T DONE DANCING -- I KNEW ANOTHER JUMPIN' JOINT WHERE MY MOVES WOULD FIT RIGHT IN.
AKELEY'S PLACE.
BZZ
ZZZ
BZZ

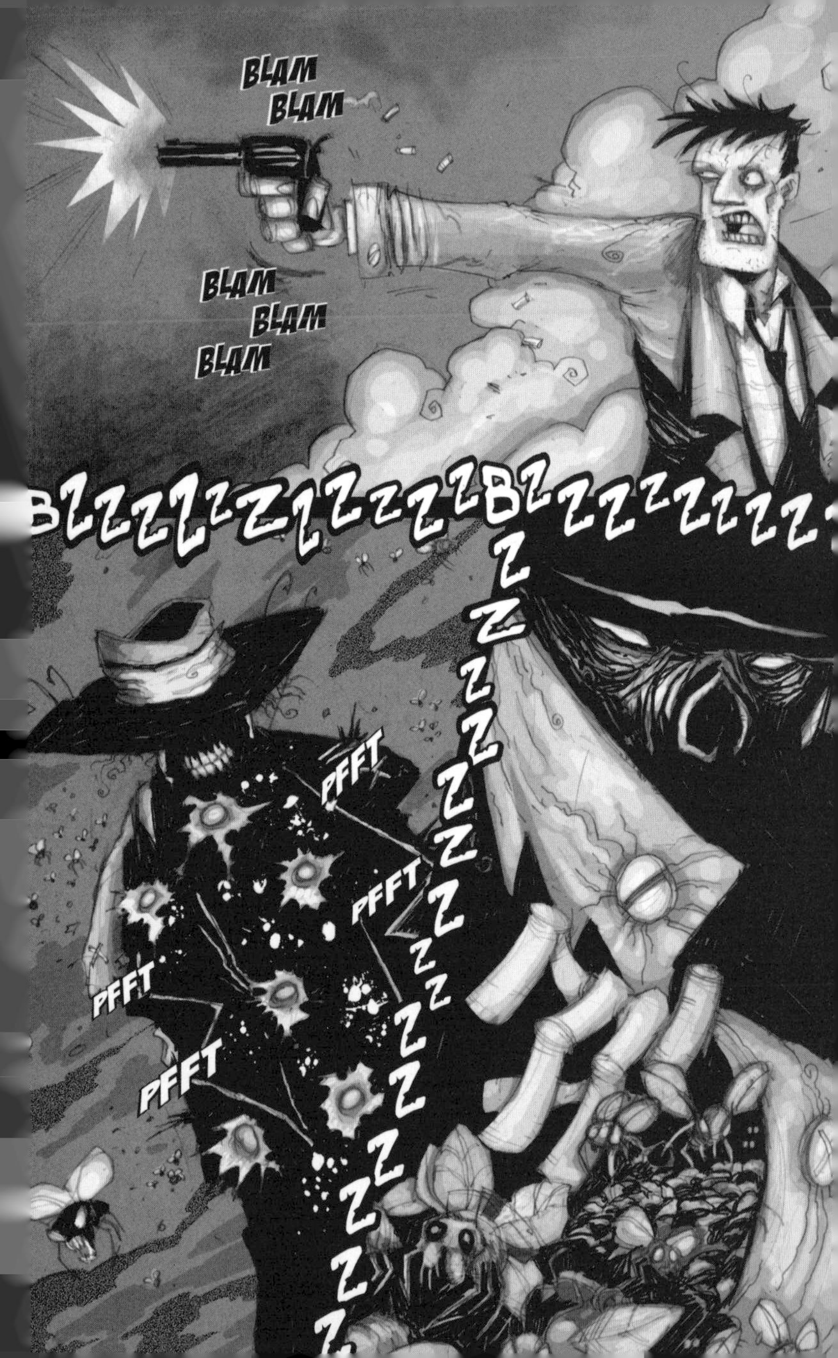
BLAM
BLAM
BLAM
BLAM
BLAM
BZZZZZZZZZZZZZBZZZZZZZZZ
ZZZZZZZZZZZZZZZZZ
PFFT
PFFT
PFFT
PFFT

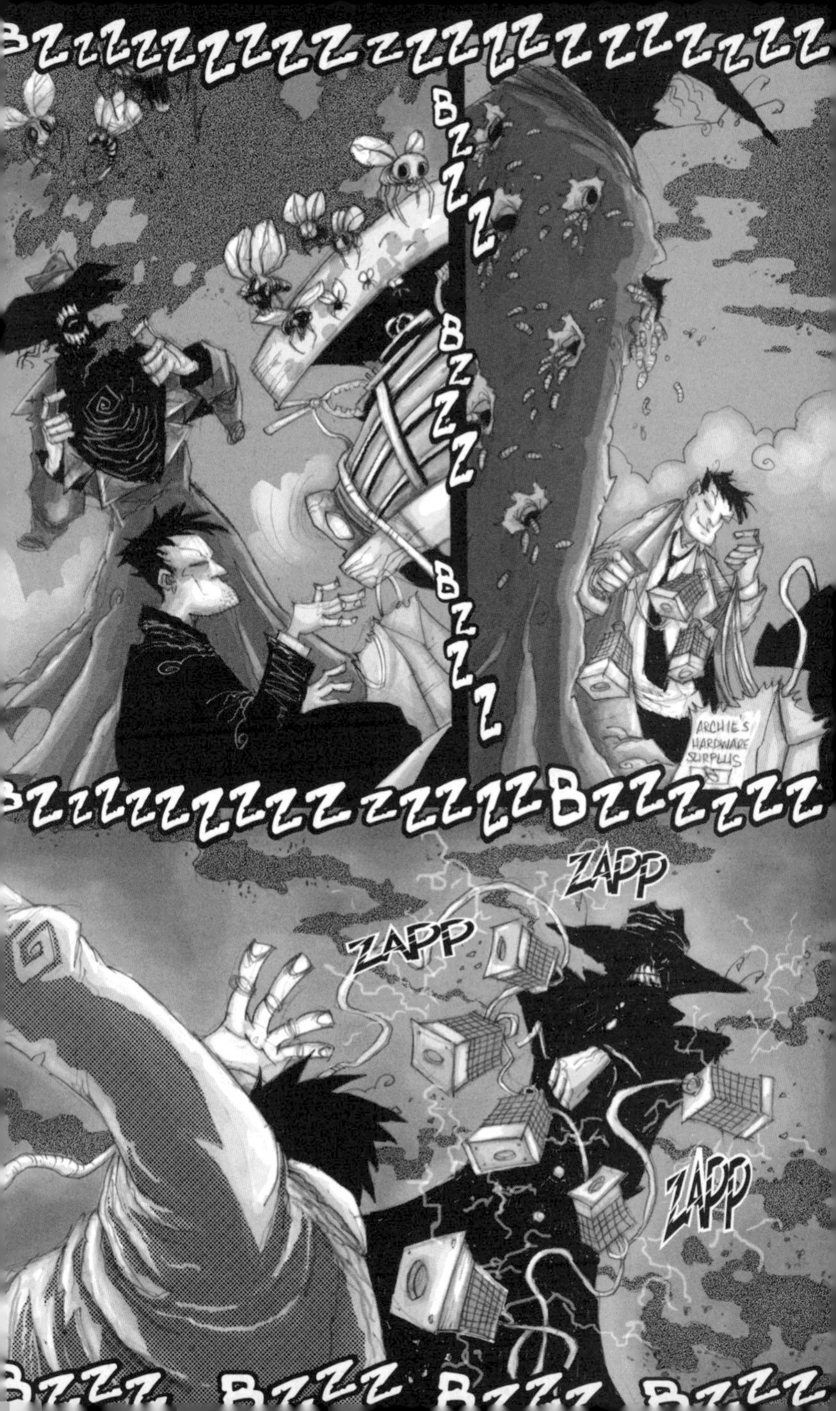

BZZZZZZZZZZZZZZZZZZZZ
BZZZ
BZZZ
BZZZZ
ARCHIE'S HARDWARE SURPLUS
BZZZZZZZZZZZZZZBZZZZZZ
ZAPP
ZAPP
ZAPP
BZZZZ BZZZZ BZZZZ BZZZZ

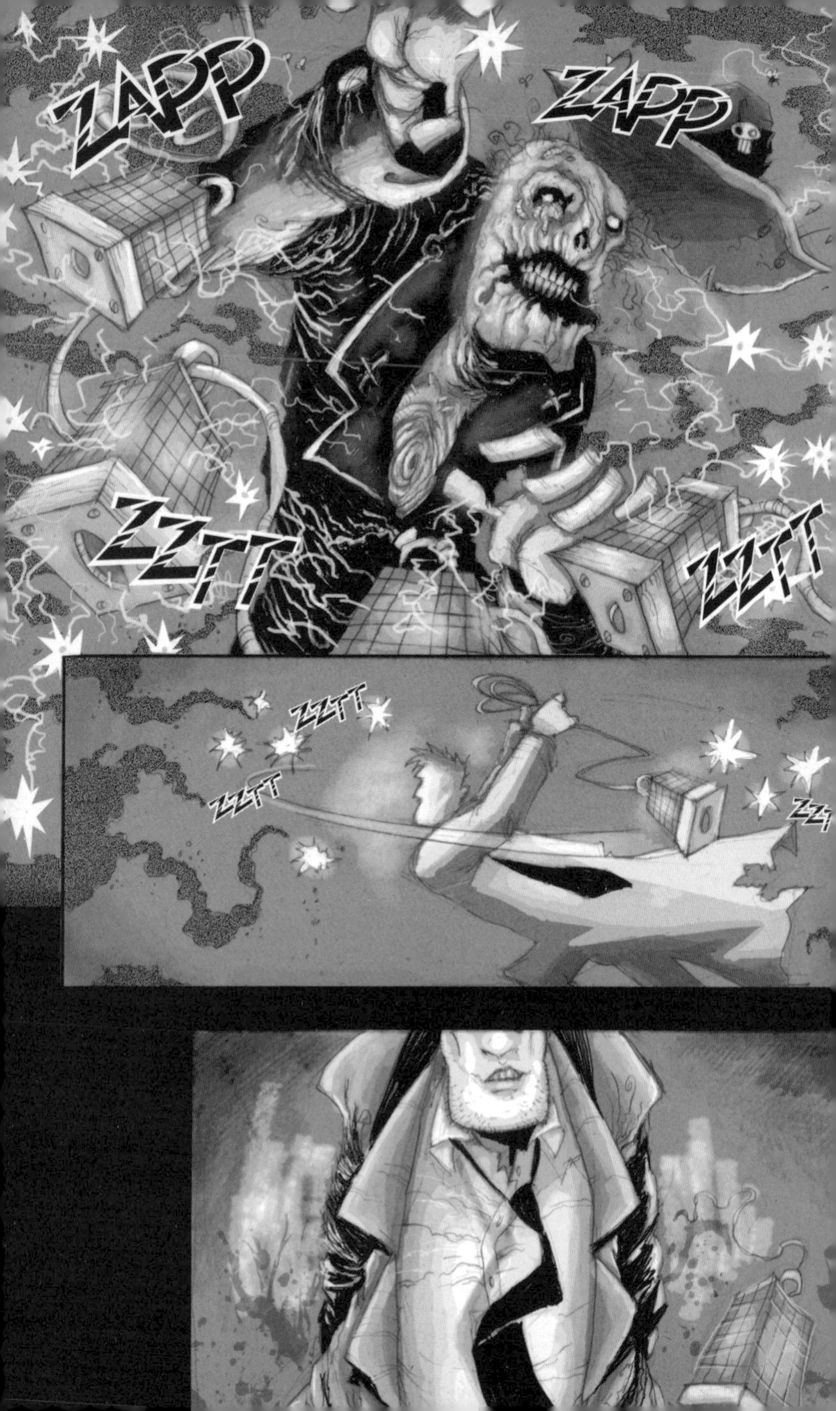
ZAPP
ZAPP
ZZTT
ZZTT
ZZTT
ZZTT

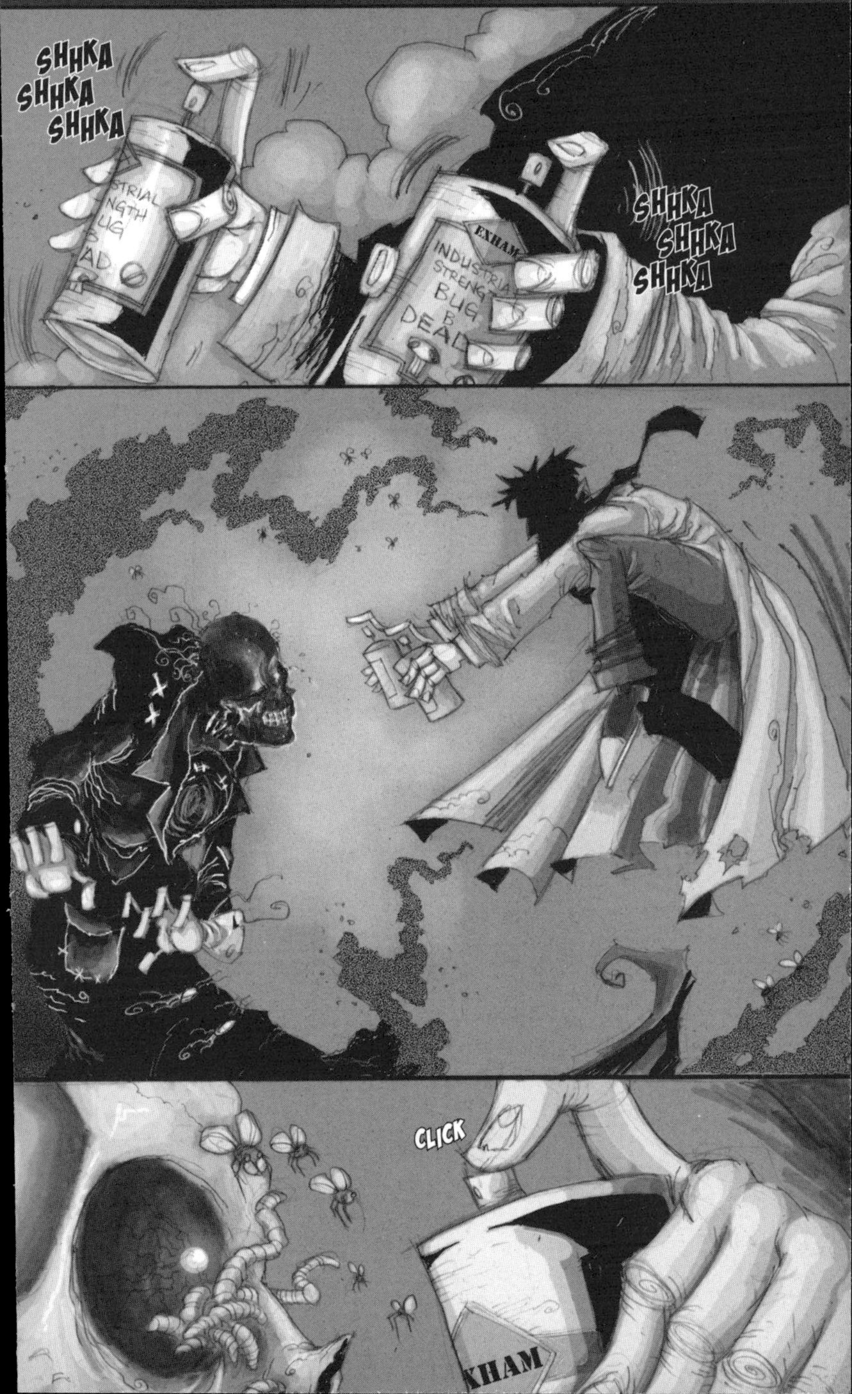
SHHKA
SHHKA
SHHKA
STRIAL NGTH UG B AD
EXHAM
INDUSTRIA STRENGT BUG B DEAD
SHHKA
SHHKA
SHHKA
CLICK
KHAM

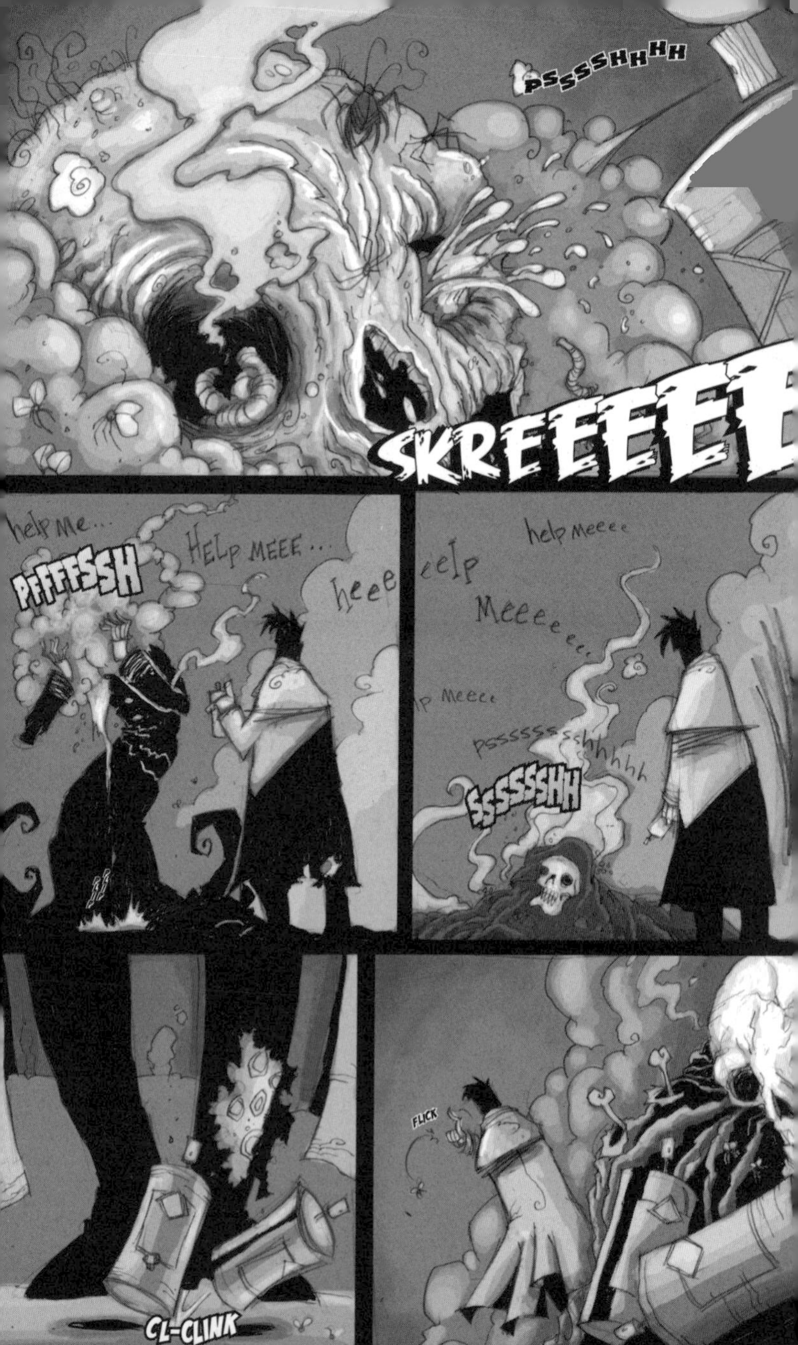
PSSSSHHHH
SKREEEEE
help me...
PFFFSSH
HELP MEEE...
heee
eelp
help meeee
Meeeeee...
lp meeee
psssssschhhhh
SSSSSSHH
CL-CLINK
FLICK

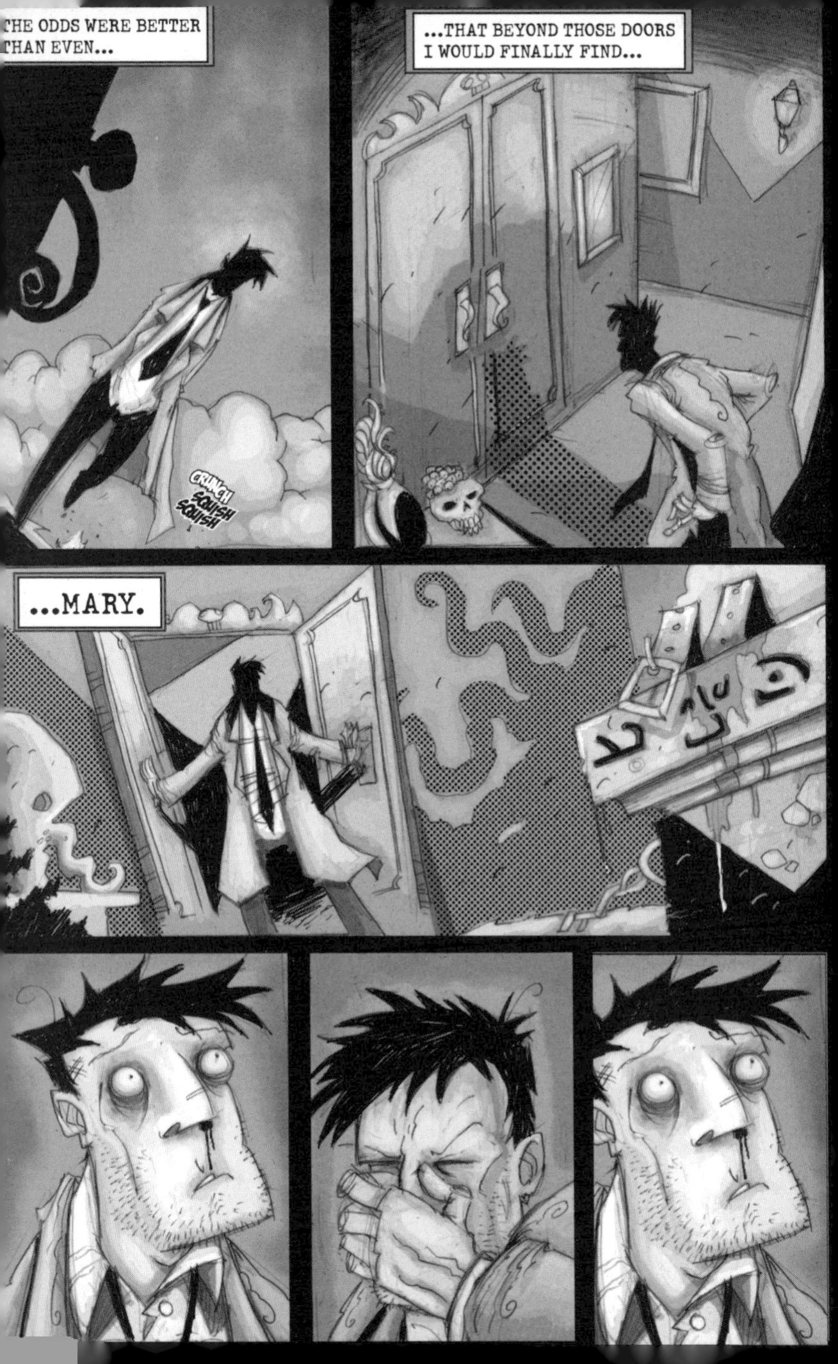
THE ODDS WERE BETTER THAN EVEN...
CRUNCH SQUISH SQUISH
...THAT BEYOND THOSE DOORS I WOULD FINALLY FIND...
...MARY.

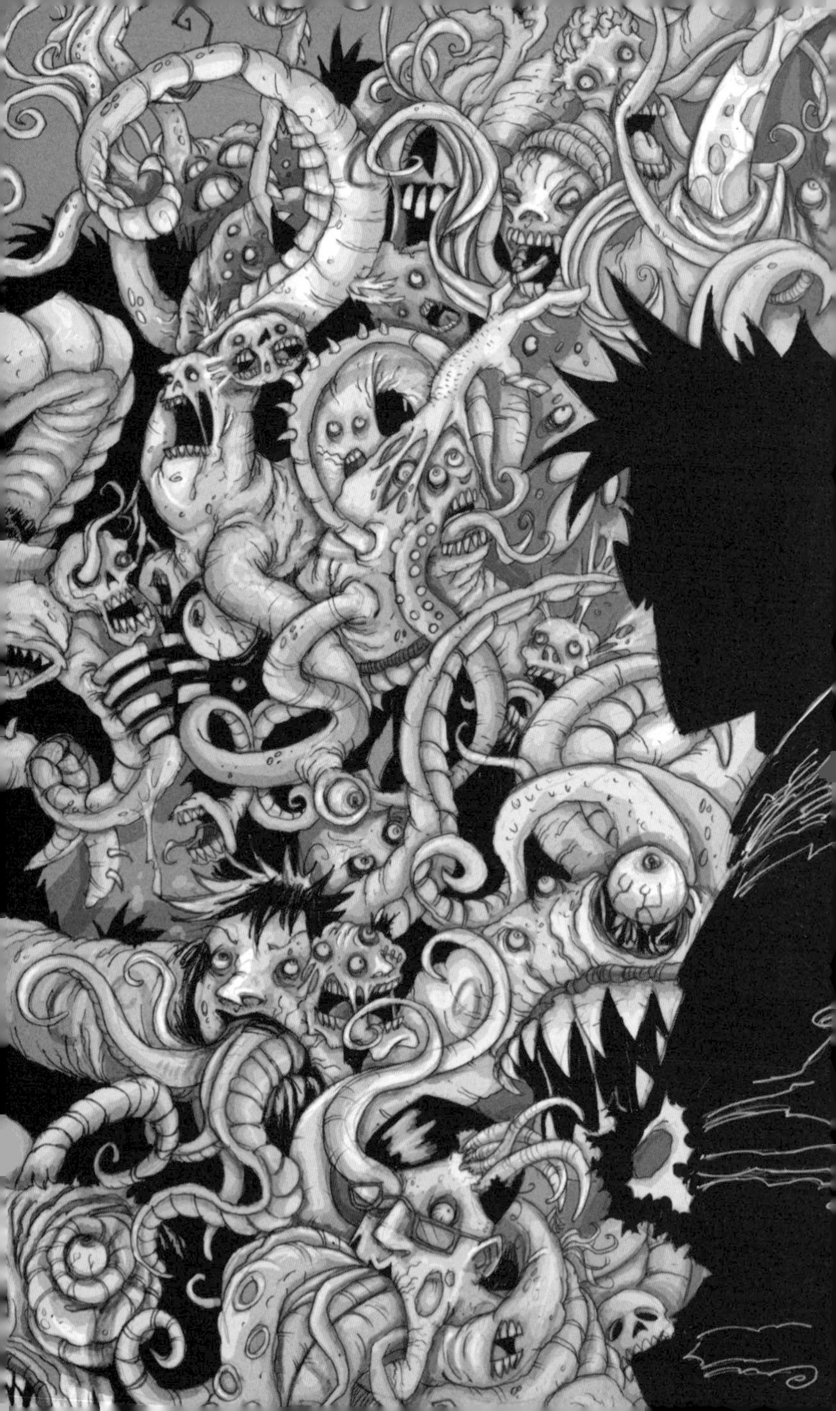

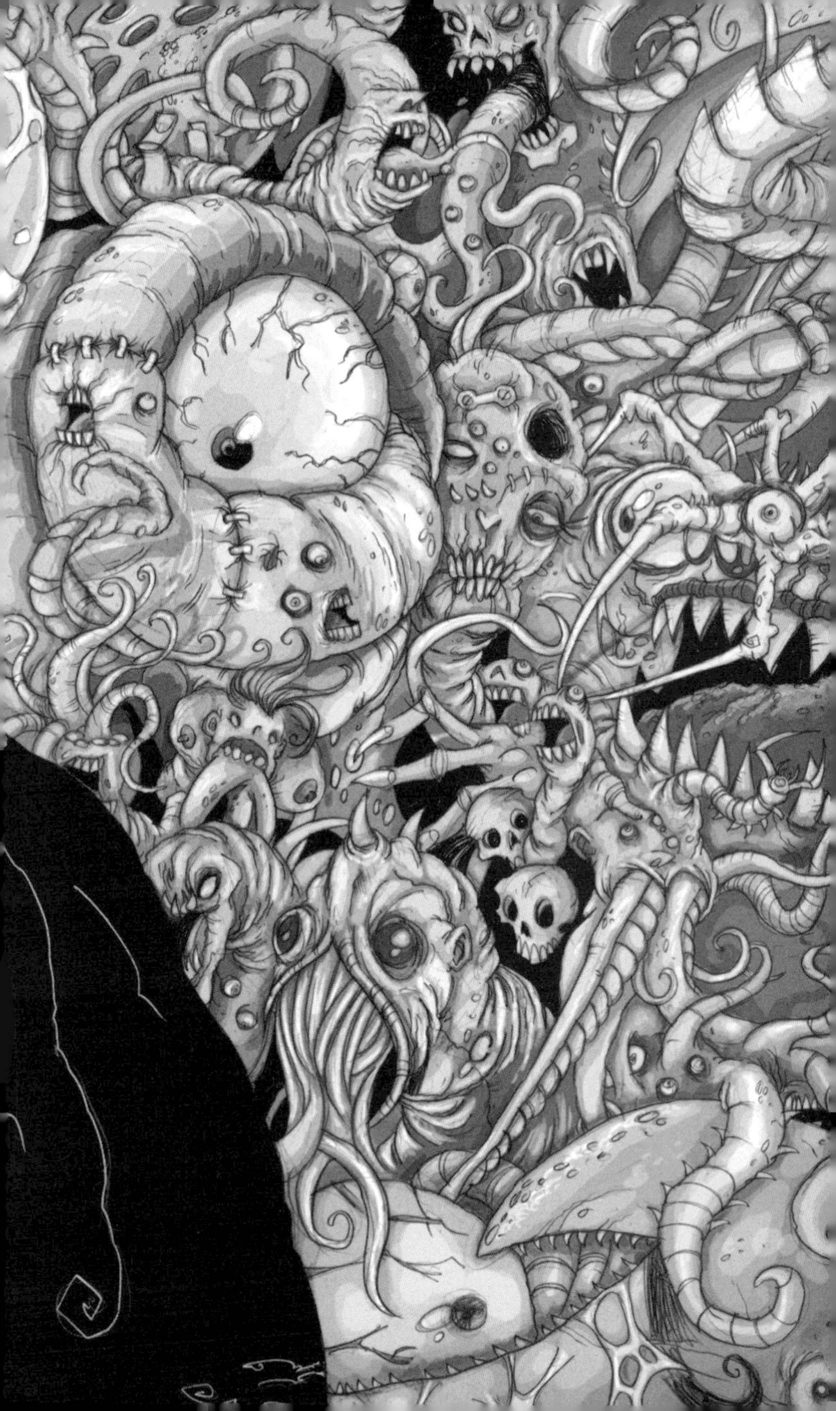

# CHAPTER 5:
## The Big Sleeper

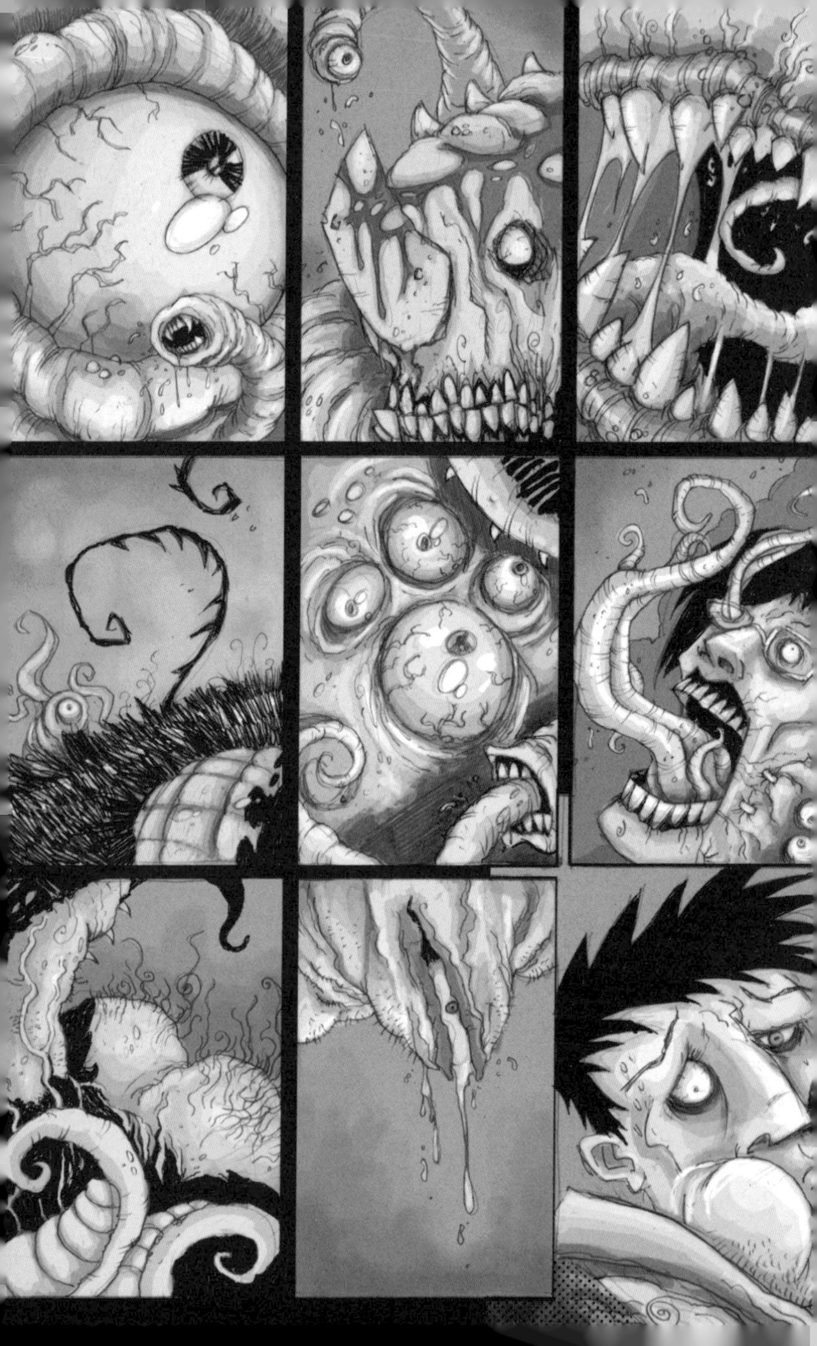

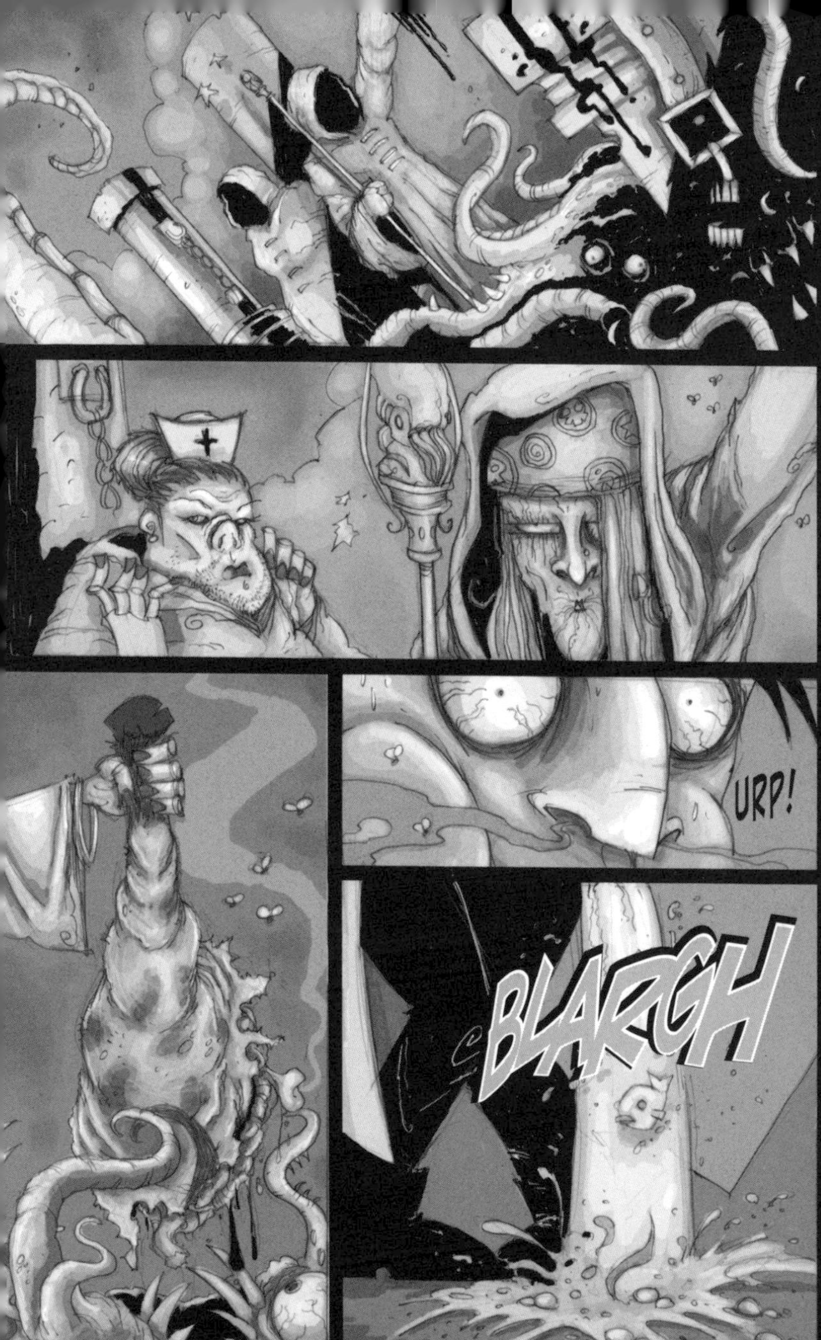
URP!
BLARGH

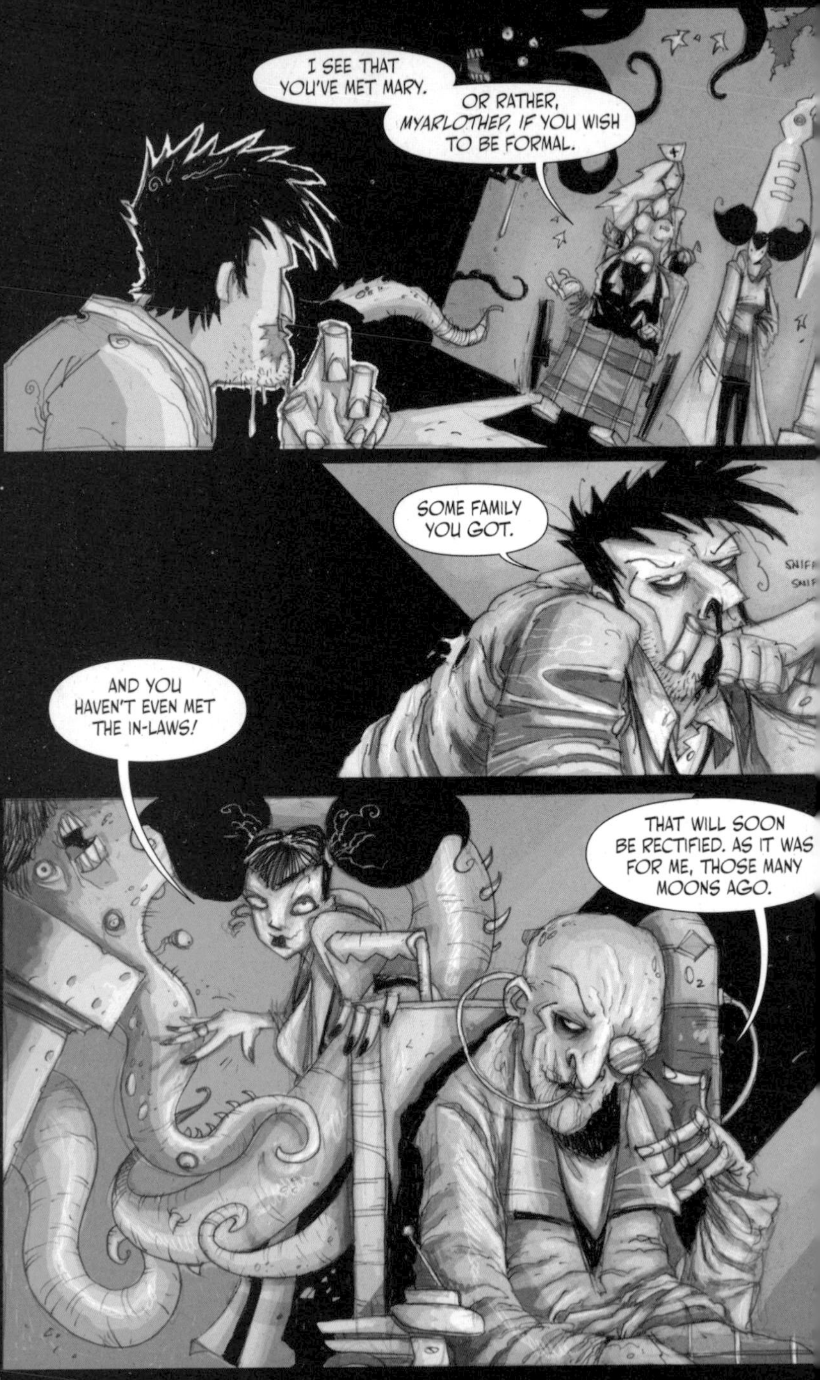
I SEE THAT YOU'VE MET MARY.
OR RATHER, MYARLOTHEP, IF YOU WISH TO BE FORMAL.
SOME FAMILY YOU GOT.
AND YOU HAVEN'T EVEN MET THE IN-LAWS!
THAT WILL SOON BE RECTIFIED. AS IT WAS FOR ME, THOSE MANY MOONS AGO.

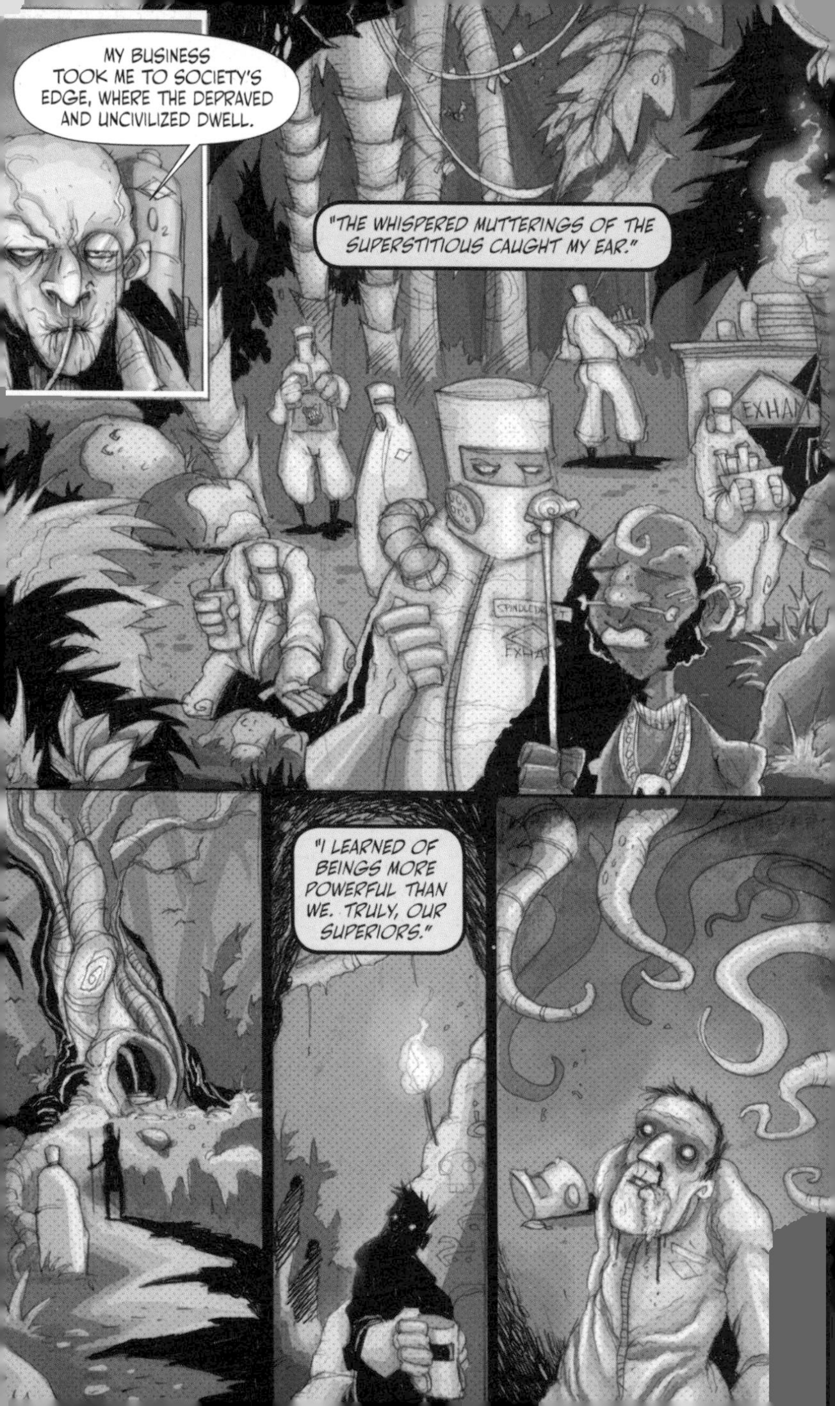
MY BUSINESS TOOK ME TO SOCIETY'S EDGE, WHERE THE DEPRAVED AND UNCIVILIZED DWELL.
O2
"THE WHISPERED MUTTERINGS OF THE SUPERSTITIOUS CAUGHT MY EAR."
EXHA
SPINDLEDRIFT
"I LEARNED OF BEINGS MORE POWERFUL THAN WE. TRULY, OUR SUPERIORS."

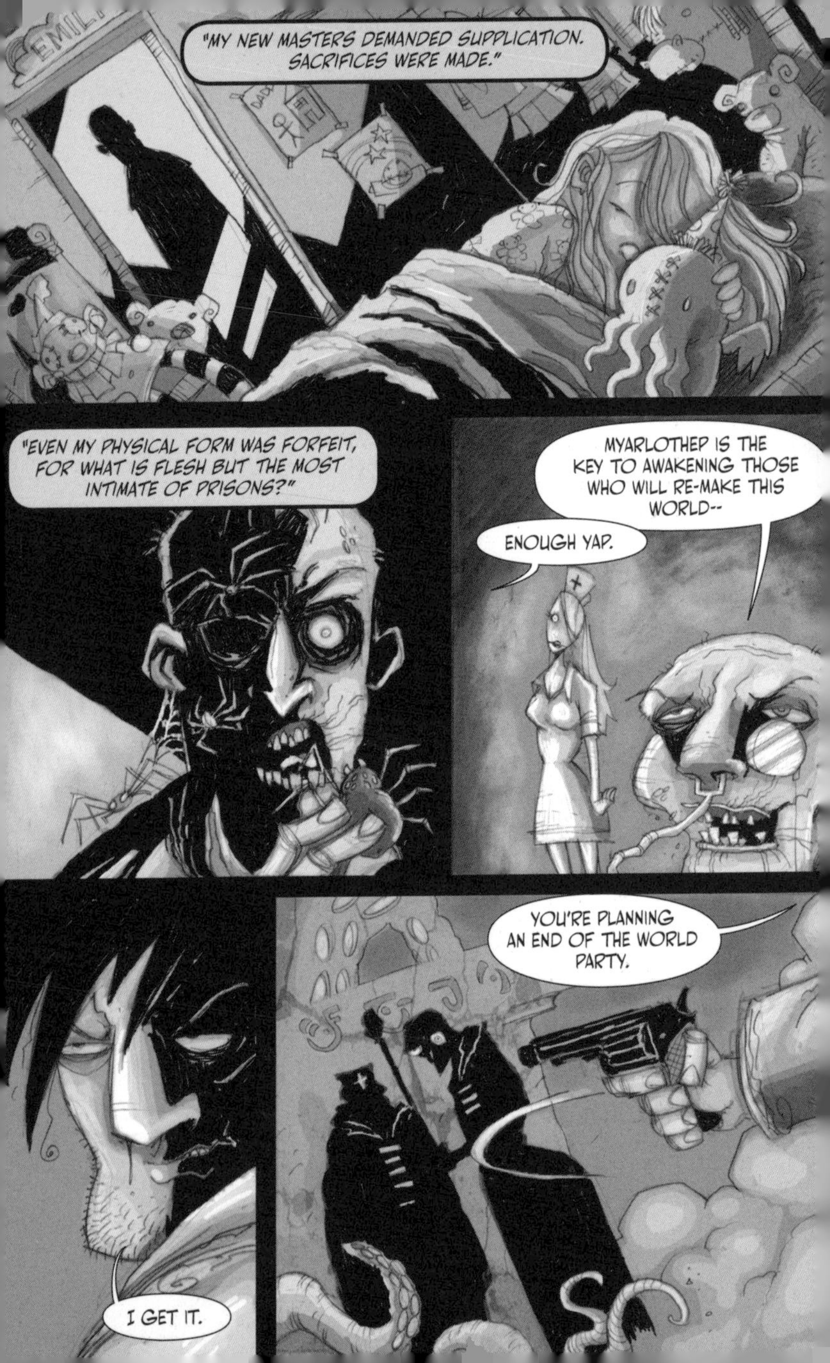
"MY NEW MASTERS DEMANDED SUPPLICATION. SACRIFICES WERE MADE."
"EVEN MY PHYSICAL FORM WAS FORFEIT, FOR WHAT IS FLESH BUT THE MOST INTIMATE OF PRISONS?"
MYARLOTHEP IS THE KEY TO AWAKENING THOSE WHO WILL RE-MAKE THIS WORLD--
ENOUGH YAP.
I GET IT.
YOU'RE PLANNING AN END OF THE WORLD PARTY.

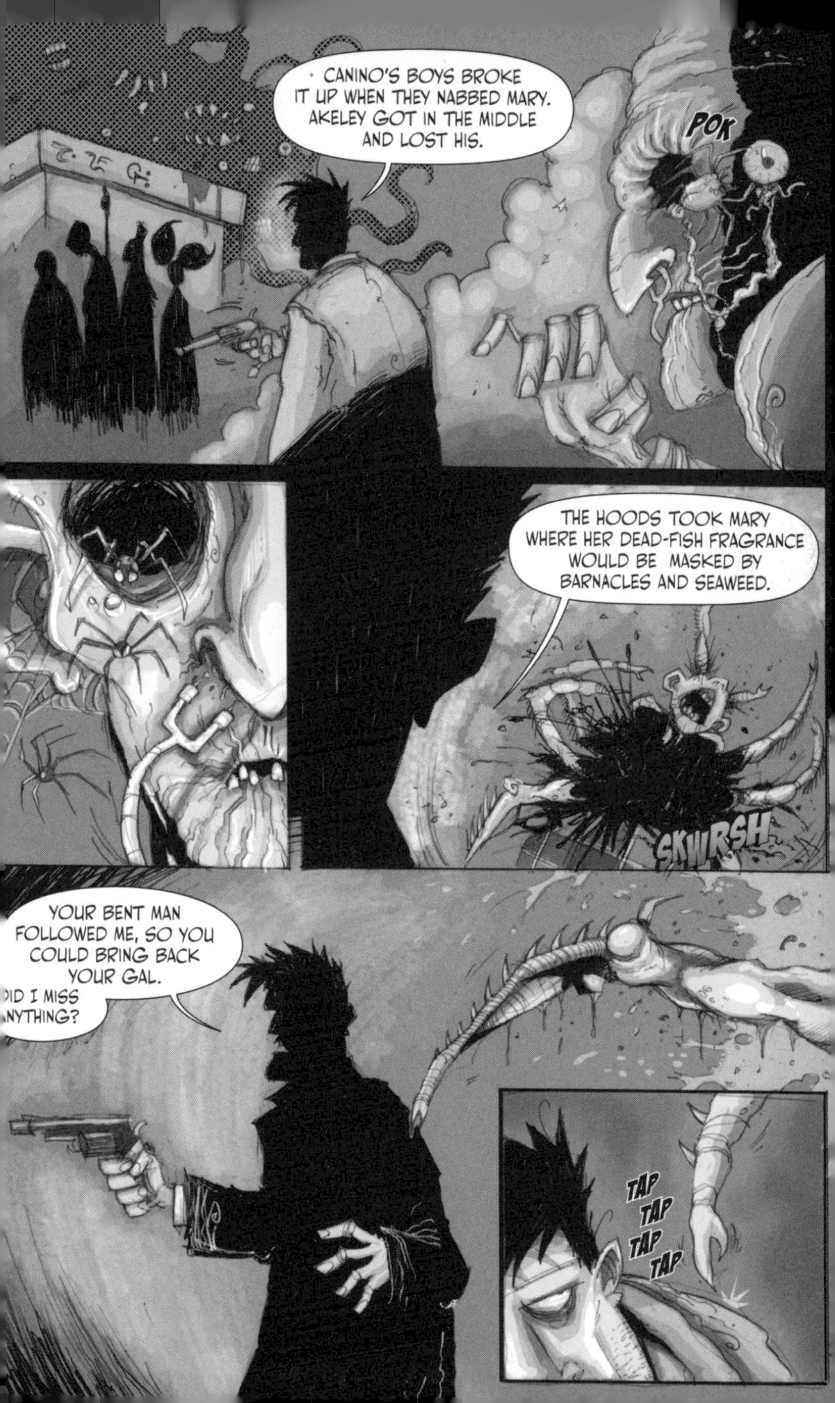
CANINO'S BOYS BROKE IT UP WHEN THEY NABBED MARY. AKELEY GOT IN THE MIDDLE AND LOST HIS.
POK
THE HOODS TOOK MARY WHERE HER DEAD-FISH FRAGRANCE WOULD BE MASKED BY BARNACLES AND SEAWEED.
SKWRSH
YOUR BENT MAN FOLLOWED ME, SO YOU COULD BRING BACK YOUR GAL.
DID I MISS ANYTHING?
TAP TAP TAP TAP

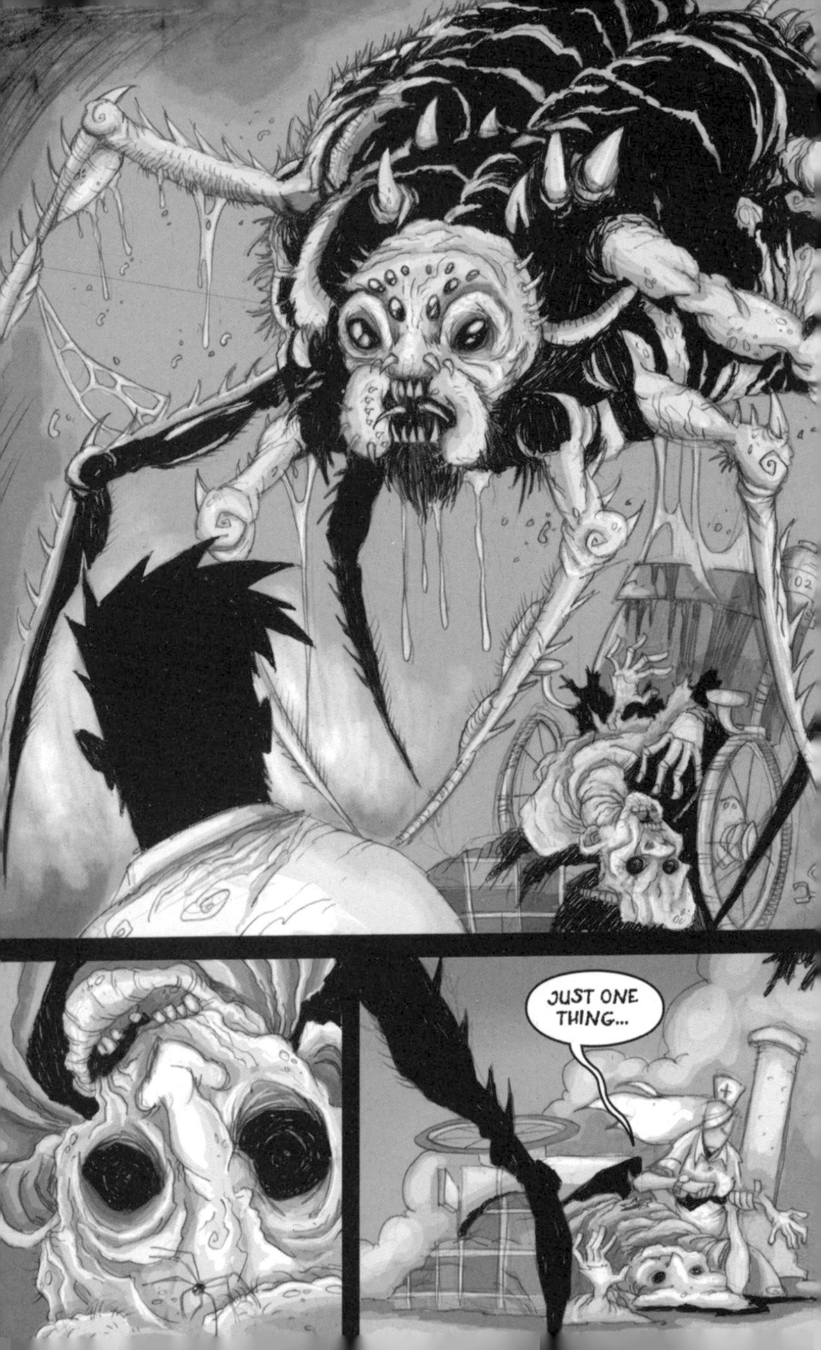
02
JUST ONE THING...

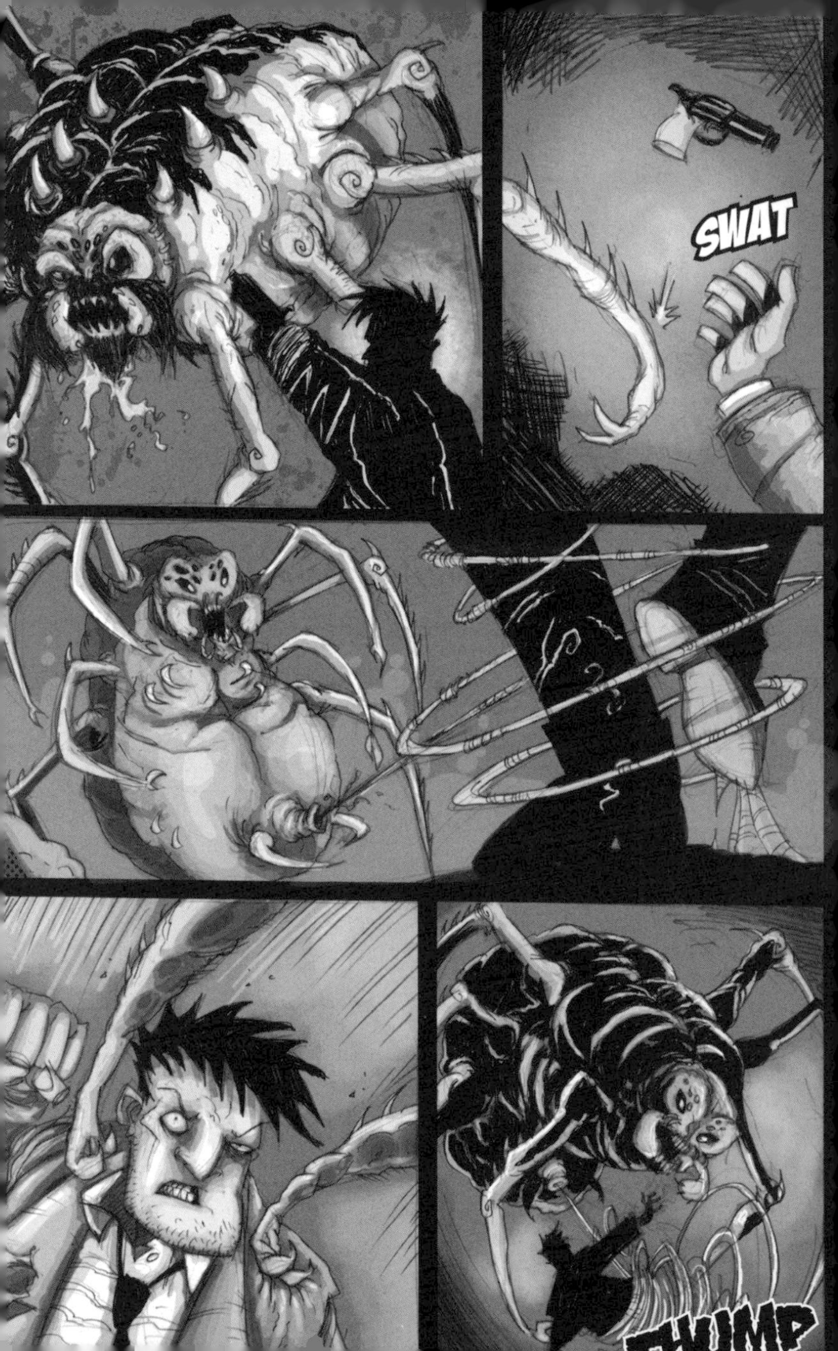
SWAT
THUMP

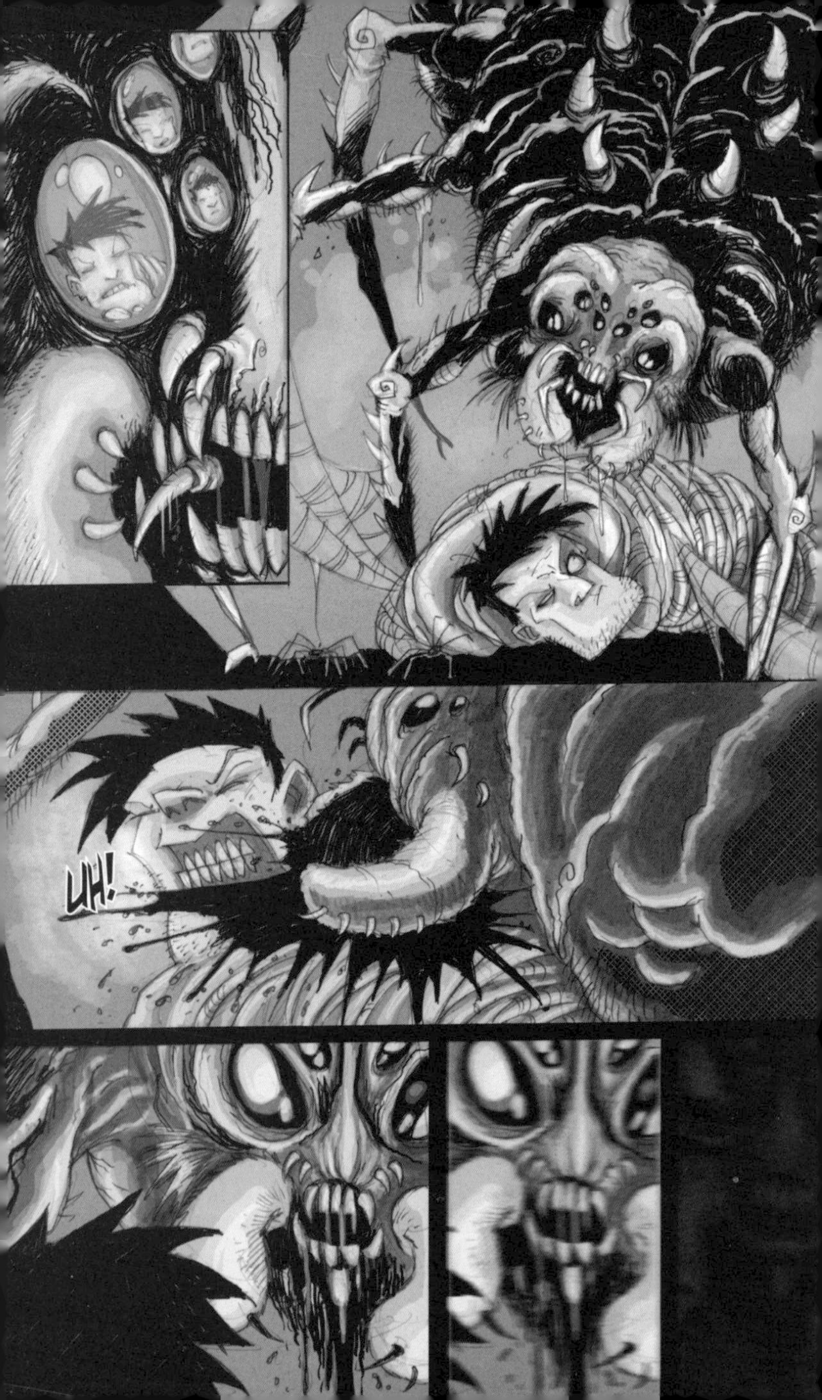
UH!

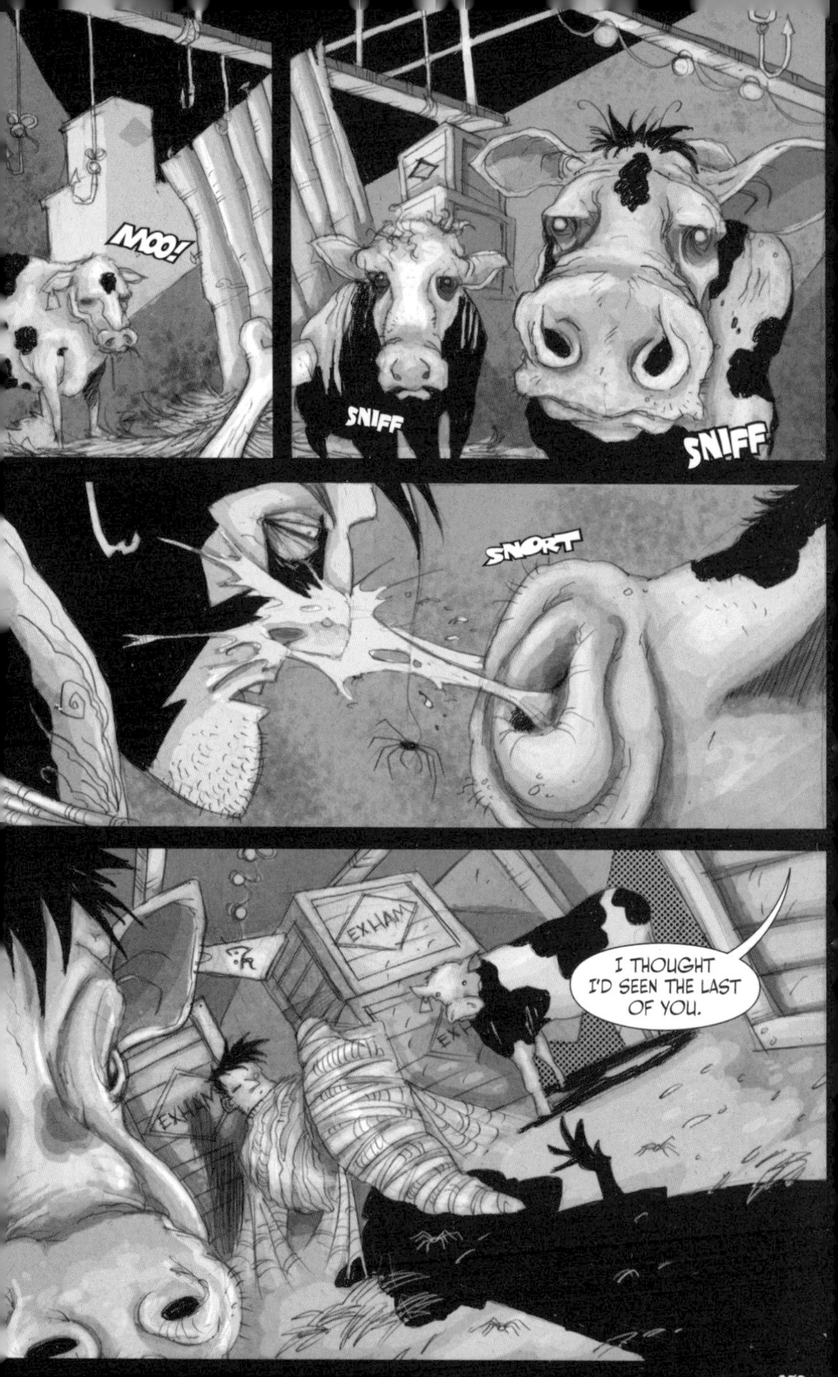
MOO!
SNIFF
SNIFF
SNORT
EXHAM
I THOUGHT I'D SEEN THE LAST OF YOU.

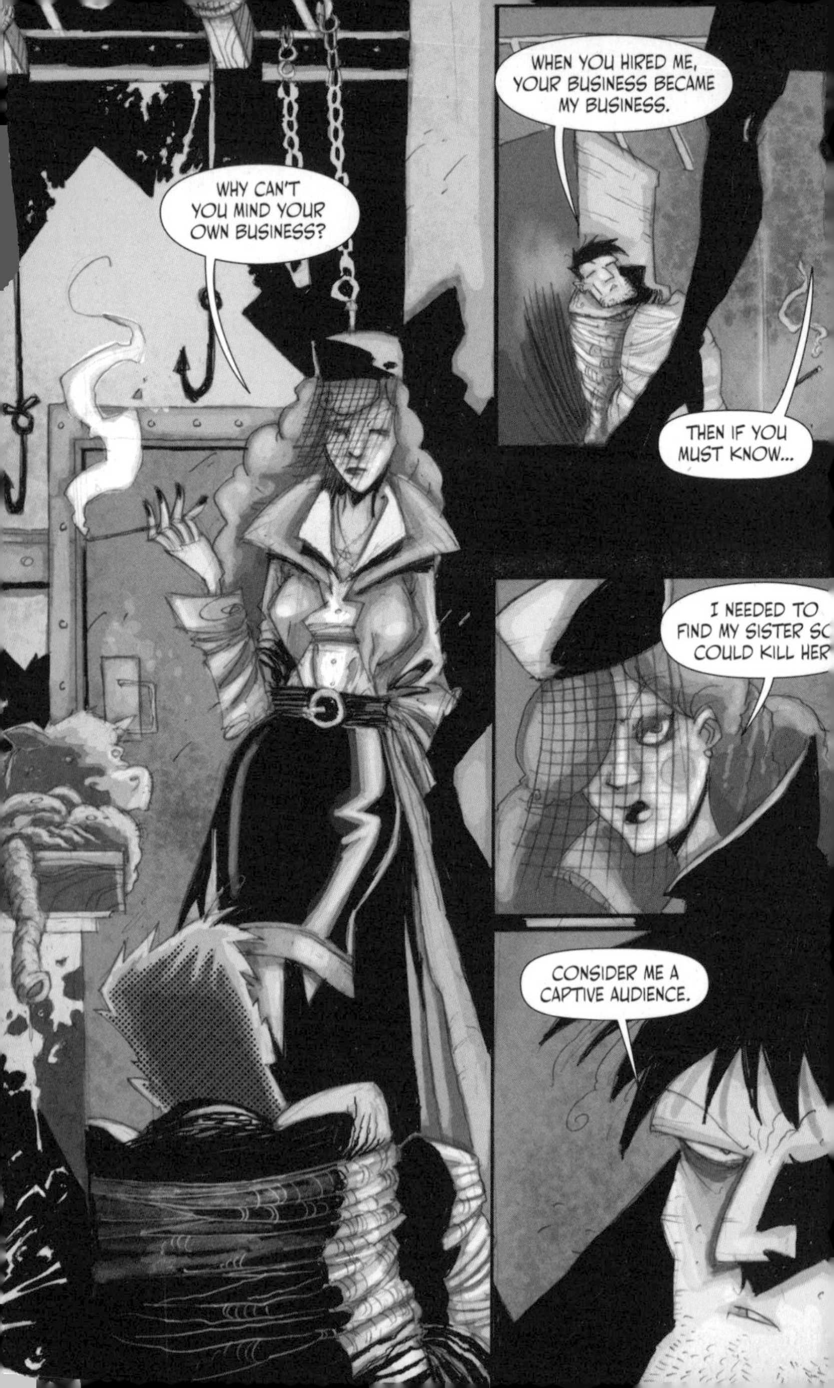
WHY CAN'T YOU MIND YOUR OWN BUSINESS?
WHEN YOU HIRED ME, YOUR BUSINESS BECAME MY BUSINESS.
THEN IF YOU MUST KNOW...
I NEEDED TO FIND MY SISTER SC COULD KILL HER
CONSIDER ME A CAPTIVE AUDIENCE.

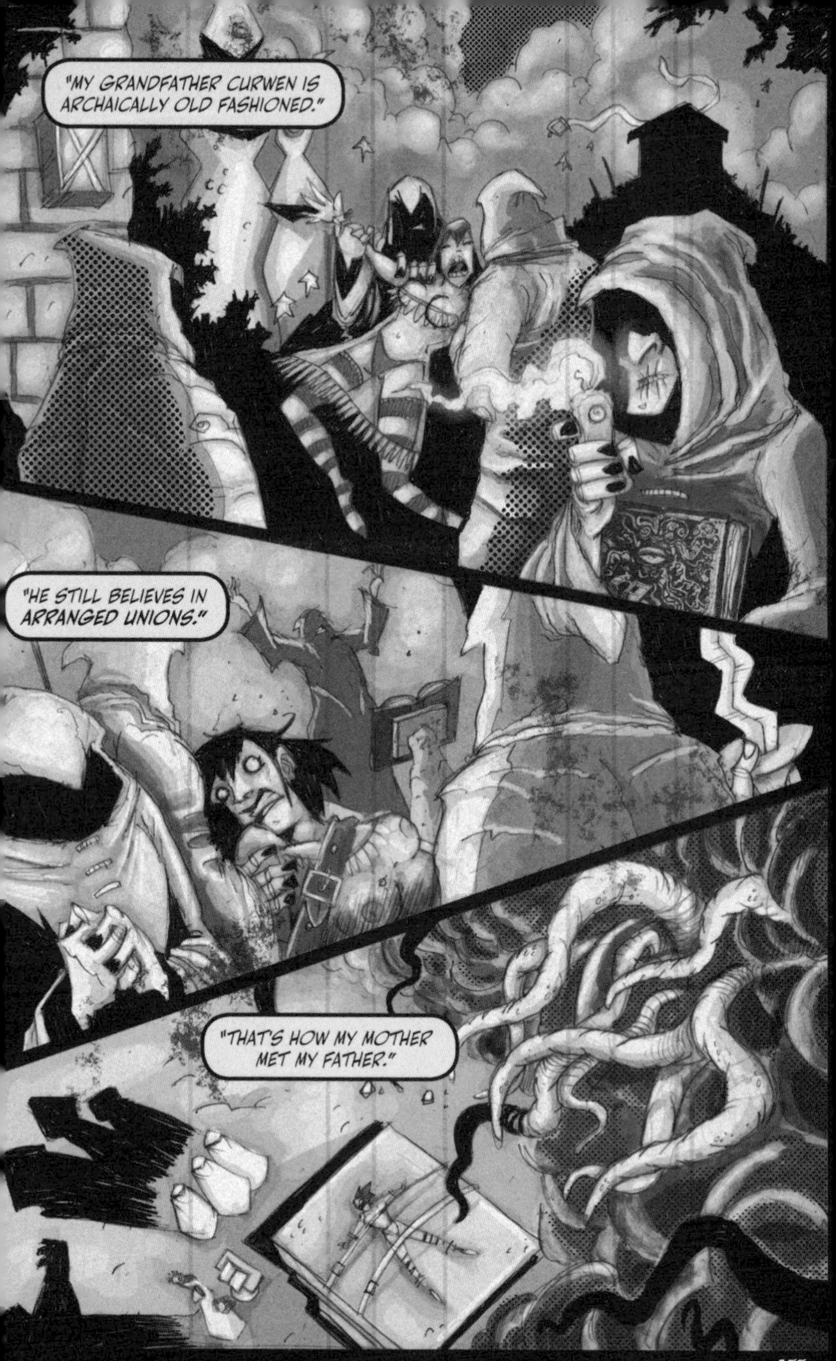
"MY GRANDFATHER CURWEN IS ARCHAICALLY OLD FASHIONED."
"HE STILL BELIEVES IN ARRANGED UNIONS."
"THAT'S HOW MY MOTHER MET MY FATHER."

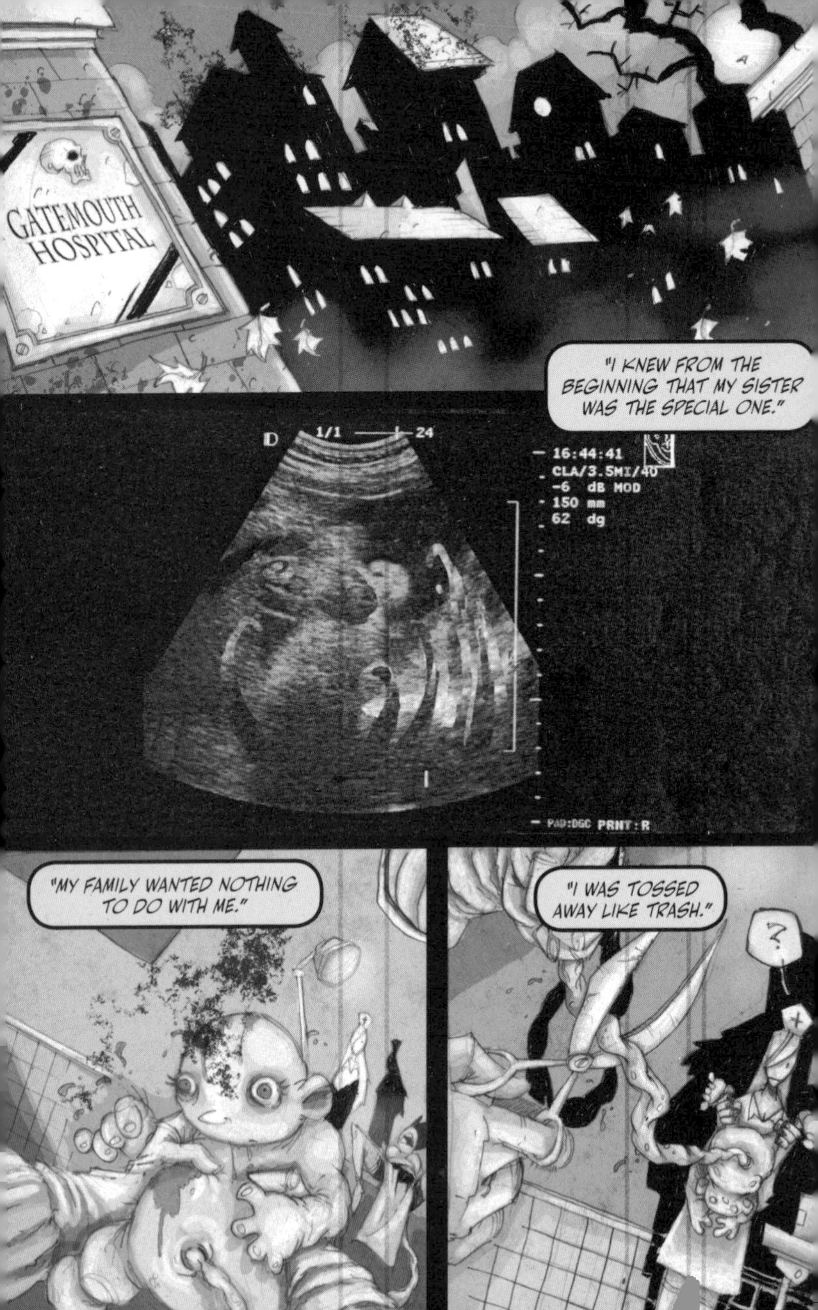
GATEMOUTH HOSPITAL
"I KNEW FROM THE BEGINNING THAT MY SISTER WAS THE SPECIAL ONE."
D 1/1 24
16:44:41
CLA/3.5MI/40
-6 dB MOD
150 mm
62 dg
PAD:DGC PRNT:R
"MY FAMILY WANTED NOTHING TO DO WITH ME."
"I WAS TOSSED AWAY LIKE TRASH."
?

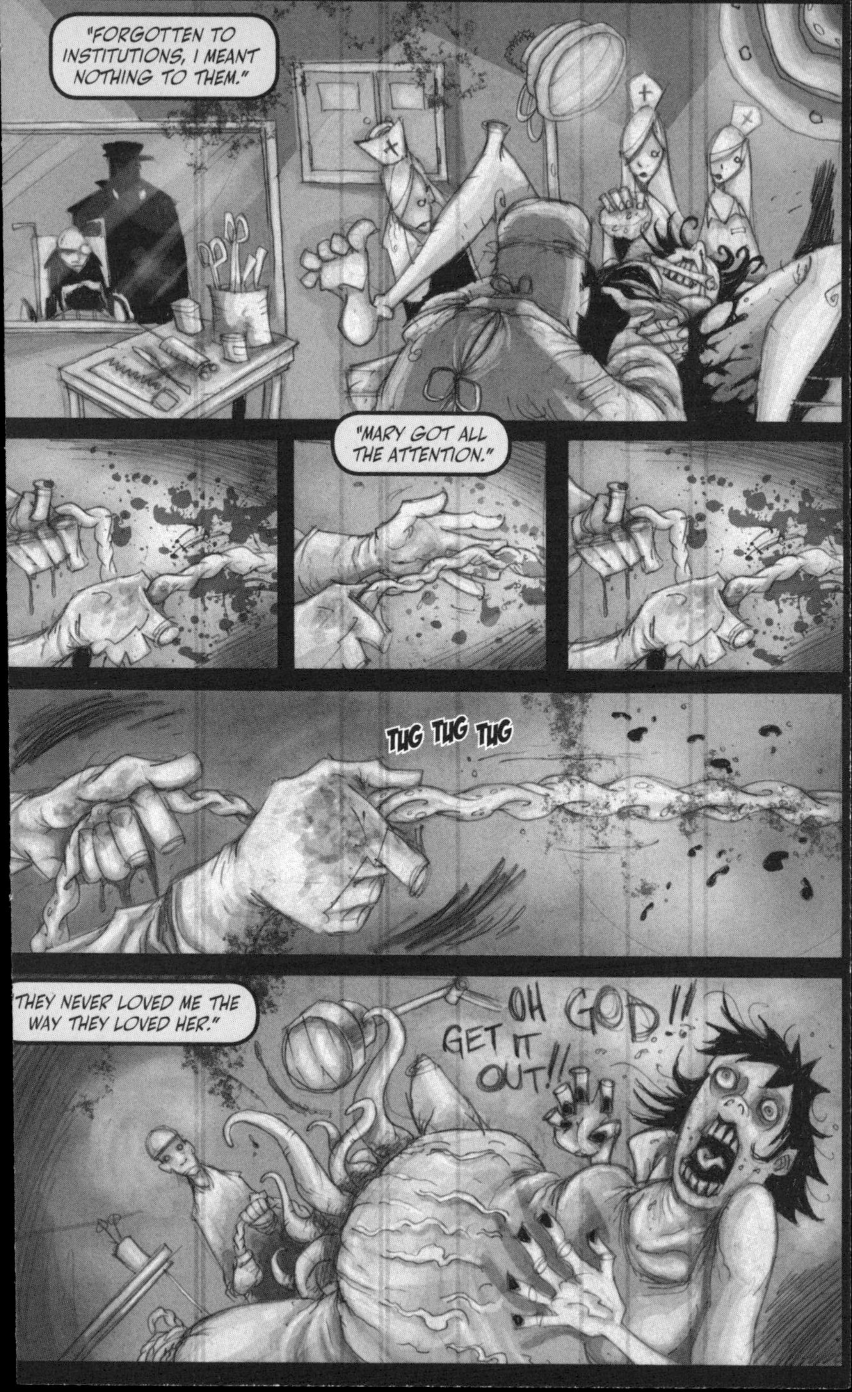
"FORGOTTEN TO INSTITUTIONS, I MEANT NOTHING TO THEM."
"MARY GOT ALL THE ATTENTION."
TUG TUG TUG
"THEY NEVER LOVED ME THE WAY THEY LOVED HER."
OH GOD!!
GET IT OUT!!

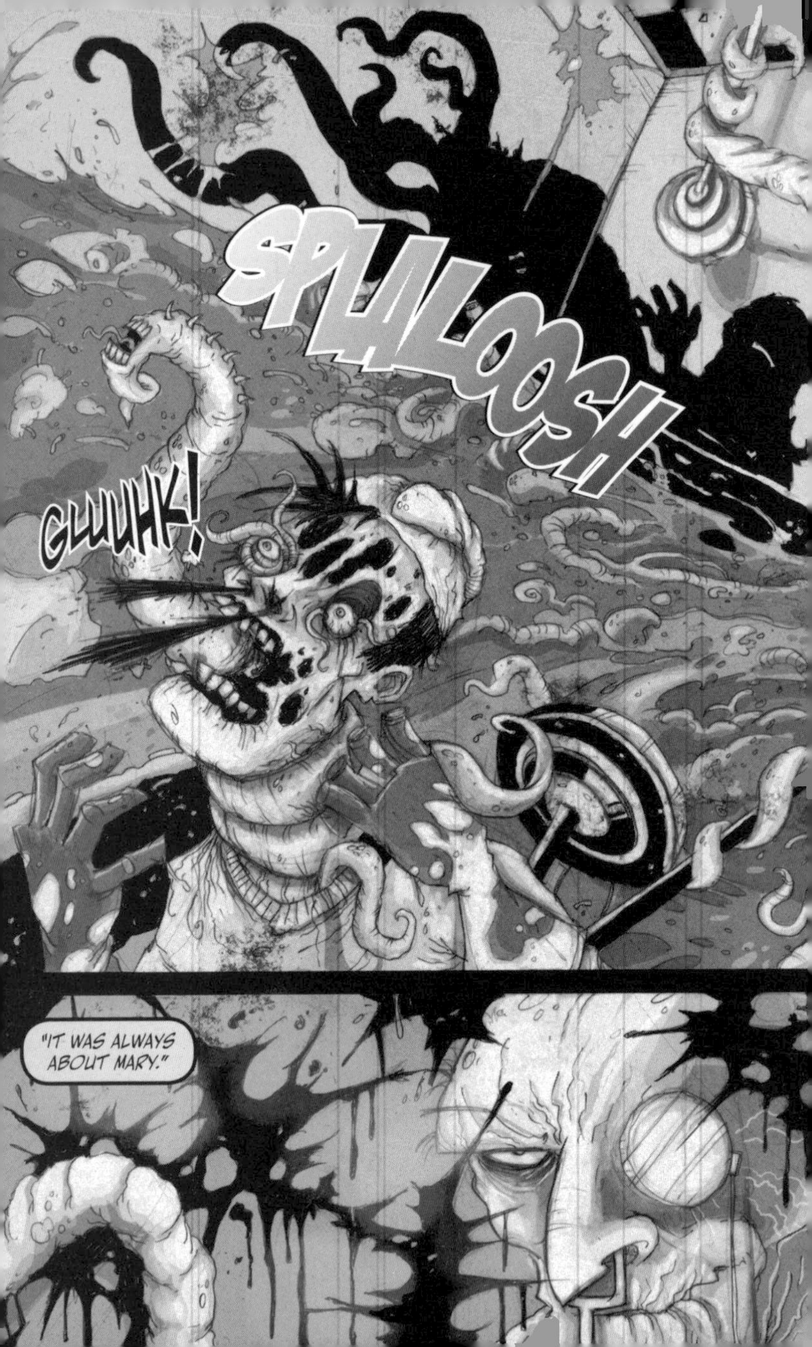
SPLULOOSH
GLUUHK!
"IT WAS ALWAYS ABOUT MARY."

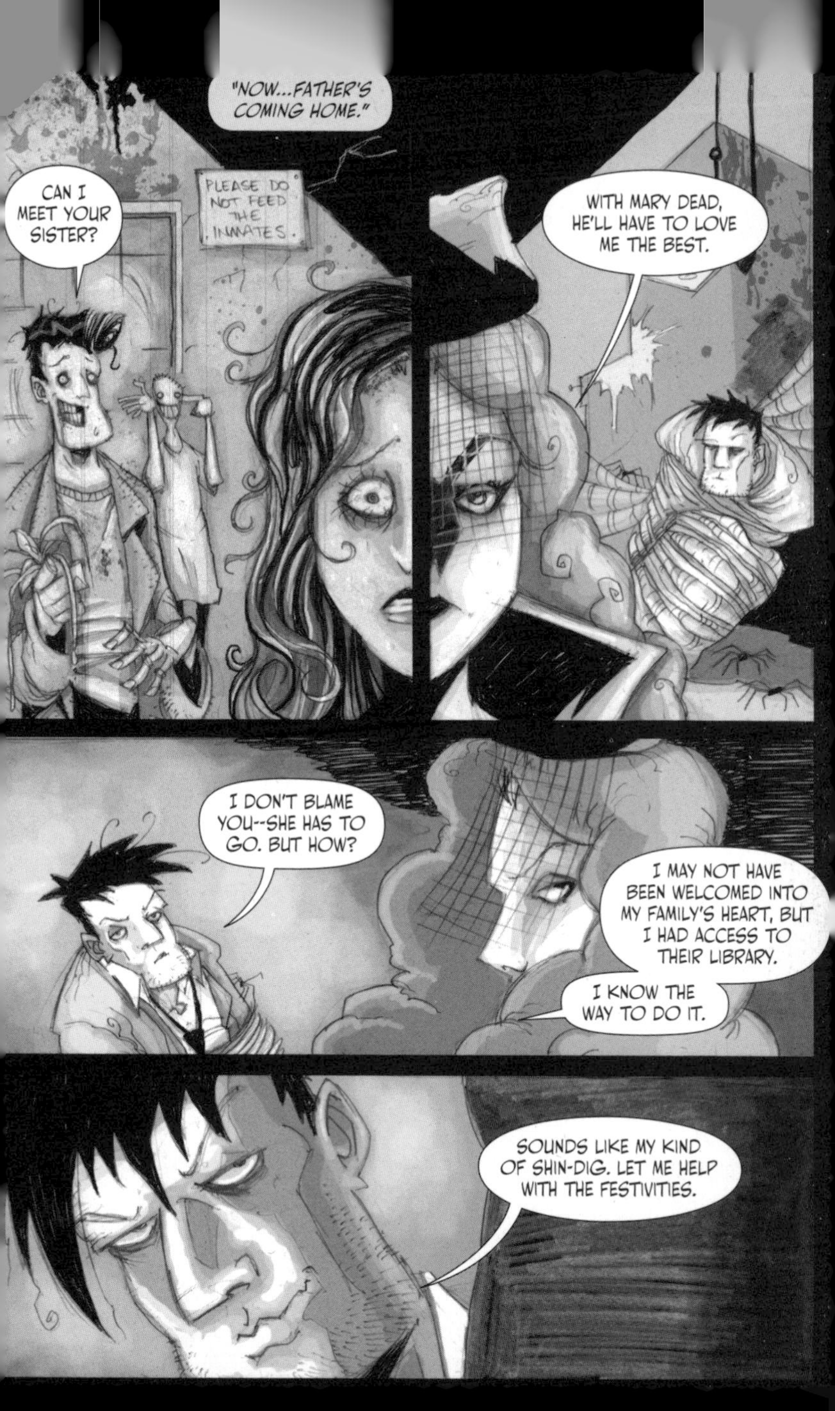
"NOW...FATHER'S COMING HOME."
CAN I MEET YOUR SISTER?
PLEASE DO NOT FEED THE INMATES.
WITH MARY DEAD, HE'LL HAVE TO LOVE ME THE BEST.
I DON'T BLAME YOU--SHE HAS TO GO. BUT HOW?
I MAY NOT HAVE BEEN WELCOMED INTO MY FAMILY'S HEART, BUT I HAD ACCESS TO THEIR LIBRARY.
I KNOW THE WAY TO DO IT.
SOUNDS LIKE MY KIND OF SHIN-DIG. LET ME HELP WITH THE FESTIVITIES.

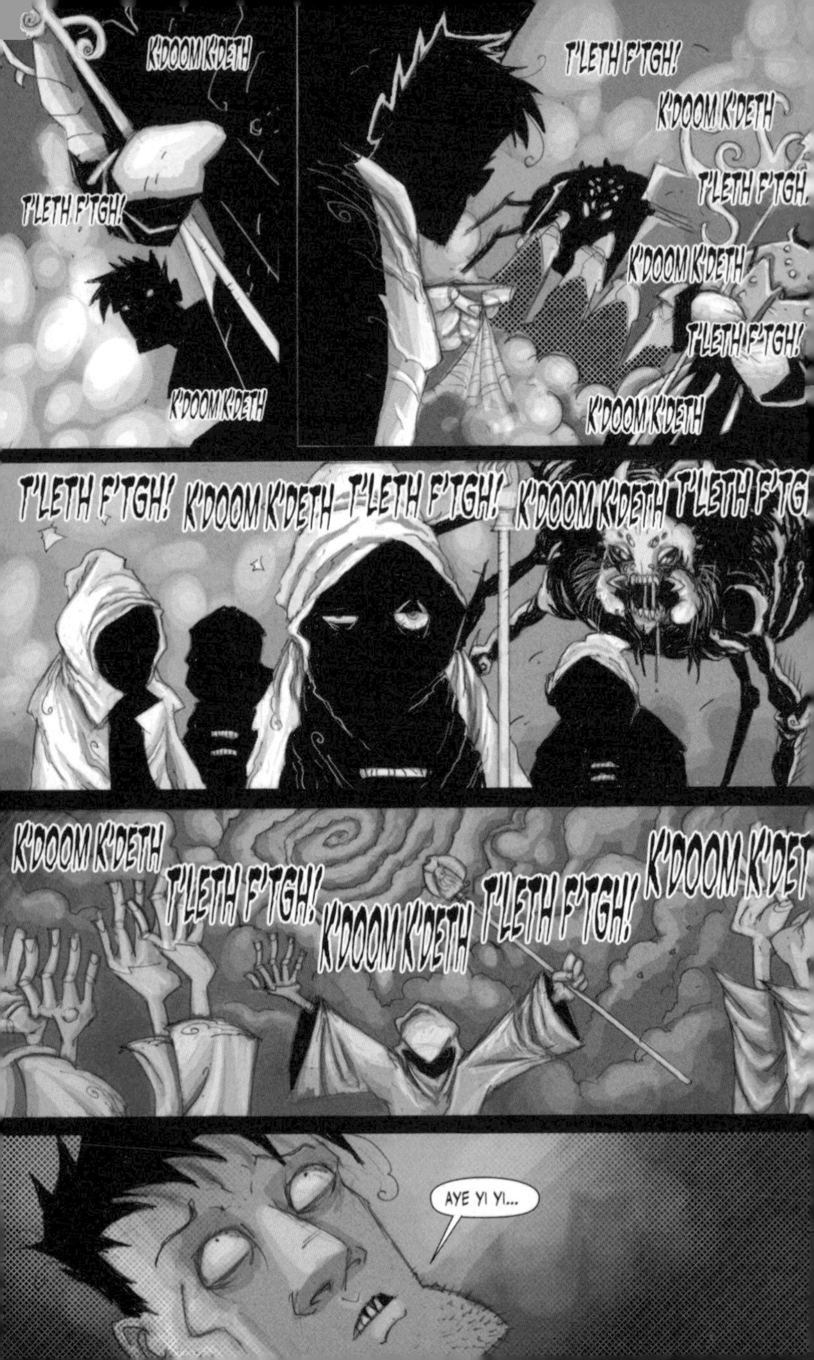
K'DOOM K'DETH
T'LETH F'TGH!
K'DOOM K'DETH
T'LETH F'TGH!
K'DOOM K'DETH
T'LETH F'TGH
K'DOOM K'DETH
T'LETH F'TGH!
K'DOOM K'DETH
T'LETH F'TGH!
K'DOOM K'DETH
T'LETH F'TGH!
K'DOOM K'DETH
T'LETH F'TG
K'DOOM K'DETH
T'LETH F'TGH!
K'DOOM K'DETH
T'LETH F'TGH!
K'DOOM K'DET
AYE YI YI...

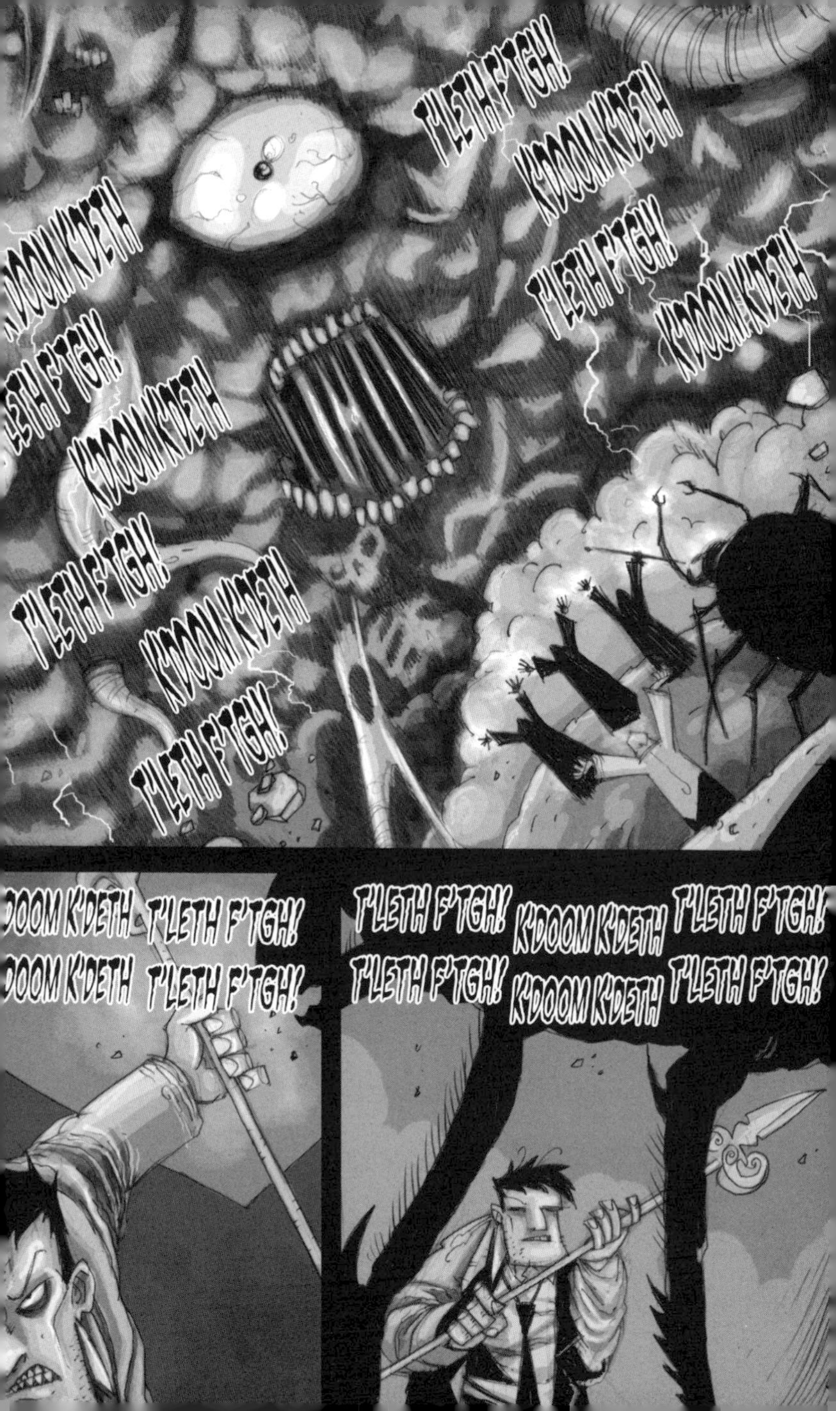

T'LETH F'TGH!
K'DOOM K'DETH
DOOM K'DETH
T'LETH F'TGH!
K'DOOM K'DETH
LETH F'TGH!
K'DOOM K'DETH
T'LETH F'TGH!
K'DOOM K'DETH
T'LETH F'TGH!
DOOM K'DETH
T'LETH F'TGH!
DOOM K'DETH
T'LETH F'TGH!
T'LETH F'TGH!
K'DOOM K'DETH
T'LETH F'TGH!
T'LETH F'TGH!
K'DOOM K'DETH
T'LETH F'TGH!

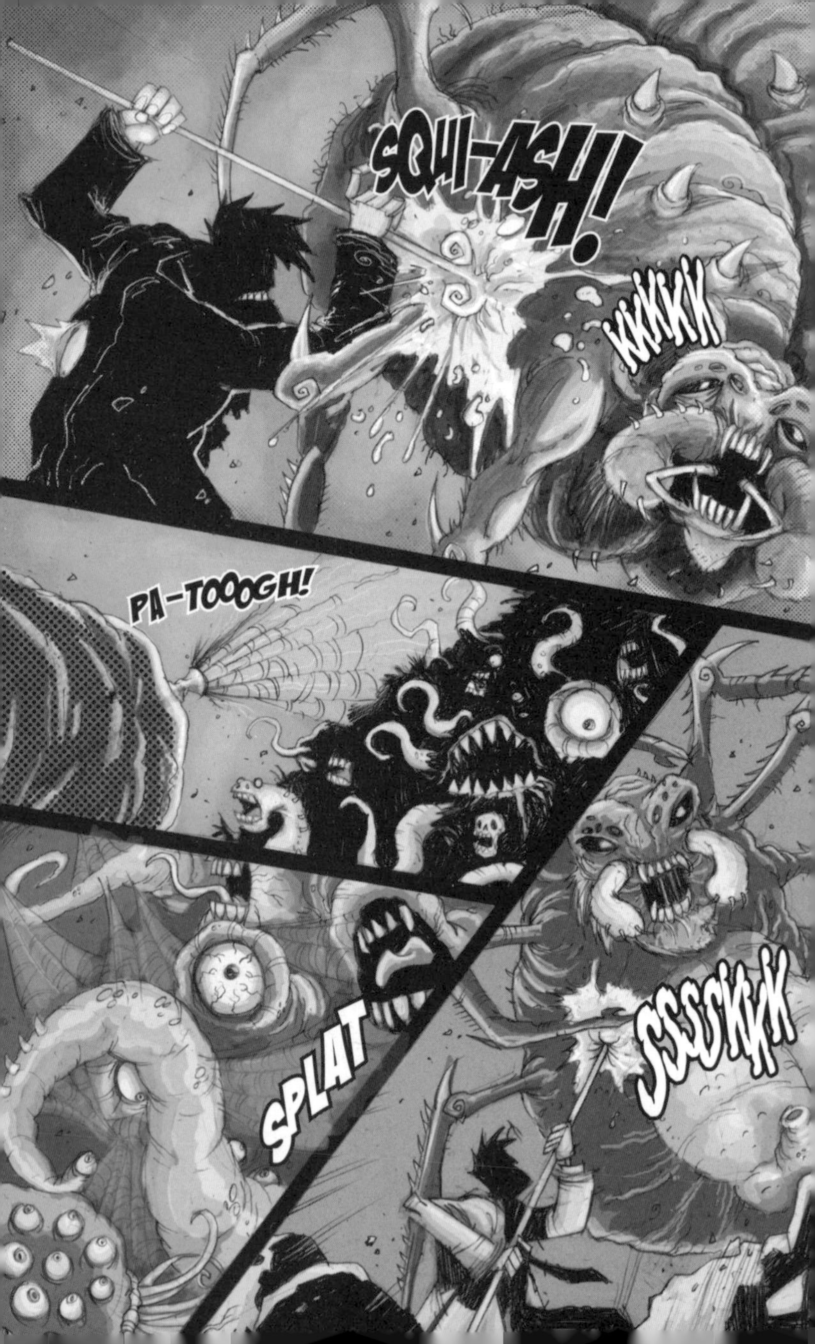
SQUI-ASH!
KKKKK
PA-TOOOGH!
SPLAT
SSSCKKK

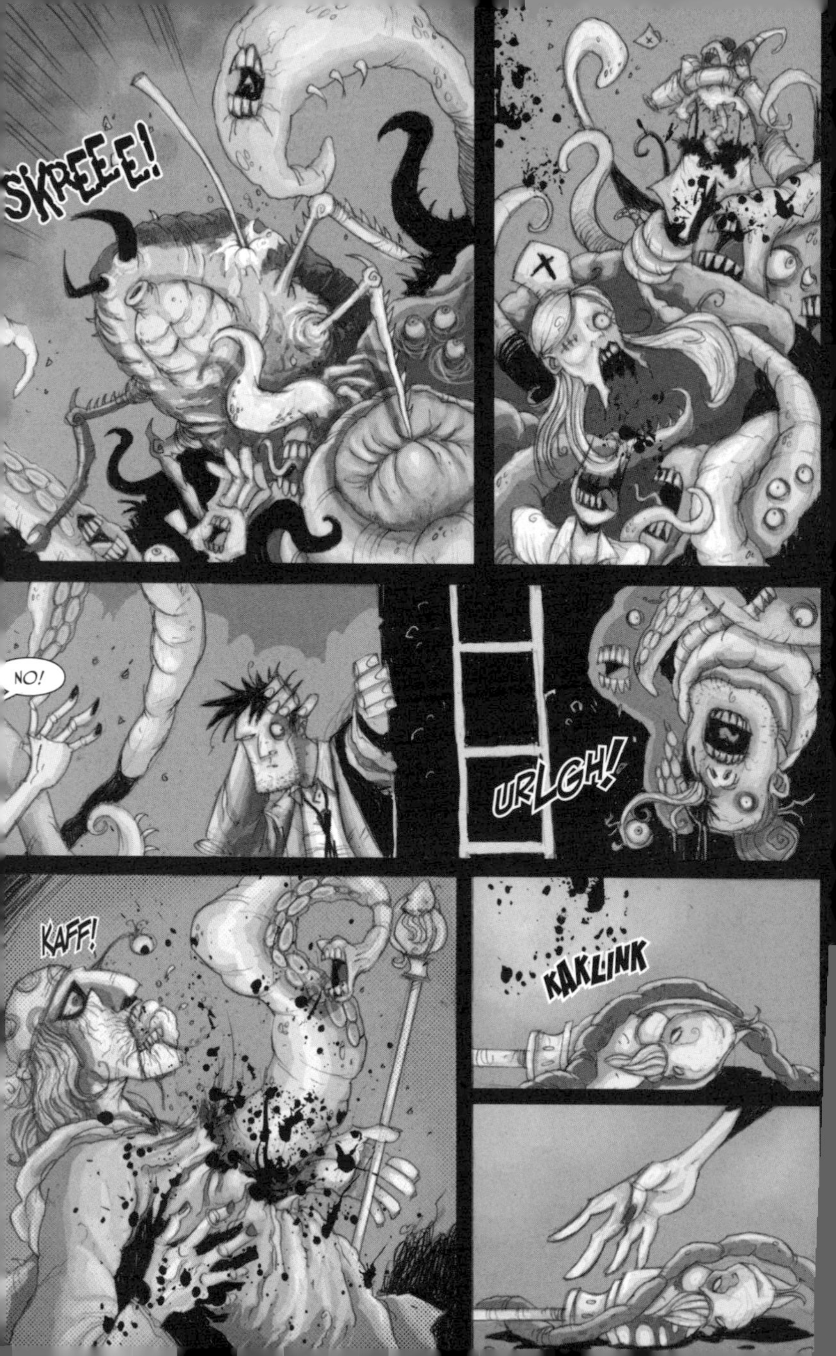
SKREEE!
NO!
URLCH!
KAFF!
KAKLINK

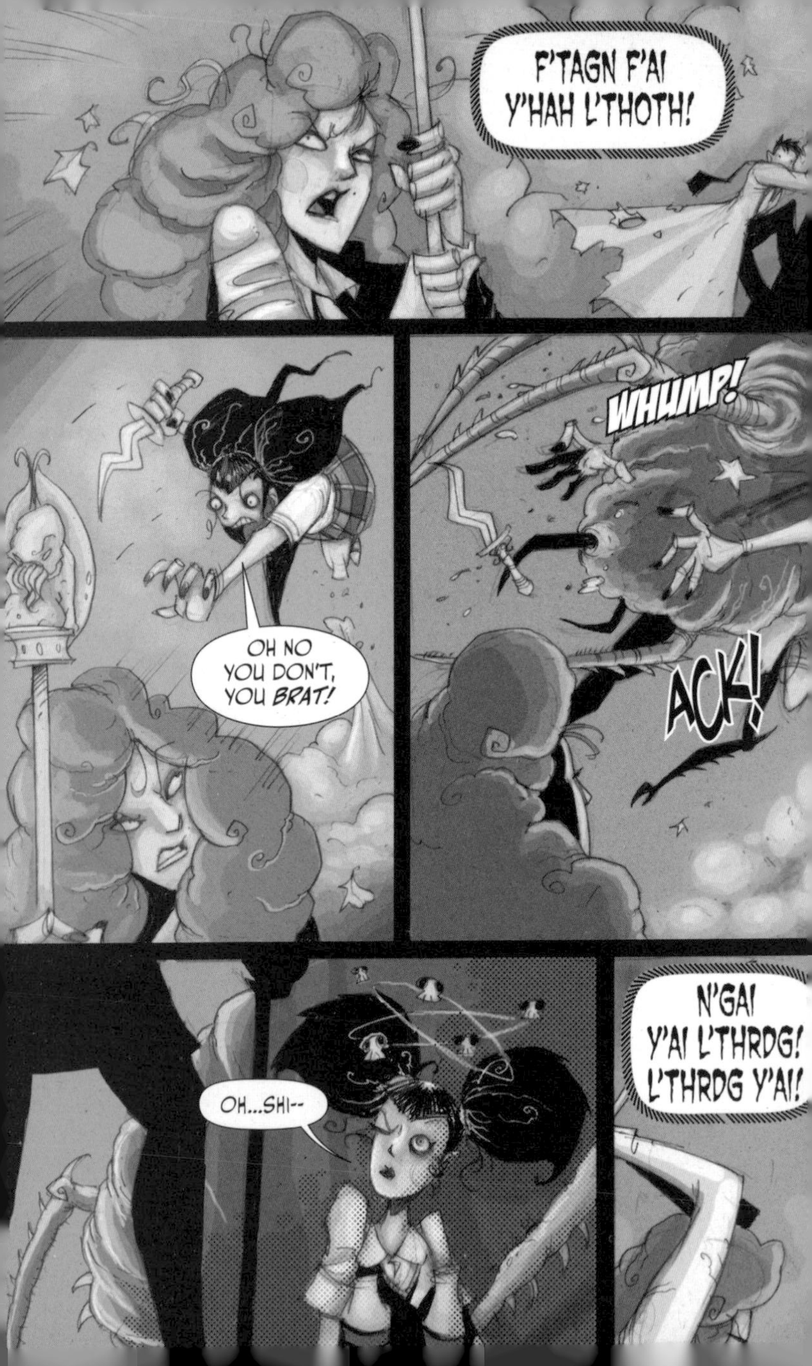
F'TAGN F'AI Y'HAH L'THOTH!
OH NO YOU DON'T, YOU *BRAT!*
WHUMP!
ACK!
OH...SHI--
N'GAI Y'AI L'THRDG! L'THRDG Y'AI!

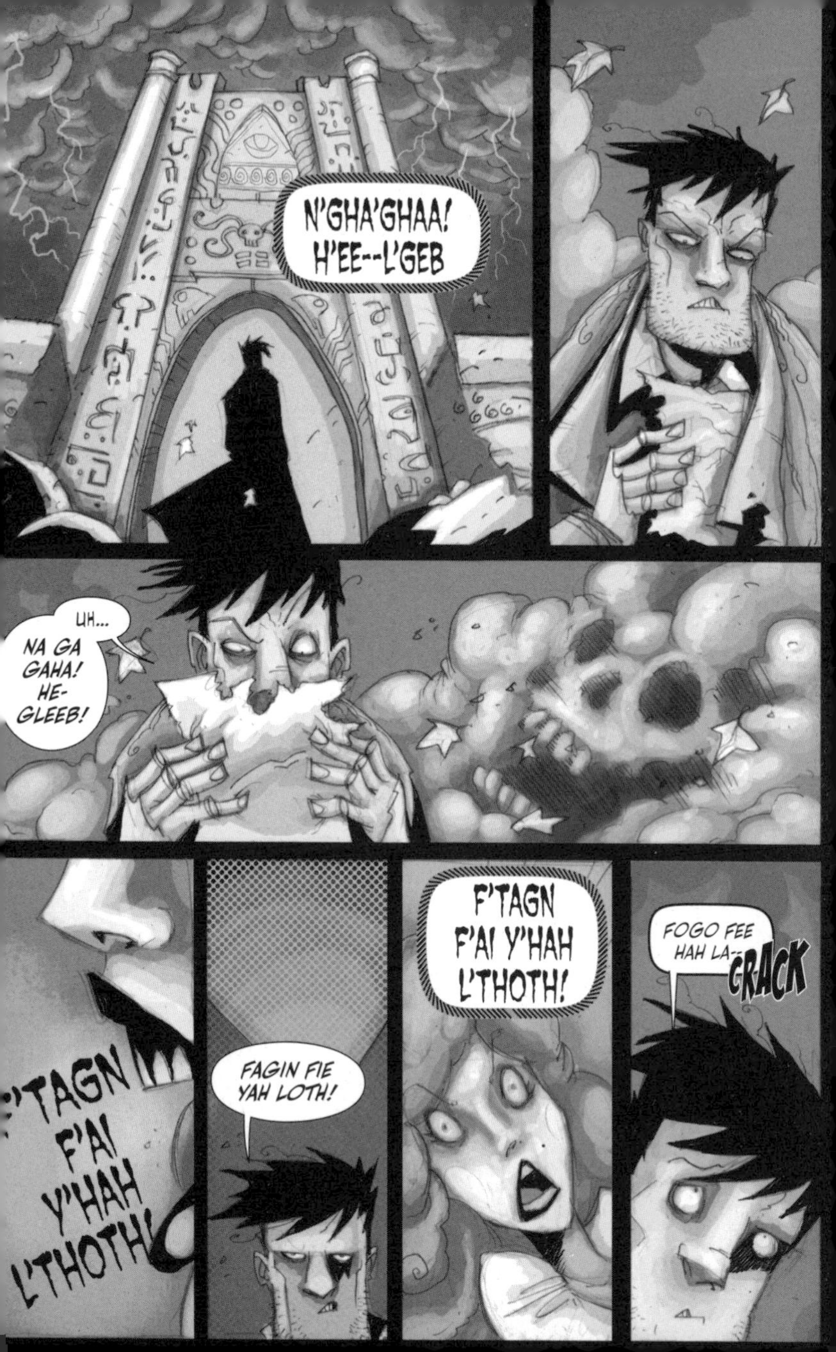
N'GHA'GHAA! H'EE--L'GEB
UH...
NA GA GAHA! HE-GLEEB!
'TAGN F'AI Y'HAH L'THOTH!
FAGIN FIE YAH LOTH!
F'TAGN F'AI Y'HAH L'THOTH!
FOGO FEE HAH LA--
CRACK

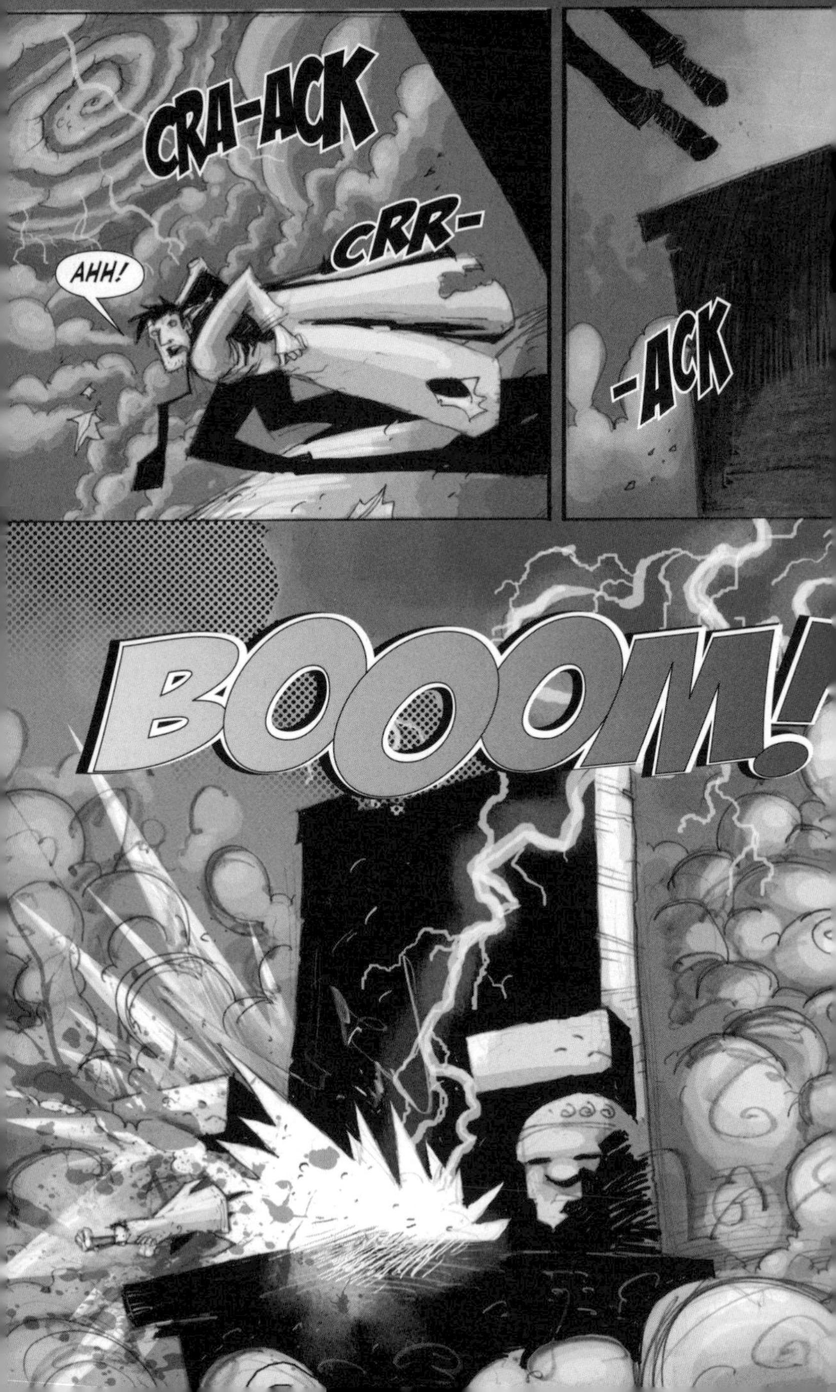
CRA-ACK
CRR-
AHH!
-ACK
BOOOM!

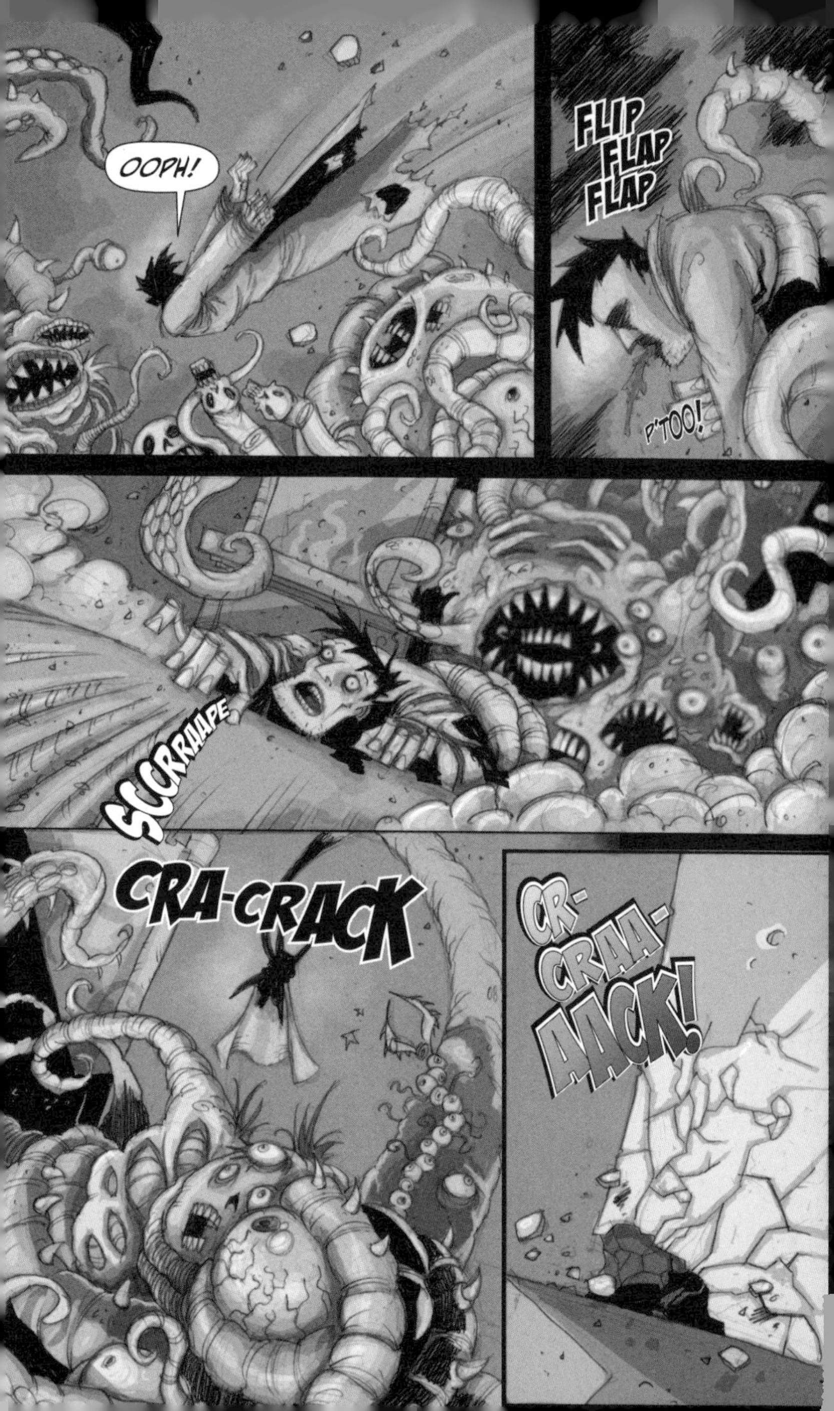
OOPH!
FLIP
FLAP
FLAP
P'TOO!
SCCRRAAPE
CRA-CRACK
CR-
CRAA-
AACK!

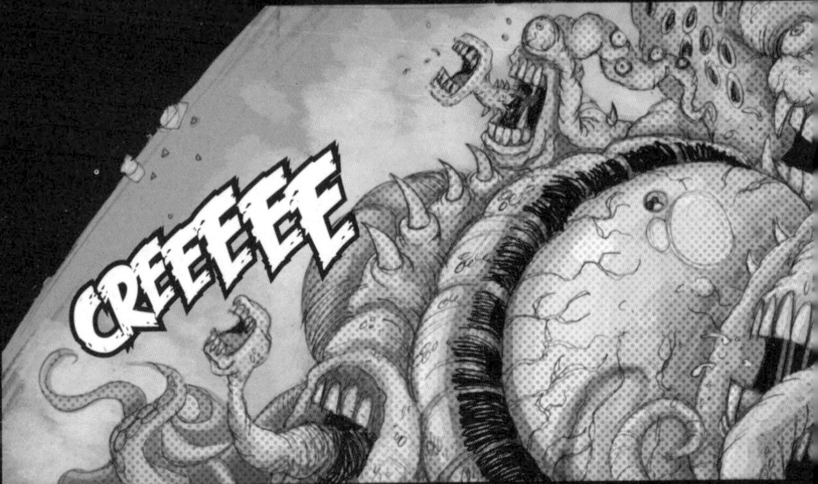
CREEEEE
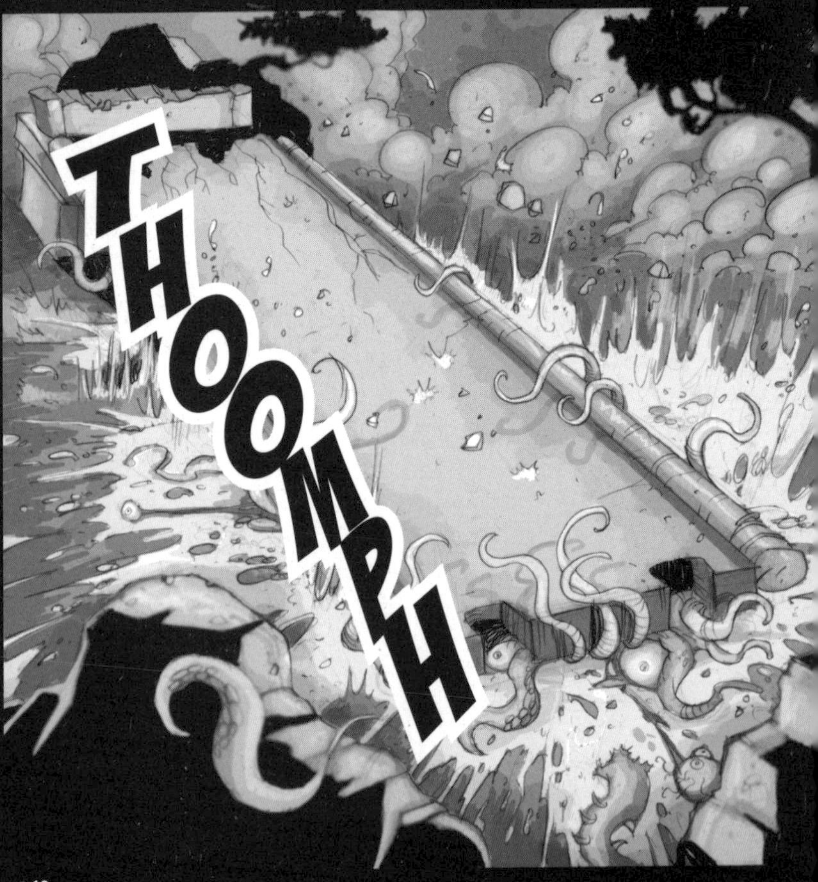
THOOMPH

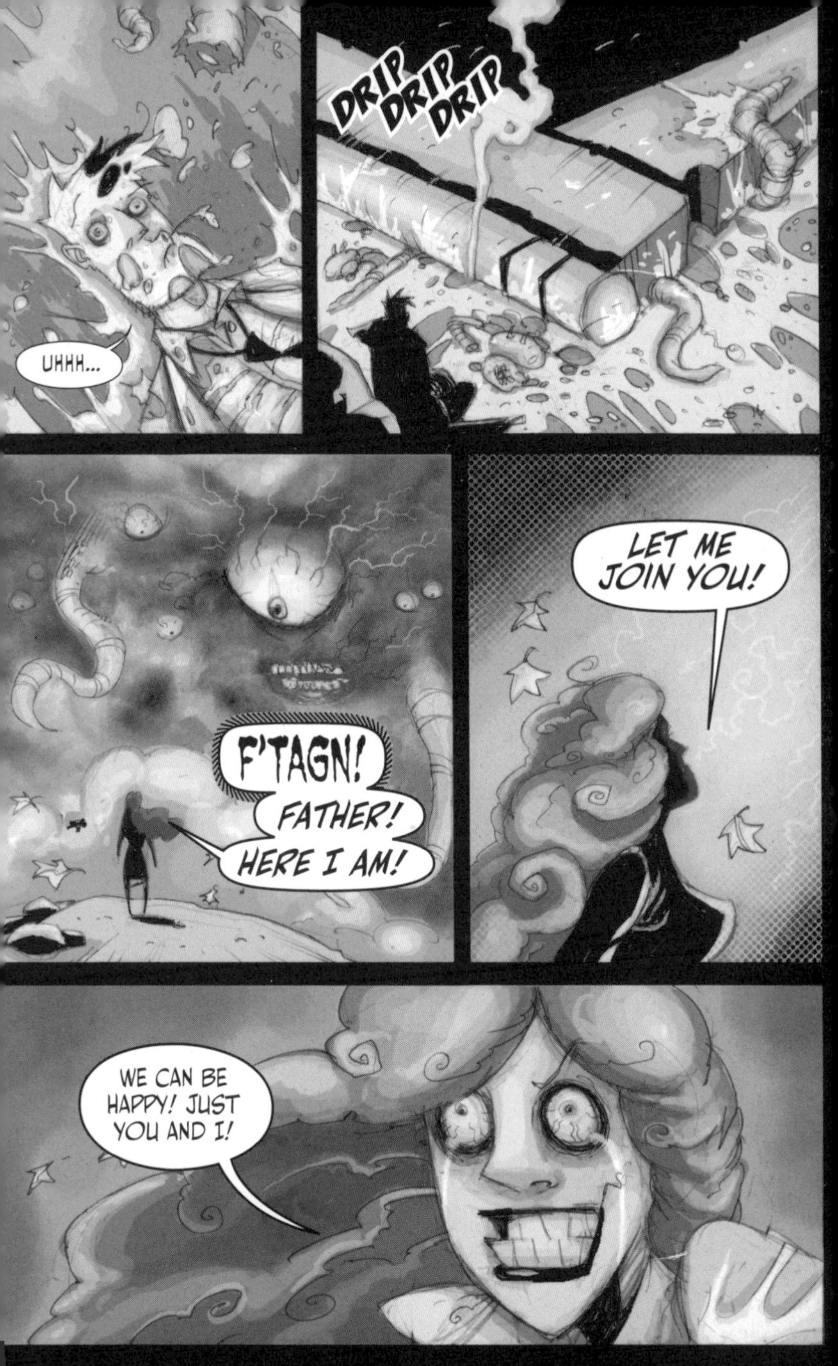
UHHH...
DRIP DRIP DRIP
F'TAGN!
FATHER! HERE I AM!
LET ME JOIN YOU!
WE CAN BE HAPPY! JUST YOU AND I!

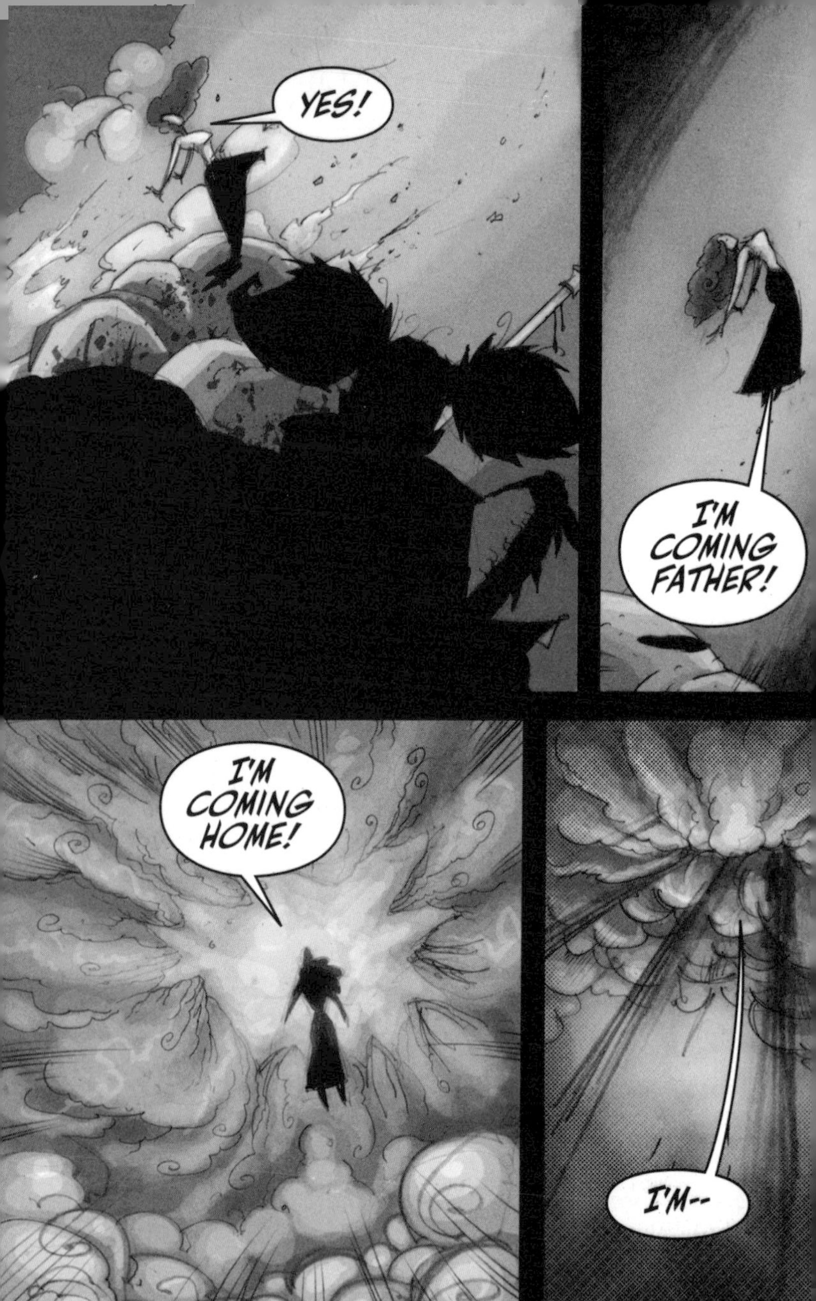
YES!
I'M COMING FATHER!
I'M COMING HOME!
I'M--

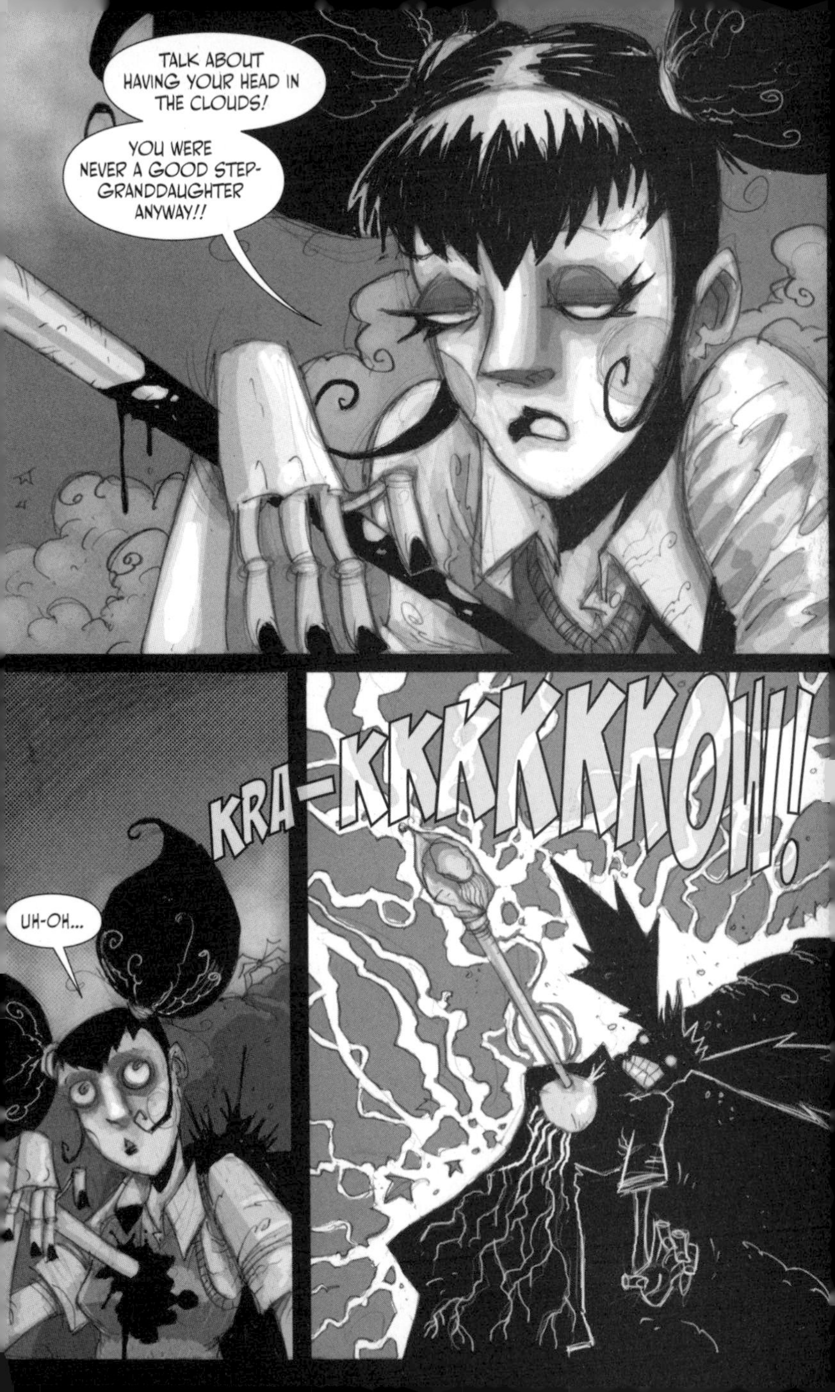
TALK ABOUT HAVING YOUR HEAD IN THE CLOUDS!
YOU WERE NEVER A GOOD STEP-GRANDDAUGHTER ANYWAY!!
KRA-KKKKKKOW!!
UH-OH...

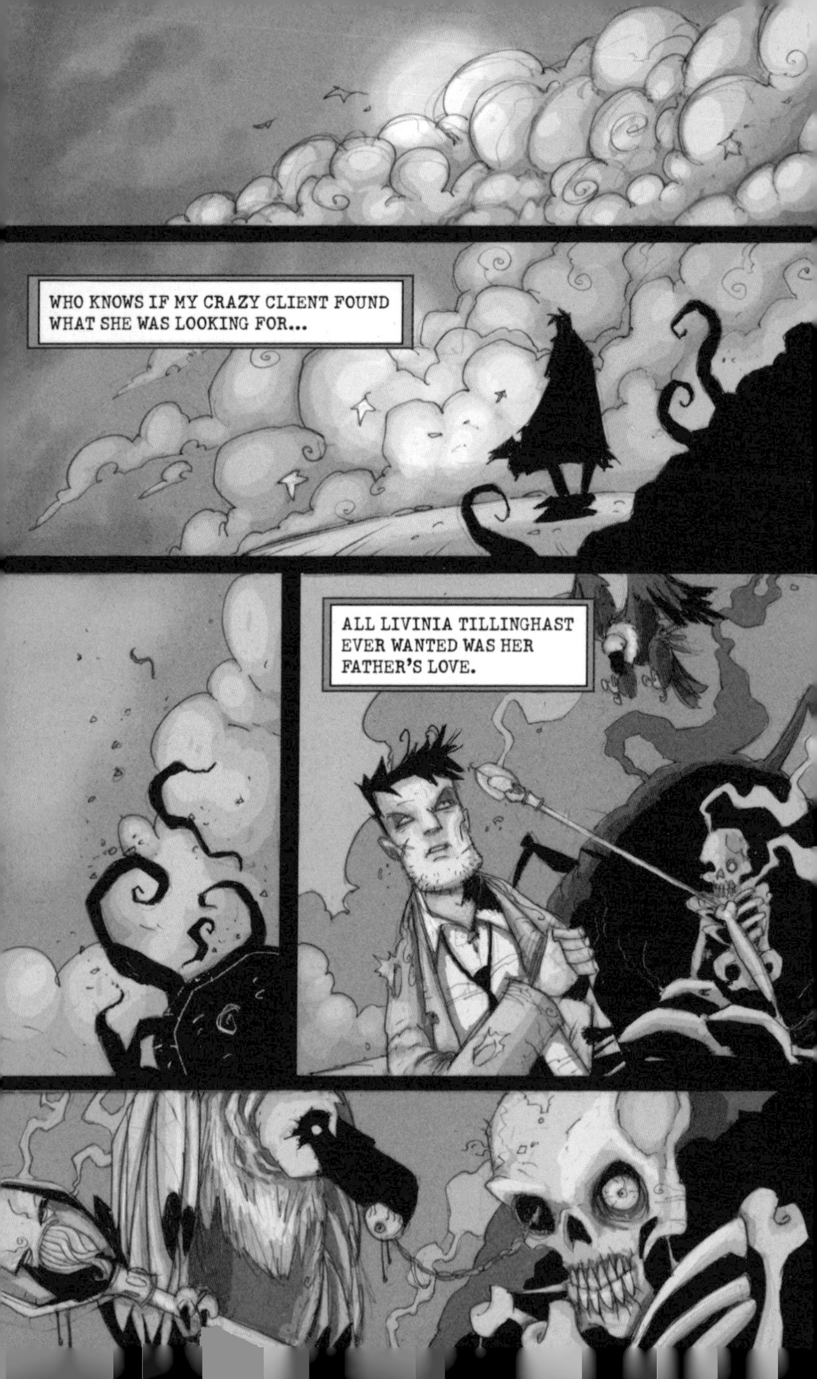
WHO KNOWS IF MY CRAZY CLIENT FOUND WHAT SHE WAS LOOKING FOR...
ALL LIVINIA TILLINGHAST EVER WANTED WAS HER FATHER'S LOVE.

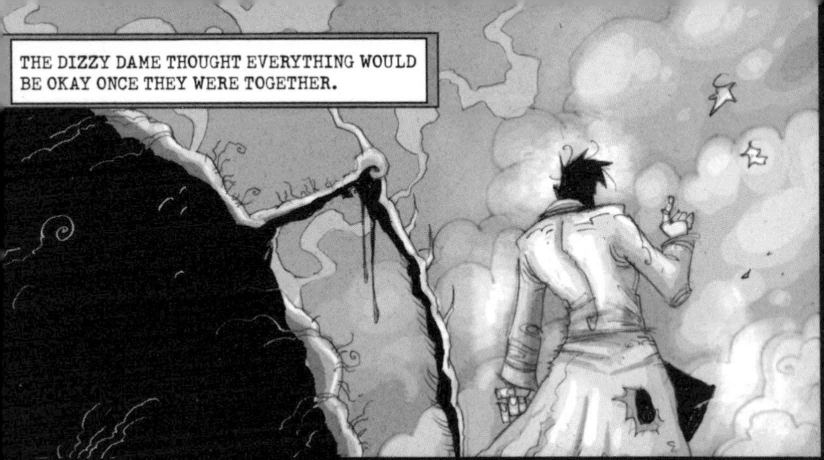
THE DIZZY DAME THOUGHT EVERYTHING WOULD BE OKAY ONCE THEY WERE TOGETHER.
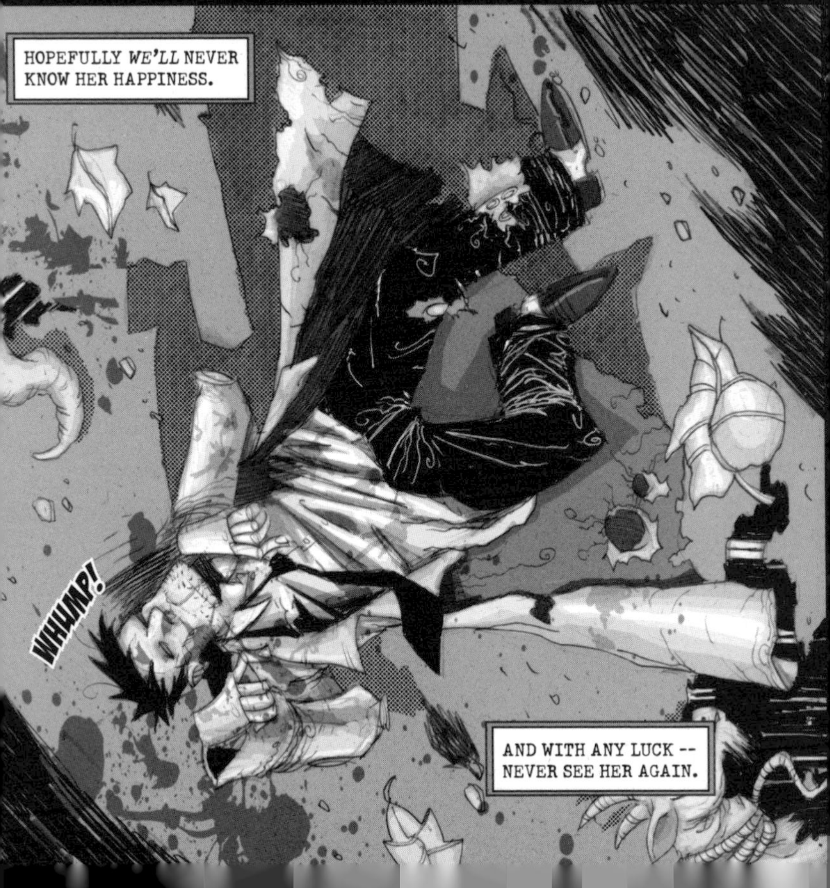
HOPEFULLY *WE'LL* NEVER KNOW HER HAPPINESS.
WHUMP!
AND WITH ANY LUCK -- NEVER SEE HER AGAIN.

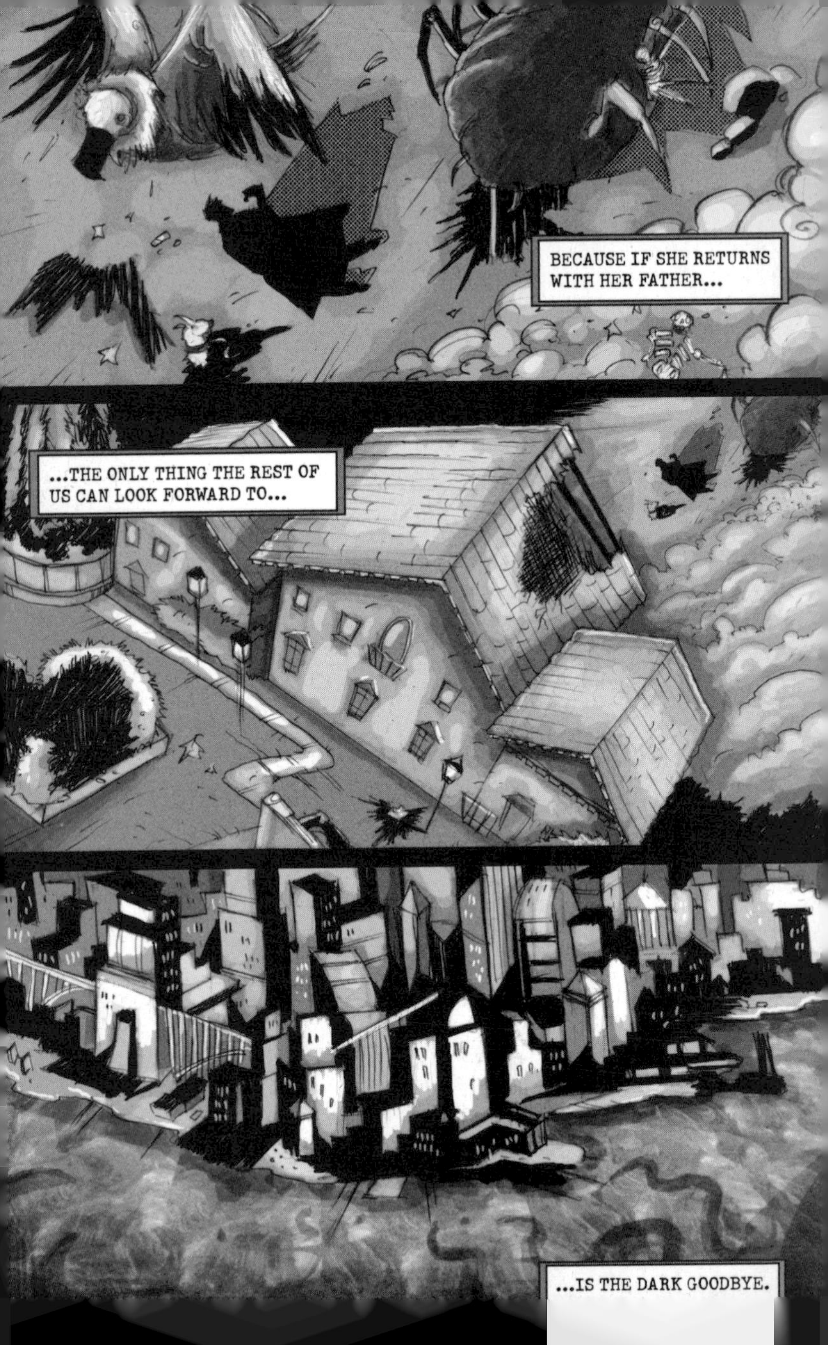
BECAUSE IF SHE RETURNS WITH HER FATHER...
...THE ONLY THING THE REST OF US CAN LOOK FORWARD TO...
...IS THE DARK GOODBYE.

END VOLUME 1
THE DARK GOODBYE

# From the Desk of
# Max Mason

Los Allende. Loss Ah-len-day.
A Mr. Coleman from the local Historical Society tells me that the name of our unfair city is short for "Puerta a los Allende." Roughly translated, he says it means something like "gateway to the other side" but I figure the old coot is just having me on.

The history of this burg is as twisted and hard to navigate as its local mean streets. A few Native American creation myths from the area sound like things I'd dream up after an all-night binge-bender. I imagine the tales were meant to scare their kids into behaving themselves.

But then again... The first story of the area from white men doesn't make much sense either. In the 1500's the Spanish arrived looking for gold. Instead they found an obsidian-like black ore littered about. Ignoring the pleas of the local Indians (big surprise) they stockpiled these jewels onto the vessels of their expeditionary fleet.

A surviving ship's log states that something caused the Spanish to not only return all of their newfound loot to land, but also to carry it to the highest peak and dump it down the other side. While sailing empty-handed back to Spain a series of calamities struck the small fleet and nearly all hands were lost. The only survivors, from the scout ship Pizicarro, made a convincing argument for never returning. Hell, I bet I could convince folks never to show up in the first place.

The one lasting influence of that Spanish expedition comes from the Franciscan monk traveling with them who gave the area its original title: Puerta a los Allende. Interesting how that name stuck...

The next documented use of the land is from the first half of the 1800's. A revolutionary practitioner of the psychiatric arts founded a hospice and retreat here. Some claimed that the mentally infirmed greatly benefited from their distance away from "normal" society. Most accounts, however, dispel this notion and explain that the remote hospital worked so well because families could dispose of inconveniently afflicted members, and then claim that it was too far away to visit. It proved incredibly successful, and led to the building of that grand cathedral of the perplexed mind which is still in operation today, Gatemouth Hospital.

By the 1850's Gatemouth was already one of the largest asylums in the world, although it proved exceedingly slow to adopt the more humane treatment methods that were already commonplace in eastern states.

Also in the mid-1800's, the rich marine treasures of the bay had begun to be mined. Immigrant Japanese built shanties along the rocky coastline and successfully plumbed the rich bounty of abalone, yellowtail and the amazingly abundant shellfish and crustaceans.

At about the same time gold rush fever hit Los Allende, perhaps spurred on by uncovered accounts of the Spanish galleys, which had arrived so many years before. Prospectors hoping to plunder the mineral rich soil found only the same dark rocks, which had caused all that unpleasantness years before. The black gold proved valueless in this new era and most prospectors departed. Those who stayed turned their attention to fishing opportunities. In typical fashion, the newer fishermen allowed prejudices to lead to mistrust and suspicion of the Japanese fishing community who had paved the way for them. The reek of dying fish probably didn't help any.

The matter was settled in 1906 when a fire of mysterious origin swept through the Japanese-American shanty community, destroying both homes and fishing gear. European immigrants were never able to successfully imitate the earlier fishing success, due to a series of earthquakes and resulting fires.

The last remnants of this community were swept away in the 20's when an unusual plague broke out. It would make sense that this was a strain of influenza, but accounts from this time don't support that theory. Regardless, the federal government isolated the community for health reasons and destroyed the infected areas.

The U.S. military took control of the region, and in the years during World War II it is said that dumping of spent armaments took place here, which might explain the purple fumes sometimes seen escaping upwards from the earth. The manufacturing giant Exhampton-InterDynamics placed a research facility above town to develop top-secret weapons. Conspiracy theorists like to posit that they also performed nerve tests on "volunteers" from nearby Gatemouth Hospital.

The cold war that followed was a boon to military contractors, and for Exhampton it was no different. As their business grew, the city was re-opened and the influx of new employees necessitated the development of Los Allende's first, and only, suburban neighborhood.

A concerted effort by town elders led to much of the city being labeled with Landmark Status, a move that prevents remodeling and new construction. The most modern building hails from the 70's - the worldwide headquarters of, then newly re-named, Exham Industries, which has since turned its attention to medicine, chemicals and...various other undisclosed pursuits.

# Dark Denizens:
# Early Character Designs for
# The Dark Goodbye

MAX "MUTT" MASON

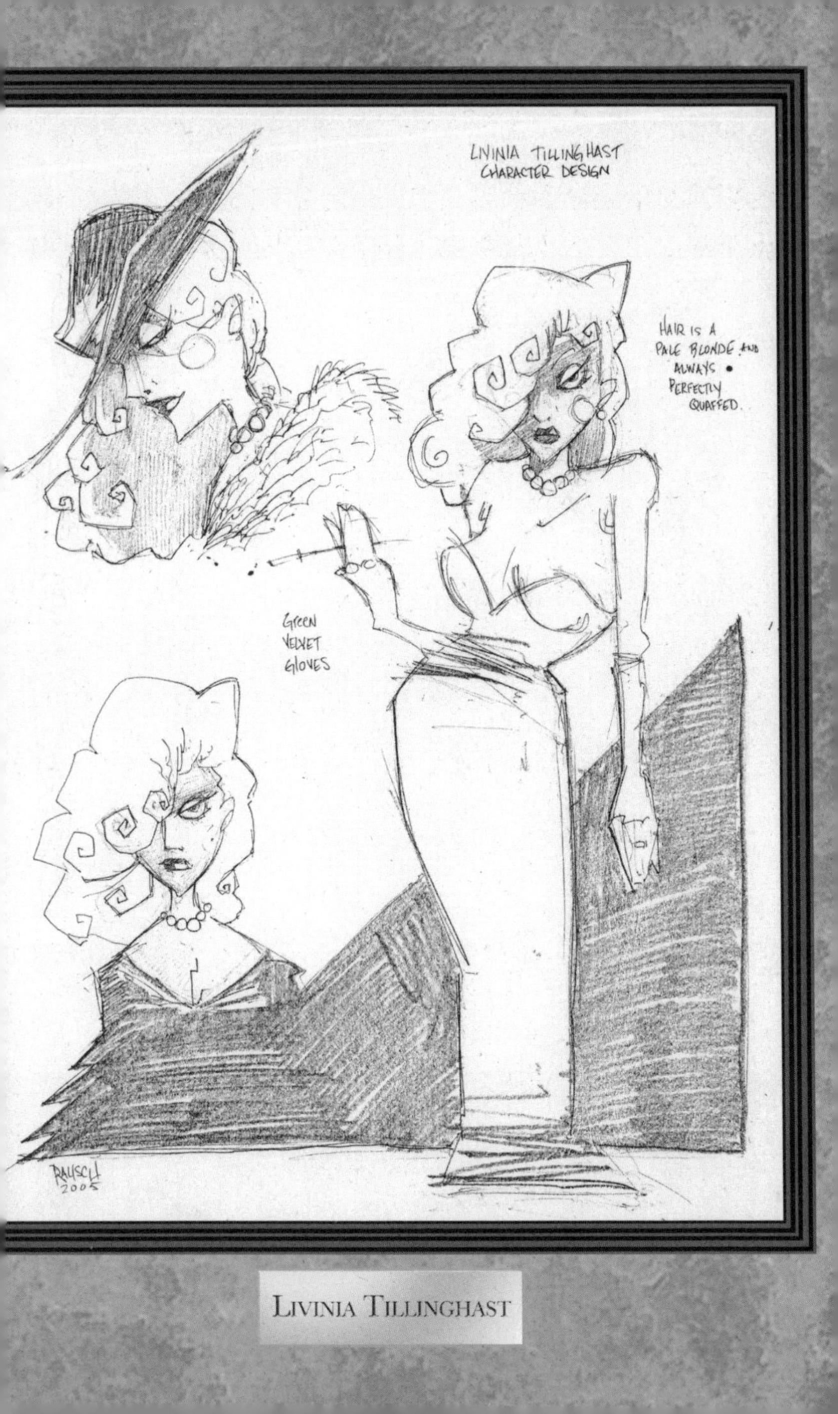
LIVINIA TILLINGHAST
CHARACTER DESIGN
HAIR IS A
PALE BLONDE AND
ALWAYS
PERFECTLY
QUAFFED.
GREEN
VELVET
GLOVES
RAUSCH
2005

LIVINIA TILLINGHAST

"RAFT"
CHARACTER
ROUGHS

DOT SPINDLEDRIFT

DOT

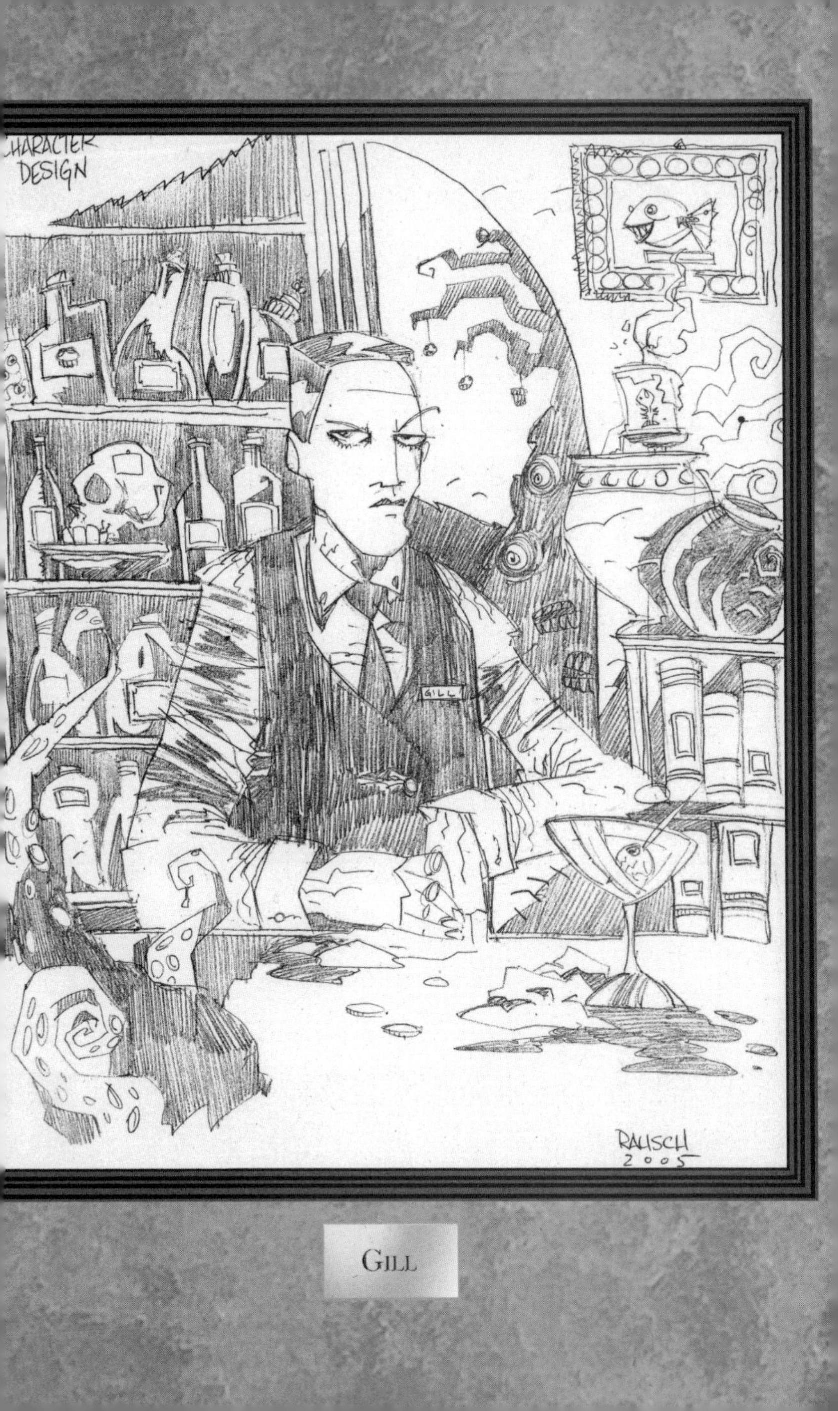
CHARACTER DESIGN
GILL
RAUSCH 2005

GILL

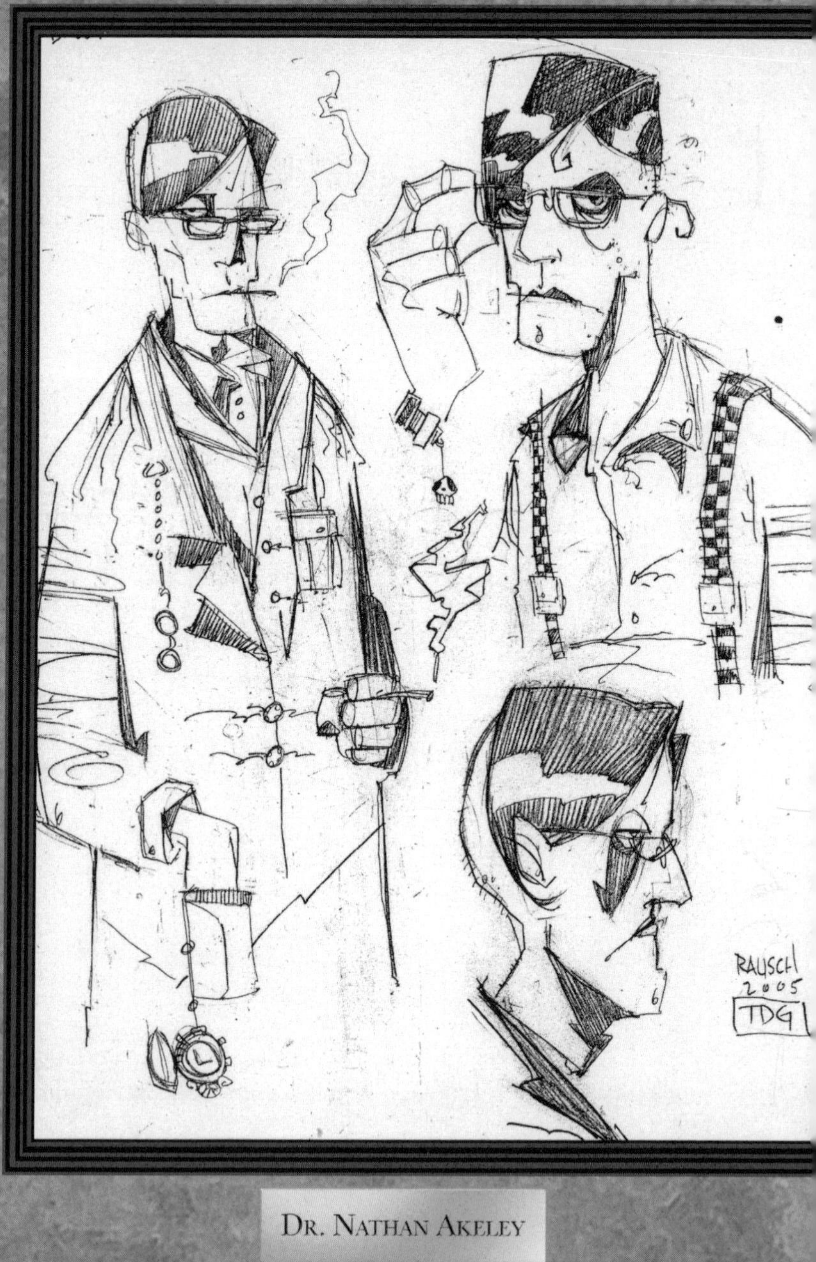
RAUSCH
2005
TDG

Dr. Nathan Akeley

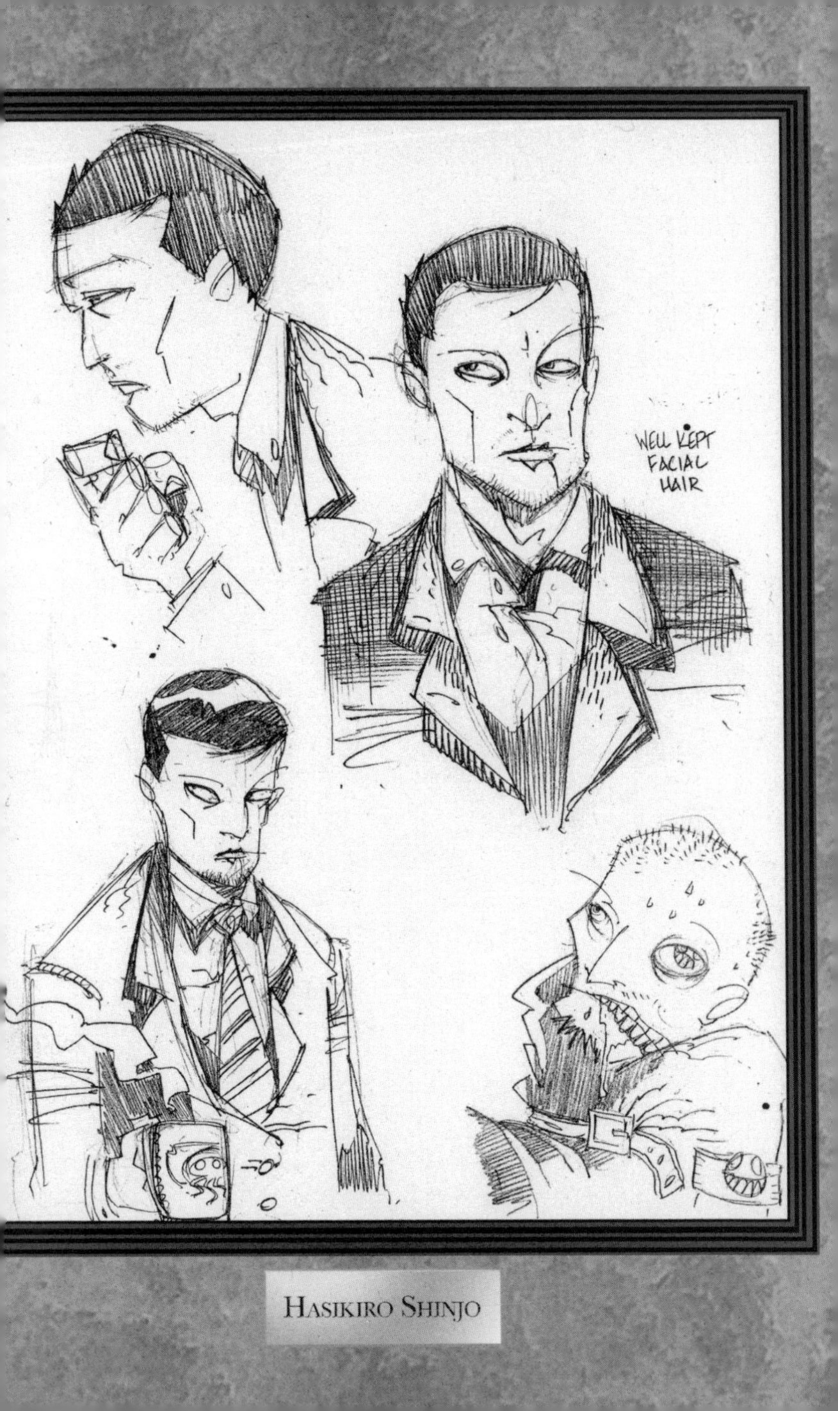
WELL KEPT FACIAL HAIR

Hasikiro Shinjo

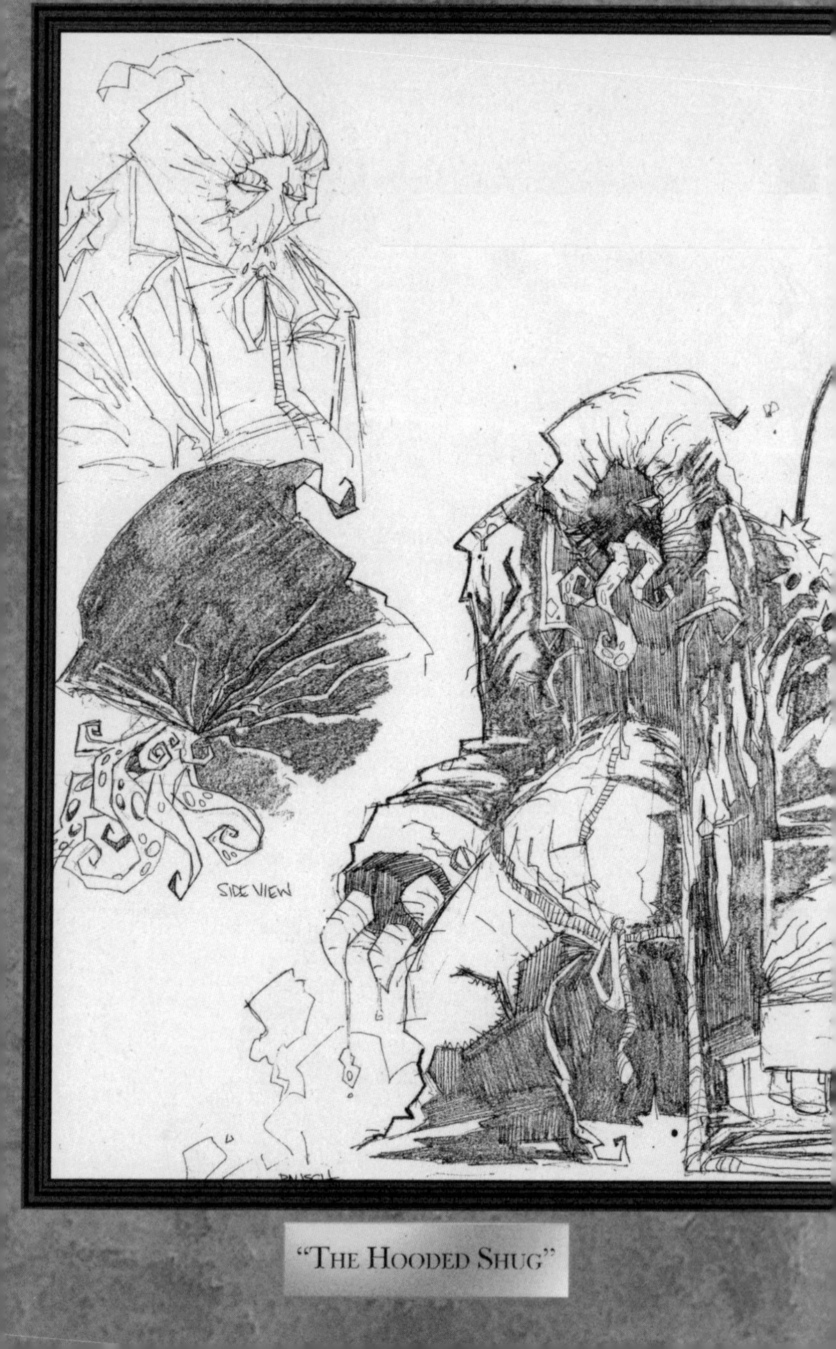
SIDE VIEW

"THE HOODED SHUG"

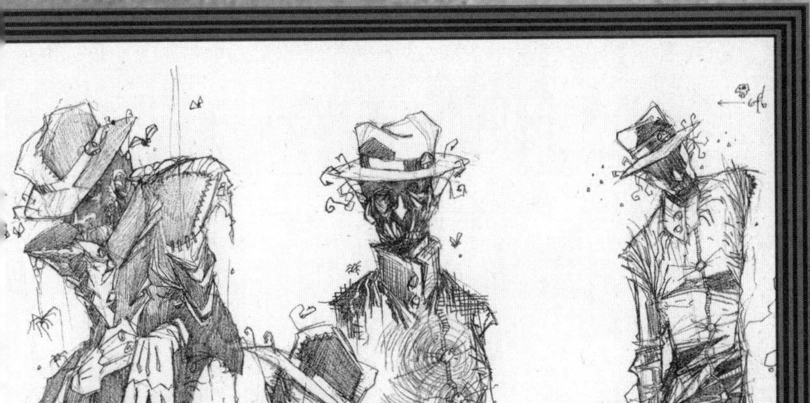

ENT MAN
RAUSCH
05


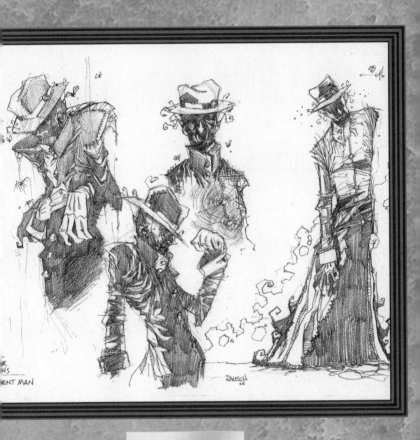

"The Bent Man"

IN THE NEXT
INSTALLMENT OF

*The*

# DARK GOODBYE

Mutt's back on the case, when he investigates the suspicious death of an esteemed astronomer. Before his untimely, and decidedly grisly demise, the scientist had made unsettling connections between the recent discovery of an unusual cluster of pods in a nearby marsh and an unprecedented meteor shower passing close to the earth.

Don't try to make sense of it, friend. This is Los Allende, and "The Dark Goodbye" lurks down every alleyway, awaiting us all.

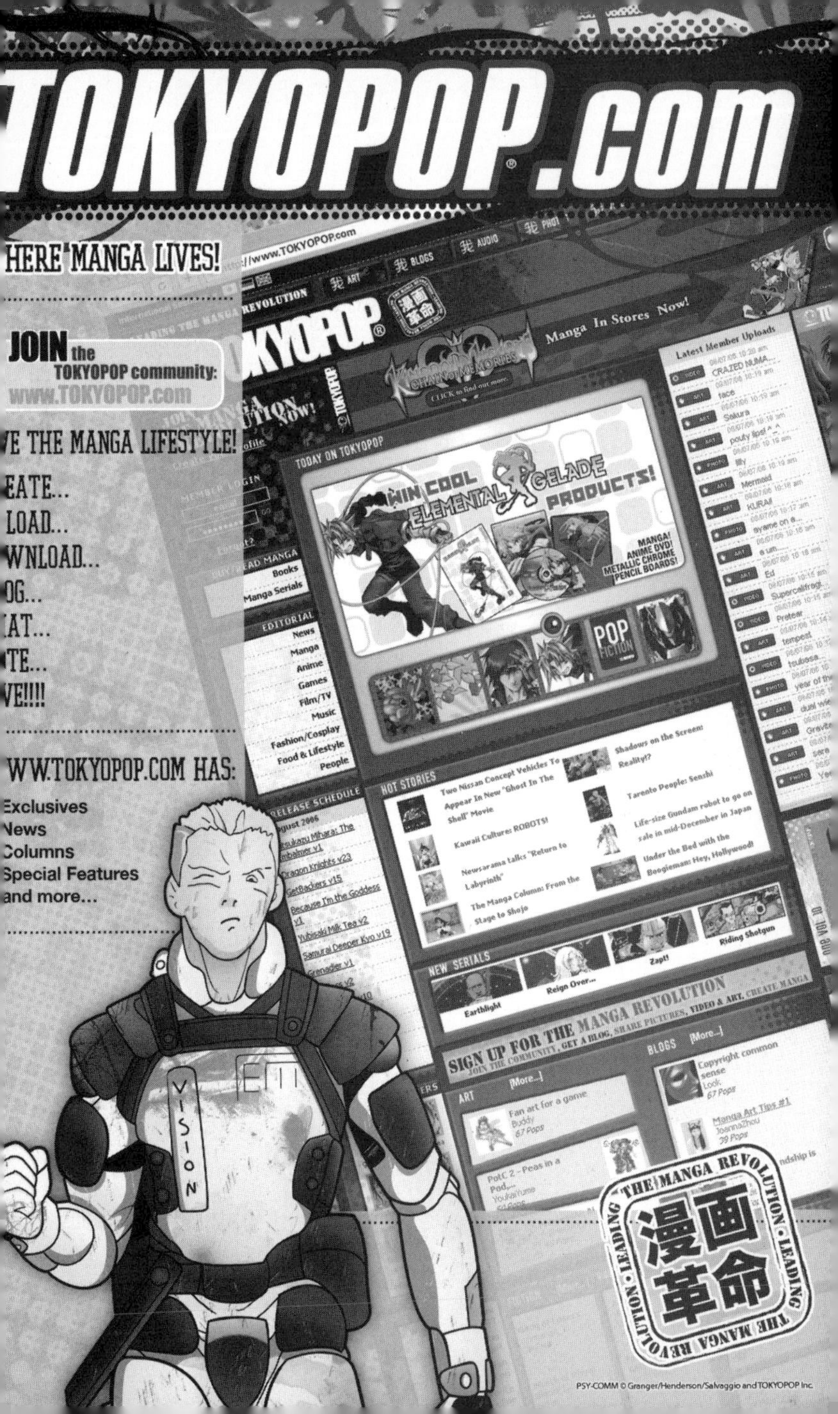

TOKYOPOP.com
HERE MANGA LIVES!
JOIN the TOKYOPOP community: www.TOKYOPOP.com
E THE MANGA LIFESTYLE!
EATE...
LOAD...
WNLOAD...
OG...
AT...
TE...
E!!!!
WW.TOKYOPOP.COM HAS:
Exclusives
News
Columns
Special Features
and more...
THE MANGA REVOLUTION
漫画革命
LEADING
PSY-COMM © Granger/Henderson/Salvaggio and TOKYOPOP Inc.

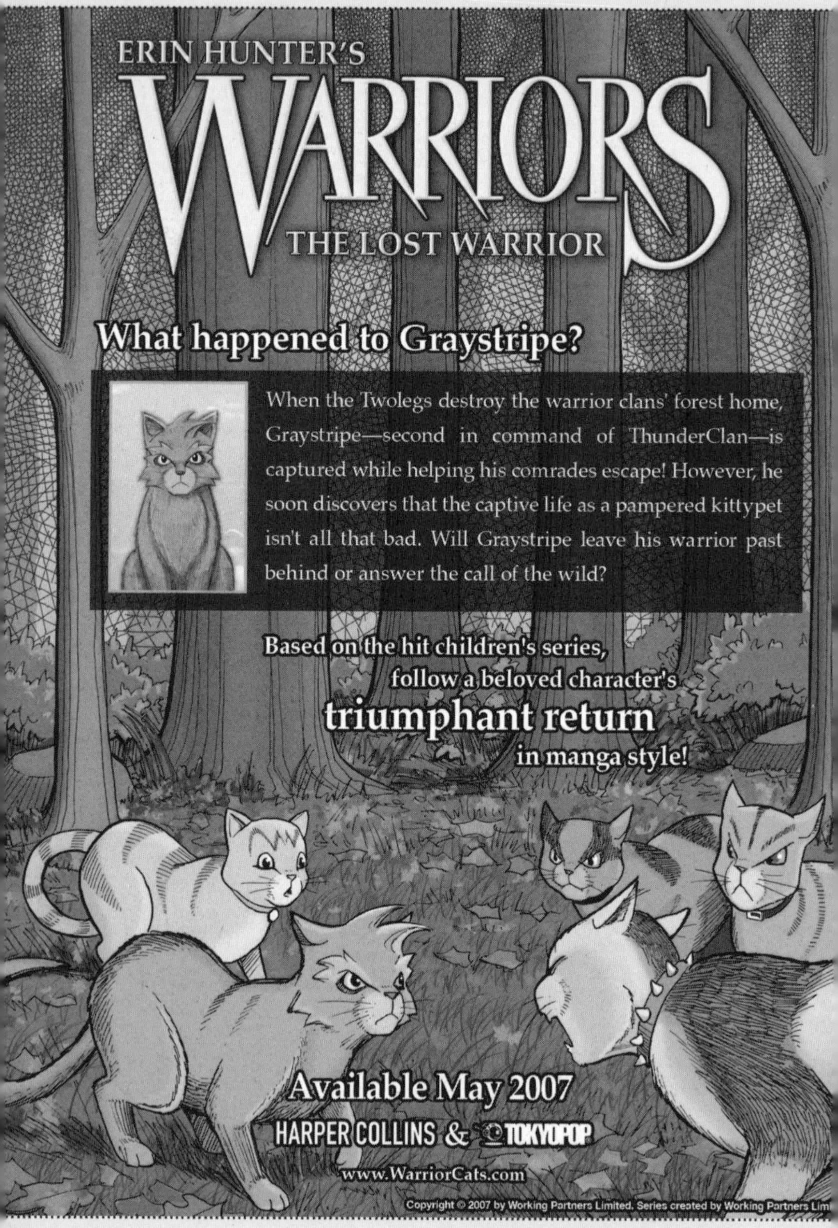
ERIN HUNTER'S
WARRIORS
THE LOST WARRIOR
What happened to Graystripe?
When the Twolegs destroy the warrior clans' forest home, Graystripe—second in command of ThunderClan—is captured while helping his comrades escape! However, he soon discovers that the captive life as a pampered kittypet isn't all that bad. Will Graystripe leave his warrior past behind or answer the call of the wild?
Based on the hit children's series, follow a beloved character's triumphant return in manga style!
Available May 2007
HARPER COLLINS & TOKYOPOP
www.WarriorCats.com
Copyright © 2007 by Working Partners Limited. Series created by Working Partners Limi